Sex Slang

'In the world of slang, sex slang is about as good as it gets. You can pretend to be appalled by this slang, if not the sexual practices described, but if you weren't amused with the wit and creativity of unconventional vocabulary you wouldn't be holding this book in your hands in the first place.'

From the preface by **Tom Dalzell** and **Terry Victor**

Sex Slang

Tom Dalzell and **Terry Victor**

Routledge
Taylor & Francis Group

LONDON AND NEW YORK

First published 2008 by Routledge
2 Park Square, Milton Park, Abingdon, OX14 4RN
Simultaneously published in the USA and Canada
by Routledge
270 Madison Ave, New York, NY 10016

Routledge is an imprint of the Taylor & Francis Group, an informa business

© 2008 Tom Dalzell and Terry Victor

Typeset in India by Alden Prepress Services Private Limited, Chennai, TN
Printed and bound in Great Britain by TJ International Ltd, Padstow, Cornwall

British Library Cataloguing in Publication Data
A catalogue record for this book is available from the British Library

Library of Congress Cataloging in Publication Data
Dalzell, Tom, 1951
Sex slang / Tom Dalzell and Terry Victor.
p. cm.
1. Sex – Terminology 2. Sex – Slang – Dictionaries. I. Victor, Terry. II. Title
HQ9.D325 2007
306.7703–dc22
2007028913

ISBN10: 0-415-37180-5 (pbk)
ISBN10: 0-203-93577-2 (ebk)

ISBN13: 978-0-415-37180-3 (pbk)
ISBN13: 978-0-203-93577-4 (ebk)

CONTENTS

PREFACE

In the world of slang, sex slang is about as good as it gets. You can pretend to be appalled by this slang, if not the sexual practices described, but if you weren't amused with the wit and creativity of unconventional vocabulary you wouldn't be holding this book in your hands in the first place.

We are hard-wired for a linguistic resourcefulness that always matches, and usually surpasses, our physical and sexual invention. Most sexual slang represents practices as old as the ages – newly discovered, of course, by the next generation. New sexual activity is extremely rare but you will find there's always a word for it in these pages.

The need for slang as an intimate language and defender of moral transgression is readily apparent. As the next generation is always inventing sex for the first time sex can never be entirely conventional. The excitement of discovery and danger, of outrage and rebellion against the mainstream, is evident in this small dictionary of sex slang.

This volume consists of approximately 3,000 headword entries drawn in large part from our *New Partridge Dictionary of Slang and Unconventional English*, in which we recorded slang and unconventional English heard anywhere in the English-speaking world any time since 1945. In that work and here we included pidgin, Creolized English and borrowed foreign terms used by English speakers in primarily English-language conversation. We excluded no term on the ground that it might be considered offensive as a racial, ethnic, religious, sexual or other slur. This dictionary contains many entries and citations that will, and should, offend.

We used UK spelling for definitions and our commentary but used indigenous spelling for headwords and citations. This is especially relevant in the case of the UK **arse** and US **ass**. For Yiddish words, we used Leo Rostens spelling, which favours sh- over sch-. An initialism is shown in upper case without full stops (for example, **BJ**), except that acronyms (pronounced like individual lexical items) are lower case (for example, **milf**).

Phrases are, as a rule, placed under their first significant word. For example, the phrase 'get your ashes hauled' is listed as a phrase under the headword **ash**. By this placement scheme, we sought to avoid the endless pages of entries starting with prepositions or common verbs such as get.

In dealing with slang from all seven continents, we encountered more than a few culture-specific term's. For such terms, we identified the domain or geographic location of the term's usage. We used conventional English in the definitions, turning to slang only when it is both substantially more economical than the use of conventional English and readily understood by the average reader.

The country of origin reflects the origin of the earliest citation found for the headword. As is the case with dating, further research will undoubtedly produce a shift in the country of origin for a number of our entries. We resolutely avoided guesswork and informed opinion.

We recognize that the accurate dating of slang is far more difficult than dating conventional language. Virtually every word in our lexicon is spoken before it is written, and this is especially true of unconventional terms. We dated a term to indicate the earliest citation that we discovered.

For each entry, we included a quotation, a citation or a gloss explaining where the term was collected. Sheer joy is often found expressed in these quotations, while the citations and glosses give a sense of when and where the term was found.

No more foreplay! Enough beating about the bush! Time to get down to some serious reading and it just doesn't get much better than sexual slang.

But remember: too much of a good thing may make you go blind.

Tom Dalzell, Berkeley, California
Terry Victor, Caerwent, Wales
Late Spring 2007

ACKNOWLEDGEMENTS

Our debt to Sophie Oliver defies description. With good humour and a saintly tolerance for our so-called wit and attempts to corrupt, she herded this project through from a glimmer in the eye to print on the page.

We bow to and thank the following who helped along the way: Mary Ann Kernan, who was charged with putting this project together in 1999 and 2000; John Williams, who must be credited for all that is right about our lexicography and excused for anything that is not; our contributors to the *New Partridge*, Richard Allsopp, Diane Bardsley, James Lambert, John Loftus, Lewis Poteet; and our Sex and Vice task-mistress Sonja van Leeuwen.

Tom Dalzell and Terry Victor

This dictionary would never have seen the light of day without the time and support given me by my family. To protect the innocent from the dubious honour of being thanked in a context such as this, they will remain for these purposes nameless.

I thank: my slang mentors Paul Dickson and Madeline Kripke (and better mentors you could not hope for); Archie Green, who saved Peter Tamony's work for posterity and encouraged me throughout this project; Reinold Aman, Jesse Sheidlower, Jonathan Green and Susan Ford, slang lexicographers, friends and comrades-in-words; Dr. Jerry Zientara, the learned, witty and helpful librarian at the Institute for Advanced Study of Human Sexuality in San Francisco, which kindly opened its incomparable library to me; Tom Miller, Bill Stolz, John Konzal and Patricia Walker, archivists at the Western Historical Manuscript Collection, University of Missouri at Columbia, for their help and insights during my work with the Peter Tamony archives; Jim Holliday for his help on the slang of pornography; Jennifer Goldstein for her help on the slang of sex dancers; and Richard Perlman for his patient technological help.

Lastly, I acknowledge Terry Victor. With his joy of life and sexual puns, he has made a consider-able mark on the last eight years.

Tom Dalzell

Liz, for her patience and tolerance, and above all for her smiles that seem to say 'Well, what else could I expect from the man I married?' My Liz. Thank you.

My inspirations cannot go unacknowledged; the seductive swirl of their slang led a young man astray, especially Barry Took and Marty Feldman for 'Jules & Sand'; Ray Galton and Alan Simpson for 'Steptoe & Son', Barry Humphries for 'Barry McKenzie', and Ronnie Barker for 'Fletcher'. They got me started, long before I had ever heard of Eric Partridge.

But, above all, Tom Dalzell must be named and shamed as the Sultan of Slang, for his scholarship and generosity - my passionate affair with the dark niches of our tongue would be just a secret fantasy without him.

Terry Victor

Aa

A *adjective*
anal *US, 1997*
- Now every scene I do is pretty much an "A" scene. (Quoting Nici Sterling). — Anthony Petkovich, *The X Factory* 1997

ABC's *noun*
underwear *US, 1949*
- I took off the a b c's and her stockings. — Hal Ellson, *Duke* 1949

abort *verb*
to defecate after being the passive partner in anal sex *US, 1972*
- — Bruce Rodgers, *The Queens' Vernacular* 1972

ace of spades *noun*
the vulva *US, 1960*
- — Harold Wentworth and Stuart Berg Flexner, *Dictionary of American Slang* 1960

acey-deucy *adjective*
bisexual *US, 1972*
A probable elaboration of 'AC/DC'.
- — Bruce Rodgers, *The Queens' Vernacular* 1972

Adam *noun*
a homosexual's first sexual partner *US, 1972*
The first man.
- — Bruce Rodgers, *The Queens' Vernacular* 1972

adult baby *noun*
a person, often a prostitute's client, whose sexual needs are manifested in a desire to be dressed and treated as an infant *UK, 1995*
- Ben refused to see anything wrong with being an adult baby. — Kitty Churchill, *Thinking of England* 1995

afgay *noun*
a homosexual *US, 1972*
Formed by a pig Latin-like construction called 'Anyway'.
- — Robert A. Wilson, *Playboy's Book of Forbidden Words* 1972

African queen *noun*
a white homosexual man who finds black men attractive *US, 1979*
Punning on the Bogart film.
- — *Maledicta* 1979: 'Kinks and queens: linguistic and cultural aspects of the terminology for gays'

afternoon delight *noun*
extra-marital sex *US, 1982*
- adultery: afternoon delight — Sherri Foxman, *Classified Love* 1982

agate *noun*
a small penis *US, 1967*
- — Dale Gordon, *The Dominion Sex Dictionary* 1967

Agent Scully *noun*
oral sex *US, 2001*
A reference to the name of the female lead in the *X-Files* television series, punning on her name and SKULL (oral sex).
- Brooks and his colleagues also provide police with glossaries of street slang – "Agent Scully" = "oral sex," "getting my cake" = "dating my girl." — *Washington Post* 20th August 2001

a-hole *noun*
the anus *US, 1942*
A euphemism that calls more attention to that which is being skirted than would a direct reference.
- Cum dribbles down her crack, ultimately resting upon her a-hole. — Anthony Petkovich, *The X Factory* 1997

air *noun*
in the pornography industry, an ejaculation that cannot be seen leaving the penis and travelling through the air *US, 1995*
In a situation which calls for visual proof of the ejaculation, air is not good.
- — *Adult Video News* August, 1995

air-conditioned *adjective*
sexually frigid *UK, 1983*
- — Tom Hibbert, *Rockspeak!* 1983

ala-ala's *noun*
the testicles *US, 1981*
Hawaiian youth usage.
- Wow, da guy when keec mah ala-alas! Ah t'ought da buggah goin bus'! — Douglas Simonson, *Pidgin to da Max* 1981

a-la-beff *noun*
vaginal intercourse, the woman on hands and knees and the man entering her from behind *TRINIDAD AND TOBAGO, 1980*
An allusion to the mating of cattle and the French *boeuf*.
• — Lise Winer, *Dictionary of the English/Creole of Trinidad & Tobago* 2003

a-levels *noun*
anal sex, especially when advertised as a service offered by a prostitute *UK, 2003*
A play on the name given to 'advanced-level' examinations in the British education system.
• — Caroline Archer, *Tart Cards* 2003

alley cat *noun*
a sexually promiscuous person, especially a woman *UK, 1926*
• He goes on the prowl each night / Like an alley cat / Looking for some new delight / Like an alley cat / She can't trust him out of sight[.] — Jack Harlen, *The Alley Cat Song* 1963

Amy-John *noun*
a lesbian *US, 1968*
• There are harsher and more widely used expressions: "Bulldyke," "Amy-John," "Cat-lapper," "Les," and so on. — L. Reinhard, *Oral Sex Techniques and Sex Practices Illustrated* 1968

angel food *noun*
a member of the US Air Force as an object of homosexual desire *US, 1988*
• — H. Max, *Gay (S)language* 1988

angry *adjective*
(used of a penis) sexually aroused, erect *US, 1970*
• Ah'd purely love to see it angry. — *M*A*S*H* 1970

Antarctic 10 *noun*
any moderately good looking person of the sex that attracts you *ANTARCTICA, 1991*
The humour lies in the fact that a 'ten' in Antarctica would be a 'five' anywhere else.
• — Carnegie Mellon Astrophysics Peterson Group, *Antarctic Vocabulary* 19th September 1997

anteater *noun*
an uncircumcised penis *US, 1970*
• You get bored you might amuse yourselves by betting quarters whether the next guy in will be a helmet or an anteater. — Joseph Wambaugh, *The New Centurions* 1970

A-plug *noun*
a plug inserted in the rectum as part of a sadomasochistic encounter *US, 1979*
An abbreviation for '*ass-plug*'.
• My world of s/m is full of pleasure and is full of toys and goodies — hand-crafted leather dildoes, A-plugs[.] — *What Color is Your Handkerchief* 1979

apples *noun*
the female breasts *US, 1942*
• — Vincent J. Monteleone, *Criminal Slang* 1949

around the world *noun*
the oral stimulation of all parts of a partner's body *US, 1951*
• [T]hey say she gives a super around the world and also knows about massage[.] — Gore Vidal, *Myra Breckinridge* 1968

arse *noun*
the posterior, the buttocks *UK, 1954*
In conventional usage from Old English until early C18, at which time it was deemed impolite language and began a celebrated existence in slang, rarely appearing in print with all four letters in place. B.E.'s *Dictionary of the Canting Crew*, probably 1698–9, gives 'ar-'; Francis Grose's *Dictionary of the Vulgar Tongue*, five editions from 1785–1823 omits the 'r'. It was not until 1860 that the American **ASS** appeared. The spelling in Australia is 'arse', but pronounced with a long 'a' and no 'r'. Since the 1980s there has been some encroachment of 'ass', but this is still strongly associated with the US.
• [S]lag birds used to go trotting upstairs with him [...] arses wagging and bristols [breasts] going[.] — Derek Raymond (Robin Cook), *The Crust on its Uppers* 1962

arsehole *noun*
the anus *UK, 1400*
• You talk to your average lesbian about two men shoving their engorged pricks up each other's sweating arse-holes and they will practically vomit on you. — *Kink* 1993

arse like a wizard's sleeve *noun*
an unusually loose rectum and anus *UK, 2002*

• Fackin' slag. Cunt like a Grimsby welly, arse like a wizard's sleeve. — Andrew Holmes, *Sleb* 2002

arva; harva *noun*
sexual intercourse *UK, 2002*
Derives from Romany **charva** (to interfere with). Anal intercourse is the 'full harva'.
• [T]o have the arva. — Paul Baker, *Polari* 2002

A-sex *noun*
sex experienced while under the influence of amphetamine *US, 1975*
• Others joined them writing in insatiable A-sex. — Ed Sanders, *Tales of Beatnik Glory* 1975

ashes *noun*
▶ **get your ashes hauled**
to be brought to ejaculation *US, 1906*
• "Get the old ashes hauled." Billy and Mule look at each other. "Ashes hauled?" "That's an expression, kinda like, that means, you know, to do it, get it done." — Darryl Ponicsan, *The Last Detail* 1970

asparagus *noun*
a boy's penis *US, 2003*
From the language of child pornography.
• In court Monday, Schopp said his computer had inadvertently downloaded some of the images as he searched the Internet for asparagus recipes. Wilken noted that asparagus is apparently a slang term for boys' genitalia. — *San Francisco Chronicle* 28th October 2003

ass *noun*
1 the vagina *UK, 1684*
• I had saved my hankie that I wiped Ruth's ass out with after we had had our taste of sex, because I had a real freak of a nigger that I was gonna sell a smell of it to after I got back in the joint. — A.S. Jackson, *Gentleman Pimp* 1973
2 sex; a person as a sexual object *US, 1910*
• The other numerous downtown clubs would not serve us, nor would the white prostitutes sell black G.I.s any ass. — Bobby Seale, *A Lonely Rage* 1978
▶ **take it in the ass**
3 to take the passive role in anal intercourse *US, 1983*
• "There's a lady lawyer at the end of the bar that likes to take it in the ass," he

said. — Gerald Petievich, *To Die in Beverly Hills* 1983

ass *verb*
to engage in prostitution *US, 1991*
• — William T. Vollman, *Whores for Gloria* 1991

ass bandit; arse bandit; asshole bandit *noun*
a male homosexual especially the active partner in anal sex *US, 1968*
Usually derogatory; combines **ass**, with 'bandit' – or 'brigand', conventionally a generally romantic image of a villain who will take what he wants.
• Which is, dear reader, the true story of this particular asshole bandit[.] — Angelo d'Arcangelo, *The Homosexual Handbook* 1968

ass burglar *noun*
the active partner in anal sex; more generally, a male homosexual *US, 1979*
• — Maledicta 1979: 'Kings and queens; lingustic and cultural aspects of the terminology for gays'

ass cunt *noun*
the anus *US, 1974*
• Wowee, will you look at that little white kid's ass-cunt. That's a cherry if I ever saw one. — Piri Thomas, *Seven Long Times* 1974

ass fuck *noun*
anal sex *US, 1940*
• It seems like they were having more fun back then. Now it's like, um, you want to do an ass fuck for $250 real quick? — *LA Weekly* 19th November 1999

ass-fuck *verb*
to engage in anal sex, especially in the active role *US, 1940*
• He denies saying he wanted to "ass fuck" the man, but agrees he was out of line. — *Cleveland Scene* 2nd August 2001

ass fucking *noun*
anal sex *US, 1970*
• Ass-fucking in general, never so much as crossed my mind until about two years ago[.] — *Screw* 15th March 1970

asshole eating *noun*
oral-anal sex *US, 1988*
• For asshole eating, I would charge, I would charge him thirty dollars extra. — Dolores French, *Working* 1988

ass hound *noun*
a man who obsessively engages in the pursuit of women for sex *US*, *1952*
- Corbett, who had the reputation of being a real ass hound, was embarassed and could not look Hal in the eye. — Ralph McInerny, *Body and Soil* 1991

ass juice *noun*
rectal secretions and/or lubrication *US*, *2001*
- This fat cock likes dark and damp places where it can gather up the stench of sweat and cum and ass-juice. — Mark Hemry, *Tales from the Bear Cult* 2001

ass man; arse man *noun*
a man who considers that the (suggestive) appearance of a woman's posterior provides the supreme initial sexual attraction *US*, *1972*
- [A]n ageing pornographer who specialised in videos devoted to anal sex – "the arse man of the millennium". — *The Guardian* 8th May 2000

ass queen *noun*
a homosexual man who is particularly attracted to other men's buttocks *US*, *1978*
- — Anon., *King Smut's Wet Dreams Interpreted* 1978

at it *adjective*
engaged in sexual intercourse *AUSTRALIA*, *1972*
- She's got another one now. She's at it again. — Dorothy Hewett, *The Chapel Perilous* 1972

auld lang syne *noun*
mutual, simultaneous oral sex between two people *UK*, *2003*
Rhyming slang for **69**.
- I'm lucky if my wife gives me a hand job, let alone join me in Auld Lang Syne. — Bodmin Dark, *Dirty Cockney Rhyming Slang* 2003

aunt *noun*
the manager of a brothel *UK*, *1606*
- — Vincent J. Monteleone, *Criminal Slang* 1949

Aussie kiss *noun*
oral-genital stimulation *UK*, *2002*
Described as 'similar to a French Kiss, but given down under'.
- — Chris Donald, *Roger's Profanisaurus* 2002

Bb

baby *noun*

1 a prostitute's customer *US, 1957*

- Still and all, she had a small minute of indecision when he brought the first hundred-dollar baby to his apartment to meet her. — John M. Murtagh and Sara Harris, *Cast the First Stone* 1957

2 a young performer new to the pornography industry who looks even younger than he or she is *US, 1995*

- — *Adult Video News* August, 1995

baby batter *noun*

semen *US, 1997*

- [I]t's because you ain't got the baby batter in your brain any more. — *Something About Mary* 1998

baby fucker *noun*

a child molestor *US, 1985*

- The third was a child molestor who perhaps was not the best choice that the Colebrook Unified School District might have made as the driver of its bus for junior high school students. "The baby-fucker," I said. — George V. Higgins, *Penance for Jerry Kennedy* 1985

babylons *noun*

the female breasts *UK, 2001*

- BEING FIT DONT JUST MEAN HAVIN GREAT BABYLONS AND A NICE PUNANI. — Sacha Baron-Cohen, *Da Gospel According to Ali G* 2001

baby pro *noun*

a very, very young prostitute *US, 1961*

- — Burgess Laughlin, *Job Opportunities in the Black Market* 1978

bacalao *noun*

the unwashed vagina *JAMAICA, 1996*

From the Spanish for 'codfish'.

- — Richard Allsopp, *Dictionary of Caribbean English Usage* 1996

back door; backdoor *noun*

the anus and rectum *UK, 1694*

- She says, "Sweetie, I ain't gonna go three way with you for no sawbuck. You gotta gimme fifteen." He says, "I'll spring for that if you can guarantee a tight back door and quim." — Iceberg Slim (Robert Beck), *Doom Fox* 1978

back-door; backdoor *adjective*

adulterous *US, 1947*

- He was your mother's back-door man, I thought. — Ralph Ellison, *Invisible Man* 1947

backdoor Betty *noun*

a woman who enjoys anal sex *US, 2000*

- The people who've volunteered to get done are always self-proclaimed backdoor betties, but when push comes to penetration, they get shy. — *The Village Voice* 8th August 2000

backdoor delivery *noun*

anal sex *US, 1973*

- I find "back door deliveries" very painful – even when a man uses lots of lubricant. — Jennifer Sills, *Massage Parlor* 1973

backdooring *noun*

anal intercourse *UK, 1997*

- ["]Bradley is referring to the rusty bullet-hole," said Mikey. "The what?" Mario was still struggling. "The chocolate starfish." "Backdooring." "Uphill gardening." [...] "What, you mean shoving it up their arse?" exclaimed Mario. — Colin Butts, *Is Harry on the Boat?* 1997

back-scuttle *verb*

to play the active role in sex, anal or vaginal, from behind *US, 1885*

- — Dale Gordon, *The Dominion Sex Dictionary* 1967

back stairs *noun*

the anus and rectum considered as a sexual passage *UK, 2001*

- [B]ecause women can, and do, let men take the back stairs[.] — *GQ* July, 2001

back wheels *noun*

the testicles *UK, 1998*

- Right up to the back wheels[.] — *www.LondonSlang.com* 26th June 2002

backyard *noun*

1 the buttocks *US, 1972*

- — John A. Holm, *Dictionary of Bahamian English* 1982

2 the anus *US, 1967*

- — Dale Gordon, *The Dominion Sex Dictionary* 1967

badger scratching *noun*
the act of fondling a woman's vagina *UK,*
2002
- I wouldn't mind doin' a bit of badger
  scratching with her.
  — *www.londonSlang.com* 26th June
  2002

badly packed kebab *noun*
the vagina *UK, 2002*
A visual similarity.
- — Chris Lewis, *The Dictionary of
  Playground Slang* 2003

bad sick *noun*
any sexually transmitted infection *ANTIGUA
AND BARBUDA, 1996*
- — Richard Allsopp, *Dictionary of
  Caribbean English Usage* 1996

bag *noun*
1 the scrotum *US, 1938*
- — Anon., *King Smut's Wet Dreams
  Interpreted* 1978
2 a diaphragm *US, 1964*
- — Roger Blake, *The American Dictionary
  of Sexual Terms* 1964

baggage *noun*
a boyfriend, agent or other male who
accompanies a female pornography
performer to the set *US, 1995*
Not flattering.
- — *Adult Video News* October, 1995

bagpipe *verb*
to stimulate the penis to orgasm under the
armpit of a lover *UK, 1904*
Homosexual use.
- He's a real case for bagpiping guys
  with big hairy arms. — Bruce Rodgers,
  The Queens' Vernacular 1972

bag up *verb*
to put a condom on a penis *UK, 2002*
Also variant construction of 'bag it up'.
- Ah couldn'a found a fellah's dick, let
  alone discreetly bagged it up. — Ben
  Elton, *High Society* 2002

bahookie *noun*
the buttocks; the anus *UK, 1985*
- [A] member of the Scottish executive
  having a dildo jammed up his
  bahookie by a piece of telegenic jailbait[.] — Christopher Brookmyre,
  Boiling a Frog 2000

baked-bean *noun*
a sexual interlude *UK, 2000*
Rhyming slang for SCENE.

- I'm about to press the little green
  button to connect me to her number, to
  arrange a little baked bean, my old
  gent's getting twitchy at the very
  thought[.] — J.J. Connolly, *Layer Cake*
  2000

balcony *noun*
the female breasts *US, 1964*
- Polly's balcony might not be something
  to inflame the pimple-faced readers of
  Playboy, but it had exactly what a
  grown man wanted[.] — Max Shulman,
  Anyone Got a Match? 1964

baldy lad *noun*
the penis *UK, 2001*
- Is there a famous person who looks
  like your baldy lad, would you say?
  Who'd yew say yewer knob looks like,
  if anyone? — Niall Griffiths,
  Sheepshagger 2001

ball *noun*
an act of sexual intercourse *US, 1970*
- Ball: The accepted word for the sex act.
  — *Screw* 12th October 1970

ball *verb*
1 to have sex *US, 1952*
- In that time, Dean is balling Marylou at
  the hotel and gives me time to change
  and dress. — Jack Kerouac, *On the
  Road* 1957
2 to insert amphetamine or methampheta-
mine in the vagina before sexual
intercourse *US, 1971*
- — Eugene Landy, *The Underground
  Dictionary* 1971

balls *noun*
the testicles *UK, 1325*
- I joined the university karate class (not
  because I wanted a code of honour but
  so I could kick anyone in the balls who
  attacked me when I walked home late
  at night). — *The Guardian* 20th January
  2004

baloney *noun*
the penis *US, 1928*
- Man, wouldn't I love to play hide the
  baloney with that. — Charles Whited,
  Chiodo 1973

baloney pony *noun*
the penis *US, 2002*
- DUANE: How big is your johnson?
  RAMU: Johnson? DUANE: Your wand,
  your pork sword, your baloney pony.
  — *The Guru* 2002

balsa boy *noun*
a male pornography performer who has
trouble maintaining an erection *US, 1995*
One of many **wood** images.
- — *Adult Video News* August, 1995

bam-bam *noun*
the buttocks *TRINIDAD AND TOBAGO, 2003*
- — Lise Winer, *Dictionary of the
English/Creole of Trinidad & Tobago*
2003

- I shall keep my word, and you shall
keep your banana tree. — Petra
Christian, *The Sexploiters* 1973

B and D; B/D *noun*
bondage and domination (or discipline) as
sexual activities *US, 1974*
- Real-life S/M activity, unlike the cliches
of S/M ficiton, rarely is bizarre or
extreme; most of it involves biting,
hitting, slapping and the like, rather

PENIS

baloney *noun, US, 1928*
- Man, wouldn't I love to play hide the
baloney with that. — Charles Whited,
Chiodo 1973
beef *noun, US, 2001*
- "The boy is masturbating" [...] Beef Strokin'
off[.] — Erica Orloff and JoAnn Baker, *Dirty
Little Secrets* 2001
bone *noun, US, 1916*
the penis, especially when erect
- "Why, if you mean do I think I could get a
bone up over that old buzzard, no, I don't
believe I could..." — Ken Kesey, *One Flew
Over the Cuckoo's Nest* 1962
dingus *noun, US, 1888*
- Half-and-half still costs you more than
straight, so if you need the girl's mouth on
your dingus to get you up it will set you
back a total of thirty dollars[.] — Gerald
Paine, *A Bachelor's Guide to the Brothels of
Nevada* 1978

swanz *noun, US, 1985*
- They wore wigs and tied their cocks up with
pantyhose back toward their ass, so if the
guy reached down there he couldn't feel the
swanz hanging there to give the guy away.
— Mark Baker, *Cops* 1985
tool *noun, UK, 1553*
Conventional English at first – found in
Shakespeare's *Henry VIII* – and then
rediscovered in the C20 as handy slang.
- Men wake up every morning and look at
their tools standing at attention. — Anka
Radakovich, *The Wild Girls Club* 1994
wang; whang *noun, US, 1935*
- Filipinos come quick; colored men are built
abnormally large ("Their wangs look like a
baby's arm with an apple in its fist"); ladies
with short hair are Lesbians; if you want to
keep your man, rub alum on your pussy.
— Lenny Bruce, *How to Talk Dirty and
Influence People* 1965

bamsie *noun*
the buttocks *BARBADOS, 1996*
- — Richard Allsopp, *Dictionary of
Caribbean English Usage* 1996

bamsie man *noun*
a male homosexual *TRINIDAD AND TOBAGO,
1996*
- — Richard Allsopp, *Dictionary of
Caribbean English Usage* 1996

banana *noun*
the penis *US, 1916*
- — Anon., *King Smut's Wet Dreams
Interpreted* 1978

banana hammock *noun*
a brief male bikini *US, 1997*
- — Vann Wesson, *Generation X Field
Guide and Lexicon* 1997

banana tree *noun*
the penis *UK, 1973*

than heavy B and D (bondage and
discipline). — *Playboy* March, 1974

bandit *noun*
an obvious homosexual *UK, 2001*
An abbreviation of **ass/arse bandit**.
- [T]his pure fucking bandit comes
mincing in[.] — Kevin Sampson,
Outlaws 2001

bang *noun*
an instance of sexual intercourse *UK, 1691*
- Bob had his bang; he came out and
called Big Lug; Big Lug went down and
got his bang[.] — Jack Kerouac, *Letter
to Neal Cassady* 10 January 1951

bang *verb*
1 to have sex *UK, 1720*
- Because I haven't banged anybody, not
anybody, since we picked up Dinah,
except her, of course, and this Margo is

real cute. — John Clellon Holmes,
Go 1952

2 to stimulate a woman's vagina by
introducing and withdrawing a finger in
rapid order *US, 1971*

- — Eugene Landy, *The Underground
Dictionary* 1971

▶ **bang the crap out of**

3 of a male, to exhaust a sex-partner by
vigorous sexual activity *UK, 2003*

An intensification of BANG (to have sex) on the
model of 'beat the crap out of' (to thrash).

- Their favourite [porn film] star is Rocco,
a Brazilian guy who bangs the crap out
of girls[.] — *Mixmag* April, 2003

bang-bang *noun*

the penis *BAHAMAS, 1982*

- — John A. Holm, *Dictionary of
Bahamian English* 1982

banged up *adjective*

pregnant *NEW ZEALAND, 2002*

- — Sonya Plowman, *Great Kiwi Slang*
2002

baps *noun*

the female breasts *AUSTRALIA, 1992*

After the small soft bread rolls.

- Another survey – this time by British
bra makers – found that Pommy
sheilas' baps are getting bigger and
bigger and that soon the average girlie
will sport enormous 38D-sized noras.
— *Picture* 5th February 1992

bareback *adverb*

(used of sex) without a condom *US, 1960*

- I always ride bareback myself. Take a
chance my way, though. — Joseph
Wambaugh, *The Glitter Dome* 1981

bareback rider *noun*

a man who has sex without using a condom
US, 1960

- — Harold Wentworth and Stuart Berg
Flexner, *Dictionary of American Slang*
1960

Baseball Annie *noun*

a woman who makes herself available
sexually to professional baseball players
US, 1949

- It is permissible, in the scheme of
things, to promise a Baseball Annie
dinner and a show in return for certain
quick services for a pair of roommates.
— Jim Bouton, *Ball Four* 1970

bash *noun*

an act of sexual intercourse *UK, 1979*

- And then you can whip her up top for a
quick bash! — Lance Peters, *The Dirty
Half-Mile* 1979

bash *verb*

▶ **bash one out**

(of a male) to masturbate *UK, 2002*

- I didn't like the thought of him just
doing it so cheap, so routine – just
bashing one out like that. — Kevin
Sampson, *Clubland* 2002

▶ **bash the bishop**

(of a male) to masturbate *UK, 2000*

- [M]y left hand Bashing the Bishop.
— Stuart Browne, *Dangerous Parking*
2000

basket *noun*

1 the male genitals as seen through tight
trousers *US, 1941*

- What a low-cut gown to a faggot must
be is like tight Levis with a padded
basket. — Lenny Bruce, *The Essential
Lenny Bruce* 1967

2 a woman's labia *US, 1949*

- — Vincent J. Monteleone, *Criminal
Slang* 1949

basket days *noun*

days of good weather *US, 1965*

- Basket days – A period of mild weather
that permits men to wear garments
light enough to reveal the contours of
their baskets. — *Fact* January-February,
1965

basket shopping *noun*

the practice of observing the crotch of a
clothed male to gauge the size of his penis
US, 1964

Also known as 'basket watching'.

- — Roger Blake, *The American Dictionary
of Sexual Terms* 1964

bat and balls *noun*

the male genitals with the penis erect *UK,
2003*

- She [...] took off her glasses and went
straight to work with that long tongue
of hers licking my bat and balls.
— *The Sucker's Kiss* (excerpted in 'The
Guardian' under the headline 'The Bad
Sex award shortlisted passages') 4th
December 2003

batch *noun*

an ejaculation's worth of semen *US, 1973*

- The sounds this bitch was making
damn near had me ready to unload this
batch right in her hand[.] — A.S.
Jackson, *Gentleman Pimp* 1973

baths *noun*
Turkish baths where the main attraction is sex between homosexual men *US, 1968*
- You'll never learn to stay out of the baths, will you. — Mart Crowley, *The Boys in the Band* 1968

battle scar *noun*
a bruise on the skin caused by sucking *US, 1982*
Hawaiian youth usage.
- — Douglas Simonson, *Pidgin to da Max Hana Hou* 1982

batty *noun*
the buttocks *JAMAICA, 1935*
Also variant 'bati'.
- If yuh touch me batty again, me gwan chop off yuh han'. — Donald Gorgon, *Cop Killer* 1994

batty man *noun*
a male homosexual *ANTIGUA AND BARBUDA, 1977*
- Being gay or lesbian – a "chi-chi" man'gal or a "battyman," is the ultimate sin in Jamaica. — *San Diego Union-Tribune* 26th August 2001

batty wash *noun*
the act of licking an anus with your tongue *UK, 2000*
West Indies origins.
- Tunde made him give him a batty wash [...] And he had to suck out Tunde's arsehole. — *Dog Eat Dog* 2000

bayonet *noun*
▶ **take the bayonet course**
to participate in bismuth subcarbonate and neoarsphenamine therapy for syphilis *US, 1981*
- — *Maledicta* Summer/Winter, 1981: 'Sex and the single soldier'

bazooka *noun*
the penis *US, 1984*
- — Brigid McConville and John Shearlaw, *The Slanguage of Sex* 1984

bazookas *noun*
the female breasts *US, 2005*
- Thonged buttage backed up by booming bazookas when Bobbie boogies on the stage at a club. — Mr. Skin, *Mr. Skin's Skincyclopedia* 2005

bazoomas; bazoombas *noun*
the female breasts *UK, 1984*
- Do you wish you played drums so you could peek at her bazoomas on stage? — *FHM* June, 2003

bazooms *noun*
the female breasts *US, 1936*
Originally a corruption of 'bosom' with the same sense, then evolved to mean 'breasts'; almost always phrased in the plural.
- Yeahh, but howdja like them bazooms on that P.R. chick? — Richard Price, *The Wanderers* 1974

bazooties *noun*
the female breasts *US, 1997*
- — Anna Scotti and Paul Young, *Buzzwords* 1997

BDSM; BD/SM *noun*
bondage, domination, sadism and masochism or sado-masochism, unified as a sexual subculture *US, 1969*
- Even fashion is taking a lead from the BDSM scene. Black leather, chokers, spikes and high heels have all graced the catwalks over the last year or so. — *Code* January, 2002

beach boy *noun*
a handsome, young black man who takes white female tourists as lovers *BARBADOS, 1996*
- — Richard Allsopp, *Dictionary of Caribbean English Usage* 1996

beam *noun*
▶ **to have your high beams on**
(used of a female) to experience erect nipples *US, 2003*
Related to describing such a female as having her HIGH BEAMS on.
- — Chris Lewis, *The Dictionary of Playground Slang* 2003

bean *noun*
the clitoris *UK, 2001*
- The scenes with her flicking her bean [masturbating] are fucking good. — Kevin Sampson, *Outlaws* 2001

bean queen *noun*
a homosexual who prefers Latin Americans as sexual partners *US, 1988*
- — H. Max, *Gay (S)language* 1988

beans *noun*
sexual satisfaction *UK, 1997*
A meal that 'fills you up'.
- I told him I's givin' her beans before him so he calls me a cunt an' we had

a scrap. — Nick Barlay, *Curvy Lovebox*
1997

beard *noun*
a woman's pubic hair *US, 2005*
- [S]he strips down to bumpers and
beard, then climbs aboard his Oscar
Meyer-mobile. — Mr. Skin, *Mr. Skin's
Skincyclopedia* 2005

bearded clam *noun*
the vulva *US, 1965*
- He gobbles one beaver and gets
promoted. I've ate close to three
hundred bearded clams in my time and
never even got a commendation.
— Joseph Wambaugh, *The Choirboys*
1975

beast *noun*
the penis *UK, 2001*
- [H]e iz very mesculin [masculine] and iz
got a beast dat iz well in hadvance of
hiz age. — Sacha Baron-Cohen,
Da Gospel According to Ali G 2001

beast *verb*
to have anal sex *UK, 1999*
- "What you been up to then, Lisa?"
"Well, you know, getting beasted by
Jason. What with him being inside for
so long, one of the problems is they
always want to do it up the arse."
— Jeff Pope and Terry Winsor, *Essex
Boys* 1999

beasting *noun*
from a male perspective, an act of sexual
intercourse *UK, 2003*
Possibly inspired by the BEAST WITH TWO BACKS.
- [T]onight I'm planning to give her a
beasting she won't forget. — Colin
Butts, *Is Harry Still on the Boat?* 2003

beast with two backs *noun*
vaginal, face-to-face sexual intercourse
between a heterosexual couple; sex
between two people *UK, 1604*
From Shakespeare.
- Hey you!! Did you make the beast with
two backs with my little ewe? — Barry
Humphries, *The Wonderful World of
Barry McKenzie* 1968

beat *verb*
▶ **beat about the bush; beat around the
bush**
1 (of a female) to masturbate *UK, 1991*
Wordplay on 'beat' (used in many terms of
male masturbation) and BUSH (the pubic hair).

- Forgive me. I probably don't have time
to beat about your bush. — Terry Victor,
Return of the Menu Monster 1991
▶ **beat it**
2 (of a male) to masturbate *US, 1995*
- The plane started spinning around,
going out of control. So my cousin
decides it's all over, and he whips it
out and starts beating it right there.
— *Mallrats* 1995
▶ **beat the pup**
3 (of a male) to masturbate *US, 1950*
- — Hyman E. Goldin et al., *Dictionary of
American Underworld Lingo* 1950
▶ **beat your baloney**
4 (of a male) to masturbate *US, 1969*
- One maverick among those polled got
his kicks beating his baloney during TV
commercials. — *Screw* 10th November
1969
▶ **beat your bishop**
5 (of a male) to masturbate *US, 1916*
- In fact you can sit here and rest or
beat your bishop while I go ramblin
around there, I like to ramble by
myself. — Jack Kerouac, *The Dharma
Bums* 1958
▶ **beat your meat; beat the meat**
6 (of a male) to masturbate *US, 1936*
- Suppose you just sit down and beat
your meat if you're getting anxious.
— Norman Mailer, *The Naked and the
Dead* 1948

beat off *verb*
(of a male) to masturbate *US, 1962*
- [T]hen there was only emptiness and
the same sort of something-wasted
feeling he'd had when he was his little
brother's age and beat off in the
bathroom. — Jess Mowry, *Way Past
Cool* 1992

beat sheet *noun*
a pornographic magazine *US, 1997*
- — Anna Scotti and Paul Young,
Buzzwords 1997

beaver *noun*
a woman's pubic region; a woman as a sex
object; sex with a woman *US, 1927*
- Hey, you know what the cryptic term
"Beaver" refers to in those nudie movie
ads? Then you're sharper than a
Gillette. — *San Francisco Chronicle* 27th
September 1967

beaver cleaver *noun*
a womaniser; the penis *UK, 1981*

- Do black men truly have such
  burdensome Beaver Cleavers?
  — Richard Herring, *Talking Cock* 2003

beaver creek *noun*
▶ **have a bite at beaver creek**
to perform oral sex on a woman *US, 2001*
- Another way to say "cunnilingus" [...]
  Having a bite at beaver creek[.] — Erica
  Orloff and JoAnn Baker, *Dirty Little
  Secrets* 2001

beaver fever *noun*
an obsession with women and sex *US, 1997*
- — Anna Scotti and Paul Young,
  Buzzwords 1997

beaver flick *noun*
a pornographic film *US, 1970*
- "We know we've got a long way to go
  but we're trying not to make just
  beaver flicks." (Quoting Jim Mitchell).
  — *The Berkeley Tribe* 22nd-28th August
  1970

beaver loop *noun*
a repeating video featuring female frontal
nudity *US, 1971*
- During my career, I've probably seen
  close to 500 beaver loops and maybe
  200 hard-core shorts[.] — *Screw* 2nd
  August 1971

beaver pie *noun*
the female genitals, especially as the object
of sucking and licking *UK, 1983*
- — Tom Hibbert, *Rockspeak!* 1983

beaver red *noun*
a photograph or film depiction of a
woman's vulva, showing a hint of pink but
not the vaginal lips *US, 1970*
- No, that's what we call "beaver red."
  It's not prosecutable as long as you
  don't have the lips showing or hanging
  out all through the picture. — Roger
  Blake, *The Porno Movies* 1970

beaver-shooting *noun*
a concerted voyeuristic effort to find women
whose genitals or pubic hair can be seen
US, 1970
- I better explain about beaver-shooting.
  A beaver-shooter is, at bottom, a
  Peeping Tom. It can be anything from
  peering over the top of the dugout to
  look up dresses to hanging from the
  fire escape on the twentieth floor of
  some hotel to look into a window.
  — Jim Bouton, *Ball Four* 1970

beaver shot *noun*
a photograph or filming of a woman's
genitals *US, 1970*
In the early 1960s LA-based band The
Periscopes recorded a rock'n'roll tune called
'Beaver Shot' which was banned from the
radio after two plays.
- In commercial film prior to this, other
  than documentaries on nudism, a view
  of the pubic region – the "beaver shot"
  it was called – occurred only as a brief
  glimpse[.] — Terry Southern, *Blue Movie*
  1970

beaver-with-stick *noun*
full frontal male nudity *US, 1977*
- Back in the good old days, like the
  middle '60s, when female "beaver"
  films were all the rage, the industry
  catered primarily to the heterosexual
  trade. Oh, sure, there was the
  occasional male "beaver-with-stick"
  flick, but these were the exception.
  — *San Francisco Chronicle* 24th January
  1977

beef *noun*
1 the vagina; an attractive and sexual
woman *BARBADOS, 1982*
- — John A. Holm, *Dictionary of
  Bahamian English* 1982
2 the penis *US, 2001*
- "The boy is masturbating" [...] Beef
  Strokin' off[.] — Erica Orloff and JoAnn
  Baker, *Dirty Little Secrets* 2001

beef *verb*
to have sex *US, 1975*
- There were sounds from Connell's
  bedroom [...] Connell was beefing her.
  — G.F. Newman, *The Gurnor* 1997

beef-a-roni *noun*
a muscular, handsome male *US, 1985*
Punning with the name of a food product
and the many meat images involved in
sexual slang.
- — Connie Eble (Editor), *UNC-CH
  Campus Slang* April, 1985

beef bugle *noun*
the penis, especially as an object of oral
sex *AUSTRALIA, 1971*
- Have youse tried blowin' the old beef
  bugle? — Barry Humphries, *Bazza Pulls
  It Off!* 1971

beefcake *noun*
artistic or photographic depictions of nude
or partially nude muscular men *US, 1949*

The sexual reciprocal of CHEESECAKE.
- Lesbian periodicals, male "beefcake," pamphlets, cards, buttons, and a host of fine fiction on the homosexual theme adorn the shelves of Craig's bookstore. — *Screw* 21st February 1969

beef curtains *noun*
the labia *US, 1998*
- — Paul Baker, *Polari* 2002

beef injection; hot beef injection *noun*
sexual intercourse *US, 1968*
- [W]hat Rollo really needs is love, affection, understanding, etc., etc. In other words, a beef injection. — Angelo d'Arcangelo, *The Homosexual Handbook* 1968

been around *adjective*
sexually experienced *US, 1979*
- Brad and Dell both told me "for my own good" that Deb "has been around." — Beatrice Sparks (writing as 'Anonymous'), *Jay's Journal* 1979

been there *adjective*
said of a person with whom the speaker has had sex *FIJI, 1996*
- She's a fuck-around man. Lotsa fellas been there. — Jan Tent, 1996

bee stings *noun*
small female breasts *US, 1964*
- — Michael Dalton Johnson, *Talking Trash with Redd Foxx* 1994

behind-the-behind *noun*
anal sex *US, 1967*
- — Dale Gordon, *The Dominion Sex Dictionary* 1967

bejonkers *noun*
the female breasts *AUSTRALIA, 1988*
- — James McDonald, *A Dictionary of Obscenity, Taboo and Euphemism* 1988

bell *noun*
the clitoris *AUSTRALIA, 1988*
- — James McDonald, *A Dictionary of Obscenity, Taboo and Euphemism* 1988

bell end *noun*
the head of the penis *UK, 1997*
- [H] brushed his bell end up and down her lips before ramming himself inside her — Colin Butts, *Is Harry on the Boat?* 1997

belly queen *noun*
a male homosexual who prefers face-to-face intercourse *US, 1965*

- — Robert A. Wilson, *Playboy's Book of Forbidden Words* 1972

belly ride *noun*
sexual intercourse *US, 1993*
- — Kenn 'Naz' Young, *Naz's Dictionary of Teen Slang* 1993

Benny boy *noun*
a young transvestite prostitute found in Manila and other Southeast Asian cities *PHILIPPINES, 1967*
- The Benny Boy is a man who is dressed as a woman and uses adhesive tape to keep his genitals flat against his abdomen. — Charles Winick and Paul Kinsie, *The Lively Commerce* 1972

bent *adjective*
1 sexually deviant *UK, 1957*
- Being tall I could pass for a foreign soldier, albeit a slightly bent one. — Fiona Pitt-Kethley, *Red Light Districts of the World* 2000
2 homosexual *UK, 1959*
- Does your family know you're bent? — Armistead Maupin, *Babycakes* 1984

best friend *noun*
your penis *AUSTRALIA, 1992*
- So I wrapped a $50 note around my best friend (*he means his* DICK *readers*) and fastened it on with a rubber band. I woke up next morning with my Morning Glory being choked. — *Picture* 5th February 1992

bi *noun*
a bisexual person *US, 1956*
- If he were a "bi" he'd want to get into the act and maybe hump his buddy while ol' buddy is humping you. — *Screw* 16th May 1969

bi *adjective*
bisexual *US, 1956*
- Met this quietly sensual "bi" friend of Martin's, wearing a clerical collar. — Jefferson Poland and Valerie Alison, *The Records of the San Francisco Sexual Freedom League* 1971

Bianca blast *noun*
oral sex performed with a mouth full of Bianca mouth wash *US, 1993*
- — J.R. Schwartz, *The Official Guide to the Best Cat Houses in Nevada* 1993

bi-curious *adjective*
interested in experimenting with bisexuality *US, 2002*

● [T]o check if I have missed this week's edition of Bi-Curious Girls. — *The Guardian* 28th October 2002

bicycle *noun*
a sexually promiscuous female *UK, 1989*
● A fellow might easily marry a girl whose oul' one had been getting her oats morning, noon and night, tongue hanging out for it, the town bicycle, like, only she never got caught. — Hugh Leonard, *Out After Dark* 1989

biffer *noun*
a prostitute *US, 1971*
● "Biffer," "prossie," "she-she," "pig-meat" are some other slang designations. — Charles Winick, *The Lively Commerce* 1971

big *verb*
to impregnate someone *US, 1917*
● He tu blame fuh biggin yu. — Iceberg Slim (Robert Beck), *Mama Black Widow* 1969

big brown eye *noun*
the female breast *US, 1971*
● — Eugene Landy, *The Underground Dictionary* 1971

big casino *noun*
any sexually transmitted infection *US, 1948*
● Nitti, like Capone, had picked up in his travels the occupational malady of the underworld, euphemistically known as the capital prize, or big casino. — *San Francisco Call-Bulletin* 23rd February 1948

Big O *noun*
an orgasm *US, 1968*
● Then, just as I was about to reach the big O, shrieking with pleasure, he hurled me down the stairs[.] — Gore Vidal, *Myra Breckinridge* 1968

big tender *noun*
a scene in a pornographic film when the participants hug each other *US, 1991*
● Now, this [on screen] is what we call "the big tender," only the dialogue is a little different[.] — Robert Stoller and I.S. Levine, *Coming Attractions* 1991

big-up *adjective*
pregnant *BAHAMAS, 1995*
● — Patricia Clinton-Meicholas, *More Talkin' Bahamian* 1995

bike *noun*
a promiscuous woman *AUSTRALIA, 1945*
Suggests 'easy availability for a ride'. Often in compound as 'office bike', 'school bike', 'town bike', 'village bike', etc; occasionally, if reputation demands, 'the bike'.
● What an ugly old bike. I wouldn't ride her for practice!!! — Barry Humphries, *Bazza Pulls It Off!* 1971

bike space *noun*
the vagina *UK, 2001*
From the phrase 'I know "where i'd like to park my bike"', said by a man considering a woman as a sexual object.
● — *Sky Magazine* July, 2001

bilingual *adjective*
bisexual *US, 1964*
● — Roger Blake, *The American Dictionary of Sexual Terms* 1964

billiards *noun*
the testicles *AUSTRALIA, 1988*
● — James McDonald, *A Dictionary of Obscenity, Taboo and Euphemism* 1988

bimbo *noun*
a well-built, attractive, somewhat dim woman *US, 1920*
● New York has the most beautiful bimbos on earth and it will amuse you to learn that few of them come from New York. — Jack Lait and Lee Mortimer, *New York Confidential* 1948

bint *noun*
a promiscuous woman *UK, 1855*
Derogatory.
● Roger takes a great swig of his lager and says, quietly: – slags. Ianto sniggers and agrees. – Bints. — Niall Griffiths, *Sheepshagger* 2001

bird *noun*
the penis *US, 1969*
● "Bird" – the male organ. Used in jovial greeting, as in "How's your bird?" — *Washington Post* 17th January 1985

bird bandit *noun*
a womaniser *UK, 1984*
● I walk into a well-known bird-bandit's lair and find a comely Richard [woman] flaunting her Arris [buttocks] around the gaff[.] — Anthony Masters, *Minder* 1984

birdcage *noun*
the anus *US, 1972*

● — Bruce Rodgers, *The Queens' Vernacular* 1972

birdie *noun*
a passive, effeminate male homosexual *US, 1921*
  ● He didn't turn around even when he heard the crunch of boots on the gravel, or felt the heavy body of the bulldog creature filling the space at his back, or even when the sodomite spoke. "You're a birdie and I'm going to have your ass." — Robert Campbell, *Alice in La-La Land* 1987

bitchsplitter *noun*
the penis *US, 2003*
Used on-air in the telling of a joke by syndicated US broadcaster Mancow Muller, adopted as a name by a Canadian death metal band.
  ● — Chris Lewis, *The Dictionary of Playground Slang* 2003

bite *verb*
1 to flex, and thus contract, the sphincter during anal sex *US, 1972*
  ● — Bruce Rodgers, *The Queens' Vernacular* 1972

ERECT PENIS

blue steeler *noun, US, 1997*
a particularly erect erection
  ● — Vann Wesson, *Generation X Field Guide and Lexicon* 1997

boner *noun, US, 1961*
  ● [D]eep inside of me still burned the soul of a stupid and simple girl, who wanted nothing more out of life than to induce in every man she met a good hard boner. — Rita Ciresi, *Pink Slip* 1999

chubby *adjective, UK, 1998*
  ● [T]he sight of her big old arse is getting me chubby. — *Loaded* June, 2003

diamond cutter *noun, US, 1975*
  ● Then she slowly twists 360 degrees, all the while impaled on your diamond-cutter.
  — *The FHM Little Book of Bloke* June, 2003

pride of the morning *noun, US, 1972*
the erection experienced by a man upon awakening in the morning
  ● — Robert A. Wilson, *Playboy's Book of Forbidden Words* 1972

---

biscuit *noun*
1 a promiscuous woman *US, 1993*
  ● — Kenn 'Naz' Young, *Naz's Dictionary of Teen Slang* 1993
2 the buttocks *US, 1950*
  ● — Hyman E. Goldin et al., *Dictionary of American Underworld Lingo* 1950

bishop *noun*
the penis *US, 1916*
Used in a variety of expressions that refer to male masturbation.
  ● I banged the bishop over this one more times than I care to count. — Armistead Maupin, *Babycakes* 1984

bitch *noun*
a sexual submissive of either gender in a sado-masochistic relationship *UK, 2002*
Generally attached to a possessive pronoun.
  ● The sound of a voice I barely recognize as mine, moaning, "I'm your bitch, fuck me harder." — Val McDermid (Editors: Stella Duffy and Lauren Henderson), *Metamorphosis [Tart Noir]* 2002

▶ **bite the brown**
2 to perform mouth-to-anus sex *US, 1972*
  ● — Robert A. Wilson, *Playboy's Book of Forbidden Words* 1972

biter *noun*
the vagina *US, 1998*
  ● And out on the floor, after a long sexy masturbatory dance, her miniskirt around her hips; her rosy biter winking its hairy eye at me where I sat[.]
  — Clarence Major, *All-Night Visitors* 1998

bit of black *noun*
a black person objectified sexually *UK, 1974*
  ● I'd like to see how you'd handle a bit of black. Or vice versa. — Ted Lewis, *Jack Carter's Law* 1974

bit of brush *noun*
a woman regarded and categorised as a sexual object; the act of sex *AUSTRALIA, 1965*
  ● — William Dick, *A Bunch of Ratbags* 1965

bit of cunt *noun*
a woman regarded and categorised as a sex
object; an act of sexual intercourse *UK, 1984*
- It's all a MaccLad wants / Beer 'n' 'sex'
  'n' chips 'n' gravy / Tasty bit of cunt.
  — *The Macc Lads, Beer 'n' 'Sex' 'n'
  Chips 'n' Gravy* 1985

bit of elastic *noun*
the penis *UK, 1999*
- For me though, you can reserve your
  nice bit of elastic down there Nicky, do
  the trick just nicely. — Jeremy Cameron,
  Brown Bread in Wengen 1999

bit of hard *noun*
an erection *UK, 1978*
- [G]ive a bit of hard for a bit of soft [of
  a man, to have sex]. — Laurie Atkinson,
  1978

bit of rough *noun*
a male lover, categorised as of a lower
social status, or a rougher background than
the partner *UK, 1999*
- They're howling for a bit of rough, this
  lot! — Kevin Sampson, *Powder* 1999

bit of spare *noun*
anyone providing sexual favours, even on a
short-term or occasional basis; an
unattached woman *UK, 1978*
'Bit of' plus conventional use of 'spare'
(available).
- I always got the impression that
  Maurice was down her on the look out
  for a bit of spare. — Roger Busley,
  Garvey's Code 1978

bit of stray *noun*
a casual sexual acquaintance, usually
female *UK, 2001*
- She was posh, too, and a lot brighter
  than his usual bits of stray. — Garry
  Bushell, *The Face* 2001

bit of the other *noun*
sexual intercourse *UK, 1984*
- Life is, after all, a bit at this, a bit at
  that and a bit of the other. — *The
  Observer*, 29th June 2003

bit of tit *noun*
a woman regarded as a sexual object; sex
with a woman *UK, 1984*
- "I fancy a bit of tit tonight." "Lovely bit
  of tit, she was." — Beale, 1984

bit on the side *noun*
a lover; a love affair; extra-marital sex *UK,
2001*

- [A] ladies' man who regarded a bit-on-
  the-side as harmless[.] — Mark Powell,
  Snap 2001

BJ *noun*
an act of oral sex, a blow job *US, 1949*
- And what should be this film's finest
  sex scene, the finale between Ashlyn
  and Jamie, turns out to be mainly a
  simple b.j. ending in a facia. — *Adult
  Video News* February, 1993

black jack *noun*
the penis of a black man *US, 1965*
Homosexual usage.
- — *The Guild Dictionary of Homosexual
  Terms* 1965

black velvet *noun*
a black woman's vagina *US, 1967*
- — Dale Gordon, *The Dominion Sex
  Dictionary* 1967

black wings *noun*
oral sex with a black woman *US, 2000*
- You got your Red Wings by eating a girl
  on her period and your Black Wings by
  eating a black girl. — Ralph 'Sonny'
  Barger, *Hell's Angel* 2000

blanket drill *noun*
sex in bed *US, 1964*
- — Roger Blake, *The American Dictionary
  of Sexual Terms* 1964

blister *noun*
a prostitute *US, 1905*
- — Dale Gordon, *The Dominion Sex
  Dictionary* 1967

block *noun*
▶ **on the block**
1 engaged in prostitution on the street *US,
1941*
- Have all the players and working girls
  smiling on her, lapping up the news
  that Inez been put out on the block
  again, handed over her little black
  book and gone back in harness.
  — John Sayles, *Union Dues* 1977
2 subjected to serial rape *NEW ZEALAND,
1973*
- Home had told the girl: "You've got
  between now and the time I finish this
  cigarette until you go into the bedroom
  and go on the block." — *Truth* 4th
  December 1973

block *verb*
to sodomise someone or subject them to
serial rape *NEW ZEALAND, 1978*

- When a sheila came she knew what was going to happen, she was going to be blocked, gang raped. — Bill Payne, *Staunch* 1991

blocks *noun*
▶ **put the blocks to**
to have sex with someone *US, 1888*
- Guys who spoke of "putting the blocks to" a chick were bound to be assholes too[.] — *Screw* 3rd January 1972

blow *noun*
an act of oral sex performed on a man *US, 1946*
An abbreviation of **BLOW JOB**.
- Oh J-A-N-E-T *I want a blow* I love you so. — Sal Piro and Michael Hess, *The Official 'Rocky Horror Picture Show' Audience Participation Guide* 1991

blow *verb*
1 to perform oral sex *US, 1930*
- I, anticipating even more pleasure, wouldn't allow her to blow me on the bus[.] — Neal Cassady, *The First Third* 1947
▶ **blow a load**
2 to ejaculate *US, 1995*
- Lois could never have Superman's baby. Do you think her fallopian tubes could handle his sperm? I guarantee he blows a load like a shotgun. — *Mallrats* 1995
▶ **blow a nut**
3 to ejaculate *US, 1994*
- JAY: So I blow a nut on her belly, and I get out of there, just as my uncle walks in. — *Clerks* 1994
▶ **blow your beans**
4 to orgasm *AUSTRALIA, 1985*
- — Recorded by Thommo, *The Dictionary of Australian Swearing and Sex Sayings* 1985
▶ **blow your cookies**
5 to ejaculate *UK, 2000*
- I got a coachload of Japanese booked in [to a massage parlour] for the weekend. Don't want 'em to blow their cookies in the first five minutes and refuse to pay for the whole hour. — Chris Baker and Andrew Day, *Lock, Stock... & a Fist Full of Jack and Jills* 2000

blow bath *noun*
during the war in Vietnam, a bath, massage and sex *US, 1991*
- — Linda Reinberg, *In the Field* 1991

blowboy *noun*
a male homosexual *US, 1935*

- — Michael Dalton Johnson, *Talking Trash with Redd Foxx* 1994

blow job *noun*
an act of oral sex performed on a man, or, occasionally, a woman *US, 1942*
- Mario and Greg emerged triumphant from the same toilet, having received a wank and a blow-job respectively from a girl called Geraldine. — Colin Butts, *Is Harry on the Boat?* 1997

blue *adjective*
sexually explicit, pornographic *UK, 1864*
- [B]ut then one night he took us to a blue movie, and what do you suppose? There he was on the screen — Truman Capote, *Breakfast at Tiffany's* 1958

blue balls *noun*
1 a pain in the testicles caused by long periods of sexual arousal without release *US, 1916*
Also South African variant 'blou balles'.
- She's taken their blood pressures on a wild-goose chase, and abandoned them with blueballs. — Josh Alan Friedman, *Tales of Times Square* 1986
2 any sexually transmitted infection *US, 1912*
- — Roger Blake, *The American Dictionary of Sexual Terms* 1964

blue steeler *noun*
a particularly erect erection *US, 1997*
- — Vann Wesson, *Generation X Field Guide and Lexicon* 1997

blue veiner *noun*
a rigid erection *US, 1975*
- During his one month convalescence Rosco was unable to raise what Harold Bloomguard called a "diamond cutter" or even a "blue veiner" due to the shooting pains in his groin. — Joseph Wambaugh, *The Choirboys* 1975

bob *verb*
to perform oral sex on a man *US, 1995*
- How much more can I bob here? — *Kids* 1995

bobo *noun*
the vagina *BAHAMAS, 1982*
- — John A. Holm, *Dictionary of Bahamian English* 1982

body shop *noun*
a bar catering to an unmarried clientele with sexual agendas *US, 1970*

● Pete Rozelle was in town this weekend. He popped into one of those body shops on Union Street Friday night, squeezing past the sweet young things and the hot-to-trot hustlers. — *San Francisco Examiner* 24th September 1970

body-to-body *noun*
a sexual service offered in some massage parlours in which a girl will massage her client with her body *UK, 2003*
● [T]wo-way body-to-body: the girl will massage her client with her body and vice versa. — Caroline Archer, *Tart Cards* 2003

boff *noun*
sex; an act of sexual intercourse *US, 1956*
● Ladies flock to kiss him, pay respects, and, in some cases, hope for a little boff. — Josh Alan Friedman, *Tales of Times Square* 1986

boff *verb*
to have sex *US, 1937*
● And yet, go understand people – it is her pleasure while being boffed to have one or the other of my forefingers lodged snugly up her anus. — Philip Roth, *Portnoy's Complaint* 1969

bog bird *noun*
a woman who is willing to have sex in a public lavatory *UK, 2003*
● Just a dirty old bog-bird. — Colin Butts, *Is Harry Still on the Boat?* 2003

boink *verb*
to have sex with someone *US, 1897*
● On one call-out Anne had told the pathologist that she wouldn't have had any problem at all with a first-date boinking of the actor who'd played Hari. — Joseph Wambaugh, *Floaters* 1996

boinking *noun*
sexual intercourse *US, 2005*
● Julia joins a horned-up farmhand for some boinking in the barn. — Mr. Skin, *Mr. Skin's Skincyclopedia* 2005

bombs *noun*
the female breasts *US, 1968*
● — Collin Baker et al., *College Undergraduate Slang Study Conducted at Brown University* 1968

bone *noun*
the penis, especially when erect *US, 1916*

● "Why, if you mean do I think I could get a bone up over that old buzzard, no, I don't believe I could..." — Ken Kesey, *One Flew Over the Cuckoo's Nest* 1962

bone *verb*
to have sex from the male point of view *US, 1971*
● It's a lot more interesting than just flinging off your clothes and boning away on the neighbor's swing set. — *Heathers* 1988

bone-on *noun*
an erection *US, 1927*
● I swear to Christ, B., I never got such a terrific bone-on in my life! Like a fucking rock[.] — Terry Southern, *Blue Movie* 1970

bone queen *noun*
a male homosexual who favours performing oral sex *US, 1964*
● — Roger Blake, *The American Dictionary of Sexual Terms* 1964

boner *noun*
an erection *US, 1961*
● [D]eep inside of me still burned the soul of a stupid and simple girl, who wanted nothing more out of life than to induce in every man she met a good hard boner. — Rita Ciresi, *Pink Slip* 1999

boneyard *noun*
a conjugal visit in prison *US, 1989*
● — James Harris, *A Convict's Dictionary* 1989

boning tool *noun*
the penis *US, 2001*
● — Erica Orloff and JoAnn Baker, *Dirty Little Secrets* 2001

bonk *noun*
sexual intercourse *UK, 2000*
● I had a really funny bonk in Tenerife once. Or was it twice, no, I only did her once but it was a good one. — Dave Courtney, *Raving Lunacy* 2000

bonk *verb*
to have sex *UK, 1975*
● His plan was to shack up with some fat girlfriend of his, piping [smoking crack cocaine] and bonking the night away[.] — Lanre Fehintola, *Charlie Says...* 2000

boob *noun*
the female breast *US, 1931*

- Her breasts weren't especially big, or little, or round, or pointy or any of those magazine-writer tit fetish cliches. They were just nice boobs on a nice woman. — Gurney Norman, *Divine Right's Trip (Last Whole Earth Catalog)* 1971

boobitas; boobititas *noun*
small female breasts *US, 1963*
A borrowed use of the Spanish diminutive.
- — Carol Ann Preusse, *Jargon Used by University of Texas Co-Eds* 1963

boob man *noun*
a male with a primary interest in a woman's breasts as a point of attraction *US, 1073*
- Like, most of 'em got small little titties and are skinny, so if you're a boob man your hands feel kinda empty. — Cherokee Paul McDonald, *Into the Green* 2001

boo-boos *noun*
the testicles *US, 1951*
- — Dale Gordon, *The Dominion Sex Dictionary* 1967

booby; boobie *noun*
a female breast *US, 1916*
- Sitting in the back seat with the pudgy girl was his date – big boobies, he remembered, they jiggled. — Bernard Wolfe, *The Late Risers* 1954

boogie *noun*
the vagina *US, 1969*
- — J. E. Lighter, *Historical Dictionary of American Slang, Volume 1* 1994

boogie *verb*
to have sex *US, 1960*
- — *The Sunday Telegraph Magazine* 11th March 1979

boom-boom *noun*
sex *US, 1964*
From Asian pidgin. Major use in Vietnam during the war.
- [A]nd I get to wondering what the fuck am I doing sleeping on the couch in my own house instead of in there doing boom-boom with the little woman[.] — Robert Campbell, *Juice* 1988

boom-boom *verb*
to copulate *US, 1971*
- Hey, baby-san, you boum-boum G.I.? — *Screw* 15th February 1971

boom-boom girl *noun*
a prostitute *US, 1966*
- The rest of the day was spent in finding a boom-boom girl. — Charles Anderson, *The Grunts* 1976

boom-boom house; boom-boom parlor *noun*
a brothel *US, 1966*
- — *American-Statesman (Austin, Texas)* 9th January 1966

boom-dee-boom *noun*
sex *US, 1984*
- Some of the boom-dee-boom girls. Some of the owners of the boom-dee-boom clubs. — Wallace Terry, *Bloods* 1984

boomers *noun*
large female breasts *US, 2005*
- Kinked-up Lisa dons a leather outfit that showcases her boomers and buncakes while she drips hot wax on her man-friend. — Mr. Skin, *Mr. Skin's Skincyclopedia* 2005

boongy *noun*
the buttocks *BAHAMAS, 1995*
- — Patricia Clinton-Meicholas, *More Talkin' Bahamian* 1995

boots *noun*
▶ **put the boots to**
to have sex with someone *US, 1933*
- I'd rather put the boots to Mrs. A. than Mrs. S. — *Screw* 18th July 1969

booty; bootie *noun*
1 the buttocks *US, 1928*
- He's Cyndia Lauper's boyfriend, so no skin search; Cyndi wouldn't want us looking up his boodie. — James Ellroy, *Suicide Hill* 1986
2 the vagina *US, 1925*
- I've got a body as well as a booty. — Parlet, *Booty Snatchers* 1979

booty bandit *noun*
an aggressive, predatory male homosexual *US, 1962*
- Inmates subject to rape ("punks") face threats and violence perpetrated by stronger inmates ("daddies," "jockers," or "booty bandits") who initiate unwanted sexual acts. — *Corrections Today* December, 1996

booty call *noun*
a date made for the sole purpose of engaging in sex *US, 1997*

• He cruises the streets of L.A. in one long booty call. — Ana Loria, *1 2 3 Be A Porn Star!* 2000

bootylicious *adjective*
sexually attractive, especially with reference to the buttocks *US, 2001*
• I don't think you / Ready for this / 'Cause my body too / Bootylicious for ya babe — Destiny's Child *Bootylicious* 2001

bop *verb*
1 to have sex with someone *US, 1974*
• Your dick been limp for a year, 'cept when you're bopping your buddy Tony up there. — *Platoon* 1986
▶ **bop the baloney**
2 (of a male) to masturbate *US, 1983*
• Do you ever bop your baloney? — *National Lampoon's Vacation* 1983

border *noun*
a woman's pubic hair *UK, 2001*
A cultivated variation of the 'garden' theme.
• I love the way the girls in Nirvana do their borders. It's like they're having a little contest to see who can shave their minge in the most eye-catching way. — Kevin Sampson, *Outlaws* 2001

Boston tea party *noun*
a sexual fetish in which the sadist defecates or urinates on the masochist *US, 1967*
• — Dale Gordon, *The Dominion Sex Dictionary* 1967

both ways *adverb*
to be bisexual *US, 1988*
• You trying to tell me if I don't like spiders it means I go both ways? — Elmore Leonard, *Freaky Deaky* 1988

bottom *noun*
1 the pimp's favourite of the prostitutes working for him *US, 2002*
An abbreviation of 'bottom bitch' or 'bottom lady'.
• His bottom was Rudy, a seasoned ho from Georgia. — Tracy Funches, *Pimpnosis* 2002
2 the submissive partner in a homosexual or sado-masochistic relationship *US, 1961*
• Boots could take either the top or the bottom, without the least show of emotion. — Donald Goines, *Whoreson* 1972

bottom man *noun*
the passive partner in a homosexual relationship *US, 1972*

• Bottom man is the masochist in an S/M relationship (antonym: top man). The term refers exclusively to the hierarchial contrast of the two partners, one subject to the other, and need not correspond to the actual physical position — Wayne Dynes, *Homolexis* 1985

bouncy-bouncy *noun*
sexual intercourse *US, 1960*
• — Kenn 'Naz' Young, *Naz's Dictionary of Teen Slang* 1993

boungy; bungy *noun*
the anus *BAHAMAS, 1982*
• — John A. Holm, *Dictionary of Bahamian English* 1982

box *noun*
1 the vagina; a woman *UK, 1605*
• I grabbed her by the shoulders, kissed her, and right quick from some instinctive sense shoved my hand right up her dress and came up with her box shining golden in the golden sun. — Jack Kerouac, *Letter to Neal Cassady* 10th January 1951
2 the posterior, the buttocks *US, 1965*
Originally black, then gay usage.
• — Paul Baker, *Polari* 2002

box-chaser *noun*
a man who relentlessly pursues women *US, 1969*
• He was a real triple-threat man – boozer, Bible-thumper and box-chaser. — Joey V., *Portrait of Joey* 1969

box lunch; box lunch at the Y *noun*
oral sex on a woman *US, 1964*
The character Y resembles a woman's groin and plays on **box** (the vagina).
• [C]omments such as "likes to make," "frigid," "the picture does her too much justice," "box lunch," "a real roller," "get laid," ad infinitum. — John Nichols, *The Sterile Cuckoo* 1965

boy in the boat *noun*
the clitoris *US, 1916*
• [T]hose who felt that the ladies should have big bursts but could have them only in that highly localized surface nodule known in the trade as the vestigial phallus, or button, or boy in the boat. — Bernard Wolfe, *The Magic of Their Singing* 1961

boy toy *noun*
a young, attractive woman or man who is the object of sexual desire of their elders, homosexual or heterosexual *US, 1989*
- After two months he started complaining about being used as a boy toy – in bed he had no objection to being a sex object, but afterward he wanted me to respect him for his mind. — Anka Radakovich, *The Wild Girls Club* 1994

bozack *noun*
the penis; the entire male genitalia *US, 1990*
Sometimes shortened to 'zack'.
- And the bitches? They'll do anything for it. I got my bozack done every day last week. Several times a time. — *New Jack City* 1990

brandy *noun*
lubricant applied to the anus in preparation for anal sex *UK, 2002*
- — Paul Baker, *Polari* 2002

Brazilian landing strip; Brazilian *noun*
the trimming of a woman's pubic hair such that only a narrow strip remains; the result thereof *US, 2001*
- Maybe one percent of my clients have stuck to the old conservative bikini line wax – the rest have converted to Brazilians. — *Nerve* December 2000 – January, 2001

break *verb*
▶ **break luck**
(of a prostitute) to have sex with the first customer of the day or night *US, 1969*
- Several of her stable prosses were chatting over too hot cups of coffee, eager to break luck, anxious for Leila to tell them where to turn the first trick of their workday. — Emmett Grogan, *Final Score* 1976

break-luck *noun*
a prostitute's first customer of the day *US, 1993*
- — *Washington Post* 7th November 1993

brick *verb*
to have sex leaning against a brick wall for balance and purchase *UK, 2001*
- [D]escribe a sex act (eg: "bricking" means shagging against a brick wall)[.] — *Sky Magazine* May, 2001

bricks *noun*
▶ **on the bricks**

working as a street prostitute *US, 1981*
- "Oh, they might treat you real nice at first, talk to you pretty, show you a good time, buy you pretty things, but before you know what's happening they got you out on the bricks." — Alix Shulman, *On the Stroll* 1981

brick shithouse *noun*
a woman, or rarely a homosexual man, with a curvaceous figure; a powerfully built man *US, 1928*
Sometimes euphemised to a simple 'house'.
- The girl is underage but built like a brick shit-house, and there's no corroboration. — Edwin Torres, *Q & A* 1977

bridal suite *noun*
a two-man prison cell *NEW ZEALAND, 1999*
A frank allusion to homosexual sex in prison.
- — Harry Orsman, *A Dictionary of Modern New Zealand Slang* 1999

bring off *verb*
to induce and achieve an orgasm *UK, 1984*
- "Bring me off," I'm saying. "Finger me. Fuck me." — Kevin Sampson, *Clubland* 2002

British Standard Handful *noun*
the average female breast *UK, 1977*
A play on standards established by the British Standards Institute.
- A third nurse complained that Dr. Galea, a married man, squeezed one of her breasts and told her: "You are the three British standard handfuls." — *The Mirror* 1999

bronski *verb*
to sandwich a face between female breasts *US, 1995*
- Ludwig Vogel managed to get bronskied by that night's headliner, Colt 45. — Howard Stern, *Miss America* 1995

brothel spout *noun*
a prostitute who is physically and emotionally worn out by her work *US, 1993*
- — J.R. Schwartz, *The Official Guide to the Best Cat Houses in Nevada* 1993

brown *noun*
the anus and/or rectum *US, 1916*
- Then, I'll wanna pinky you and put it in your friend's brown. — Kevin Smith, *Jay and Silent Bob Strike Back* 2001

brown *verb*
to perform anal sex upon someone *US,*
1933
- Let's just say a little friendly browning,
OK? — Angelo d'Arcangelo,
The Homosexual Handbook 1968

brown *adjective*
used for describing sexual activities
involving excrement *UK, 2002*
- I leans back in my chair thinking about
my brown adventures and the way we
was both fucking covered in shite.
— Kevin Sampson, *Clubland* 2002

brownie queen *noun*
a male homosexual who enjoys the passive
role in anal sex *US, 1968*
- A "brownie queen" is a homosexual
male interested primarily in being the
passive partner in anal intercourse.
— James Harper, *Homo Laws in all 50
States* 1968

brownies *noun*
the female breasts, especially the nipples
US, 1982
- — *Maledicta* Summer/Winter, 1982:
'Dyke diction: the language of lesbians'

FLACCID PENIS

deadwood *noun, US, 1995*
Extended from wood (the erect penis).
- — *Adult Video News* October, 1995

dolphin *noun, US, 1995*
- — *Adult Video News* October, 1995

flapper *noun, US, 1980*
- — *Maledicta* Winter, 1980: 'A new erotic
vocabulary'

flop on *noun, UK, 2003*
the penis that has become flaccid when an
erection is to be preferred
- [A]bout ten minutes into it I got a flop on.
— Richard Herring, *Talking Cock*
2003

hanging Johnny *noun, US, 1980*
- — *Maledicta* Winter, 1980: 'A new erotic
vocabulary'

Irish horse *noun, US, 1987*
a flaccid or impotent penis
- — *Maledicta* 1986–1987: 'A continuation of
a glossary of ethnic slurs in American
English'

Mister Floppy; Mr Floppy *noun, UK, 2003*
the penis that has become flaccid when an
erection is to be preferred
- [A]nxiety causes us to say hello to Mr Floppy[.]
— Richard Herring, *Talking Cock* 2003

softy *noun, US, 1995*
- — *Adult Video News* October, 1995

brown eye *noun*
the anus *US, 1954*
- The video continues as Stag fucks
Trinity's brown eye while she finishes
reaming North. — *Adult Video*
August/September, 1986

brown eyes *noun*
the female breasts, especially the nipples
US, 1932
- — Collin Baker et al., *College
Undergraduate Slang Study Conducted
at Brown University* 1968

Brownie Girls *noun*
lesbian mutual oral-anal sex *US,*
1968
- Analingus, in which one one of the
partners will be tongued, or playing
"Brownie Girls" in which the two take
turns upon each other. — L. Reinhard,
*Oral Sex Techniques and Sex Practices
Illustrated* 196

brown job *noun*
oral-anal sex *US, 1971*
- — Eugene Landy, *The Underground
Dictionary* 1971

brown lover *noun*
a person with a fetishistic love of
excrement *US, 1996*
- This series was started by some brown
lovers like yourself[.] — Peter Sotos,
Index 1996

brown shower *noun*
an act of defecation as part of
sadomasochistic sex play *UK, 2003*
- — Caroline Archer, *Tart Cards* 2003

brown wings *noun*
experience of anal intercourse, or anal-oral
sexual contact, considered as an
achievement *US, 1971*
Originally Hell's Angel usage; 'brown' (the
colour associated with the anus) plus
'wings' (badge of honour).

- But if you're the proud owner of an enormous penis and you still want to get your brown wings, the way is not to ask, it's to do. — *GQ* July, 2001

bub *noun*
the female breast *UK, 1826*
- A flask that fits over her bubs. — Irving Shulman, *The Amboy Dukes* 1947

bubby *noun*
the female breast *UK, 1655*
Usually in the plural.
- Their secondary sex characteristics are simply too conspicuous to pass without insult, and we were unmerciful towards them: tits, boobs, knockers, jugs, bubbies, bazooms, lungs, flaps and hooters we called them, and there was no way to be polite about it. — *Screw* 3rd January 1972

bucket *noun*
1 the vagina *UK, 2001*
- Women's genitalia were represented as (potential) containers (e.g., bucket, box, hair goblet), places to put things in (e.g., furry letterbox, disk drive, socket, slot), containers for semen (e.g., gism pot, spunk bin, honey pot), and containers for the penis/sex (e.g., willy warmer, wank shaft, shagbox). — *Journal of Sex Research* 2001
2 the buttocks; the anus *US, 1938*
- — Ellen C. Bellone (Editor), *Dictionary of Slang* 1989

bud *noun*
the female nipple *US, 1990*
- Your buds is as hard as two frozen huckleberries. — Robert Campbell, *Sweet La-La Land* 1990

buddy window *noun*
a hole between private video booths in a pornography arcade designed for sexual contact where none is officially permitted *US, 1996*
- The peep show has lost its popularity. The buddy window, glory hole. — James Ridgeway, *Red Light* 1996

buds *noun*
small female breasts *US, 1967*
- — Dale Gordon, *The Dominion Sex Dictionary* 1967

buff *verb*
▶ **buff the banana**
(of a male) to masturbate *US, 2001*

- Another way to say "the boy is masturbating" [...] Buffing the banana[.] — Erica Orloff and JoAnn Baker, *Dirty Little Secrets* 2001

buffers *noun*
the female breasts *US, 1964*
- — Roger Blake, *The American Dictionary of Sexual Terms* 1964

bugger *verb*
to play the active role in anal sex *UK, 1598*
- Don't try to analyze it. The quarterback buggering the linebacker. What a waste. — *Heathers* 1988

bugle *noun*
the erect penis *IRELAND, 1991*
- He could'ev given himself a bugle now, out there in the hall, just remembering what she was like and her smile; no problem. — Roddy Doyle, *The Van* 1991

bulldag *verb*
to perform oral sex on a woman *US, 1954*
- Cause, whore, I'm gonna sleigh-ride you and bulldag you too. — Bruce Jackson, *Get Your Ass in the Water and Swim Like Me* 1965

bullet *noun*
a single spurt of semen during male ejaculation *US, 1966*
Plays on SHOOT (to ejaculate).
- — David Rowan, *A Glossary for the 90s* 1998

bullhead *noun*
an extremely large penis *US, 1973*
- I told her to make a guy think he has a bullhead for a dick even if it's not as large as her clitoris. — A.S. Jackson, *Gentleman Pimp* 1973

bull ring *noun*
a strongly-muscled anus; in terms of anal intercourse, a virgin anus *UK, 2003*
- — *Gayness Explained, The FHM Little Book of Bloke* June, 2003

bum *verb*
to engage in anal intercourse *UK, 1999*
- I thought he was bumming Keva! Honest to God! I hears this mad moaning [...] just mad talking really... Oh my God! You've got your cock up me... fuck my butt, you bastard! — Kevin Sampson, *Powder* 1999

bum bandit *noun*
a male homosexual *UK, 1983*

● — Tom Hibbert, *Rockspeak!* 1983

bum boy *noun*
a homosexual male, especially a youthful, sexually inexperienced male who is the object of an older homosexual's desire *UK, 1929*
  ● You can find Christians as well as meths men, tear offs, outcasts, bum boys, prostitutes and head breakers on Skid Row. — Geoffrey Fletcher, *Down Among the Meths Men* 1966

bum-bum *noun*
the buttocks *TRINIDAD AND TOBAGO, 2003*
  ● — Lise Winer, *Dictionary of the English/Creole of Trinidad & Tobago* 2003

bumfuck *verb*
to have anal intercourse, to sodomise someone *US, 1866*
  ● I love being fucked up the arse, I just love it! Will you bum fuck me? — Stewart Home, *Sex Kick [britpulp] (else where)* 1999

bum fun *noun*
an intimate fondling of another's bottom *UK, 2000*
  ● [N]o snogging, lap dancing or bum fun. — Pete McCarthy, *McCarthy's Bar* 2000

bump *noun*
in a striptease or other sexual dance, a forceful pelvic thrust *US, 1931*
  ● A lot of white vocalists, even some with the big name bands today, are either as stiff as a stuffed owl or else they go through more wringing and twisting than a shake dancer, doing grinds and bumps all over the place[.] — Mezz Mezzrow, *Really the Blues* 1946

bump *verb*
1 in a striptease or other sexual dance, to thrust the hips forward as if copulating *US, 1936*
  ● Dancing boys strip-tease with intestines, women stick severed genitals in their cunts, grind, bump, and flick it at the man of their choice. — William Burroughs, *Naked Lunch* 1957
  ▶ **bump fuzz**
2 (used of a female) to have sex with another woman *US, 1997*
  ● — Pamela Munro, *U.C.L.A. Slang* 1997
  ▶ **bump pussies**

3 (used of lesbians) to have sex, especially by engaging in vulva-to-vulva friction *US, 1967*
  ● Two girls can, by interlacing themselves like forks, "bump pussies" as we used to say when I was a lad, and enjoy all of the thrills and chills of intercourse without even fingering themselves. — Angelo d'Arcangelo, *The Homosexual Handbook* 1968
  ▶ **bump the blanket**
4 to masturbate in bed *UK, 2000*
  ● If you need a toss [masturbation] you wait till association. We take it in turns, the rest of us go out [of the prison cell]. Don't wanna hear you bumping the blanket in the middle of the night. — Chris Baker and Andrew Day, *Lock, Stock... & A Good Slopping Out* 2000
  ▶ **bump uglies**
5 to have sex *US, 1989*
  ● And Tango adds a phrase to the popular lexicon when Sly's Tango asks Russell's Cash, "Did you bump uglies with my sister?" — *USA Today* 22nd December 1989

bumper *noun*
the buttocks *US, 1963*
  ● I'll moor it on the Chicago River and put on a big sign, "Babes with Big Bumpers Wanted." — Red Rudensky, *The Gonif* 1970

bum puncher *noun*
a male taking the active role in anal sex, especially when finesse is not an issue *AUSTRALIA, 1985*
  ● — Thommo, *The Dictionary of Australian Swearing and Sex Sayings* 1985

bumpy *noun*
the buttocks *BERMUDA, 1985*
  ● — Peter A. Smith and Fred M. Barritt, *Bermewjan Vurds* 1985

bun *noun*
the vagina *US, 1970*
  ● [He is] hung like a stud horse, too. If she can't feel what he's throwing her she must have a bun full of novocaine. — Lawrence Block, *No Score [The Affairs of Chip Harrison Omnibus]* 1970

bunch punch *noun*
sex involving multiple males and a single female *US, 1975*
  ● — *American Speech* Spring-Summer, 1975: 'Razorback slang'

bunghole *noun*
the anus *UK, 1611*
- The way you were banging the bunghole, you damned near fell in — Jim Thompson, *Pop. 1280* 1964

bunk-up *noun*
an act of sexual intercourse *UK, 1958*
Originally military, post-World War 2.
- I'll have a leavy [levy] at the same time and imagine that I'm haveing [sic] a bunk up instead of you. — Frank Norman, *Bang To Rights* 1958

bunny *noun*
1 the vulva and vagina *US, 1969*
- Especially when I reached around and started playing with her big, beautiful tits and fingering her slick-furry bunny. — Joey V., *Portrait of Joey* 1969
2 a homosexual male prostitute *US, 1967*
- — Dale Gordon, *The Dominion Sex Dictionary* 1967

buns *noun*
the buttocks *US, 1877*
- It was a drag with all the whiteys looking at a brother getting his buns kicked. — Babs Gonzales, *Movin' On Down De Line* 1975

bunt *noun*
the buttocks *US, 1967*
A blend of 'buttocks' and 'cunt'.
- — Dale Gordon, *The Dominion Sex Dictionary* 1967

bunty *noun*
semen *UK, 2000*
- I'd give that a good service I can tell you. Pump a couple of gallons of bunty up it any day of the week. — John King, *Human Punk* 2000

burley; burly *noun*
burlesque *US, 1934*
- — Harold Wentorth and Stuart Berg Flexner, *Dictionary of American Slang* 1960

burleycue *noun*
burlesque *US, 1923*
- There was also burly burleycue queen Carrie Finnell, who could make the tassels on her breasts swing in multiple directions. — Samuel L. Letter, *The Encyclopedia of the New York Stage, 1940–1950* 1992

burn *verb*
1 to masturbate *US, 1975*

- BURN. *** To masturbate while looking at a provocative picture of a woman. — Miguel Pinero, *Short Eyes* 1975
2 to infect someone with a sexually transmitted disease *US, 1967*
- — Dale Gordon, *The Dominion Sex Dictionary* 1967

bury *verb*
▶ **bury the stiffy**
from a male perspective, to have sex *US, 1994*
- — Michael Dalton Johnson, *Talking Trash with Redd Foxx* 1994

bush *noun*
pubic hair, especially a woman's pubic hair *UK, 1650*
- Know what the biggest change is for me? Broads shavin' their bushes. I went over to Silvio's, it's like the Girl Scouts in there. — *The Sopranos (Episode 53)* 2004

bush light *noun*
in the pornography industry, a light used to illuminate the genitals of the performers *US, 1995*
- — *Adult Video News* October, 1995

bush mag *noun*
a magazine featuring photographs of naked women, focusing on their pubic hair and vulvas *US, 1972*
- The "tit magazines" of the Fifties and Sixties, which were fit only for the garbage pail, have transformed themselves of late into "bush mags." — *Screw* 3rd July 1972

business *noun*
▶ **the business**
prostitution *US, 1957*
- Prostitutes, from the very young beauties to the shabbiest old fleabags, say that you can measure women in the "business" by the kinds of operations in which they engage[.] — John M. Murtagh and Sara Harris, *Cast the First Stone* 1957

bust *verb*
▶ **bust her vee**
to take a female's virginity *UK, 2006*
Black urban youth slang.
- I busted her vee last year. Pussy was live! — Noel Clarke, *Kidulthood* 2006
▶ **bust someone's drawers**

to have sex, seen as a conquest *US, 1990*
- Yeah, I've bust them draws once. But I just met her. I need time to get to know her. — *New Jack City* 1990

▶ **bust your nuts**
to experience an orgasm *US, 1964*
- She lay with her arms spread, like a female Christ or a woman who has just busted her nuts[.] — Clarence Cooper Jr, *The Farm* 1967

bustle-punching *noun*
frottage; an act of unwanted intimacy, usually in a crowded place, when a man rubs his penis against the hindquarters of an unsuspecting woman *UK, 1977*
- The practice, not uncommon in dense crowds, of a male rubbing his penis against the buttocks of females. The penis may or may not be exposed. — David Powis, *The Signs of Crime* 1977

butch dike *noun*
a aggressive, mannish lesbian *US, 1969*
- Rumors have it that a truly "butch dike" can whip any muscleman with her little finger. — *Screw* 27th June 1969

butch trade *noun*
a seemingly heterosexual man who consents to homosexual sex in the male role, receiving orally or giving anally *US, 1970*
- They want their men to be "butch trade." — *Screw* 22nd June 1970

buttered bun *noun*
a prostitute, or, less specifically any woman, who has already had sex with several customers/men *UK, 1699*
Also heard in the plural.
- She knew that some men were inflamed by a woman who had just been with another man – April had told her the slang term for a woman in that state, a buttered bun – and she knew intuitively that Edward was such a man. — Ken Follett, *A Dangerous Fortune* 1993

butterfly girl *noun*
a prostitute *US, 2004*
- — David Hart, *First Air Cavalry Division Vietnam Dictionary* 2004

butter legs *noun*
a promiscuous woman *AUSTRALIA, 1985*
Because, like butter, her legs are 'easy to spread'.
- — Thommo, *The Dictionary of Australian Swearing and Sex Sayings* 1985

butt floss *noun*
a thong or string bikini with only a slender piece of fabric passing between the cheeks of the buttocks *US, 1991*
- — Trevor Cralle, *The Surfin'ary* 1991

butt-fuck *verb*
to copulate anally *US, 1968*
- He'll be at the Betty Ford Clinic while you and me do twenty-five at Raiford, getting butt-fucked in the showers. — Carl Hiaasen, *Tourist Season* 1986

butt fucking *noun*
anal sex *US, 1999*
- The Back Door Boys go for all the fag subtext of these homoerotic groups, exploring their interpretation of the hit song "I Want It That Way" – it's all about butt fucking. — *The Village Voice* 5th October 1999

butthole *noun*
the anus *US, 1951*
- We want to be phalluses ramming in the butthole of pop. — *Jabberrock* [quoting Gibby Haines of the band Butthole Surfers] 1997

button *noun*
the clitoris *UK, 1900*
- [T]hose who felt that the ladies should have big bursts but could have them only in that highly localized surface nodule known in the trade as the vestigial phallus, or button, or boy in the boat. — Bernard Wolfe, *The Magic of Their Singing* 1961

button-dicked *adjective*
possessing a small penis *US, 1994*
- — Michael Dalton Johnson, *Talking Trash with Redd Foxx* 1994

butt pirate *noun*
an anal sex enthusiast *US, 1997*
- Francesca lived for butt-pirate porn and the old slap and tickle. — Mr. Skin, *Mr. Skin's Skincyclopedia* 2005

Cc

cabaret *verb*
to lie in bed masturbating *US, 1950*
- You better knock off reading that hot stuff and going carbareting or you'll wind up bugged — Hyman E. Goldin et al., *Dictionary of American Underworld Lingo* 1950

cabbage *noun*
the vagina *US, 1967*
- — Dale Gordon, *The Dominion Sex Dictionary* 1967

cabin stabbing *noun*
(from a male perspective) an act of conventional sexual intercourse *JAMAICA, 2001*
- Real Rasta man to come / And sprinkle di lawn / And give her di cabin stabbing dem / From evenings to dawn. — Damien Marley, *MiBrenda* 2001

caboose *noun*
1 the buttocks *US, 1919*
- He cussed her as he drove his needle-toed shoe into her wide caboose several times. — Iceberg Slim (Robert Beck), *Pimp* 1969
2 the final participant in serial sex *US, 1970*
From the phrase PULL A TRAIN used to describe the practice.
- — *Current Slang* Spring, 1970

cake *noun*
1 the female breast *US, 1957*
- What they want is shows where one guy kicks another guy in the belly while a dame leans over 'em with her cakes falling out of her negligee. — Max Shulman, *Rally Round the Flag, Boys!* 1957
2 the vagina *US, 1967*
- — John A. Holm, *Dictionary of Bahamian English* 1982

cake-eater *noun*
a person who enjoys performing oral sex on women *US, 1967*
- — Robert A. Wilson, *Playboy's Book of Forbidden Words* 1972

cakes *noun*
the buttocks, especially female buttocks *US, 1993*

- — Judi Sanders, *Faced and Faded, Hanging to Hurl* 1993

cam *verb*
to use a webcam in sexual play *UK, 2006*
- — Ashley Lister, *Swingers* 2006

camel toe *noun*
the condition that exists when a tight-fitting pair of trousers, shorts, bathing suit or other garment forms a wedge or cleft between a woman's labia, accentuating their shape *US, 1994*
- Camel lips, an offensive name from the '50s when women wear their pants too tight. Also known as camel toes. The pants were designed to capitalize on that. — *USA Today* 12th April 1994

cammer *noun*
a person who uses a webcam in sexual play *UK, 2006*
- Those cammers less inclined to such public displays[.] — Ashley Lister, *Swingers* 2006

can *noun*
the buttocks *US, 1914*
- Mr. Preston overheard him ask Miss Pliny how long she'd been "parking her pretty can at Regressive Plywood." — C.D. Payne, *Youth in Revolt* 1993

candy maker *noun*
a male homosexual who masturbates a partner to ejaculation and then licks and swallows the semen *US, 1964*
- — Roger Blake, *The American Dictionary of Sexual Terms* 1964

cane *verb*
to have sex *US, 1966*
- Fuck me, was I caning last night. — Colin Butts, *Is Harry on the Boat?* 1997

can house *noun*
a brothel *US, 1906*
- The Roamer Inn was like a model of all the canhouses I ever saw around Chicago[.] — Mezz Mezzrow, *Really the Blues* 1946

canned goods *noun*
a virgin *US, 1967*
- — Anon., *King Smut's Wet Dreams Interpreted* 1978

canoe inspection *noun*
a medical inspection of a woman's genitals for signs of a sexually transmitted disease *US, 1964*

- — Robert A. Wilson, *Playboy's Book of Forbidden Words* 1972

canoe licking *noun*
the act of oral sex on a woman *US, 2001*
- — Erica Orloff and JoAnn Baker, *Dirty Little Secrets* 2001

cans *noun*
the female breasts *US, 1959*
- Cans up to her chin and an ass like a brick shithouse. — Oscar Zeta Acosta, *The Autobiography of a Brown Buffalo* 1972

- "Natalie Wood, a carpenter's dream. Flat as a board an' easy to screw."
— Richard Price, *The Wanderers* 1974

carpet *noun*
▶ **clean the carpet**
(of a female) to masturbate *US, 2001*
- Another way to say "the girl is masturbating" [...] Cleaning the carpet[.] — Erica Orloff and JoAnn Baker, *Dirty Little Secrets* 2001

carpet burger *noun*
oral sex performed on a woman *US, 2001*

TESTICLES

balls *noun, UK, 1325*
- I joined the university karate class (not because I wanted a code of honour but so I could kick anyone in the balls who attacked me when I walked home late at night). — *The Guardian* 20th January 2004

clangers *noun, UK, 1961*
- You like real clangers? I'll show you a pair that gong like Big Ben! — Joseph Wambaugh, *The Secrets of Harry Bright* 1985

cods *noun, UK, 1632*
- He don't have cods enough to steal and all he wants to do is stand around and whip

some gal, you know. — Bruce Jackson, *Outside the Law* 1972

knackers *noun, UK, 1866*
From an earlier sense (castanets).
- I turned again, and – yeeeooooowww! – a spade handle leapt up at me as I stepped on the end of it, and gave me a resounding whack in the crutch, right in the knackers, de-balling me. — *Alvin Purple* 1974

nuts *noun, US, 1863*
- If another one of these chairs hits me in the nuts, I'm gonna go postal. — *Austin Powers* 1999

cantaloupes *noun*
large female breasts *US, 1974*
- [H]e took 1 gander at those bouncing cantalopes and gave "Bebe" the Bye-Bye. — Leo Rosten, *Dear Herm* 1974

canyon *noun*
the vagina *US, 1980*
- — Edith A. Folb, *runnin' down some lines* 1980

canyon-dive *noun*
oral sex performed on a woman *US, 1980*
- — Edith A. Folb, *runnin' down some lines* 1980

captain's log *noun*
the penis *US, 2001*
A *Star Trek* cliché punning on **wood** (the erect penis).
- — Erica Orloff and JoAnn Baker, *Dirty Little Secrets* 2001

carpenter's dream *noun*
a flat-chested woman *US, 1974*
From the pun 'flat as a board, and easy to screw'.

- — Pamela Munro, *U.C.L.A. Slang* 2001

car wash *noun*
during the Vietnam war, an establishment where a man went for a haircut, bath, massage and sex *US, 1977*
- And finally the convoy would crank and crash past the strip of car-wash and hand-laundry whorehouses outside the Tay Ninh Base Camp gate, where the housecats got laid. — Larry Heinemann, *Close Quarters* 1977

casabas *noun*
the female breasts *US, 1970*
Spanish for "gourds".
- What ever happened to comparing breasts to fruit – casabas, melons, peaches? [Letter to Editor] — *New York Times* 19th September 1993

case *verb*
▶ **go case**
to have sex with someone *UK, 1950*
From 'case' (a love affair).

- [S]he went case with some geezer now she's liveing [sic] with him. — Frank Norman, *Bang To Rights* 1958

cat *noun*
the vagina *UK, 1720*
- That puckered gash looked like she had grown an extra "cat." — Iceberg Slim (Robert Beck), *Pimp* 1969

catcher *noun*
the passive partner in homosexual sex *US, 1966*
- I've been known to pitch, but I'm no catcher. — Malcolm Braly, *On the Yard* 1967

cat lapper *noun*
a lesbian; someone who enjoys performing oral sex on women *US, 1967*
- — Dale Gordon, *The Dominion Sex Dictionary* 1967

cat pan *noun*
a bowl used for washing the vagina *TRINIDAD AND TOBAGO, 2003*
- — Lise Winer, *Dictionary of the English/Creole of Trinidad & Tobago* 2003

cave *noun*
the vagina *UK, 2001*
- — *Sky Magazine* July, 2001

caviar *noun*
human faecal matter in the context of a sexual fetish *UK, 2002*
A euphemism used in pornography.
- I had never seen a "caviar" video before, and was fascinated by the sight of a well-dressed German couple working on their plate of faeces with forks and knives[.] — Anabel Chong, *Life Beyond the Bidet [Inappropriate Behaviour]* 2002

CBT *noun*
in the subculture of consensual sado-masochism, the infliction of discomfort and pain on a male's genitals *UK, 2002*
An initialism of COCK (the penis), 'ball' (the testicle) and 'torture'.
- She wanted pretty severe CBT, and no, I'm not going to describe what it involved in this case[.] — Claire Mansfield and John Mendelssohn, *Dominatrix* 2002

cement mixer *noun*
a dancer who rotates her pelvis in a simulation of sexual intercourse *US, 1951*

- Belly down she's a cement mixer. — Thurston Scott, *Cure it with Honey* 1951

CFM *adjective*
sexually suggestive *US, 1989*
An abbreviation of COME-FUCK-ME.
- — Pamela Munro, *U.C.L.A. Slang* 1989

CFNM *noun*
clothed female naked/nude male, as a sexual subculture and pornographic genre *US, 2004*
- — www.cfnm.net 2004

chabobs *noun*
the female breasts *US, 1962*
- McMurphy starts. "She's got one hell of a set of chabobs," is all he can think of. — Ken Kesey, *One Flew Over the Cuckoo's Nest* 1962

chach *noun*
the vagina; a despised woman *US, 2003*
- — Connie Eble (Editor), *UNC-CH Campus Slang* November, 2003

chains and canes *noun*
restraint and corporal punishment as a sexual fetish *UK, 2003*
- — Caroline Archer, *Tart Cards* 2003

chair cheeks *noun*
the buttocks *US, 2005*
- [H]er exquisitely formed chair cheeks and her perfecting thrusting, ever-so-slightly swaying top tier are impossible to look away from? — Mr. Skin, *Mr. Skin's Skincyclopedia* 2005

chamber of commerce *noun*
a brothel *US, 1949*
- — Vincent J. Monteleone, *Criminal Slang* 1949

champagne *noun*
human urine in the context of a sexual fetish *US, 1987*
- — Thomas E Murray and Thomas R Murrell, *The Language of Sadomasochism* 1989

chancre mechanic *noun*
a military medic, especially one assigned to diagnose and treat sexually transmitted infections *US, 1944*
- [H]e had been doc of Baker Company, survivor of the Makin Raid, as opposed to your typical natty, run-of-the-mill chancre mechanic. — W.E.B. Griffin, *The Corps Book II* 1987

change *verb*
▶ **change your luck**
(used of a white person) to have sex with a black person; to have sex with a person of the sex with whom one would not ordinarily have sex *US, 1916*
● Hey, Flo, gonna take the little monkey home with you, change your luck? — Dick Gregory, *Nigger* 1964

change of luck *noun*
(used of a white person) sex with a black person *US, 1916*
● I know you, you after a change of luck. — Bernard Wolfe, *The Magic of Their Singing* 1961

charity fuck *noun*
sexual intercourse engaged in by one partner as an act of generosity *US, 1978*
● [A]sk her for an affair, a charity fuck, anything[.] — Joel Rose, *Kill Kill Faster Faster* 1997

charity girl *noun*
an amateur prostitute or promiscuous woman *US, 1916*
● — Dale Gordon, *The Dominion Sex Dictionary* 1967

charity goods *noun*
a promiscuous woman who does not expect payment for sex *US, 1966*
● — Rose Giallombardo, *Society of Women* 1966: Glossary of Prison Terms

charity stuff *noun*
a woman who, while promiscuous, does not prostitute herself *US, 1950*
● — Hyman E. Goldin et al., *Dictionary of American Underworld Lingo* 1950

charleys *noun*
the testicles *US, 1964*
● — Roger Blake, *The American Dictionary of Sexual Terms* 1964

Charlie Chester; charlie *noun*
a paedophile, a child mol*ester*; often used as a nickname for a headmaster *UK, 2003*
Rhyming slang, used by schoolchildren, formed, for no reason other than a convenient rhyme, from the name of the comedian and broadcaster, 1914–96.
● — Chris Lewis, *The Dictionary of Playground Slang* 2003

charlie willy *noun*
a real or imagined state of sexual arousal as a result of cocaine usage, *1999*

Combines 'charlie' (cocaine) with **WILLY** (the penis).
● — Alon Shulman, *The Style Bible* 1999

charver *noun*
a woman, especially when objectified sexually; an act of heterosexual intercourse with a woman *UK, 1979*
● I need a good charver, a bitta freestyle, a good bunk-up. — J.J. Connolly, *Layer Cake* 2000

charver; charva *verb*
to have sex *UK, 1962*
From Romany *charvo* (to interfere with).
● Marchmare walloping a strange bird he later charvered — Derek Raymond (Robin Cook), *The Crust on its Uppers* 1962

chassis *noun*
the female breasts *US, 1957*
● They really had no idea what was coming off – even though Barbara had a couple of fangled chassis that would put Jayne Mansfield to shame. — Frederick Kohner, *Gidget* 1957

cheaters *noun*
padding that enhances the apparent size of a female's breasts *US, 1972*
● — Helen Dahlskog (Editor), *A Dictionary of Contemporary and Colloquial Usage* 1972

check *verb*
▶ **check the oil level**
to pentrate a vagina with your finger *CANADA, 2003*
● — Chris Lewis, *The Dictionary of Playground Slang* 2003

cheese *noun*
smegma, matter secreted by the sebaceous gland that collects between the glans penis and the foreskin or around the clitoris and labia minora *US, 1927*
G. Legman wrote in his 1941 homosexual glossary that 'The term is derived from the dull whitish color of the smegma.'
● We pushed heavily on the new moral outlook: get a VD test often or face the fact that you're just as dirty as a person who never washes the cheese off his uncircumcised cock[.] — *Screw* 6th November 1972

cheesecake *noun*
a scantily clad woman as the subject of a photograph or artwork *US, 1934*

- I had done only cheesecake photos before – never anything nude – but I did the centerfold for December 1959 because I knew it would please him. — Kathryn Leigh Scott, *The Bunny Years* 1998

cherry *noun*
1 the hymen; virginity (male or female); the state of sustained sexual abstinence *US*, *1918*
- Not when he's about to cash in his cherry. — Ken Kesey, *One Flew Over the Cuckoo's Nest* 1962
2 a virgin; someone who because of extenuating circumstances has abstained from sex for a long period *US*, *1942*
- The puzzled expectant look on his face excited her. She had a cherry. — Hubert Selby Jr, *Last Exit to Brooklyn* 1957
3 a young woman regarded as the object or subject of a transitory sexual relationship *SOUTH AFRICA*, *2005*
Scamto youth street slang (South African townships).
- — *The Times* 12th February 2005
4 of a male, the 'virginity' of the anus *US*, *1997*
- MISTRESS: [...] Now let's dress you – let's get you ready for your defloration. DAMEN [a male 'slave']: I'm going to lose my cherry. MISTRESS: You're just a little girl, an innocent thing[.] — Terence Sellers, *Dungeon Evidence* 1997
5 the clitoris *AUSTRALIA*, *1985*
- — Thommo, *The Dictionary of Australian Swearing and Sex Sayings* 1985
6 a female nipple *US*, *1964*
- — Roger Blake, *The American Dictionary of Sexual Terms* 1964

cherry *adjective*
virginal *US*, *1933*
- I know you thought I was cherry, your number-one size / But I was balling Tony, and you weren't wise. — Dennis Wepman et al., *The Life* 1976

cherry bomb *noun*
a virgin *US*, *2001*
- "A lot of 'em like little girls. And if I tell 'em I'm a cherry bomb ... a virgin." — J.T. LeRoy, *The Heart is Deceitful Above All Things* 2001

cherry picker *noun*
1 a person who targets virgins for seduction *US*, *1960*
- They call me Rap the dicker the ass kicker / The cherry picker the city slicker the titty licker. — H. Rap Brown, *Die Nigger Die!* 1969
2 the penis *UK*, *2003*
- — Richard Herring, *Talking Cock* 2003

cherry-popping *noun*
the act of taking someone's virginity *US*, *1975*
- — Xaviera Hollander, *The Best Part of a Man* 1975

chew *noun*
an act of oral sex *UK*, *1962*
- When I was pissed I wouldn't refuse anything, slut, beef, chews, anything. — *Heart* 1962

chew *verb*
▶ **chew face**
to kiss *US*, *1980*
- "Who can tell me what petting means?" asked subsitute teacher Sharon Simon, who has a master's degree in psychology. "You mean chewing face?" queried one student. — *Los Angeles Times* 3rd February 1986
▶ **chew pillows**
to be the passive partner in anal sex *UK*, *1979*
- [A] scrounger, parasite, pervert, a worm, a self-confessed player of the pink oboe, a man or woman who by his own admission chews pillows. — Peter Cook, *Entirely a Matter for You* 1979

Chicago G-string *noun*
a g-string designed to break open, revealing the dancer's completely naked state *US*, *1981*
- — Don Wilmeth, *The Language of American Popular Entertainment* 1981

chi-chis *noun*
a woman's breasts *US*, *1961*
- I, on the other hand, seize the synchronous opportunity to stare at those Monster Chi-Chis for ninety splendid minutes. — Marty Beckerman, *Death to All Cheerleaders* 2000

chicken *noun*
1 a young prostitute *US*, *2002*
- Sunny put me in charge of making a chicken out of her, and I was taking my

responsibility seriously. — David Henry Sterry, *Chicken* 2002

2 a boy, usually under the age of consent, who is the target of homosexual advances *US, 1914*

- Like seeing a big new car with Ohio plates come driving up in front of that skinny little ten-year-old chicken selling his tender ass for a night's bed and board — Robert Campbell, *Alice in La-La Land* 1987

chickenhawk *noun*

1 a mature homosexual man who seeks much younger men as sexual partners *US, 1965*

- Basically the Flamingo Isles was a dive for pimps, chicken hawks, and hookers. — Carl Hiaasen, *Tourist Season* 1986

2 by extension, a woman who seeks out young male lovers *US, 1978*

- "She's a chickenhawk!" Natalie sneered. "These kids come and go hourly through her zoo." — Joseph Wambaugh, *The Black Marble* 1978

chicken ranch *noun*

a rural brothel *US, 1973*

Originally the name of a brothel in LaGrange, Texas, and then spread to more generic use.

- Hey, you don't make a thousand bucks tax-free by staying in bed unless you're working at one of those chicken ranches in Nevada. — Joseph Wambaugh, *Fugitive Nights* 1992

chick with a dick *noun*

a transsexual or, rarely, a hermaphrodite *US, 1991*

Almost always plural.

- Asserting that neither the "glamorized" movie stars nor the queens are desirable (they are "asexual," despite the evidence of star fan clubs and Chicks-with-Dicks phone sex numbers) Bersani condemns them to/for masturbation. — Diana Fuss, *Inside/Out* 1991

chile pimp *noun*

a pimp, especially a Mexican-American pimp, who has no professional pride and only mediocre success in the field *US, 1972*

- Black pimps never solicit for their women if they are "true pimps," and call a man who does a cigarette pimp, popcorn pimp, or chile pimp. — Christina and Richard Milner, *Black Players* 1972

chippy; chippie *noun*

a young woman, usually of loose morals, at times a semi-professional prostitute *US, 1886*

- [W]hy would I fool around with some chippy when I had you? — Jim Thompson, *The Killer Inside* 1952

chippy; chippie *verb*

to be unfaithful sexually *US, 1930*

- "You ever chippied on your wife?" "Never." "Never chippied on your wife one time in eighteen years?" "Never." — Lenny Bruce, *How to Talk Dirty and Influence People* 1965

choad *noun*

the penis *US, 1968*

- [N]obody to my knowledge spoke of "choad," "rod," "stem" or any other more strictly pornographic term. — *Screw* 3rd January 1972

chocha *noun*

the vagina *US, 2002*

From Spanish.

- It shouldn't be an issue whether you arrive in possession of a Johnson or a chocha as long as you show up with your records — Frank Broughton and Bill Brewster, *How to DJ Right* 2002

chockers *adjective*

(of a man) with the penis entirely inserted into a sexual partner *AUSTRALIA, 1975*

- Her brothers sprang me one night when I was chockers outside her house, and they beat the shit out of me. — William Nagel, *The Odd Angry Shot* 1975

chocolate highway *noun*

the anus and rectum *US, 1977*

- I rode her chocolate highway in eighth gear. — Zane, *Carmel Flava* 2006

chocolate starfish *noun*

the anus *UK, 1997*

- ["]Bradley is referring to the rusty bullet-hole," said Mikey. "The what?" Mario was still struggling. "The chocolate starfish." — Colin Butts, *Is Harry on the Boat?* 1997

choir practice *noun*

an after-hours gathering of policemen, involving liberal amounts of alcohol and sex, usually in a remote public place *US, 1975*

- According to Hart, many officers participate in a rite of passage in many police departments – the so-called "choir practice" or heavy after-hours drinking. — *Boston Globe* 30th October 1991

choke *noun*
▶ **pull your choke**
to masturbate *US, 1992*
- [M]asturbation – "pulling your choke" – becomes something to brag about. — Pete Earley, *The Hot House* 1992

choke *verb*
▶ **choke the chicken**
1 (of a male) to masturbate *US, 1976*
- He likes killin ... the way you like chokin your chicken. — Seth Morgan, *Homeboy* 1990

2 (of a male) to masturbate with the adrenaline-inducing agency of autoerotic strangulation or suffocation *UK, 2002*
- Guide to "The Choking of the Chicken"[.] Please note: all the following are extremely hazardous to health[.] — *Loaded* June, 2002

chomo *noun*
a child molester *US, 1997*
- Like the "chomos" (child molesters) and rapists, he [Charles Manson] needed protection. — Edward George, *Taming the Beast* 1998

chopper *noun*
the penis *UK, 1973*
- Now, guys, brace yourselves, there's no avoiding this, and I'm not talking about my chopper. — Ben Elton and Rik Mayall, *The Young Ones* 8th May 1984

chopsticks *noun*
mutual, simultaneous masturbation *US, 1941*
From the crossing of hands in the piano piece 'Chopsticks'.
- — Robert A. Wilson, *Playboy's Book of Forbidden Words* 1972

chub *noun*
the penis *US, 1997*
- — Anna Scotti and Paul Young, *Buzzwords* 1997

chub-a-dub *noun*
an act of masturbation *CANADA, 2002*
- Eli performs a "chub-a-dub" on his morning erection, still scenting Jezebel's hair on his pillow. — *Toronto Globe and Mail* 27th April 2002

chubbies *noun*
large female breasts *US, 1964*

- — Roger Blake, *The American Dictionary of Sexual Terms* 1964

chubby *noun*
an erection *US, 1997*
- — Pamela Munro, *U.C.L.A. Slang* 1997

chubby *adjective*
(of the penis) erect *UK, 1998*
- [T]he sight of her big old arse is getting me chubby. — *Loaded* June, 2003

chubby-chaser *noun*
a person who is sexually attracted to overweight people *US, 1976*
- Are there any straight bars for chubbies and chubby-chasers? — *Screw* 2 August 1971

chuff *noun*
1 the vagina *UK, 1997*
- — *Roger's Profanisaurus* December, 1997
2 pubic hair *US, 1967*
- — *Maledicta* Summer/Winter, 1982: 'Dyke diction: The language of lesbians'

chuffdruff; muffdruff *noun*
dried flakes of sexual secretions (male and/or female) clinging to the female pubic hair *UK*

chute *noun*
the rectum *US, 1976*
- [S]lim blonde anal lover Chrissy Ann, who lets Cal Jammer slide up her chute. — *Adult Video News* February, 1993

cigarette pimp *noun*
a pimp whose lack of professional pride leads him to solicit customers for his prostitutes *US, 1972*
- Black pimps never solicit for their women if they are "true pimps," and call a man who does a cigarette pimp, popcorn pimp, or chile pimp. — Christina and Richard Milner, *Black Players* 1972

circle jerk *noun*
group male masturbation, sometimes mutual and sometimes simply a shared solitary experience *US, 1958*
- If there are several persons present, and somehow it has been determined that all are "O.K.", a circle jerk will result. — John Francis Hunter, *The Gay Insider* 1971

circle-jerk *verb*
to participate in group male masturbation
US, 1971
- [F]or some reason the idea of circle
  jerking with a needle-dicked lard-arse
  didn't appeal. — Kitty Churchill,
  Thinking of England 1995

circus *noun*
sexual behaviour that is public, fetishistic
or both *US, 1878*
- When I came in here, our deal included
  no circuses, no shows, no peeping.
  — Robert Leslie, *Confessions of a
  Lesbian Prostitute* 1965

circus tent *noun*
an apartment or house where customers
pay to view sexual exhibitions *US, 1959*
- And behind the respectable-looking
  facades of the apartment buildings
  were the plush flesh cribs and poppy
  pads and circus tents of Harlem.
  — Chester Himes, *The Real Cool Killers*
  1959

clam *noun*
1 the vagina *US, 1916*
- I was gobblin' her clam like it was the
  last supper. — Richard Price, *The
  Wanderers* 1974
2 the anus *US, 1983*
- — *Maledicta* 1983: 'Ritual and personal
  insults in stigmatized subcultures'

clangers *noun*
testicles *UK, 1961*
- You like real clangers? I'll show you a
  pair that gong like Big Ben! — Joseph
  Wambaugh, *The Secrets of Harry Bright*
  1985

clap *noun*
gonorrhoea *UK, 1587*
From old French *clapoir* (a sore caused by
venereal disease); the term was normal
register for centuries, slipping into colloquial
or slang in mid-C19.
- But how do you get the clap? By doing
  it, and anybody who does that dirty
  thing obviously deserves to get the
  clap. — Lenny Bruce, *How to Talk Dirty
  and Influence People* 1965

clean *verb*
▶ **clean the cage out**
to perform oral sex on a woman *UK, 2002*
- — Paul Baker, *Polari* 2002
▶ **clean the kitchen**
to lick your sex-partner's anus *UK, 2002*

- — Paul Baker, *Polari* 2002
▶ **clean the pipes**
to ejaculate; to masturbate *US, 1998*
- DOM: You know, clean the pipes. TED:
  Pipes? What are you talking about?
  DOM: You jerk off before all big dates,
  right? — *Something About Mary* 1998
▶ **clean the tube**
(of a male) to masturbate *US, 2001*
Using 'tube' to mean 'the penis'.
- "The boy is masturbating" [...] Cleaning
  the tube[.] — Erica Orloff and JoAnn
  Baker, *Dirty Little Secrets* 2001

C light *noun*
in the pornography industry, a light used to
illuminate the genitals of the performers
US, 1991
'C' as in **CUNT**.
- This is Randy's dick here. We lit it so it
  wouldn't look so white and unreal: a
  little light called the C light. — Robert
  Stoller and I.S. Levine, *Coming
  Attractions* 1991

clit *noun*
the clitoris *US, 1958*
- Why, I've only to give my clit a tiny flick
  right now and I'd be sopping. — Terry
  Southern, *Candy* 1958

clit stick *noun*
a small vibrating sex-aid designed for
clitoral stimulation *UK, 2002*
- Oh, it's a clit-stick! — *A – Z of Rude
  Health* 11th January 2002

clitty
the clitoris *UK, 1866*
- She may want you to use your best
  soft, sloppy tongue for caressing her
  clit, or if she has a tough li'l clitty, a
  firm tongue might be just fine. — Jamie
  Goddard, *Lesbian Sex Secrets for Men*
  2000

clitty clamp *noun*
a device that is attached to a clitoris and is
designed to cause discomfort or pain in the
cause of sexual stimulation *UK, 1995*
- Her punishment from her master took a
  variety of forms "from the caning of my
  bottom and breasts through torturous
  bondage, inflatable appendages, nipple
  and clitty clamps, enemas and
  electrical stimulation". — Kitty
  Churchill, *Thinking of England* 1995

clitwobble *noun*
a woman's desire for sex *UK, 1998*

- [W]hen he has a knob throb for her and she has a clitwobble for him. — Ray Puxley, *Fresh Rabbit* 1998

clockweights noun
the testicles *UK, 2003*
- [T]he ward sister whips off his bed sheets, strips him and has a good poke round his clockweights. — *FHM* June, 2003

clodge noun
the vagina *UK, 2001*
- [H]ave my hand brush against the teacher's stocking-top rather than thump into her red-hot clodge. — Frank Skinner, *Frank Skinner* 2001

People Our Parents Warned Us Against 1967

clutch-butt noun
sex *US, 1967*
- "That big old gal is ready for some rib-rattling clutch butt," said Nails. — Elaine Shepard, *The Doom Pussy* 1967

coachman's knob noun
an erection of the penis caused by the vibrations whilst travelling on public transport *UK, 2003*
- — Chris Lewis, *The Dictionary of Playground Slang* 2003

coal noun
▶ burn coal; deal in coal

SEMEN

baby batter noun, *US, 1997*
- [I]t's because you ain't got the baby batter in your brain any more. — *Something About Mary* 1998

creampie noun, *US, 2002*
semen seeping from a vagina, anus or mouth
- Creampie vids mean to correct this by showing sex as it actually happens, plus bodily fluids getting licked off the floor. — *Village Voice* 23rd April 2002

felching noun, *US, 1981*
the act of sucking semen from another's rectum
- [A]cts such as "felching." — Noretta Koertge, *The Nature and Causes of Homosexuality* 1981

funk noun, *US, 1976*
semen; smegma
- They had fried shit choplets and hot funk custard/ Drank spit out of cocktail glasses and used afterbirth for mustard. — Dennis Wepman et al., *The Life* 1976

Irish confetti noun, *US, 1987*
semen spilled on a woman's body
- — *Maledicta* 1986–1987: 'A continuation of a glossary of ethnic slurs in American English'

jazz noun, *US, 1932*
- Momo wipes the jazz off Jasmin. — Anthony Petkovich, *The X Factory* 1997

jizz verb, *US, 1983*
to ejaculate
- Then, I want you to flick at my nuts while your friend spanks me into the same Dixie cup Silent Bob jizzed in. — Kevin Smith, *Jay and Silent Bob Strike Back* 2001

joy juice noun, *US, 1969*
- He wanted her ass to be good and strong and filled to the brim with the joy juice of the men she'd had that day, and the more the merrier. — A.S. Jackson, *Gentleman Pimp* 1973

clunkers noun
the testicles *US, 1976*
- If you don't print this letter or pic, I'll cut your clunkers off! — *Punk* July, 1976

clusterfuck noun
group sex, heterosexual or homosexual *US, 1966*
- Oh, those big cluster fucks! I can't stand them. I think it's revolting, you know, more or less getting punked by anybody who happens to be standing near you, man, woman, child, or dog. — Nicholas Von Hoffman, *We Are The*

(of a white person) to have sex with a black person *US, 1922*
- The Harlem community accepts – though it despises – these Caucasians who cross the color line, or as it is known above 110th Street, "change their luck" or "deal in coal." — Jack Lait and Lee Mortimer, *New York Confidential* 1948

coal hole noun
the anus *UK, 2003*
- Sugar paste [...] can also be used directly on your coal-hole, unlike

paraffin-based waxes. — *The FHM Little Book of Bloke* June, 2003

cock *noun*
1 the penis *UK, 1450*
- "I want to feel your cock, your hard cock spreading me wide apart and tearing me apart." — *Final Report of the Attorney General's Commission on Pornography* 1986
2 the vagina *US, 1867*
- Cock mean pussy down here, boy. so don't you go takin' no offense, y'hear. — Emmett Grogan, *Ringolevio* 1972

cockblock *verb*
to interfere with someone's intentions to have sex *US, 1971*
- So you both jus' gonna set dere and cock block and neither one o' you gonna get nothin. — Geneva Smitherman, *Talkin that Talk* 1999

cock book *noun*
a sexually explicit book *US, 1968*
- — Carl Fleischhauer, *A Glossary of Army Slang* 1968

cock custard *noun*
semen *UK, 2001*
- He's a jumped up squirt of cock custard. — Harry Enfield, *We Know Where You Live* 2001

cockeater *noun*
a person who enjoys performing oral sex on men *US, 1967*
- — Dale Gordon, *The Dominion Sex Dictionary* 1967

cock hound *noun*
a man obsessed with sex *US, 1947*
- Everyone in Hollywood knows my father as a real cockhound. Once when I came home from boarding school he had these two Puerto Rican women in his bedroom. — Gerald Petievich, *To Die in Beverly Hills* 1983

cockie *noun*
the penis *UK, 2001*
- I don't mean cockies in general li ke, but they don't want the real thing. No way. — Niall Griffiths, *Sheepshagger* 2001

cock-jockey *noun*
a man who thinks that sex is more important than anything else and that his contribution is paramount *UK, 2002*

- One thing, tho; cock-jockey forgot to ask for his change before he stamped off. — Niall Griffiths, *Kelly + Victor* 2002

cockmeat *noun*
the penis, specifically or as a generality *US, 1995*
- Hey girls, who needs some cockmeat from a real man? — Howard Stern, *Miss America* 1995

cockpit *noun*
the vagina *UK, 1891*
- — Dale Gordon, *The Dominion Sex Dictio nary* 1967

cock ring *noun*
a device worn on the penis to enhance sexual performance *US, 1977*
- The other man wears a cock ring – a current fad, a ring of metal, like his, or of studded leather, around the base of the cock and balls, supposedly insuring harder hard-ons, better orgasms. — John Rechy, *The Sexual Outlaw* 1977

cocksman *noun*
a man who prides himself on his sexual prowess *US, 1896*
- The adolescent cocksman having made his conquest barely broods at home the loss of the love of the conquered lass[.] — Jack Kerouac, *The Subterraneans* 1958

cocksmith *noun*
a sexually expert man *US, 1959*
- Nevertheless, the latter scene is one of the most scorching four-ways ever committed to film with Siffredi proving to be arguably the best living cocksmith in the business. — *Adult Video News* February, 1993

cockstand; stand *noun*
an erection *UK, 1866*
- Fighting gives ye a terrible cockstand, after. Ye want me, do ye no? — Diana Gabaldon, *Outlander* 1991

cocksucker *noun*
1 a person who performs oral sex on a man, especially a male homosexual *UK, 1891*
The most well-known use of the term in the US is in a statement attributed to former President Richard Nixon, who upon learning of the death of FBI Director J. Edgar Hoover on 2nd May 1972, is reported to have said 'Jesus Christ! That old cocksucker!' Nixon

was reflecting the widespread belief that Hoover was homosexual.

- I know I have always been a beat cocksucker in your imagination.
  — Allen Ginsberg, *Letter to Carolyn Cassady* 30th May 1952

2 a person who performs oral sex on a woman *US, 1942*

- The man said, "I'm a cocksucker [a performer of cunnilingus]." — Roger Abrahams, *Positively Black* 1970

cocktease *verb*
to tempt a man with the suggestion of sex *UK, 1957*

- I knew I couldn't cocktease him any lower without walking off the lot[.]
  — Rita Ciresi, *Pink Slip* 1999

cods *noun*
the testicles *UK, 1632*

- He don't have cods enough to steal and all he wants to do is stand around and whip some gal, you know. — Bruce Jackson, *Outside the Law* 1972

coffee grinder *noun*
a sexual dancer who makes grinding motions with her pelvis *US, 1960*

- — Harold Wentworth and Stuart Berg Flexner, *Dictionary of American Slang* 1960

cold comfort *noun*
in necrophile usage, sexual activity with a corpse *US, 1987*

- — *Maledicta* Summer/Winter, 1986–1987: 'Sexual slang: prostitutes, pedophiles, flagellators, transvestites, and necrophiles'

colly *noun*
an erection *UK, 1960*
Derives from earlier rhyming slang, 'colleen bawn' for HORN; formed on the name of the heroine of *The Lily of Killarney*, an 1862 opera by Julius Benedict.

- — Julian Franklyn, *A Dictionary of Rhyming Slang* 1960

combat jack *noun*
an act of masturbation by a combat soldier to relieve the tension or boredom of combat *US, 2003*

- After surviving their first ambush at Al Gharraf, a couple of Marines even admitted to an almost frenzied need to get off combat jacks. — *Rolling Stone* 24th July 2003

come; cum *noun*
1 semen *US, 1923*

- His rich rich come made the bitch's body numb / And the whore went blind in both eyes. — Dennis Wepman et al., *The Life* 1976

2 an orgasm *US, 1967*
From the verb sense (to experience an orgasm).

- [In Cairo, 1992] the price was about 50 piastres (8p) for one come whether you took a minute or hours. — Fiona Pitt-Kethley, *Red Light Districts of the World* 2000

come; cum *verb*
1 to experience an orgasm *UK, 1600*

- In a jiff I was in; but for some strange reason I couldn't come; all 19-year-old cockmasters can't come, you know this as well as I do. — Jack Kerouac, *Letter to Neal Cassady* 10th January 1951
▶ **come over all unnecessary; go all unnecessary**

2 to become sexually excited *UK, 1984*

- The Bride Stripped Bare might sound like the sort of novel to make a chap come over all unnecessary[.] — *The Times* 2nd July 2003
▶ **come your lot**

3 to experience an orgasm *UK, 1964*
An elaboration of COME.

- I got the feeling that he was coming his lot in his trousers. — John Peter Jones, *Feather Pluckers* 1964

come freak; cum freak *noun*
a person who is obsessed with sex *US, 1966*

- Body have to be stuck with a mean case of horniness to even think about it in this weather, much less do anything about it. Have to be a stone come-freak. — John Sayles, *Union Dues* 1977

come-fuck-me *adjective*
sexually alluring *US, 1986*

- Then Paco hears Cathy and Marty-boy leave her apartment (the two of them dressed for a hot day's traveling; Cathy in one of her famous low-cut, summery "come-fuck-me" dresses). — Larry Heinemann, *Paco's Story* 1986

come scab *noun*
a dried-on patch of semen on skin *UK, 2002*

- [E]xhaust-soot and dried sweat, come scabs [...] all down the plug an into the

Mersey[.] — Niall Griffiths, *Kelly + Victor* 2002

come shot; cum shot *noun*
a scene in a pornographic film or a photograph of a man ejaculating *US, 1972*
- The film [Deep Throat] features a couple of ass-fucking sequences and three come shots, two in that wonderful mouth. — *Screw* 19th June 1972

commando *adjective*
wearing no underwear *US, 2001*
Commandos are always ready for action.
- Knowing her daughter's penchant for going commando, the first thing she did was whip off her pants for Letitia to wear while she was examined. — *Ariel* 12th August 2003

conductor *noun*
the second active participant in serial sex with a single passive partner *US, 1975*
From PULL A TRAIN (serial sex).
- Carolina Moon announced that she was going to take her blanket into the bushes and pull the train. "I'm first! I'm the engineer!" cried Harold Bloomguard. "I'm second! I'm conductor!" cried Spencer Van Moot. — Joseph Wambaugh, *The Choirboys* 1975

conky *noun*
the penis BAHAMAS, 1982
- — John A. Holm, *Dictionary of Bahamian English* 1982

cooch *noun*
the vagina; sex with a woman *US, 2001*
- There are plenty of queer women who work as porn stars, strippers, and sex workers, but there are a lot fewer of us willing to fork over cash for cooch. — *The Village Voice* 7th August 2001

coochie *noun*
the vagina; sex with a woman; a woman as a sex object *US, 1995*
- So what you had your little coochie in your dad's mouth? — Eminem (Marshall Mathers), *My Fault* 1999

cookie *noun*
▶ **get your cookies**
to experience pleasure, especially in a perverted way *US, 1956*
- A fart smeller, way over in the corner, grabbed them, started sniffing, getting his cookies. — Steve Cannon, *Groove, Bang, and Jive Around* 1969

coot *noun*
the vagina; a woman as a sex object; sex with a woman *US, 1975*
- — *American Speech* Spring-Summer, 1975: 'Razorback slang'

cootch dancer; cooch dancer *noun*
a woman who performs a sexually suggestive dance *US, 1910*
A shortened form of HOOCHY KOOCHY.
- In sentencing the Cootch-Dancer Schmidt to 15 years for manslaughter (Time, Beb. 2), the judges had chided her for "appearing nude on the deck of [Mee's] yacht like a nymph," and for "swimming naked in [Havana] Bay." — *Time* 11th October 1948

cooter *noun*
the vagina *US, 1986*
- — Connie Eble (Editor), *UNC-CH Campus Slang* Fall, 1986

cooze; coozie *noun*
the vulva; the female genitals *US, 1927*
- She also possesses a truly attractive cunt: cooze lips which aren't flappy, crinkly, or rundown[.] — Anthony Petkovich, *The X Factory* 1997

cooze light *noun*
in the pornography industry, a light used to illuminate the genitals of the performers *US, 1995*
- — *Adult Video News* October, 1995

cop *verb*
▶ **cop a feel**
to touch someone sexually without their consent *US, 1935*
- She was the only woman that I've ever met that I could kiss without copping a feel. Except for my mama and sisters, of course, and I'm not too sure about my sisters. — Tom Robbins, *Another Roadside Attraction* 1971
▶ **cop a joint**
to perform oral sex on a man *US, 1962*
- I was staying at the Y once, and this guy kept following me in the showers, wanting to cop my joint. — John Rechy, *Numbers* 1967

cop off *verb*
1 to fondle someone intimately; to engage in foreplay; to have sex *UK, 2001*
- He shoves The Joy of Sex at me, and I can't help looking at a few pages: endless pictures of horrible hippies

copping off. — *The Guardian* 28th November 2001

2 to masturbate *UK, 2000*
● Well, we'd better get those tapes back cos I've got a couple of 'undred desperate perverts itching to cop off on 'em. — Chris Baker and Andrew Day, *Lock, Stock... & Spaghetti Sauce* 2000

corey; cory; corie *noun*
the penis *UK, 2000*
English gypsy use; probably from Romany *kori* (a thorn).
● 12 red-faced young men energetically shaking the drips from their coreys — Jimmy Stockin, *On The Cobbles* 2000

cornhole *noun*
the anus *US, 1922*
● They may want you to show your corn hole. A lot of them are very anal. — James Ridgeway, *Red Light* 1996

cornhole *verb*
to take the active role in anal sex *US, 1938*
● Fans expressed their profound interest in dirty, unsheathed cornholing by expressing total uninterest in such safe sex features[.] — Anthony Petkovich, *The X Factory* 1997

corral *noun*
a group of prostitutes working for a single pimp *US, 1971*
● — Eugene Landy, *The Underground Dictionary* 1971

corybungus *noun*
the buttocks *UK, 2002*
Homosexual usage; perhaps from COREY (the penis).
● — Paul Baker, *Polari* 2002

cottage *verb*
to seek homosexual contact in a public urinal *UK, 1971*
After COTTAGE (a public lavatory).
● Did you see anything? Were you perhaps cottaging in the area that night[?] — Christopher Brookmyre, *Boiling a Frog* 2000

cottager *noun*
a homosexual man who seeks sexual contact in public toilets *UK, 2000*
● hanging around secluded highland public conveniences all night, in the hope of running into the headhunter, or at least some would-be cottager they

could accuse — Christopher Brookmyre, *Boiling a Frog* 2000

cotton *noun*
female pubic hair *US, 1970*
● — Roger D. Abrahams, *Deep Down in the Jungle* 1970

couch checkers *noun*
sexual foreplay *US, 1967*
● What sports do you like? Couch checkers? — Elaine Shepard, *The Doom Pussy* 1967

cow *noun*
a prostitute attached to a pimp *US, 1859*
● Her tricks, when she functioned as an independent instead of a cow, had been hundred-dollar babies who came highly recommended. — John M. Murtagh and Sara Harris, *Cast the First Stone* 1957

cow-cunted *adjective*
possessing a slack and distended vagina *US, 1980*
● — Michael Dalton Johnson, *Talking Trash with Redd Foxx* 1994

cowgirl *noun*
a sexual position in which the woman is on top, astride and facing her partner *US, 1995*
● [I]n describing one of these positions (called the "cowgirl," in which the woman is facing the man and sitting up, or the "reverse cowgirl," in which she faces away from him) a pornographic director has said: "Very unnatural position. The girls hate it.["] — Gail Dines, *Pornography* 1998

coyote date *noun*
a date with an ugly woman *US, 1985*
● When you wake up in the morning and she's laying on your arm, you chew your arm off so she won't wake up as you leave. That's a coyote date. — Mark Baker, *Cops* 1985

crabs *noun*
pubic lice *UK, 1707*
● When we were kids in the Navy, he had such a bad case of crabs, we used to call him the Governor of Maryland. — *The Sopranos* (Episode 60) 2004

crack *noun*
the vagina *UK, 1775*
● "Snatch," "hole," "kooze," "slash," "pussy" and "crack" were other terms

referring variously to women's genitals, to women as individuals, or to women as a species. — *Screw* 3rd January 1972

crack *verb*
1 to have sex with a girl who is a virgin *FIJI, 1992*
- She too young to crack, man. — Jan Tent, 1995
► **crack a fat**
2 to achieve an erection *AUSTRALIA, 1968*
- Pommy sheilas? Aw, they're apples I s'pose – but the way I feel now I don't reckon I could crack a fat! — Barry Humphries, *The Wonderful World of Barry McKenzie* 1968
► **crack a Judy; crack a Judy's tea-cup**
3 to take a woman's virginity *UK, 1937*
- Baby baby baby let me pick your cherry / Go star-gazin' on yer back / To crack a Judy's teacup I'll give you a little upshot / Doncha say your mama's comin' back — Savage Garden, *Smashed 'n' Trashed* 1995

crack off *verb*
(of a male) to masturbate *UK, 2003*
- I had cracked off twice that day – so it was understandable. — Richard Herring, *Talking Cock* 2003

cradle-snatch *verb*
to have a sexual relationship with someone much younger than yourself *UK, 1938*
- The women, he meant. Too fucking young for the most part. Even the ones where it wasn't out and out cradle-snatching[.] — John Williams, *Cardiff Dead* 2000

crank *noun*
1 the penis *US, 1968*
- Right soon after that, his crank was hard. It rose up like it wanted to have a look around. — Tom Abrams, *A Piece of Luck* 1994
2 an act of masturbation *AUSTRALIA, 1985*
- — Thommo, *The Dictionary of Australian Swearing and Sex Sayings* 1985

cream *verb*
to ejaculate; to secrete vaginal lubricants during sexual arousal *US, 1915*
- Sometimes, though, I'd go home afterwards, after having had a hard-on for four hours of making out on the floor and in the bleachers, but without creaming, and it really gave you a sore dick. — *The Berkeley Tribe* 5th-12th September 1969

creamdown *noun*
sex focused on the pleasure of the active male participant *US, 1997*
- He basically liked them leaning over, braced against the wall, legs wide, a good fast pump. Back in San they call that a creamdown. — Ethan Morden, *Some Men Are Lookers* 1997

creamed *adjective*
soiled by vaginal secretions as a result of sexual arousal *UK, 1997*
- [W]e exchanged numbers like French kisses, at 2 a.m. / my creamed knickers rode the night bus home — Bernadine Evaristo, *Lara* 1997

creamies *noun*
the viscuous discharge of a sexually transmitted infection *US, 1969*
- — *Kiss* 1969

cream off *verb*
to orgasm *UK, 2000*
- JAMIE: Yer not lookin' for that kind of movie then? DEEP THROAT: I could cream off quicker to "Aerobics Oz Style". — Chris Baker and Andrew Day, *Lock, Stock... & Spaghetti Sauce* 2000

creampie *noun*
semen seeping from a vagina, anus or mouth *US, 2002*
- Creampie vids mean to correct this by showing sex as it actually happens, plus bodily fluids getting licked off the floor. — *Village Voice* 23rd April 2002

creep *noun*
a sex offender *US, 1975*
- Creeps never "get a hang-out card" (command enough respect to mingle and converse freely with other prisoners). — Miguel Pinero, *Short Eyes* 1975

creep house *noun*
a brothel where customers are routinely robbed *US, 1913*
- Warnings of immorality were probably less effective than warnings that some brothels were creep houses or panel houses wherein visitors were robbed of money and gold watches. — Irving Lewis Allen, *The City in Slang* 1993

crib *noun*
a room or shack where a prostitute plies her trade *US, 1846*
- All of nigger Chicago is lousy with police stations, gambling joints, and

whore cribs. — Iceberg Slim (Robert Beck), *Mama Black Widow* 1969

cribhouse *noun*
a brothel *US, 1916*
- He wasn't anything, for he got cut by a coke-frisky piano player in a cribhouse where he had gone to take out a little in trade on his protection account. — Robert Penn Warren, *All the King's Men* 1946

crotch light *noun*
in the pornography industry, a light used to illuminate the genitals of the performers *US, 1977*
- They said, "What am I doing here" and see all these strange faces and people holding crotch lights. — Stephen Ziplow, *The Film Maker's Guide to Pornography* 1977

crotch magazine *noun*
a pornographic magazine *US, 1986*
- "My name's Whistler," he said when the attendant looked up from his crotch magazine, open to the centerfold in which a girl of stunning beauty opened her legs for anyone who cared to ogle her. — Robert Campbell, *In La-La Land We Trust* 1986

crotch row *noun*
in a striptease performance, seats very near the performers *US, 1973*
- — Sherman Louis Sergel, *The Language of Show Biz* 1973

crotch shot *noun*
a photograph focused on a person's genitals *US, 1973*
- The explicitness of the crotch shots was made for pigs like you who need the anatomy lesson. — *The Village Voice* 25th July 2000

cruise *verb*
to search for a casual sex-partner, usually homosexual; to pursue a person as a casual sex-partner, especially by eye contact *US, 1925*
- A man who spends long evenings in a "gay bar" hoping to "cruise" what he knows is going to be a one-night stand cannot fulfill his office functions the next morning. — Antony James, *America's Homosexual Underground* 1965

cruiser *noun*
a person who habitually searches regular haunts for casual sex-partners, usually homosexual *UK, 1996*
- — Angela Devlin, *Prison Patter* 1996

cummy face *noun*
in a pornographic film or photograph, a close-up shot of a man's face as he ejaculates *US, 1995*
- — *Adult Video News* August, 1995

cunny *noun*
the vagina *UK, 1615*
A play on CUNT (the vagina) and 'con(e)y' (a rabbit).
- I kept touching her breasts and her cunny (that's what she calls it) and at last I got on her between her legs and she guided my prick into her cunt[.] — Frank Harris, *My Life and Loves (Grove Press Reader)* 1963

cunt *noun*
1 the vagina *UK, 1230*
The most carefully avoided, heavily tabooed word in the English language.
- Then he said, "Allright bitch, I want to taste a little bit of your cunt." — *Final Report of the Attorney General's Commission on Pornography* 1986
2 a woman, especially as an object of sexual desire *UK, 1674*
- After that, Mexico, and this time a cunt will live with me. — Jack Kerouac, *Letter to Neal Cassady* April, 1953
3 sex with a woman *UK, 1670*
- [P]rostitutes are our political prisoners – in jail for cunt. — Kate Millett, *The Prostitution Papers* 1976
4 among homosexuals, the buttocks, anus and rectum *US, 1972*
- Move your cunt – Mama wants to sit down. — Bruce Rodgers, *The Queens' Vernacular* 1972
5 among homosexuals, the mouth *US, 1972*
- Close your filthy cunt; I don't want to hear any more about it. — Bruce Rodgers, *The Queens' Vernacular* 1972

cunt book *noun*
a pornographic book, especially one with photographs or illustrations *US, 1969*
- Goldstein showed that it wasn't just perverts that bought cunt books. — *Screw* 4th July 1969

cunt collar *noun*
a desire for sex *US, 1965*
- Spoon's cunt collar was tight / which was understandably right / after serving three years and day. — Lightnin' Rod, *Hustlers Convention* 1973

cunt-lapper *noun*
a person who performs oral sex on a woman *US, 1916*
- Well, cock-suckers and reluctant cunt-lappers, the revolution is here! — *Screw* 12th June 1972

VAGINA

box *noun, UK, 1605*
the vagina; a woman
- I grabbed her by the shoulders, kissed her, and right quick from some instinctive sense shoved my hand right up her dress and came up with her box shining golden in the golden sun. — Jack Kerouac, *Letter to Neal Cassady* 10th January 1951

chuff *noun, UK, 1997*
- — *Roger's Profanisaurus* December, 1997

clam *noun, US, 1916*
- I was gobblin' her clam like it was the last supper. — Richard Price, *The Wanderers* 1974

cooch *noun, US, 2001*
the vagina; sex with a woman
- There are plenty of queer women who work as porn stars, strippers, and sex workers, but there are a lot fewer of us willing to fork over cash for cooch. — *The Village Voice* 7th August 2001

fuckhole *noun, UK, 1893*
- Four young wannabe sex stars get their nearly cherry fuckholes stretched, slammed, and jizzed on by big-dicked professional porn studs in the latest installment of this raunchy, hot series. — Penthouse Magazine, *The Penthouse Erotic Video Guide* 2003

holy of holies *noun, US, 1984*
- Look, maybe your method of massage differs from mine, but touchin' his lady's feet, and stickin' your tongue in her holyiest of holyies, ain't the same ballpark, ain't the same league, ain't even the same fuckin' sport. — *Pulp Fiction* 1994

honeypot *noun, US, 1958*
Recorded as rhyming slang for TWAT (the vagina) It certainly rhymes, but must surely be influenced – if not inspired – by senses that are conventional, figurative and slang. Found once in the UK in 1719, and then in general slang usage with 'Candy'.
- "Now I am inserting the member," he explained, as he parted the tender quavering lips of the pink honeypot and allowed his stout member to be drawn slowly into the seething thermal pudding of the darling girl. — Terry Southern, *Candy* 1958

minge *noun, UK, 1903*
From the Latin *mingere* (to urinate) and the mistaken belief that urine passes through the vagina.
- If nothing else, most women will feel they have cut their losses if you get down there and lick her minge! — Richard Herring, *Talking Cock* 2003

quim *noun, UK, 1735*
the vagina; used objectively as a collective noun for women, especially sexually available women
- With his pal filling her quim and Butler's dick sliding in and out of her luscious lips, Kari gets a heaping helping of the living needle from both ends at once. — *Adult Video* August/September, 1986

twat *noun, UK, 1656*
- I just love the sound of a bird with a posh accent bellowing obscenities as I batter her twat with my love truncheon. — Stewart Home, *Sex Kick [britpulp]* 1999

cunt hound *noun*
a man obsessed with the seduction of women *US, 1960*
- It was shocking, but I knew Joe was 1 helluva cunthound, or so he said[.] — Clarence Cooper Jr, *The Farm* 1967

cunt juice *noun*
vaginal secretions *US, 1990*
- My cock slides in almost too easily – her cunt is too wet, drenched with her own cunt juice and Christie's saliva, and there's no friction. — Brett Easton Ellis, *American Psycho* 1991

cunt-lapping *noun*
oral sex on a woman *US, 1970*
- Is Cunt-Lapping Better Than the Pill? (Headline) — *Screw* 22nd March 1970

cunt-licking *noun*
oral sex on a woman *US, 1996*
- Elsewhere there's all the stuffed cunts, finger jobs, and cunt-licking you can handle – and then some. — *The Penthouse Erotic Video Guide* 2003

cunt light noun
in the pornography industry, a light used to illuminate the genitals of the performers US, 1995
- — Adult Video News October, 1995

cunt like a Grimsby welly noun
an unusually large and pungent vagina UK, 2002
Grimsby is a fishing port on the north east coast of England; a 'welly' is a Wellington boot.
- Fackin' slag. Cunt like a Grimsby welly, arse like a wizard's sleeve. — Andrew Holmes, Sleb 2002

cunt man noun
a heterosexual man; a womaniser UK, 1999
- I hear you're a bit of a cunt man, Mr Dunford. So I apologise for the vile content of these snaps. — David Peace, Nineteen Seventy-Four 1999

cunt pie noun
the vagina, especially as an object of oral sex US, 1980
- There, in public, making herself hotter and hotter, finger in cunt pie going round and round, as finger slips black panties lower, she breathes harder and harder. — Kathy Acker, Portrait of an Eye 1980

cunt-simple adjective
obsessed with sex; easily distracted by women US, 1982
- With her mind, and with her body, she had to organize Louis Palo, that cunt-simple schmuck, and her own husband, to steal the money then to take the fall for her. — Richard Condon, Prizzi's Honor 1982

cunt-struck adjective
obsessed with sex with a woman or women UK, 1866
- I do not agree, for instance, that he is a philosopher, or a thinker. He is cunt-struck, that's all. — Henry Miller, Tropic of Cancer 1961

cunt-sucker noun
a person who performs oral sex on women UK, 1868
- He can become a world-class cunt sucker who will have women standing in line waiting to be next. — Betty Dodson, Orgasms for Two 2002

cunt-sucking noun
oral sex on a woman US, 1998
- I sat right down on Joe's mouth and he gave me the most comprehensive cunt-sucking that I've ever had in my life. — Graham, Masterson, Secrets of the Sexually Irresistible Woman 1998

cunt tease noun
a woman who signals an interest in sex with another woman but does not have sex with her US, 1971
- — Eugene Landy, The Underground Dictionary 1971

cunt-tickler noun
a moustache US, 1967
- I was you was an Italianate Jew, all earthy and Levantine and suave and had a cunt-tickler of a mustache[.] — Norman Mailer, Why Are We in Vietnam? 1967

cup noun
the vagina US, 1973
- Satin was a bitch that had one of those real rare fuzzy cups, the kind a man runs into once in a lifetime. — A.S. Jackson, Gentleman Pimp 1973

cupcakes noun
1 the female breasts US, 2001
- "Yeah, well, nice cupcakes!" he said, eyes locked onto the woman's breasts. — Kregg Jorgenson, Very Crazy G.I. 2001

2 well-defined, well-rounded buttocks US, 1972
- — H. Max, Gay (S)language 1988

cupid's itch noun
any sexually transmitted infection US, 1930
- "So your client goes in on Monday complaining that he is," she reads from a page, "as he describes it, 'pissing battery acid,' and wondering if he has to tell his wife about a little bout of Cupid's itch." — Richard Dooling, Brain Storm 1998

curlies noun
pubic hair US, 1973
Used both literally and figuratively to suggest complete control over someone.
- You're in no position to make deals. We got you by the curlies. — Joseph Wambaugh, The Blue Knight 1973

curtains noun
the labia majora US, 1982

● — *Maledicta* Summer/Winter, 1982:
'Dyke diction: the language of lesbians'

cush *noun*
the vagina; sex; a woman as a sexual
object *US, 1960*
● No, it was a walking, living round balloon
with a fat "poke" [wallet] and a flaming
itch for black "Cush." — Iceberg Slim
(Robert Beck), *Pimp* 1969

cut *verb*
▶ **cut the mustard**
to have sex *UK, 1977*
● A lady from New Zealand expressed
dismay at the sight of a pair [of lovers]
energetically cutting the mustard in
broad daylight. — *Sunday Telegraph*
9th October 1977

cut *adjective*
circumcised *US, 1998*
● I've got six-pack abs. I'm eight inches
cut. — *The Village Voice* 4th April
2000

cut and tuck *noun*
a male transsexual who has had his penis
removed and an artificial vagina surgically
constructed *AUSTRALIA, 1985*
● — Thommo, *The Dictionary of
Australian Swearing and Sex Sayings*
1985

cutta *noun*
the buttocks *US, 1957*
● "Man, dig that crazy cutta on the big
beast in the plaid skirt." — Herbert
Simmons, *Corner Boy* 1957

Dd

daddy *noun*
an aggressive, predatory male homosexual
US, 1996
- Inmates subject to rape ("punks") face threats and violence perpetrated by stronger inmates ("daddies," "jockers," or "booty bandits") who initiate unwanted sexual acts. — *Corrections Today* December, 1996

dadger *noun*
the penis *UK, 1997*
Variation of 'tadger' (the penis).
- ["I]s it true what they all say about black men?" "What? That we all make great lawyers, accountants, politicians?" "No, yer pillock, that you've all got cowin' big dadgers." — Colin Butts, *Is Harry on the Boat?* 1997

dairy; dairies *noun*
the female breast(s) *UK, 1788*
Elaborated as 'dairy arrangements' in 1923.
- — *The Times* 12th February 2005

daisy chain *noun*
a group of people, arranged roughly in a circle, in which each person is both actively and passively engaged in oral, anal, or vaginal sex with the person in front of and behind them in the circle *US, 1927*
A term that is much more common than the practice.
- Past the Horseshoe Club, with its modified burlesque, and where for five bucks extra you can watch three naked women form a daisy chain on the floor of a basement room anytime after one a.m. — *Rogue for Men* June, 1956

damaged goods *noun*
an ex-virgin *US, 1916*
- — Vincent J. Monteleone, *Criminal Slang* 1949

danger wank *noun*
an act of masturbation with the threat of being discovered as an added stimulus *UK, 2003*
- Danger wank: [T]hrill-seeking masturbation, while your mum is walking upstairs to your bedroom after

you have called her. The object of the game is to come before she opens the door and catches you. — Chris Lewis, *(The Dictionary of Playground Slang)* 2003

dangle *noun*
the penis *US, 1936*
- On the wall was a nude drawing of Dean, enormous dangle and all, done by Camille. — Jack Kerouac, *On the Road* 1957

dangler *noun*
the penis *US, 1971*
- At which point he unzipped his fly and yanked out his dangler and waved it at me. — John Francis Hunter, *The Gay Insider* 1971

Danish *noun*
sexual intercourse with full penetration *US, 1981*
- [S]tick to Swedish massage (by hand), or French (by mouth), and only go Spanish (between the breasts), Russian (between the thighs), American (a body roll) or Danish (inside) if it's worth the money. — Alix Shulman, *On the Stroll* 1981

dartboard *adjective*
▶ **had more pricks than a second-hand dartboard**
used of a sexually promiscuous woman *UK, 1982*
As the punch-line of a joke from the early 1980s 'second-hand' is dispensable.
- — Ted Walker, *High Path* 1982

date with DiPalma *verb*
(of a male) an act of masturbation *US, 2001*
DiPalma alias 'the hand'.
- Another way to say "the boy is masturbating" [...] a date with DiPalma[.] — Erica Orloff and JoAnn Baker, *Dirty Little Secrets* 2001

dawner *noun*
an engagement between a prostitute and customer that lasts all night, until dawn *US, 1987*
- Rialto was supposed to be waitin' on Felita to say was it going to be a quick trick or a dawner. But Rialto wasn't there. — Robert Campbell, *Alice in La-La Land* 1987

deadwood *noun*
a flaccid penis *US, 1995*

Extended from **wood** (the erect penis).
● — *Adult Video News* October, 1995

debaucherama *noun*
an orgy *UK, 2000*
● Makes sense they'd put a tail on me at a debaucherama like that, I suppose, and unfortunately I didn't disappoint. — Christopher Brookmyre, *Boiling a Frog* 2000

deep-dick *verb*
(from the male point of view) to have sex *US, 1997*
● Can I at least tell people that all you needed was some serious deep-dicking? — *Chasing Amy* 1997

deep throat *noun*
oral sex performed on a man in which the person doing the performing takes the penis completely into their mouth and throat *US, 1991*
A term from the so-named 1972 classic pornography film.
● Once you've mastered the basic techniques of fellatio and cunnilingus, you might want to experiment with '69', deep throat and other oral tricks for adventurous lovers! — Siobhan Kelly, *The Wild Guide to Sex and Loving* 2002

deep throat *verb*
to take a man's penis completely into the mouth and throat *US, 1991*
● I know he is ready to shoot his thick creamy come down my throat, as I deep-throat him. — Nancy Friday, *Women on Top* 1991

derrière *noun*
the vagina *US, 1998*
From French *derrière* (behind), a familiar euphemism for 'the buttocks', 'the behind', adopted here for a new location.
● There's "powderbox," "derriere," a "poochi," a "poopi," a "peepe["·] — Eve Ensler, *The Vagina Monologues* 1998

diamond cutter *noun*
the erect penis *US, 1975*
● Then she slowly twists 360 degrees, all the while impaled on your diamond-cutter. — *The FHM Little Book of Bloke* June, 2003

dibbler *noun*
the penis *US, 1998*
● The attraction of my hand, my fingers at her clitoris, only distracts from her

skill on my dibbler. — Clarence Major, *All-Night Visitors* 1998

dick *noun*
1 the penis *US, 1888*
● [T]he thick cunt who stands at the door pretending to be a security guard, biceps for brains and a dick the size of my clit[.] — Stella Duffy, *Jail Bait* 1999
2 the clitoris *US, 1964*
● She had a dick so long she had to be circumcized. — Bruce Jackson, *Get Your Ass in the Water and Swim Like Me* 1964
3 sex with a man *US, 1956*
● Women are tricky. You ask a woman how many men she's fucked, and she'll tell you how many boyfriends she's had instead. A woman doesn't count all the miscellaneous dick. — Chris Rock, *Rock This!* 1997

dick *verb*
(from the male point of view) to have sex with *US, 1942*
● He said, "Did I ask him, you want to know, if he's dicking her? No, I didn't." — Elmore Leonard, *Split Images* 1981

dick cheese *noun*
smegma *CANADA, 2002*
● Is dick cheese a major problem with uncircumcised gay slobs? — Suroosh Alvi et al., *The Vice Guide* 2002

dickey *noun*
the penis *US, 1962*
● The hair around my dickey has been there since I was fourteen, and I have hair under my arms. — Charles Perry, *Portrait of a Young Man Drowning* 1962

dicklicker *noun*
a 'cocksucker' in all its senses *US, 1968*
● "Dicklickers!" she calls her two dads. — Naomi Odenkirk, *Mr. Show* 2002

dickory dock *noun*
the penis *UK, 1961*
Rhyming slang for **cock** (the penis), not an elaboration of **dick**.
● — Julian Franklyn, *A Dictionary of Rhyming Slang* 2nd 1961

dick-skinner *noun*
the hand *US, 1971*
● You ain't going to have no skin on those dick-skinners. Remember them hands is your best girl. Rosie Palms. — Daniel Buckman, *The Names of Rivers* 2003

dick teaser *noun*
a girl who suggests that she will engage in sex but will not *US*, *1962*
- I wanted to, but my muscles had atrophied. I didn't want him to think of me as a dick teaser. — Maya Angelou, *Gather Together in My Name* 1974

dicky *noun*
the penis *UK*, *1891*
- Your pa sticks his dicky boy in your ma, see, and shoots this stuff into the hole that your mother pees from. — Herman Wouk, *Inside, Outside* 1985

dicky-dunking *noun*
sex from the male perspective *US*, *1994*
- When the frost is on the pumpkin, it's time for dicky dunkin. — Michael Dalton Johnson, *Talking Trash with Redd Foxx* 1994

diddle *noun*
an act of masturbation *US*, *2001*
- "You can keep the twenty [dollars]." "Do you want a diddle for it?" "No!" — Janet Evanovich, *Seven Up* 2001

diddle *verb*
1 (from the male perspective) to have sex *US*, *1870*
- I used to could diddle all night long/ but since I got the age I am/ it takes me all night to diddle. — Bruce Jackson, *Get Your Ass in the Water and Swim Like Me* 1964
2 to masturbate *US*, *1934*
- [I]f I was you I would just go right back out that door and let her diddle herself in the powder room. — George V. Higgins, *The Rat on Fire* 1981

diddler *noun*
the penis *US*, *1969*
- If I see a queer, I wave my diddler at him and show him how big it is. — *Screw* 4th July 1969

diddling Miss Daisy *noun*
an act of female masturbation *UK*, *2004*
After the 1989 film *Driving Miss Daisy*.
- — Michelle Baker and Steven Tropiano, *Queer Facts* 2004

diddy *noun*
the female breast or nipple *UK*, *1991*
- If Sophia Loren came up to yeh an' stuck her diddies in your face would you say tha' she was nice enough? — Roddy Doyle, *The Van* 1991

DILF *noun*
a sexually attractive father *US*, *2003*
A gender variation of **MILF** (a sexually appealing mother); an acronym of 'dad I'd like to fuck'.
- — Chris Lewis, *The Dictionary of Playground Slang* 2003

dill *noun*
the penis *AUSTRALIA*, *1988*
- — James McDonald, *A Dictionary of Obscenity, Taboo and Euphemism* 1988

dill-dock *noun*
a dildo *US*, *1949*
- Dill-dock – Artificial penis strapped on by active Lesbian partner. — Anon., *The Gay Girl's Guide* 1949

dill piece *noun*
the penis *US*, *2001*
- — Rick Ayers (Editor), *Slang Dictionary* 2001

dillzy *noun*
the penis *US*, *1999*
- She on the dillzy, I take advantage — Dr. Dre *Housewife* 1999

dine *verb*
▶ **dine at the Y; eat at the Y**
to perform oral sex on a woman *US*, *1971*
The Y is an effective pictogram for the groin of a woman.
- BARRY: Well, I dunno about you Suke – but I feel like dining at the Y. SUKE: Well darls [darling] if you wanted to yodel up the valley youse had your chance[.] — Barry Humphries, *Bazza Pulls It Off!* 1971

ding *noun*
the penis *US*, *1965*
- I say to you, Legion of Decency – you with your dings scrubbed with holy water and Rokeach soap – you're dirty. — Lenny Bruce, *How to Talk Dirty and Influence People* 1965

ding-a-ling *noun*
the penis *US*, *1952*
- She may be your wife but I stick my dingaling in her every night so that make her mine. — *Boyz N The Hood* 1990

dingdong *noun*
the penis *US*, *1944*
- [T]he man had used his handkerchief to wipe up the "funny white juice that came out of his dingdong"[.] — James Harper, *Homo Laws in all 50 States* 1968

dinge queen *noun*
a white homosexual man who finds black men attractive; a black homosexual man *US, 1964*
- — Florida Legislative Investigation Committee (Johns Committee), *Homosexuality and Citizenship in Florida* 1964: 'Glossary of homosexual terms and deviate acts'

dinghy *noun*
the penis *BAHAMAS, 1982*
- — John A. Holm, *Dictionary of Bahamian English* 1982

dingleberry *noun*
a glob of dried faeces accumulated on anal hairs *US, 1938*
- Some of your cruds are going to wipe just half-assed, so I do not want to see any – and I mean any – dingleberries in your skivvies. — Zell Miller, *Corps Values* 1996

dingle-dangle *noun*
the penis *UK, 1937*
- I won't let my dingle-dangle dangle in the dirt / Gonna pick up my dingle-dangle, tie it to my shirt. — Sandee Johnson, *Cadences: The Jody Call Book, No. 2* 1986

dingus *noun*
1 the penis *US, 1888*
- Half-and-half still costs you more than straight, so if you need the girl's mouth on your dingus to get you up it will set you back a total of thirty dollars[.] — Gerald Paine, *A Bachelor's Guide to the Brothels of Nevada* 1978
2 an artificial penis *US, 1957*
- She greases the dingus, shoves the boy's legs over his head and works it up his ass with a series of corkscrew movements of her fluid hips. — William Burroughs, *Naked Lunch* 1957

dink *noun*
the penis *US, 1888*
- Lube the shit out of her ass and your dink, and place your dink's face right at the anus. — Suroosh Alvi et al., *The Vice Guide* 2002

dinky *noun*
the penis *US, 1962*
- They they start to pressing him, grabbing at his dinky. — Charles Perry, *Portrait of a Young Man Drowning* 1962

dinny *noun*
the vagina *BAHAMAS, 1982*
- — John A. Holm, *Dictionary of Bahamian English* 1982

dip *verb*
▶ **dip your wick**
to have sex *UK, 1958*
- You're gonna find out if you mastrebate (sic) instead of dippin' your wick, you'll conserve energy. — Dan Jenkins, *Life Its Ownself* 1984

dipstick *noun*
the penis *US, 1973*
- I wouldn't mind checking her oil with my dipstick. — Craig Lesley, *Winterkill* 1984

dirtbox *noun*
the anus; the rectum *UK, 1984*
- Is this love at first sight? / I'll let you know when I've seen her dirt-box. — Susan Nickson, *Two Pints of Lager and a Packet of Crisps*, 12th April 2004

dirt chute *noun*
the rectum *US, 1971*
- It would have been so sweet to know she'd felt that last big bang, and to feel her guts spasm as I greased her dirt chute! — Brian Lumley, *Necroscope: Invaders* 1999

dirt road *noun*
the anus and rectum *US, 1922*
- "That nigga just tore me a new asshole," said Rosalyn clutching her own butt cheeks. "Girl, you let him go down the dirt road?" "Oooh." She covered her mouth. "Shut up. My ass is killing me." — Antoine Thomas, *Flower's Bed* 2003

dirty hustling *noun*
behavior by a prostitute during a group inspection by a potential customer that crosses the line of what is allowed by the brothel *US, 1997*
- All private parts must be covered at all times (nipples and pubic hair). It was absolutely taboo and called "Dirty Hustling" if a girl broke any of these rules during line-ups. — Sisters of the Heart, *The Brothel Bible* 1997

dirty leg *noun*
a woman with loose sexual mores; a common prostitute *US, 1966*
- A dirty leg is the $5 or $10 trick. — Bruce Jackson, *In the Life* 1972

dirty mac; dirty mackintosh *noun*
used as a generic description for any man
who habitually resorts to sex-shops, strip-
clubs and the purchase of 'top-shelf' publi-
cations *UK, 1975*
- That little newsagent round the corner's
  got so many bum and tit mags on
  display you feel like one of the dirty
  mac outfit just going in for an evening
  newspaper. — *Journal of British
  Photography* 4th January 1980

dirty mac brigade *noun*
a notional collection of sex-oriented older
men *UK, 1987*
- If the Dirty Mac brigade had been
  disappointed by the distinctly
  unstreamy output of Channel 4, Central,
  Yorkshire, and now Thames, in the wee
  small hours, what has been on offer?
  — *The Guardian Likelier* 8th June 1987

dirty old man *noun*
a lecher; especially a middle-aged or older
man with sexual appetites considered more
appropriate in someone younger *UK, 1932*
Given impetus in the UK in the late 1960s –
early 70s by television comedy series
'Steptoe and Son'.
- O'MALLY: Did you ever see such pins
  [legs], did you, did you honestly?
  TAYLOR: You're a dirty old man you are,
  Paddy. — Graeme Kent, *The Queen's
  Corporal [Six Granada Plays]* 1959

dirty Sanchez *noun*
an act of daubing your sex-partner's upper
lip with a 'moustache' of his or her faeces
US, 2003
This appears to have been contrived with an
intention to provoke shock rather than
actually as a practice, although, no doubt,
some have or will experiment.
- — Chris Lewis, *The Dictionary of
  Playground Slang* 2003

dirty water *noun*
▶ **get the dirty water(s) off your chest**
(of a male) to ejaculate, either with a
partner or as a sole practitioner *UK, 1961*
- [W]hile the other bastards are busy
  getting the dirty waters off their chests
  a bloke like me runs the risk of goin'
  blind jerkin' the gerkin!!! — Barry
  Humphries, *Bazza Pulls It Off!* 1971

dirty work *noun*
in a strip or sex show, movements made to
expose the vagina *US, 1971*

- If strippers choose a face that is shy, it
  is because they want their "floor work"
  (crouching or lying on the floor and
  simulating intercourse) and "dirty
  work" ("flashing" and spreading their
  legs) to remind the audience of demure
  girls. — Marilyn Salutin, *The Sexual
  Scene* June, 1971

disco queen *noun*
a male homosexual who frequents discos
US, 1978
- — *Maledicta* 1979: 'Kinks and queens:
  linguistic and cultural aspects of the
  terminology for gays'

dish *noun*
1 the buttocks, the anus *UK, 1965*
- JULIAN: I can't work in here. All the
  dishes are dirty. SANDY: Speak for
  yourself, ducky. — Barry Took and
  Marty Feldman, *Round the Horne*,
  1965
▶ **put on the dish**
2 to apply lubricant to the anus in preparation for anal sex *UK, 2002*
- — Paul Baker, *Polari* 2002

dishonorable discharge *noun*
ejaculation achieved through masturbation
US, 1964
- When I was in the army, a sergeant
  caught me in the shower in the process
  of giving my dick a dishonorable
  discharge. I looked him straight in the
  eye and told him it was my dick and
  I could wash it as fast as I wanted to.
  — Ken Weaver, *Texas Crude* 1984

Disneyland *nickname*
the brothel district near An Khe, Vietnam,
near the 1st Cavalry Division base *US, 1966*
- — *Time* 6th May 1966

disobey *verb*
▶ **disobey the pope**
to have sex *US, 2001*
- Another way to say "intercourse" [...]
  Disobeying the pope[.] — Erica Orloff
  and JoAnn Baker, *Dirty Little Secrets*
  2001

do *verb*
1 to have sex with *UK, 1650*
- I tried some sex banter with him but
  Axel was looking fierce. "I'd like to do
  some of them," he whispered, "I'd like
  to do some of them." — Clancy Sigal,
  Going Away 1961

▶ **do it**

2 to have sex *IRELAND, 1923*

● [D]oing it everyway we could think of any-
old place we happened to be, in fact, we
did it in so many places that Denver was
covered with our pecker-tracks. — Neal
Cassady, *The First Third* 1971

dobber *noun*

the penis *US, 1974*

● Lad had a big mad hairy dobber on
him. — Kevin Sampson, *Outlaws* 2001

dog *noun*

a sexually transmitted infection *US, 1962*

● — Joseph E. Ragen and Charles Finston,
Inside the World's Toughest Prison
1962: 'Penitentiary and underworld
glossary'

dog fashion; doggie fashion *adverb*

sexual intercourse from behind, vaginal or
anal, heterosexual or homosexual *UK, 1900*

● I'd always drop it down and fuck her
dog fashion. — A.S. Jackson,
Gentleman Pimp 1973

dogfuck *verb*

to have sex from the rear, homosexual or
heterosexual, vaginal or anal *US, 1980*

● — Edith A. Folb, *runnin' down some
lines* 1980

dogger *noun*

a person who engages in al fresco sexual
activities such as exhibitionism or
voyeurism; especially of sexual activities
(with multiple partners) in parked vehicles,
generally in the countryside *UK, 2003*
When police approached 'doggers' (before
they were so-named), the usual excuse
offered was 'walking the dog'.

● — *Farming Today* 26th July 2003

dogging *noun*

al fresco sexual activities such as
exhibitionism or voyeurism; especially of
sexual activities (with multiple partners) in
parked vehicles, generally in the
countryside *UK, 1998*

● Another curious habit for the
looker/lookee set is called dogging.
No, it doesn't mean letting your dog
watch your sexual activities. — Erica
Orloff and JoAnn Baker, *Dirty Little
Secrets* 2001

doggy *noun*

the penis *BAHAMAS, 1982*

● — John A. Holm, *Dictionary of
Bahamian English* 1982

dog's lipstick *noun*

the uncircumcised penis when erect *UK,
2003*

● — Graham Norton, *V Graham Norton*
20th May 2003

dog-style; doggy style *noun*

a sexual position in which the woman or
passive male kneels and the man enters
her from behind *US, 1962*

● Greek lads white as marble fuck dog
style on the portico of a great golden
temple. — William Burroughs, *Naked
Lunch* 1957

dog water *noun*

colourless seminal fluid *US, 1965*

● Knowing that scum was white, most of
the guys said that Horse was right and
that it was just dog water. I said that
dog water was most that he ever made.
— Claude Brown, *Manchild in the
Promised Land* 1965

doll shop *noun*

a brothel *US, 1990*

● After all, Ah Toy once worked at one of
Johnny Formosa's doll shops. — Seth
Morgan, *Homeboy* 1990

dolly *noun*

a lesbian prisoner's lover *NEW ZEALAND,
1999*

● — Harry Orsman, *A Dictionary of
Modern New Zealand Slang* 1999

dolphin *noun*

1 a flaccid penis *US, 1995*

● — *Adult Video News* October, 1995

▶ **wax the dolphin**

2 of a male, to masturbate *US, 2002*

● Most guys come in here, they wax the
dolphin. That's it — it's over. — *The
Guru* 2002

dom; domme *noun*

1 a dominatrix *US, 2002*

● [T]he most in-demand dom in the
north-west. — Niall Griffiths, *Kelly +
Victor* 2002

2 a sexual dominant in sadomasochistic
sexual relationships *US, 1989*

● — Thomas Murray and Thomas Murrell,
The Language of Sadomasochism 1989

do-me queen *noun*

a passive sexual partner with specific, self-
oriented, sexual demands *US, 1994*

● Now, it does help that I am a do-me-
queen, and have no need to have a

deep, meaningful relationship with everyone I play with. If they're willing to do me the way I want them to do me, they can do me. — *soc.subculture.bondage-bdsm* 11th April 2001

don *verb*

▶ **don the beard**

to perform oral sex on a woman *AUSTRALIA, 1971*

- — Barry Humphries, *Bazza Pulls It Off!* 1971

dong *noun*

the penis *US, 1900*

- Nevertheless, I was wholly incapable of keeping my paws from my dong once it started the climb up my belly. — Philip Roth, *Portnoy's Complaint* 1969

donkey *noun*

▶ **pull your donkey**

humping? — Mr. Skin, *Mr. Skin's Skincyclopedia* 2005

doodle *noun*

the penis *US, 1980*

- Uric acid, they say is my trouble, and I don't mind telling you this, / I've to whistle "The Last Rose of Summer", to coax the old doodle to piss. — Martin Cameron, *A Look at the Bright Side* 1988

doodle *verb*

to have sex *US, 1957*

- Well, Mr. Anker, you know yourself all a Jew wants to do is doodle a Christian girl. — William Burroughs, *Naked Lunch* 1957

doodles *noun*

the testicles *US, 2001*

- Truth is, I think naked men are kind of strange-looking, what with their

LABIA

beef curtains *noun, US, 1998*

- — Paul Baker, *Polari* 2002

camel toe *noun, US, 1994*

the condition that exists when a tight-fitting pair of trousers, shorts, bathing-suit or other garment forms a wedge or cleft between a woman's labia, accentuating their shape

- Camel lips, an offensive name from the '50s when women wear their pants too tight. Also known as camel toes. The pants were designed to capitalize on that. — *USA Today* 12th April 1994

fanny lip *noun, UK, 2002*

the vaginal lips; the labium majora or minora

- Flap dancin' I call it 'cos if you're lucky they give you the full two sets of fanny lips even though they in't s'posed to[.] — Ben Elton, *High Society* 2002

piss flaps *noun, AUSTRALIA, 1985*

the vaginal lips

- [N]aked, her breasts pendulous and flabby, her legs spread, her piss flaps all red and hairy and wet[.] — Lisa Jewell, *Labia Lobelia [Tart Noir]* 2002

pussy lips *noun, US, 1969*

- Ugh. All that hair. Then my pussy lips be black. — Alice Walker, *The Color Purple* 1982

(used of a male) to masturbate *US, 1990*

- They'd be pulling their donkeys all night, beating their meat, whispering back and forth. — Robert Campbell, *Sweet La-La Land* 1990

donkey dick *noun*

a man with a large penis; a large penis *US, 1980*

- Little fuckin' fag! Donkey dick! — *Boogie Nights* 1997

donut bumping *noun*

lesbian sex *US, 2005*

- But wouldn't we all try to make her trade her donut-bumping for cruller-

doodles and ding-dong hanging loose like they do. — Janet Evanovich, *Seven Up* 2001

dork *noun*

the penis *US, 1961*

- He sort of matter-of-factly removed his dork, pressed the length of it against her, and jizzed on her ass[.] — Josh Alan Friedman, *Tales of Times Square* 1986

dose *noun*

a case of a sexually transmitted infection *US, 1914*

- "Wait a minute," he yelled, "don't you cunt-lappers know that's Agnes, she's

got the biggest dose in Hartford,
everybody knows that." — Jack
Kerouac, *Letter to Neal Cassady* 10th
January 1951

dot *noun*
1 the anus *US, 1964*
● So, keeping a firm grip on the reins,
he scrambled over the back of the seat,
dropped his tweeds and cocked his dot
over the tail-board. — Sam Weller, *Old
Bastards I Have Met* 1979
2 the clitoris *US, 1964*
● — Roger Blake, *The American Dictionary
of Sexual Terms* 1964

dot *verb*
to have anal intercourse *UK, 2002*
● [T]o "dot" someone is to perform anal
intercourse on them (because the anus
resembles a full stop)[.]
— *www.LondonSlang.com* June, 2002

double adaptor *noun*
a bisexual *SOUTH AFRICA, 2005*
Scamto youth street slang (South African
townships).
● — *The Times* 12th February 2005

double bag *verb*
to use two condoms at once *US, 1989*
● — Geoffrey Froner, *Digging for
Diamonds* 1989

double-bagger *noun*
an ugly woman *US, 1982*
● What's a double-bagger? A woman so
ugly that before you'll screw her you
put a bag over her head, and one over
yours — just in case hers falls off.
— Blanche Knott, *Blanche Knott's Book
of Truly Tasteless Anatomy Jokes, Vol. 2*
1991

double-bass *noun*
a sexual position in which a man, having
entered a woman from behind, simultaneously applies manual stimulation to her
nipples and clitoris *AUSTRALIA, 2002*
● The position is similar to that used
when playing a double bass
instrument, but the sound produced is
slightly different. — Chris Lewis, *The
Dictionary of Playground Slang* 2003

double click your mouse; double click *verb*
of a female, to masturbate *AUSTRALIA,
2003*
● — Chris Lewis, *The Dictionary of
Playground Slang* 2003

double-cunted *adjective*
possessing a slack and distended vagina
US, 1980
● — *Maledicta* Winter, 1980: 'A new
erotic vocabulary'

double-gaited *adjective*
bisexual *US, 1927*
● A certain man, who was admittedly
double-gaited (bi-sexual), used to call
me for his entire family. — John O'Day,
Confessions of a Male Prostitute 1964

douche *verb*
to take an enema before or after anal sex
US, 1972
● — Bruce Rodgers, *The Queens'
Vernacular* 1972

downblouse *noun*
a type of voyeurism devoted specifically to
seeing a woman's breasts looking down her
blouse *US, 1994*
● "Upskirt" and "downblouse" tapes
often end up on the Internet, where
anyone over 18 can legally view and
buy them. — *Charleston (West Virginia)
Daily Mail* 10th August 1998

down south *noun*
below the waist; the genitals *US, 1982*
● — *Maledicta* Summer/Winter, 1982:
'Dyke diction: the language of lesbians'

downstairs *noun*
the genital area, especially of a female *UK,
2002*
● 3) Nipples: coarse, bulbous, lacerated
4) Downstairs: bushy, trimmed, bald
— Kevin Sampson, *Clubland* 2002

down there *noun*
the genitals *US, 1995*
● JANE: Okay. So what do you call it?
ROBIN: Down there. — *Boys on the
Side* 1995

DP *noun*
double penetration *US, 1997*
In the pornography industry, this usually
refers to a woman who is being penetrated
simultaneously in the vagina and anus.
● "While we're on the subject, what do
you think of DP's?" "They're too hard
to shoot. There's no real spontaneity in
them. You know, DP actually means a
double penetration in one hole — not
just the pussy and the ass."
— Anthony Petkovich, *The X Factory*
1997

DPP *noun*
a vagina simultaneously penetrated by two
penises *US, 2000*
An abbreviation of 'double pussy
penetration'.
- — Ana Loria, *1 2 3 Be A Porn Star!*
  2000: 'Glossary of adult sex industry
  terms'

drag *noun*
a transvestite *UK, 1974*
- I tell the drag barman to give me a
  vodka and tonic[.] — Ted Lewis, *Jack
  Carter's Law* 1974

draw drapes *noun*
the foreskin of an uncircumcized penis *US,
1979*
- — *Maledicta* 1979: 'Kinks and queens:
  linguistic and cultural aspects of the
  terminology for Gays'

dress for sale *noun*
a prostitute *US, 1979*
- — Lanie Dills, *The Official CB
  Slanguage Language Dictionary* 1976

drill *verb*
to have sex from a male perspective *UK,
2000*
- [L]ittle grains of sand ain't really knob
  friendly, know what I mean? So drilling
  away on the beach at night don't do
  your piping the world of good. — Dave
  Courtney, *Raving Lunacy* 2000

drink *verb*
▶ **drink from the furry cup**
to perform oral sex on a woman *UK, 2001*
Probably coined by comedian Sacha Baron-
Cohen (b.1970); his influence on late C20
UK slang is profound.
- DRINKIN FROM THE FURRY CUP WHILE
  AT THE EARLY STAGES OF A
  RELASHUNSHIP U IZ PROBABLY UP FOR
  EATING FROM DE BUSHY PLATE.
  — Sacha Baron-Cohen, *Da Gospel
  According to Ali G* 2001

drippy faucet *noun*
the penis of a man with a sexually
transmitted infection that produces a pus
discharge *US, 1981*
- Do you know he has a drippy faucet?
  — Joseph Wambaugh, *The Glitter Dome*
  1981

dripsy *noun*
gonorrhea *US, 1981*
- — *Maledicta* Summer/Winter, 1981: 'Sex
  and the single soldier'

drop *verb*
▶ **drop them**
of a woman, to readily remove her knickers
as a practical necessity for sexual activity
UK, 1984
- Her? She's not fussy — she'll drop 'em
  for anyone. — Paul Beale, 1984
▶ **drop your oyster**
(of a woman) to experience an orgasm *US,
1971*
- I could make Gloria drop her oyster in
  five minutes effen I put my mind to it.
  — Robert Deane Pharr, *S.R.O.* 1971

drugstore cowboy *noun*
a young man who loiters in or around a
drugstore for the purpose of meeting
women *US, 1923*
- Girl-watching is a sport of the ages that
  appeals to all ages from young
  drugstore cowboys to graying roues.
  — *Life* 27th October 1961

dry balls *noun*
an ache in the testicles from sexual activity
not resulting in ejaculation *BAHAMAS, 1982*
- — John A. Holm, *Dictionary of
  Bahamian English* 1982

dry fuck *noun*
sex simulated while clothed *US, 1938*
- Well, Dan said, "why don't you say that
  you got a dry fuck and I'll say that I got
  bare tit." — Bob Greene, *Be True to
  Your School* 1987

dry-fuck *verb*
to penetrate a vagina or rectum without
benefit of lubricant *US, 1979*
- — *Maledicta* 1979

dry fucking *noun*
sex simulated while clothed *US, 1967*
- I'll go, but that little bit of dry-fucking
  isn't what's making me go. — Robert
  Deane Pharr, *S.R.O.* 1971

dry-hump *verb*
to simulate sexual intercourse while clothed
US, 1964
- They would swing me around, with my
  bad haircut and plucked eyebrows, and
  dry hump me on the dance floor.
  — Sandra Bernhard, *Confessions of a
  Pretty Lady* 1988

dry lay *noun*
sexual intercourse simulated through
clothing *US, 1951*
- You get a chance, grab the down-draft
  blonde bumping the Marine by the

post there. Dry lay? Man, she'll grind it off. — Thurston Scott, *Cure it with Honey* 1951

dry waltz *noun*
masturbation *US, 1949*
- "I know you don't get detective trainin' doin' a dry waltz with yourself on somebody else's fire escape," she assured him. — Nelson Algren, *The Man with the Golden Arm* 1949

dubbies *noun*
the female breasts *US, 1966*
- Christ, the dubbies on Lumper.
— Richard Farina, *Been Down So Long, Looks Like Up to Me* 1966

duck butter *noun*
smegma or other secretions that collect on and around the genitals *US, 1933*
- Plus, his fucksman's got a bit fist-raised dick that gotta be washed because it stays loaded with duckbutter and stinks like hell. — A.S. Jackson, *Gentleman Pimp* 1973

dugs *noun*
the female breasts *US, 2005*
- And then she went and misbehaved like any mutt from the neighborhood, pulling out her dugs, nipples and all, for a naked-chest make-out session[.] — Mr. Skin, *Mr. Skin's Skincyclopedia* 2005

duke *verb*
to have sex *US, 1993*
- — *People Magazine* 19th July 1993

dummy *noun*
1 the penis *US, 1950*
- — Hyman E. Goldin et al., *Dictionary of American Underworld Lingo* 1950
▶ **beat your dummy**
2 (used of a male) to masturbate *US, 1977*
- I'll bet some of those businessmen are licking the glass and beating their dummies for all they're worth. — *Adam Film World* 1977

dump *noun*
the buttocks *US, 1973*
- [L]ooking down at her while she was on her knees with her well-rounded dump propped up in the air really made a freak outta me[.]
— A.S. Jackson, *Gentleman Pimp* 1973

dump *verb*
to derive sexual pleasure from sadistic acts *US, 1957*

Tricks pay a hundred dollars to dump girls. Sometimes more. — John M. Murtagh and Sara Harris, *Cast the First Stone* 1957

dumper *noun*
a person who takes sexual pleasure from sadistic acts *US, 1957*
- I have always refused to take "dumpers," men who beat you. — Sara Harris, *The Lords of Hell* 1967

dumping *noun*
a beating in the context of sadistic sex *US, 1957*
- I'd never take a dumping myself for less than a hundred. — John M. Murtagh and Sara Harris, *Cast the First Stone* 1957

dungeon *noun*
a nightclub catering to sado-masochistic fetishists *US, 1996*
- The theater of choice for many devotees of sadomasochism, or S/M, is the dungeon, a kind of specialized club catering to those with a taste for domination, bondage or submission.
— James Ridgeway, *Red Light* 1996

dunger; dunga *noun*
the penis *NEW ZEALAND, 1998*
- — David McGill, *David McGill's Complete Kiwi Slang Dictionary* 1998

dungpuncher *noun*
the male playing the active role in anal sex *AUSTRALIA, 1985*
- — Thommo, *The Dictionary of Australian Swearing and Sex Sayings* 1985

dunny *noun*
the vagina *BAHAMAS, 1982*
- — John A. Holm, *Dictionary of Bahamian English* 1982

dusters *noun*
the testicles *US, 1967*
- — Dale Gordon, *The Dominion Sex Dictionary* 1967

Dutch cap *noun*
a diaphragm or pessary *US, 1950*
- — *Maledicta* Winter, 1980: 'A new erotic vocabulary'

Dutch door action *noun*
bisexual activity *US, 1997*
- — Vann Wesson, *Generation X Field Guide and Lexicon* 1997

Ee

early morn *noun*
the erect penis *UK, 1992*
Rhyming slang for HORN.
- — Ray Puxley, *Cockney Rabbit* 1992

easy rider *noun*
a pimp *US, 1914*
- — Robert A. Wilson, *Playboy's Book of Forbidden Words* 1972

eat *verb*
1 to perform oral sex *US, 1916*
- There is the type who likes to eat his woman up after you get through piling her. — Eldridge Cleaver, *Soul on Ice* 1968

▶ **eat dick**
4 to perform oral sex on a man *US, 1988*
- Instead of making him eat dick, the other prisoners kept out of his way right from the beginning. — Gerald Petievich, *Shakedown* 1988
▶ **eat dim sum**
5 to take the passive role in anal intercourse *UK, 2003*
Rhyming slang for 'take it up the bum'.
- Every time we go to bed she wants to eat dim sum. — Bodmin Dark, *Dirty Cockney Rhyming Slang* 2003
▶ **eat face**
6 to kiss in a sustained and passionate manner *US, 1966*
- — Andy Anonymous, *A Basic Guide to Campusology* 1966
▶ **eat from the bushy plate**
7 to engage in oral sex on a woman *UK, 2001*
- WHILE AT THE EARLY STAGES OF A RELASHUNSHIP U IZ PROBABLY UP FOR

VULVA

bearded clam *noun, US, 1965*
- He gobbles one beaver and gets promoted. I've ate close to three hundred bearded clams in my time and never even got a commendation. — Joseph Wambaugh, *The Choirboys* 1975

cooze; coozie *noun, US, 1927*
the vulva; the female genitals
- She also possesses a truly attractive cunt: cooze lips which aren't flappy, crinkly, or rundown[.] — Anthony Petkovich, *The X Factory* 1997

hairburger *noun, US, 1971*
the vulva, especially in the context of oral sex

- — Eugene Landy, *The Underground Dictionary* 1971

hair pie *noun, US, 1938*
the vulva; oral sex performed on a woman
Also spelt 'hare' pie or 'hairy' pie.
- You won't believe it when I tell you I haven't seen the old hair pie in twenty-seven years. — Elmore Leonard, *Bandits* 1987

muff *noun, UK, 1699*
the vulva; a woman as a sex object
- "She's maybe got more moves than you or me got." "That's because she's got a pair of tits and a muff." — Robert Campbell, *Juice* 1988

▶ **eat cock**
2 to perform oral sex on a man *US, 1948*
- meet her 2 weeks later & drive her (Joy is name) to Sacramento to a whorehouse & she's there now – whoring & eating cock – the bitch. — Neal Cassady, *Neal Cassady Collected Letters 1944–1967* 16th June 1948: Letter to Jack Kerouac
▶ **eat cunt**
3 to perform oral sex on a woman *US, 1972*
- They claim they don't like girls, but when I get to eating their cunts, they love it. — Roger Blake, *What you always wanted to know about porno-movies* 1972

EATING FROM DE BUSHY PLATE. — Sacha Baron-Cohen, *Da Gospel According to Ali G* 2001
▶ **eat pussy**
8 to perform oral sex on a woman *US, 1965*
- I actually experienced three climaxes during a one-hour session, all because of this incredibly adept chick who was really, but really good at eating pussy. — *Porno Films and the People who make them* 1973

eat out *verb*
to perform oral sex, usually on a woman *US, 1966*
- It's laying hands on Marsellus Wallace's new wife in a familiar way.

Is it as bad as eatin her out – no, but you're in the same fuckin' ballpark.
— *Pulp Fiction* 1994

eggs *noun*
the testicles *US, 1976*
- I mean, even if I whacked off your eggs, I don't think I'd really get to you. — Jack W. Thomas, *Heavy Number* 1976

eight-pager *noun*
a small pornographic comic book that placed well-known world figures or comic book characters in erotic situations *US, 1961*
- It would be very difficult at Hanson Elementary living down probation for selling "eight-pagers." — Clancy Sigal, *Going Away* 1961

elbow-tit *verb*
to graze or strike an unknown female's breast with your elbow *US, 1974*
- Anyways, he bumps into this fat lady an' starts elbow tittin. — Richard Price, *The Wanderers* 1974

electros *noun*
electrical equipment employed for sexual stimulation *UK, 2003*
- — Caroline Archer, *Tart Cards* 2003

end *noun*
▶ **get your end away**
to have sex *UK, 1975*
- If it moved [in Ponder's End, an area north of London], someone shagged it[...] Talk about getting your Ponder's End away! — Duncan MacLaughlin, *The Filth* 2002
▶ **get your end in**
of a man, to have sex *UK, 1966*
- It was the place in the town for getting one's end in, they said, and it was naturally very crowded. — Leslie Thomas, *The Virgin Soldiers* 1966

engineer *noun*
the first active participant in serial sex with a single passive partner *US, 1975*
From to **PULL A TRAIN** (to engage in serial sex).
- Carolina Moon announced that she was going to take her blanket into the bushes and pull the train. "I'm first! I'm the engineer!" cried Harold Bloomguard. — Joseph Wambaugh, *The Choirboys* 1975

English massage *noun*
sex with a sadistic character *US, 1973*

- "English massages? I don't think I know much about them," I said. — Jennifer Sills, *Massage Parlor* 1973

English muffins *noun*
in homosexual usage, a boy's buttocks *US, 1987*
- — *Maledicta* 1986–1987: 'A continuation of a glossary of ethnic slurs in American English'

English vice *noun*
flagellation *US, 1979*
- — *Maledicta* 1979: 'Kinks and queens: linguistic and cultural aspects of the terminology for gays'

erector *noun*
a semi-erect penis *UK, 1999*
- [S]ome of them sitting [on] the geezers' knees giving them erectors. — Jeremy Cameron, *Brown Bread in Wengen* 1999

Eskimo sisters *noun*
women who have at some point had sex with the same man *US, 1994*
- Their shared experience made them "Eskimo sisters," united by the fact that they had both slept with the same guy. — Anka Radakovich, *The Wild Girls Club* 1994

eve teasing *noun*
an act of a male outraging the modesty of a female in a public place by indecent speech or actual and unwanted physical contact *INDIA, 1979*
- A 40-year-old man was arrested from the North Campus area on Tuesday on charges of eve-teasing. The accused [...] allegedly propositioned a lady constable in plain clothes. — *The Times of India* 1st April 2004

executive services *noun*
sexual intercourse, as distinct from masturbation, when advertised as a service offered by a prostitute *UK, 2003*
- — Caroline Archer, *Tart Cards* 2003

eye *noun*
the anus *US, 1990*
- — Charles Shafer, *Folk Speech in Texas Prisons* 1990

eye-fuck *verb*
to look at with unmasked sexual intentions *US, 1916*
- I like the girl to eye-fuck the viewer. — *East Bay (Oakland, California) Express* 18th February 2004

Ff

F *noun*
oral sex *US, 1987*
An abbreviation of FRENCH used in personal advertising.
- Other turn-ons include GS [golden shower], F and S/M [sadomasochism][.] — Kevin Sampson, *Clubland* 2002

face *noun*
oral sex *US, 1968*
- — Inez Cardozo-Freeman, *The Joint* 1984

face-fucking *noun*
oral sex, from an active perspective *US, 1996*
- [T]he sucking and face fucking and rimming and fagging is done behind the closed doors of the individual booths[.] — Peter Sotos, *Index* 1996

face-off *noun*
an ejaculation of semen onto a lover's face *US, 2003*
- He gave her a face-off. — Jackie Collins, *V Graham Norton* 29th May 2003

facial *noun*
ejaculation onto a person's face *US, 1993*
- Facials are common in porn, as most male viewers like to see cum on a woman's face. Many women don't like facials but put up with them. — Ana Loria, *1 2 3 Be A Porn Star!* 2000

fag-bait *noun*
an effeminate boy or young man *US, 1974*
- He quotes a book reviewer from the New York Times who refused to review the book once it was published as referring to the book of pictures of Arnold as "fag bait." — Michael Blitz, *Why Arnold Matters* 2004

faggot's lunch box *noun*
a jock strap; an athletic supporter *US, 1964*
- — Roger Blake, *The American Dictionary of Sexual Terms* 1964

fake *noun*
an erection *UK, 2002*
- — Paul Baker, *Polari* 2002

fake it *verb*
usually of a woman, to pretend to experience an orgasm during sexual intercourse *US, 1989*
- SALLY: Why? Most women at one time or another have faked it. HARRY: Well, they haven't faked it with me. SALLY: How do you know? — Rob Reiner, *When Harry Met Sally* 1989

falsie basket *noun*
crotch padding worn by males to project the image of a large penis *US, 1957*
- They all wear enormous falsie baskets. — William Burroughs, *Naked Lunch* 1957

family jewels *noun*
the male genitals *US, 1922*
- The first time he saw Carl, Lee thought, "I could use that, if the family jewels weren't in pawn to Uncle Junk [heroin]." — William Burroughs, *Queer* 1985

fancy *verb*
▶ fancy the muff off; fancy the tits off; fancy the pants off
to find a woman extremely desirable *UK, 2000*
- She knew me from school and I'd always fancied the muff off her. — Mark Powell, *Snap* 2001

fan fuck *noun*
a heterosexual pornographic film in which male fans of the female pornography star are selected to have sex with her *US, 2000*
- First, you join the club of the star who is hosting the "fan fuck." Then you can request an application form, fill it out, and mail it back with a photo of yourself. — Ana Loria, *1 2 3 Be A Porn Star!* 2000

fanny *noun*
the vagina *UK, 1879*
John Cleland's novel *The Memoirs of Fanny Hill* (1749) features an inspirational, sexually active heroine; folk-etymology notwithstanding, over a hundred years had passed before fanny was used in this sense.
- Nice kid, that Nadia. Nice, tight, gushy fanny. — Kevin Sampson, *Outlaws* 2001

fanny batter *noun*
vaginal secretions *UK, 2002*
- [A] fanny batter bobsleigh. — Phil Jupitus, *Never Mind The Buzzcocks* 14th January 2002

fanny fart *noun*
an eruption of trapped air from the vagina, usually during sexual intercourse
AUSTRALIA, 1987
- [S]he could also execute fanny farts.
  — Kathy Lette, *Girls' Night Out* 1987

fanny-flaps *noun*
the labia *UK, 2003*
- — Chris Lewis, *The Dictionary of Playground Slang* 2003

fanny lips *noun*
the vaginal lips; the *labium majora* or *minora* *UK, 2002*
- Flap dancin' I call it 'cos if you're lucky they give you the full two sets of fanny lips even though they in't s'posed to[.]
  — Ben Elton, *High Society* 2002

fanny rag *noun*
a sanitary towel *AUSTRALIA, 1985*
- — Thommo, *The Dictionary of Australian Swearing and Sex Sayings* 1985

fast sheet setup *noun*
an apartment or motel that caters to prostitutes and their customers *US, 1969*
- In addition to being a whore, she ran a fast sheet setup for a dozen whores. They tricked out of her joint. — Iceberg Slim (Robert Beck), *Pimp* 1969

fast track *noun*
a street or area where prostitutes solicit customers *US, 1981*
- The hookers who work it know it as the stroll. Pimps call it the fast track.
  — Alix Shulman, *On the Stroll* 1981

feather merchant *noun*
a prostitute *US, 1971*
- Damn if you don't have those feather merchants under control, buddee. I didn't think you had it in you.
  — Robert Deane Pharr, *S.R.O.* 1971

feathers *noun*
body hair, especially fine hair or pubic hair *US, 1966*
- "Is it true all them white women shows theyself mother naked?" the old bum grinned, exposing a couple of dung-colored snaggleteeth. "Mother naked!" he croaked. "They ain't even that. They done shaved off the feathers."
  — Chester Himes, *Come Back Charleston Blue* 1966

feeling fine *noun*
mutual, simultaneous oral sex between two people *UK, 2003*
Rhyming slang for **69**.
- — Bodmin Dark, *Dirty Cockney Rhyming Slang* 2003

feel up *verb*
to fondle someone sexually *US, 1930*
- Have you ever been felt up? Over the bra, under the blouse, shoes off, hoping to God your parents don't walk in? — *The Breakfast Club* 1985

felch *verb*
to suck semen from another's anus and rectum *US, 1972*
- [P]olished eveyrthing off by protruding his tongue into Slave's rectum to felch.
  — Larry Kramer, *Faggots* 1978

felching *noun*
the act of sucking semen from another's rectum *US, 1981*
- [A]cts such as "felching." — Noretta Koertge, *The Nature and Causes of Homosexuality* 1981

femdom *noun*
a *fem*ale sexual *dom*inant, a dominatrix; female domination as a sexual subculture *US, 1989*
- The front cover [of a specialist magazine] hinted at the delights inside showing pictures of three pairs of women's feet and the headlines: Ladies barefeet Nylon stockings and high-heeled shoes Femdom feet.
  — Kitty Churchill, *Thinking of England* 1995

fence painting *noun*
a scene in a pornographic film or a photograph of oral sex performed on a woman in a fashion designed to maximize the camera angle, not the woman's pleasure *US, 1995*
- Fence painting. Often totally unrealistic, but necessary for viewer coverage, so it looks as if the pussy eater is painting a fence. — *Adult Video News* August, 1995

ferret *noun*
the penis *AUSTRALIA, 1971*
- [T]he randy old bastard [a ghost] can't think of anything else but puttin' his phantom ferret through the furry hoop [the vagina]! — Barry Humphries, *Bazza Pulls It Off!* 1971

fiddler noun
a paedophile NEW ZEALAND, 1999
- — Harry Orsman, A Dictionary of Modern New Zealand Slang 1999

fifi bag noun
a home-made contraption used by a masturbating male to simulate the sensation of penetration US, 1969
- Jail birds, cons, and other unfortunate victims of bad laws call this ingenious invention a Fifi Bag. — Screw 27th October 1969

final gallop noun
the hastening pace of lovemaking that climaxes at orgasm UK, 1970
- — Bill Naughton, Alfie Darling 1970

finger verb
to digitally stimulate/explore the vagina as a part of sexual foreplay UK, 1937
- {W]e'd love to knob every single one of them, except the pigs, or at least finger them, or get inside their bras[.] — John King, Human Punk 2000

fingerbang verb
to insert a finger or fingers into a partner's vagina or rectum for their sexual pleasure US, 1990
- I'm gonna finger-fuck her tight little asshole! Finger-bang ... and tea-bag my balls ... in her mouth! — Kevin Smith, Jay and Silent Bob Strike Back 2001

fingerfuck noun
the manual stimulation of another's vagina or anus US, 1971
- — Eugene Landy, The Underground Dictionary 1971

fingerfuck verb
to insert a finger or fingers into a partner's vagina or rectum UK, 1793
Plain-speaking former US President Lyndon Johnson (1963–1969) was said to have said 'Richard Milhouse Nixon has done for the United States of America what pantyhose did for finger-fucking.'
- No humping-like movements, or finger-fucking or clit chatting with their fingertips. — Screw 24th January 1969

fingertips noun
someone adept at masturbating others US, 1990
- — Charles Shafer, Folk Speech in Texas Prisons 1990

fire noun
a sexually transmitted infection NORFOLK ISLAND, 1992
- — Beryl Nobbs Palmer, A Dictionary of Norfolk Words and Usages 1992

fire verb
to ejaculate UK, 1891
- The last time that Hans fired too early in the motel room, the sneering groupie said, "You better start carrying two jizz rags." — Joseph Wambaugh, The Delta Star 1983

fire pie noun
a red-headed woman's pubic hair and vulva US, 2003
- — Chris Lewis, The Dictionary of Playground Slang 2003

first base noun
in teenage categorisation of sexual activity, a level of foreplay, most commonly referring to kissing US, 1928
The exact degree varies by region and even by school.
- Anyhow, you're just saying that 'cause you're jealous and can't get to first base with Lucky. — Hal Ellson, Tomboy 1950

fish noun
1 the vagina UK, 1891
- Other verb forms are: eat fish and chew the fish. — G. Legman, The Language of Homsexuality 1941
2 a woman, usually heterosexual UK, 1891
- But a jealous bartender, who knows, tells three sailors who want to make it with her that shes not a fish, shes a fruit[.] — John Rechy, City of Night 1963

fish fingers noun
said of fingers that have been used to stimulate a woman's vagina AUSTRALIA, 1985
- — Thommo, The Dictionary of Australian Swearing and Sex Sayings 1985

fishmonger noun
a lesbian UK, 2002
- — www.LondonSlang.com June, 2002

fist fuck; fist verb
to insert your lubricated fist into a partner's rectum or vagina, leading to sexual pleasure for both US, 1972
- "Please sir. I've never been fisted." "Just shut your fucking mouth, asshole." — Drummer 1977

fist-fucker *noun*
1 a practitioner of fist fucking *US, 1972*
- Another ugly extreme of S & M is the burgeoning of a "group" calling itself the F.F.A. (Fist Fuckers of America). — John Rechy, *The Sexual Outlaw* 1977
2 a frequent, obsessive masturbator *US, 1962*
- I feel plumb sorry for you poor Wichita fistfuckers, bein deprived of growin up without an ole cow, sheep er sow er somethin. — Earl Thompson, *Tattoo* 1974

fist-fucking; fisting *noun*
1 the practice of inserting the hand and part of the arm into a partner's anus or vagina for the sexual pleasure of all involved *US, 1972*
- Fisting, incest and anal sex. We shelve it under Viking interest. — Melanie McGrath, *Hard, Soft & Wet* 1998
2 masturbation *UK, 1891*
- FIST FUCKING! [Headline] — *Screw* 1st September 1969

fisting *noun*
the practice of inserting the hand and part of the arm into a partner's anus or vagina for the sexual pleasure of all involved *US, 1972*
- KYLE'S MOTHER: What is "fisting"? CARTMAN'S MOTHER: That's when the fist is inserted into the anus or vagina for sexual pleasure. — *South Park* 1999

five-digit disco *noun*
an act of female masturbation *UK, 2004*
- — Michelle Baker and Steven Tropiano, *Queer Facts* 2004

five-fingered Mary *noun*
a man's hand as the means of masturbation *US, 1971*
- Poor bastards, they can't get a woman from one month to the next, and so it's five-fingered Mary and her horny-palmed sister in their hammock each night. — Christopher Peachment, *Caravaggio* 2002

five-fingered widow *noun*
a man's hand as the means of masturbation *UK, 1977*
- [T]he rest of us were spending more time with the five-fingered widow than girls of our own age. — John King, *Human Punk* 2000

flabby labby *noun*
unusually pronounced labia *US, 2003*

- There was recently some hype about Britney Spears' private parts being caught on camera, and considering the lifestyle that Spears chooses to present to the media and the public at large, it can be assumed that she herself possesses such a flabby labby. — *Selbalete.livejournal.com* 25 April 2007

fladge; flage *noun*
flagellation *UK, 1948*
- — *Maledicta* 1979: 'Kinks and queens: linguistic and cultural aspects of the terminology for gays'

flagpole *noun*
the erect penis *US, 1922*
- — Erica Orloff and JoAnn Baker, *Dirty Little Secrets* 2001

flah *verb*
to have sexual intercourse *IRELAND, 2003*
The word appears to be most commonly used in Cork.
- Everybody wondered if he was having an affair with her or, as it was put, "Would you say Bert is flaain' that Protestant Lady?" — Bernard Share, *Slanguage* 2003

flange *noun*
the vagina *AUSTRALIA, 1996*
- [Q] What do you do to keep fit? [A] Shake tits and suck flange. — *Lesbians on the Loose* 1996

flap *noun*
the vaginal lips; the *labia majora* or *minora* *UK, 2002*
Although there is some evidence of 'flap' meaning 'the vagina' in C17, it is long obsolete; this sense is a shortening of the synonymous PISS FLAPS.
- Flap dancin' I call it [lap dancing] 'cos if you're lucky they give you the full two sets of fanny lips even though they in't s'posed to[.] — Ben Elton, *High Society* 2002

flapper *noun*
the penis in a flaccid state *US, 1980*
- — *Maledicta* Winter, 1980: 'A new erotic vocabulary'

flappers *noun*
the female breasts *US, 2005*
- Janet flashed her fine, full flappers again in Aragosta (1982). — Mr. Skin, *Mr. Skin's Skincyclopedia* 2005

flaps *noun*
the female breasts *US, 1972*
- Their secondary sex characteristics are simply too conspicuous to pass without insult, and we were unmerciful towards them: tits, boobs, knockers, jugs, bubbies, bazooms, lungs, flaps and hooters we called them, and there was no way to be polite about it. — *Screw* 3rd January 1972

flash *verb*
to exhibit as naked a part or parts of the body that are usually clothed *UK, 1893*
- Strippers were subject to arrest if they showed their pubic hair or "flashed." — Marilyn Salutin, *The Sexual Scene* June, 1971

flatback *noun*
a prostitute *US, 2002*
- [U]nlike some of his peers, he didn't take just any ho – he liked his flatbacks clean and innocent-looking. — Tracy Funches, *Pimpnosis* 2002

flat-back *verb*
to engage in prostitution *US, 1967*
- [W]hen push comes to shove, it is easier to rob than to flatback. — Gail Sheehy, *Hustling* 1973

flatbacker *noun*
a prostitute of an undiscerning nature *US, 1969*
- I wasn't scoring a big buck from the streets with one flat-backer. — Iceberg Slim (Robert Beck), *Airtight Willie and Me* 1979

flat fuck *noun*
sex without loss of semen *US, 1982*
- — *Maledicta* Summer/Winter, 1982: 'Dyke diction: the language of lesbians'

flesh torpedo *noun*
the erect penis *UK, 2003*
- — Richard Herring, *Talking Cock* 2003

fleshy flute *noun*
the penis *US, 2001*
- — Erica Orloff and JoAnn Baker, *Dirty Little Secrets* 2001

flick *verb*
▶ **flick your bean**
(of a woman) to masturbate *UK, 2001*
- The scenes with her flicking her bean are fucking good, by the way. — Kevin Sampson, *Outlaws* 2001

▶ **flick your switch**
to sexually excite you *UK, 2003*
- What should a chap be doing in bed then, to flick your switch? — *FHM* June, 2003

flip-flop *noun*
a homosexual who will reverse sexual roles *US, 1975*
- Flip-flops, also called "knickknacks," are dudes that begin by making the homos but wind up playing the female role themselves. — James Carr, *Bad* 1975

flog *verb*
1 to have sex *BAHAMAS, 1982*
- — John A. Holm, *Dictionary of Bahamian English* 1982
▶ **flog the bishop**
2 (of a male) to masturbate *US, 1999*
- Spanking the monkey. Flogging the bishop. Choking the chicken. Jerking the gherkin. — *American Beauty* 1999
▶ **flog the infidel**
3 (of a male) to masturbate *US, 2001*
- Another way to say "the boy is masturbating" [...] Flogging the infidel[.] — Erica Orloff and JoAnn Baker, *Dirty Little Secrets* 2001
▶ **flog your dong**
4 (used of a male) to masturbate *US, 1994*
- Meanwhile, every Tom, Dick and Dick outside is trying to flog my dong. — *Airheads* 1994
▶ **flog your dummy**
5 (used of a male) to masturbate *US, 1922*
- [W]hen I left I told him not to flog his damn dummy too much[.] — Jack Kerouac, *The Dharma Bums* 1958

floor work *noun*
in a strip or sex show, movements made on the floor simulating sexual intercourse, offering strategic and gripping views as the dancer moves her legs *US, 1965*
- Meanwhile, back at the strip show, I knew that according to all true Christian standards nudity in itself was certainly not lewd, but burlesque – with its "subtle" charades of grabbing, "floor work," pulling and touching – was lewd. — Lenny Bruce, *How to Talk Dirty and Influence People* 1965

flop on *noun*
the penis that has become flaccid when an erection is to be preferred *UK, 2003*
- [A]bout ten minutes into it I got a flop on. — Richard Herring, *Talking Cock* 2003

flower patch *noun*
a woman's vulva and pubic hair *US, 1986*
- If they get into long skirts, they got a slit up the front almost to the flower patch, and their tits is fallin' out of the tops of their blouses. — Robert Campbell, *In La-La Land We Trust* 1986

flub *verb*
▶ **flub the dub**
to masturbate *US, 1922*
- — *American Speech* October, 1946: 'World War II slang of maladjustment'

The Film Maker's Guide to Pornography 1977

fluffer *noun*
in the making of a pornographic movie, a person employed to bring the on-camera male performers to a state of sexual readiness *US, 1977*
- At the end of these two lines are fluffers who suck off the bum steers, makin' 'em hard for Jasmin (at least that's the theory). — Anthony Petkovich, *The X Factory* 1997

PUBIC HAIR

beard *noun, US, 2005*
a woman's pubic hair
- [S]he strips down to bumpers and beard, then climbs aboard his Oscar Meyer-mobile. — Mr. Skin, *Mr. Skin's Skincyclopedia* 2005

beaver *noun, US, 1927*
a woman's pubic region; a woman as a sex object; sex with a woman
- Hey, you know what the cryptic term "Beaver" refers to in those nudie movie ads? Then you're sharper than a Gillette. — *San Francisco Chronicle* 27th September 1967

Brazilian landing strip; Brazilian *noun, US, 2001*
the trimming of a woman's pubic hair such that only a narrow strip remains; the result thereof
- Maybe one percent of my clients have stuck to the old conservative bikini line wax – the rest have converted to Brazilians. — *Nerve* December 2000 -January, 2001

curlies *noun, US, 1973*
Used both literally and figuratively to suggest complete control over someone.
- You're in no position to make deals. We got you by the curlies. — Joseph Wambaugh, *The Blue Knight* 1973

feathers *noun, US, 1966*
body hair, especially fine hair or pubic hair
- "Is it true all them white women shows theyself mother naked?" the old bum grinned, exposing a couple of dung-colored snaggleteeth. "Mother naked!" he croaked. "They ain't even that. They done shaved off the feathers." — Chester Himes, *Come Back Charleston Blue* 1966

fur pie *noun, US, 1934*
the vulva and pubic hair
- Candy lay back again with a sigh, closed-eyed, hands joined behind her head, and Grindle resumed his fondling of her sweet-dripping little fur-pie. — Terry Southern, *Candy* 1958

pubes *noun, US, 1970*
- A year has passed. I'm older. I'm wiser. Garth got pubes. — *Wayne's World 2* 1993

rug *noun, US, 1964*
pubic hair, especially on a female
- — *Maledicta* Summer/Winter, 1982: 'Dyke diction: the language of lesbians'

fluff *noun*
to a homosexual who practises sado-masochism, a homosexual of simpler tastes *US, 1985*
- — Wayne Dynes, *Homolexis* 1985

fluff *verb*
to perform oral sex on a male pornography performer who is about to be filmed so that he will enter the scene with a full erection *US, 1977*
- Even though the term "fluffing" is used a lot on the set, I have never actually been on a shoot where someone was paid for this service. — Stephen Ziplow,

flute player *noun*
a person who performs oral sex on a man *US, 1916*
- — *Maledicta* 1979: 'Kinks and queens: linguistic and cultural aspects of the terminology for gays'

fluter *noun*
a male homosexual *US, 1962*
- — *Maledicta* Summer, 1977: 'A word for it!'

foofoo *noun*
the vagina *UK, 1998*
- Nonsense slang referred to vague, inoffensive terms that had little or no

meanings in standard English: terms like biff, foo-foo, minky and winkie in FGTs [female genital terms], and chod, dongce, spondoolies, and winks in MGTs [male genital terms]. — *Journal of Sex Research* 2001

four f's *noun*
used as a jocular if cynical approach to male relationships with women – find them, feel them, fuck them, forget them *US, 1942*
- — Roger Blake, *The American Dictionary of Sexual Terms* 1964

fourteenth street *noun*
▶ **go below fourteenth street**
to perform oral sex on a woman *US, 1971*
- Anal intercourse ("Greek") is popular, as is cunnilingus ("going below 14th Street"). — Charles Winick, *The Lively Commerce* 1971

four-way *adjective*
willing to engage in four types of sexual activity, the exact nature of which depends upon the person described and the context *US, 1971*
- A racehorse goes four ways. She gets tricked two ways. She eats the person up and also – actually, she does anything a man wants, that's what she does, she's all the way around. — Bruce Jackson, *In the Life* 1972

freak *noun*
a sexual fetishist *US, 1981*
- She had been working six days a week for a month, turning more than half a dozen tricks a night, and had never once pulled a cop, a gorilla, or a freak. — Alix Shulman, *On the Stroll* 1981
▶ **get your freak out**
to enjoy a sexual perversion *US, 2003*
- The price is seventy five dollars a fuck, gentlemen, you gittin your freak on or what? — *Kill Bill* 2003

freak *verb*
to have sex *US, 1999*
- Later him and her would freak in the back of his tricked-out Chevy, but for now Carmen stormed off, shoving her tit back into her bra as she went[.] — John Ridley, *Everybody Smokes in Hell* 1999

freak jacket *noun*
a reputation for unconventional sexual interests *US, 1967*

- Maybe you can ease from under the freak jacket you've been carrying. — Malcolm Braly, *On the Yard* 1967

freaknasty *noun*
a sexually active woman who shares her activity with multiple partners *US, 2001*
- — Don R. McCreary (Editor), *Dawg Speak* 2001

freak-off *noun*
a sexual deviate *US, 1973*
- Darlene happened to draw a real freak-off one night around two-thirty in the morning. — Jennifer Sills, *Massage Parlor* 1973

freak off *verb*
to have sex, especially with vigour and without restraint *US, 1967*
- Tenderloin Tim and his lady "were like married," according to Queenie, "but sometimes he would let her freak off with another woman." — Christina and Richard Milner, *Black Players* 1972

freak-out *noun*
an uninhibited sexual exhibition *US, 1969*
- Man, these motherfuckers have this restaurant, a Greek restaurant and jack if a chick wants a workout, I mean a freakout, that's where they go. These Greeks work in teams, man. They fuck the chick between the toes, in the nose, and shit like that. — Cecil Brown, *The Life & Loves of Mr. Jiveass Nigger* 1969

freak out *verb*
to engage in deviant sexual behavior *US, 1973*
- It turned out that Dirk was utterly impotent and got his kicks freaking out on the phone with other girls in between performing cunnilingus on me. — Xaviera Hollander, *The Happy Hooker* 1972

freak show *noun*
a fetishistic sexual performance *US, 2001*
- Court documents state that 50 patrons were watching 25 strippers inside a red, one-story building where West Lanvale Street dead-ends into a fenced-in industrial complex. Sources familiar with the investigation said the event was advertised as a "Freak Show." — *Baltimore Sun* 30th May 2001

freak trick *noun*
a prostitute's customer who pays for unusual sex *US, 1971*

● — Eugene Landy, *The Underground Dictionary* 1971

freaky *adjective*
sexually deviant *UK, 1977*
● — David Powis, *The Signs of Crime* 1977

freckle *noun*
the anus *AUSTRALIA, 1967*
Popularised by the Barry McKenzie cartoon strip.
● You can put it up your freckle if you don't flamin' like it, you Ikey bastard! — Barry Humphries, *The Wonderful World of Barry McKenzie* 1968

freckle-puncher *noun*
a male homosexual *AUSTRALIA, 1968*
● Bugger me if the first pom I meet turns out to be a freckle !!!puncher!!!. — Barry Humphries, *Bazza Pulls It Off!* 1971

free *verb*
▶ **free the tadpoles**
of a male, to masturbate *UK, 1999*
● — *Roger's Profanisaurus* October, 1999

freelancer *noun*
a prostitute unattached to either pimp or brothel *US, 1973*
● Freelancers operate out of their own apartments, which are usually, like those of madams, located in good buildings in the better neighborhoods. — Bernhardt J. Hurwood, *The Sensuous New York* 1973

freestyle *noun*
heterosexual intercourse *UK, 2000*
● I need a good charver, a bitta freestyle, a good bunk-up. — J.J. Connolly, *Layer Cake* 2000

free-world punk *noun*
a male prisoner who engaged in homosexual sex before prison *US, 1972*
● We classify them two ways: penitentiary punk and free-world punk. — Bruce Jackson, *Outside the Law* 1972

French *noun*
1 oral sex, especially on a man *US, 1916*
● [I]f he just wants a straight fuck or a straight French, then I say, "Why don't you spend a little extra, and we have a good time?" — John Warren Wells, *Tricks of the Trade* 1970
2 an open-mouthed, French kiss *US, 1978*

● "Yes," I said grimly, "a French kiss, he tried for French." — Terry Southern, *Now Dig This* 1978

French *verb*
1 to perform oral sex *US, 1923*
G. Legman wrote in 1941 that 'The term derives from the popular and not entirely erroneous belief that the practice is very common in France.'
● All I needed to do was to French just one. She then passed on the word to the others. — *Screw* 7th March 1969
2 to French kiss; to kiss with open lips and exploratory tongues *US, 1955*
● I can't believe you let him French you! — *200 Cigarettes* 1999

French culture *noun*
oral sex *US, 1975*
● French Culture (Fr) = oral sex — Stephen Lewis, *The Whole Bedroom Catalog* 1975

French date *noun*
oral sex performed on a man by a prostitute *US, 1972*
● At the hotel, if it's a straight date it's usually $10, and a French date, a blow job, is $20. — Bruce Jackson, *Outside the Law* 1972

French dip *noun*
precoital vaginal secretions *US, 1987*
● — *Maledicta* 1986–1987: 'A continuation of a glossary of ethnic slurs in American English'.

French kiss *verb*
to kiss with the mouth open and the tongue active *US, 1918*
● One of the boys had a lot of experience with girls, and he told me about French or tongue kissing[.] — Phyllis and Eberhard Kronhausen, *Sex Histories of American College Men* 1960

French lay *noun*
oral sex *US, 1972*
● All the sex is extra. How about a French lay? / (But, but, my massage!) Well, here goes my pay. — *Screw* 15th May 1972

French lessons *noun*
oral sex *US, 1970*
● Instead of soliciting passing males, the hookers of London remained out of sight, if not out of mind, advertising their services on discreetly euphemistic

postcards in the windows of local
newsagents. "French Lessons", "Large
Chest for Sale", "Stocks and Bonds",
"Remedial Discipline by Stern
Governess" – the oblique side of
obvious, with a local phone number.
– Mick Farren, *Give the Anarchist a
Cigarette* 2001

French massage *noun*
oral sex *AUSTRALIA, 1985*
- – Thommo, *The Dictionary of
  Australian Swearing and Sex Sayings*
  1985

French trick *noun*
oral sex performed by a prostitute *US, 1972*
- A quick French trick for $10 and if they
  wanted to stand up and perform the
  act, it was $20. – Bruce Jackson, *In the
  Life* 1972

French wank *noun*
an act of sexual gratification in which the
penis is rubbed between a female partner's
breasts *UK, 1997*
- – *Roger's Profanisaurus* December,
  1997

Frenchy; Frenchie *noun*
an act of oral sex *US, 1957*
- Okay, but only a quick Frenchie. Give
  me the hundred. – Edwin Torres, *Q & A*
  1977

fresh meat *noun*
a newly met candidate for sexual conquest
US, 1967
- The man also sees himself performing
  better with "new meat" or "fresh meat"
  than with someone familiar to him
  sexually. – Elliot Liebow, *Tally's Corner*
  1967

fresh stock *noun*
an underage prostitute *US, 1971*
- Younger girls were often called "stock,"
  and those under fifteen were "fresh
  stock." – Charles Winick, *The Lively
  Commerce* 1971

frick and frack *noun*
the testicles *US, 1980*
- – Edith A. Folb, *runnin' down some
  lines* 1980

fridge *noun*
(usually of a woman) a person who is
sexually unresponsive *US, 1996*
- Either she's a dyke or a fridge[.]
  – Kevin Sampson, *Clubland* 2002

frig *verb*
1 to masturbate *UK, 1598*
- The joy-juice flies as these girls suck,
  frig their clits, and ready their assholes
  for cock. – *Adult Video*
  August/September, 1986
2 to digitally stimulate/explore the vagina
as a part of sexual foreplay *UK, 2003*
A nuance of the sense to 'masturbate'.
- – Chris Lewis, *The Dictionary of
  Playground Slang* 2003

frog *noun*
a promiscuous girl *US, 1995*
- – Bill Valentine, *Gang Intelligence
  Manual* 1995: 'Black street gang
  terminology'

frog salad *noun*
in carnival usage, any performance that
features scantily clad women *US, 1981*
- It is an old joke in the United States
  that whenever there is a great "leg
  piece," sometimes called a "frog salad"
  (i.e., a ballet with unusual
  opportunities for studying anatomy),
  the front seats are invariably filled with
  veteran roues. – Sherman Louis Sergel,
  The Language of Show Biz 1973

frog show *noun*
a dance performance that features scantily
clad women *US, 1973*

front bottom *noun*
the vulva and vagina *UK, 2003*
- I've subsequently been told of a man
  in Japan who can facilitate a woman's
  orgasm merely by hovering his hands
  over her front bottom. – *The Sunday
  Times* 26th October 2003

front door *noun*
the vagina *UK, 1890*
As opposed to the BACK DOOR (the rectum).
- Though advised Dale to get laid
  tonight; be his last shot at some front-
  door lovin'. Dale wouldn't talk about it.
  – Elmore Leonard, *Maximum Bob* 1991

front doormat *noun*
a woman's pubic hair *UK, 1980*
- – *Maledicta* Winter, 1980: 'A new
  erotic vocabulary'

front-row Charlie *noun*
a regular audience member at a striptease
show *US, 1972*
- The lines the strippers threw at the
  front-row Charlies: "Take your hot little

hands outta your pockets, boys."
— Georgia Sothern, *My Life in Burlesque* 1972

front saddlebags *noun*
the female breasts *US, 2005*
- Allegra takes off her top, showing her front saddlebags. — Mr. Skin, *Mr. Skin's Skincyclopedia* 2005

frot *verb*
to rub against another person for sexual stimulation, usually surreptitiously *UK, 1973*
- These transvestites, nymphos, junkies are in hell. They frot and turn on – take drugs – to give them the illusion of living[.] — *The Observer* 11th February 1973

fruit basket *noun*
the male genitalia when offered to view from behind *US, 2001*
- Fruit basket for Russell Woodman! — David Duchovny, *Evolution* 2001

fruit hustler *noun*
a homosexual prostitute; a criminal who preys on homosexual victims *US, 1959*
- And malehustlers "fruithustlers"/"studhustlers": the various names for the masculine hustlers looking for lonely fruits to score from[.] — John Rechy, *City of Night* 1963

fruit salad *noun*
▶ do the fruit salad
to expose your genitals in public *US, 1994*
- Flashing, or as they say in California, "doing the fruit salad," is also curious because one almost has to ask why, out of all the sexual deviations, somebody would choose this. — Anka Radakovich, *The Wild Girls Club* 1994

fruit show *noun*
a display in which a prostitute will stimulate and masturbate herself utilising any of a variety of fruits or vegetables, especially when advertised as a service *UK, 2003*
- — Caroline Archer, *Tart Cards* 2003

fuck *noun*
1 the act of sex *UK, 1675*
- I ain't had a fuck in ages & no new girl (except whores) since 1945. — Neal Cassady, *The First Third* 1950
2 a person objectified as a sex-partner *UK, 1874*

- Too much – you hang onto her 'cause she's a good fuck / Too much – cherry cheesecake and shooting up — Viv Albertine (the Slits), *So Tough* 1979

fuck *verb*
1 to have sex *UK, 1500*
- I've heard that until you've fucked on cocaine you just haven't fucked. — Herbert Huncke, *Guilty of Everything* 1990
▶ fuck the arse off
2 to have exceptionally vigorous sex *UK, 2000*
- [H]e will fuck the arse off her tonight, he thinks, he will shag her senseless, screw her daft[.] — Niall Griffiths, *Grits* 2000
▶ fuck your fist
3 to masturbate *US, 1966*
- But therefore I was not Samson, so I fucked my fist once more/ but I taken good aim and shot it – through this keyhole in the door. — Bruce Jackson, *Get Your Ass in the Water and Swim Like Me* 1966

fuckable *adjective*
sexually appealing *UK, 1891*
- 'Don't think that sticking your boobs out and trying to look fuckable will help. Remember you're in a rock band. It's not "fuck me!" its "fuck you!"' — Simon Napier-Bell quoting Chrissie Hynde in *Black Vinyl White Powder* 2001

fuckaholic *noun*
a person obsessed with sex *US, 1981*
- I used to think that you did, and now you're just a regular fuckaholic! — Kevin E. Young, *Ghett OH Luv* 2004

fuckathon *noun*
an extended bout of sex *US, 1968*
- How could he confess to her that he had been on a fuckathon. — John M. Del Vecchio, *The 13th Valley* 1982

fuck book *noun*
a sexually explicit book, usually heavily illustrated *US, 1944*
- A Barney Google fuck book. Barney's cock like a whole bologna, radiating electric squiggles and flecking great airdrops of jiss as he galled at and rammed the thing into the cartoon women with equally electric cunts that looked like toothless mouths. — Earl Thompson, *Tattoo* 1974

fuckboy *noun*
a young man as the object of homosexual desire *US, 1971*
- In prison, the convicts who are sexually assaulted are the sissies, the effeminate, and they are called "punks" or "fuckboys." — Fox Butterfield, *All God's Children* 1996

fuck buddy *noun*
a friend who is also a sex companion *US, 1972*
- While we were looking the whore spots over, we ran into an old fuck buddy of mine. We pulled up on her and after a few minutes of rapping she slid her big tasty ass in the car. — A.S. Jackson, *Gentleman Pimp* 1973

fuck button *noun*
the clitoris *US, 1969*
- There were times when I could make her come just from the feel of my lips tugging on that little fuck-button of hers[.] — Joey V., *Portrait of Joey* 1969

fuck film; fuck flick *noun*
a pornographic film *US, 1970*
- I was waiting tables, cleaning theaters, driving taxis, and I said, "Fuck all this shit, I can make more money doing fuck films." — Stephen Ziplow, *The Film Maker's Guide to Pornography* 1977

fuckhole *noun*
the vagina *UK, 1893*
- Four young wannabe sex stars get their nearly cherry fuckholes stretched, slammed, and jizzed on by big-dicked professional porn studs in the latest installment of this raunchy, hot series. — Penthouse Magazine, *The Penthouse Erotic Video Guide* 2003

fuckie-fuckie *noun*
sex *US, 1977*
Vietnam war usage.
- I didn't want any of that "Say hey, slopehead, fuckie-fuckie?" — Larry Heinemann, *Close Quarters* 1977

fucking *noun*
sexual intercourse *UK, 1568*
- [D]iscover how to see in the forms of fucking, sucking, licking, and masturbating the transcendental formlessness of the Absolute[.] — David Ramsdale, *Red Hot Tantra* 2004

fuck-in-law *noun*
someone who has had sex with someone you have had sex with *US, 1995*
Leading to a punning exploration of the 'sex degrees of separation' between people.
- — Steven Daly and Nalthaniel Wice, *alt.culture* 1995

fuck machine *noun*
a very active sexual partner *US, 1992*
- The pain is reminding the fuck machine what it was like to be a virgin. — *Reservoir Dogs* 1992

fuck-me *adjective*
extremely sexually suggestive *US, 1974*
- I think Ginger pictured Lady Larue in that mental institution in her fuck me stripper shoes and a huge blonde wig[.] — Jennifer Blowdryer, *White Trash Debutante* 1997

fuck movie *noun*
a pornographic film *US, 1967*
- "I got some fuck-movies at home," the man tries to entice him[.] — John Rechy, *Numbers* 1967

fuck pad *noun*
a room, apartment or house maintained for the purpose of sexual liaisons *US, 1975*
- When I walk into his combination office and fuck pad I see this little jive broad from Howard or Tuskegee. — Babs Gonzales, *Movin' On Down De Line* 1975

fuckpole *noun*
the penis *US, 1966*
- The verse, what I could recall, moved him, and he would idly play with what he called his "fuck-pole," but in no provocative way. — Gore Vidal, *Palimpsest* 1995

fuck stick *noun*
the penis *US, 1976*
- "Oh, baby," she moaned, "listen to your white slut's pussy talking to your big black fuck stick!" — Penthouse Magazine, *Letters to Penthouse XVIII* 2003

fuckwad *noun*
the semen ejaculated at orgasm *UK, 2000*
- It happens all the time – you shoot a big fuckwad and bust some small blood vessel or other. — Stuart Browne, *Dangerous Parking* 2000

fucky-sucky *noun*
a combination of oral and vaginal sex *US, 1974*
- You likee me? You likee fuckee-suckee? — Earl Thompson, *Tattoo* 1974

fudgepacker *noun*
a gay man *US, 1985*
- Well, yeah – J. M. Barrie was a fudgepacker from way back, and clearly some of that forbiddenness sneaks into

full personal *noun*
sexual intercourse, as distinct from masturbation, when advertised as a service offered by a prostitute *UK, 2003*
- — Caroline Archer, *Tart Cards* 2003

fumigate *verb*
to take an enema before or after anal sex *US, 1972*
- — Bruce Rodgers, *The Queens' Vernacular* 1972

CLITORIS

boy in the boat *noun, US, 1916*
- [T]hose who felt that the ladies should have big bursts but could have them only in that highly localized surface nodule known in the trade as the vestigal phallus, or button, or boy in the boat. — Bernard Wolfe, *The Magic of Their Singing* 1961

clit *noun, US, 1958*
- Why, I've only to give my clit a tiny flick right now and I'd be sopping. — Terry Southern, *Candy* 1958

dot *noun, US, 1964*
- — Roger Blake, *The American Dictionary of Sexual Terms* 1964

fuck button *noun, US, 1969*
- There were times when I could make her come just from the feel of my lips tugging on that little fuck-button of hers[.] — Joey V., *Portrait of Joey* 1969

joy button *noun, US, 1972*
- Although it's sometimes called "the joy button," the clitoris is actually more than a single spot. — Boston Women's Health Book Collective, *Our Bodies, Ourselves* 1984

every version. — Nicholson Baker, *Vox* 1992

full French *noun*
oral sex performed on a man until he ejaculates *US, 1973*
- Before you walk a trick you must give half and half or full french for the minimum price. — George Paul Csicsery (Editor), *The Sex Industry* 1973

full hand *noun*
said of a person infected with multiple sexually transmitted diseases *US, 1964*
- — Roger Blake, *The American Dictionary of Sexual Terms* 1964

full house *noun*
said of a person infected with both gonorrhea and syphilis *US, 1981*
- — *Maledicta* Summer/Winter, 1981: 'Sex and the single soldier'

full moon *noun*
buttocks of the large variety *US, 1997*
- — Anna Scotti and Paul Young, *Buzzwords* 1997

fun bags *noun*
the female breasts *US, 1965*
- Every time her instructor let himself be thrown, he did a number on her fun bags you wouldn't believe. — Jack W. Thomas, *Heavy Number* 1976

fun button *noun*
the clitoris *US, 1973*
- The little fun button is down at the bottom of your throat. — D.M. Perkins, *Deep Throat* 1973

funk *noun*
semen; smegma *US, 1976*
- They had fried shit choplets and hot funk custard/ Drank spit out of cocktail glasses and used afterbirth for mustard. — Dennis Wepman et al., *The Life* 1976

furburger *noun*
the vagina, especially as an object of oral pleasure-giving; a woman as a sex object *US, 1965*
A term that is especially popular with Internet pornographers.

- I found it not at all disagreeable to mix up a few "tinis sours, or stumplifters" in a milk jug, jump into a "flip-top motivatin' unit," and "flazz off" in search of "furburgers." — John Nichols, *The Sterile Cuckoo* 1965

fur cup *noun*

the vagina *US*, *1966*

- Why the Fur Cup is Not Just an Inside-Out Cock (Headline) — *Screw* 8th December 1969

fur pie *noun*

the vulva and pubic hair *US*, *1934*

- Candy lay back again with a sigh, closed-eyed, hands joined behind her head, and Grindle resumed his fondling of her sweet-dripping little fur-pie. — Terry Southern, *Candy* 1958

furry hoop *noun*

the vagina *AUSTRALIA, 1971*

- [T]he randy old bastard [a ghost] can't think of anything else but puttin' his phantom ferret [the penis] through the furry hoop! — Barry Humphries, *Bazza Pulls It Off!* 1971

furry monkey *noun*

the vagina *UK, 1999*

- Do you wanna have a look at my furry monkey? — Daisy Donovan, *The 11 o'Clock Show* 1999

fuzz *noun*

the pubic hair, usually on a female *US*, *1981*

- JAMIE: Two words, three effs [fuck off]. She's got to be a Velcro [lesbian]? LEE: All bets're off if she likes fuzz on fuzz. — Bernard Dempsey and Kevin McNally, *Lock, Stock ... & Two Hundred Smoking Kalashnikovs* 2000

fuzzburger *noun*

the vagina as an object of oral pleasure-giving *US, 1967*

- — *American Speed* October, 1967: 'Some special terms used in a University of Connecticut men's dormitory'

fuzz one; fuzz two; fuzz three *noun*

used as a rating system by US forces in Vietnam for the films shown on base; the system rated films on the amount of pubic hair shown *US, 1990*

The more, the better.

- — Gregory Clark, *Words of the Vietnam War* 1990

Gg

G *noun*
a G-string *US, 1992*
- For a long time, all you can get is belly dancers willing to strip down to their G's. — Robert Campbell, *Boneyards* 1992

gadget *noun*
a G-string or similar female article of clothing *US, 1980*
- — Joe McKennon, *Circus Lingo* 1980

gam *noun*
an act of oral sex *UK, 1954*
- I heard a prostitute in Malaya, 1954, on being asked her charge, say, "I no fuck. I holiday. But, I give you gam for ten bucks." — Beale, 1984

gamahuche *noun*
an act of oral sex *UK, 1865*
Possibly a combination of Scots dialect words *gam* (gum, mouth) and *roosh* (rush), hence a 'rushing into the mouth'; more likely from French *gamahucher* which shares the same sense.
- [S]he always did it with her men, and said they were made for it; it's what they call gamahuching, the French pleasure. — William Gibson, *The Difference Engine* 1991

gang *verb*
to engage in serial, consecutive sex, homosexual or heterosexual, especially to engage in multiple rape *UK, 1972*
A shortened GANG-BANG.
- We'll [...] gang her[.] — Richard Allen, *Boot Boys* 1972

gangbang *noun*
1 successive, serial copulation between a single person and multiple partners *US, 1945*
- With luck, he'll get off with nothing more than a few fights, broken glasses or a loud and public sex rally involving anything from indecent exposure to a gang-bang in one of the booths. — Hunter S. Thompson, *Hell's Angels* 1967

2 an orgy at which several couples have sex *US, 1965*
- Sometimes these small rooms, cubby holes really, entertain as many as a dozen homosexuals engaging in what is called a gang-bang. — Antony James, *America's Homosexual Underground* 1965

gangbang *verb*
to engage in successive, serial copulation with multiple partners *US, 1949*
- I used to do it myself, but these perverts would want to gang-bang your broad. — Edwin Torres, *Carlito's Way* 1975

gang-fuck *verb*
to engage in serial, consecutive sex, homosexual or hetereosexual *US, 1916*
- These cops will go fifty bucks a head to beat her into submission and then gang-fuck her. — Hunter S. Thompson, *Fear and Loathing in Las Vegas* 1971

gang-shag *noun*
successive, serial copulation between a single person and multiple partners *US, 1927*
- If a good gang-shag has any advantage over any other sort of sexual performance, it seems to me to be its indifference to and rather neutralizing effect upon emotional love. — Angelo d'Arcangelo, *The Homosexual Handbook* 1968

gang-up *noun*
serial sex between multiple active participants and a single passive one *US, 1951*
- This is the gang-up. Men like that put you to sleep with their drops. Then one man after another goes in and takes you. Then these men go all over town next day and boast of what they've done to you. — Ethel Waters, *His Eye is on the Sparrow* 1951

gape *noun*
a completely relaxed, distended anus *US, 1999*
A term used by anal sex fetishists, especially on the Internet.
- In the adult industry, the post-fucking state of openness of an ass which you refer to is called "the gape," as in the popular vid series "Planet of the Gapes." People write to me about seeing the gape in porn videos

all the time, but usually it's in fear.
— Tristan Taormino, *puckerup.com* 1999

garbanzos *noun*
    the female breasts *US, 1982*
    ● H&S sales, based in College Point,
        Queens, N.Y., is the premiere
        manufacturer and distributor of "big
        breast oriented material" – videotapes
        and magazines fixated on woman with
        gigantic knockers, huge garbanzos[.]
        — *Adult Video* August/September, 1986

gash *noun*
    the vagina; sex with a woman; a woman as
    a sex object *US, 1866*
    ● A fucking veritable GASH – a great slit
        between the legs lookin more like
        murder than anything else. — Jack
        Kerouac, *Letter to Allen Ginsberg* 14th
        July 1955

gasp and grunt; grunt *noun*
    the vagina; a woman or women sexually
    objectified *UK, 1961*
    Rhyming slang for CUNT.
    ● — Julian Franklyn, *A Dictionary of
        Rhyming Slang* 1961

Gateshead *noun*
    ▶ **get out at Gateshead**
    during sex, to withdraw the penis from the
    vagina just before ejaculation, to practise
    coitus interruptus UK, 1970
    ● Since the nineteenth century, natives of
        Newcastle-upon-Tyne have described
        the procedure alliteratively as getting
        out at Gateshead. — *Times Literary
        Supplement* 4th December 1970

gay deceivers *noun*
    padding intended to enhance the apparent
    size of a woman's breasts *UK, 1942*
    ● Millions and millions of men were
        being deceived, hoodwinked, and
        betrayed by scientific gadgets known
        as "falsies," "gay deceivers," "pads,"
        and "cheaters." — Earl Wilson, *I Am
        Gazing Into My 8-Ball* 1945

gaymo *noun*
    a homosexual male, especially one who is
    overtly and stereotypically so *UK, 2005*
    A combination of 'gay' and 'homo'.
    ● Tony's such a gaymo. If he was a
        wizard he'd be Gandalf the Gay. — Tim
        Collins, *Mingin' or Blingin'* 2005

gazebbies *noun*
    the female breasts *US, 1965*

    ● Gazebbies!! Ga-za-beys – most always
        plural – but not in dictionary! — Tony
        Zidek, *Choi Oi* 1965

gazongas *noun*
    the female breasts *US, 1978*
    ● — Judi Sanders, *Faced and Faded,
        Hanging to Hurl* 1993

gazoony *noun*
    the passive participant in anal sex *US, 1918*
    ● He's in the big house for all day and
        night, a new fish jammed into a drum
        with a cribman, who acts like a
        gazoonie. — *San Francisco Examiner*
        17th August 1976

GB *noun*
    sex between one person and multiple,
    sequential partners *US, 1972*
    An abbreviation of GANGBANG.
    ● There was some debate between my
        chief advisers and myself, regarding the
        need to devote an entire chapter to the
        G.B. – gangbang, that is. — Larry
        Townsend, *The Leatherman's Handbook*
        1972

gear *noun*
    (of a woman) the obvious physical
    attributes *US, 1953*
    Extended from the purely genital sense.
    ● You'll be [...] having a smoke and a
        laugh with the lads, clocking the gear
        on the little honeys in the queue[.]
        — Kevin Sampson, *Outlaws* 2001

geared *adjective*
    available for homosexual relations *US, 1935*
    ● — *New York Mattachine Newsletter*
        June, 1961: 'Sex deviation in a prison
        community'

gear-lever *noun*
    the penis *UK, 1973*
    ● — B.S Johnson (Editor), *All Bull* 1973

gears *noun*
    the testicles *US, 1952*
    ● About the only part of an old pig we
        don't eat is his pizlum. That's his
        auger. But we did eat the other part of
        his male self – we call them his gears.
        Some will stay away from those things.
        — Earl Conrad, *Rock Bottom* 1952

gee *noun*
    the vagina *IRELAND, 1991*
    The term gives rise to the 'gee bag' condom,
    'missed by a gee hair' (a near miss or

accident) and the expression 'do ya the gee' said by a boy to a girl and meaning 'do you have sex'.

- But he'd had to keep feeling them up and down from her knees up to her gee after she'd said that… — Roddy Doyle, *The Van* 1991

geek *noun*
a prostitute's customer with fetishistic desires *US*, *1993*

- — *Washington Post* 7th November 1993

geeked *adjective*
sexually aroused while under the influence of a central nervous system stimulant *US*, *1989*

- Geeked means to be so hungry for sex that your tongue hangs down to your feet. — Geoffrey Froner, *Digging for Diamonds* 1989

gentleman's fever *noun*
a sexually transmitted infection *BAHAMAS*, *1982*

- — John A. Holm, *Dictionary of Bahamian English* 1982

Georgia; Georgie *verb*
to cheat, to swindle; (of a prostitute) to have sex with a customer without collecting the fee *US*, *1960*

- She ain't got no man. She's a "come" freak. She's "Georgied" three bullshit pimps since she got here a month ago. — Iceberg Slim (Robert Beck), *Pimp* 1969

get *verb*
▶ **get any; get anything; get enough; get a little bit**
to have sex *US*, *1947*

- And another thing. Every time me and my old lady try to get a little bit/ You come 'round here with that roaring shit. — Anonymous ("Arthur"), *Shine and the Titanic;The Signifying Monkey; Stackolee* 1971

▶ **get it on**
to have sex *US*, *1970*

- And if you feel, like I feel baby / Come on, oh come on / Let's get it on. — Marvin Gaye, *Let's Get It On* 1973

▶ **get it up**
to achieve an erection *US*, *1943*

- I'm surprised you could even get it up – look at the way you sweating now. — James Baldwin, *Blues for Mister Charlie* 1964

▶ **get some**
to have sex *US*, *1970*

- So he goes to England and all his pals are getting some but he stays true to his wife, and he goes to Paris and all his pals are getting some, but he stays true to his wife. — Darryl Ponicsan, *The Last Detail* 1970

▶ **get with**
to have sex with *UK*, *1987*

- I tried to get with her for four years, without much success. Then I went on "The Joan Rivers Show." It was my first TV break. Right away she slept with me. — Chris Rock, *Rock This!* 1997

get down *verb*
to have sex *US*, *1973*

- [W]e catch a cab, zoom up to my apartment in the East eighties, get down, catch a cab, and zoom back down. — Susan Hall, *Ladies of the Night* 1973

get-down time; git-down time *noun*
the time of day or night when a prostitute starts working *US*, *1972*

- As the "git-down" time neared, the women complained about having to go to work on public transportation rather than in a car. — Christina and Richard Milner, *Black Players* 1972

get-hard *adjective*
sexually arousing to men *UK*, *2000*

- [T]art called Salome does a get-hard dance for Herod, he grants her a fairy-tale wish, she plumps for the head of John the Bap. — Ken Lukowiak, *Marijuana Time* 2000

get off *verb*
to achieve sexual climax *US*, *1867*

- Annie got off on her own fingers while describing exactly what it felt like to her ex-husband on the telephone[.] — Doug Lang, *Freaks* 1973

ghetto *noun*
the anus *US*, *1973*

- Nearly in tears, he bent over and fairly begged me to penetrate his ghetto. — Richard Frank, *A Study of Sex in Prison* 1973

ghetto bootie *noun*
large buttocks *US*, *2001*

- — Don R. McCreary (Editor), *Dawg Speak* 2001

gib *noun*
a man's buttocks *US, 1986*
- Looked at Whistler's thigh and asked the white mugger if he liked "gibs," which the mugger said he liked all right when there was nothing else available. — Robert Campbell, *In La-La Land We Trust* 1986

GIB *adjective*
skilled in sex *US, 1977*
An initialism for '*good in bed*'.
- — Kevin DiLallo, *The Unofficial Gay Manual* 1988

gig *noun*
the vagina *US, 1967*
- — Dale Gordon, *The Dominion Sex Dictionary* 1967

gilf *noun*
a sexually appealing mature woman *US, 2003*
A variation of ᴍɪʟғ (a sexually appealing mother) and ᴅɪʟғ (a sexually appealing father); an acronym of '*grandma I'd like to fuck*'.
- — Chris Lewis, *The Dictionary of Playground Slang* 2003

gimp *noun*
a sexual submissive who seeks satisfaction in dehumanising fully, including fetish clothing and crippling bondage *US, 2003*
A specialisation made very familiar by Quentin Tarantino, *Pulp Fiction*, 1993 – the film featured a masked-creature (taking his pleasure at the hands of a dominatrix) known only as 'the gimp'.
- "Simon must have had a screw loose," chomped Fry, pulling an ill-fitting gimp mask over his flabby features. "And he will be punished." — *The Guardian* 22nd September 2003

gin *noun*
a black prostitute *US, 1962*
- — Joseph E. Ragen and Charles Finston, *Inside the World's Toughest Prison* 1962: 'Penitentiary and underworld glossary'

gin *verb*
(used of a woman) to have sex *US, 1976*
- Now my deadliest blow came when the whore / Took sick and couldn't gin. — Dennis Wepman et al., *The Life* 1976

ginch *noun*
1 the vagina *US, 2003*
- Thinks that it's a cinch / To get up in my ginch / And if you got the inch / Then I'll treat you like a prince — Peaches *The Inch* 2003

2 a woman; a woman as a sex object *US, 1936*
- Of the thirty or so outlaws at the El Adobe on a weekend night, less than half would take the trouble to walk across the parking lot for a go at whatever ginch is available. — Hunter S. Thompson, *Hell's Angels* 1966

giner *noun*
the vagina *US, 2004*
- — Connie Eble (Editor), *UNC-CH Campus Slang* April, 2004

girlie *noun*
a magazine that is mildly pornographic, featuring naked women but not sexual activity *US, 1970*
- The mass market magazines with the highest degree of sexual orientation (especially nudity) known as "men's sophisticates" (also as "girlie" or "East Coast girlie") devote a substantial portion to photographs of partially nude females[.] — *The Presidential Commission on Obscenity and Pornography* 1970

girls *noun*
a woman's breasts *US, 2001*
From the television situation comedy *Anything but Love* (1989–92), in which the character played by Jamie Lee Curtis proudly nicknamed her breasts 'the girls'.
- — Pamela Munro, *U.C.L.A. Slang* 2001

girl thing *noun*
the various hygiene steps taken by a female pornography performer before a sex scene *US, 1995*
Also called 'girl stuff'.
- "You do your girl thing and then you go out and they start to shoot you." (Quoting Jill Kelly) — Ana Loria, *1 2 3 Be A Porn Star!* 2000

give *verb*
▶ **give it the nifty fifty**
(used of a male) to masturbate *US, 1983*
- One of the chaplains found that out the hard way, when he was caught in his cabin one afternoon with a girlie magazine in one hand and his wife's best friend in the other. In the Marines such a practice is known as "giving it

the nifty fifty." — Robert McGowan and
Jeremy Hands, *Don't Cry For Me
Sergeant-Major* 1983
▶ **give leather**
to thrust forcefully while having sex
TRINIDAD AND TOBAGO, 2003
- — Lise Winer, *Dictionary of the
English/Creole of Trinidad & Tobago*
2003
▶ **give someone one**
to have sex with someone UK, 1974
- [I]he delights of sucking cocaine off his
cock in between giving her one in as
many positions as he could manage.
— Garry Bushell, *The Face* 2001
▶ **give the skins**
to have sex with someone US, 1990
- So you gonna give me the skins or
what? — *Boyz N The Hood* 1990

giz *noun*
the vagina US, 1975
- [H]is mouth was dry as Rose Bird's
giz[.] — Joseph Wambaugh, *The Delta
Star* 1983

glad-on *noun*
an erection UK, 2001
A happy variation of HARD-ON (an erection).
- Sight of that Britannia always, always
gives myself half a glad-on. — Kevin
Sampson, *Outlaws* 2001

glazey doughnut *noun*
the residue of vaginal secretions ringing a
cunnilinguist's mouth UK, 2002
- — www.LondonSlang.com June, 2002

gleam *verb*
▶ **gleam the tube**
(of a female) to masturbate US, 2001
- Another way to say "the girl is
masturbating" [...] Gleaming the tube[.]
— Erica Orloff and JoAnn Baker *Dirty
Little Secrets* 2001

gleesome threesome *noun*
group sex with three participants
AUSTRALIA, 1971
- OZZIE: I don't want to come betwen
youse and bazza or anything like that.
SUKI: You mean a gleesome threesome.
Don't come the raw prawn with me
Ozzie[.] — Barry Humphries, *Bazza Pulls
It Off!* 1971

globes *noun*
the female breasts US, 1889
- "I resent that," said Sheila Gomez,
glancing at the little crucifix that

dangled its gold-skinned heels above
her globes. — Tom Robbins, *Jitterbug
Perfume* 1984

glory hole *noun*
a hole between private video booths in a
pornography arcade or between stalls in a
public toilets, designed for anonymous sex
between men US, 1949
- Some reports have been received that
police themselves have cut the so-
called "glory holes" in booth partitions
which invite the curiosity of the man
who believes himself to be in privacy.
— *Mattachine Review* November, 1961

glue *noun*
semen UK, 1998
- [I] go in a corner and clean up the glue
the best I can. — John King, *Human
Punk* 2000

gluepot *noun*
the vagina UK, 1992
Rhyming slang for TWAT, combined, perhaps,
with allusive imagery.
- — Ray Puxley, *Cockney Rabbit* 1992

gnawing-the-nana *noun*
oral sex on a man AUSTRALIA, 1971
- [S]he's not that struck — as yet — on
gnawing-the-nana!!! — Barry
Humphries, *Bazza Pulls It Off!* 1971

go *verb*
▶ **go all the way**
to have sexual intercourse US, 1924
- If a girl goes all the way, a boy doesn't
have to find out. — Frederick Kohner,
Gidget 1957

goalie *noun*
the clitoris US, 1972
- — Robert A. Wilson, *Playboy's Book of
Forbidden Words* 1972

gobble *verb*
1 to perform oral sex on a man US, 1966
- Hell, I'd rather let some score do a
little gobbling on my joint than spend
all day cleaning some guy's latrine.
— Johnny Shearer, *The Male Hustler*
1966
▶ **gobble the goop**
2 to perform oral sex on a man US, 1918
- [S]he got right down in broad daylight
standin outside the car, me layin back
in the seat and gobbled the goop.
— Earl Thompson, *Tattoo* 1974

gobble alley *noun*
the upper balcony in a cinema favoured by homosexuals *US, 1966*
- In Chicago, they're called "Gobble Alley." In Los Angeles, some studs refer to the balconies as the "Last Chance." — Johnny Shearer, *The Male Hustler* 1966

gobble off *verb*
to perform oral sex on a man *UK, 2003*
- She takes a gulp of [...] Diet Coke – holds it in her mouth, then gobbles you off. — *The FHM Little Book of Bloke* June, 2003

gobbler *noun*
a person who performs oral sex *US, 1969*
- She was a gobbler. And, I guess, a pretty damned expert one, too. — Joey V., *Portrait of Joey* 1969

Rhyming slang for CHOPPER rejoicing in puns of size and sweetness.
- — Ray Puxley, *Cockney Rabbit* 1992

go down on; go down; go down south *verb*
to perform oral sex *US, 1914*
- I remembered – and I felt that strange, numb, helpless, cold fear when you realize you can't change the past – the first time someone had gone down on me in a public restroom. — John Rechy, *City of Night* 1963

go downtown *verb*
to have sex *US, 2003*
Coined for US television comedy *Seinfeld*, 1993–98.
- — Susie Dent *The Language Report* 2003

golden shower *noun*
a shared act of urine fetishism; the act of

BREASTS

balcony *noun, US, 1964*
- Polly's balcony might not be something to inflame the pimple-faced readers of Playboy, but it had exactly what a grown man wanted[.] — Max Shulman, *Anyone Got a Match?* 1964

bee stings *noun, US, 1964*
small female breasts
- — Michael Dalton Johnson, *Talking Trash with Redd Foxx* 1994

British Standard Handful *noun, UK, 1977*
the average female breast
A play on standards established by the British Standards Institute.
- A third nurse complained that Dr. Galea, a married man, squeezed one of her breasts and told her: "You are the three British standard handfuls." — *The Mirror* 25th May 1999

cupcakes *noun, US, 2001*
- "Yeah, well, nice cupcakes!" he said, eyes locked onto the woman's breasts. — Kregg Jorgenson, *Very Crazy G.I.* 2001

fun bags *noun, US, 1965*
- Every time her instructor let himself be thrown, he did a number on her fun bags you wouldn't believe. — Jack W. Thomas, *Heavy Number* 1976

hooters *noun, US, 1972*
- She thrust out her chest when she said it, and he had to admit she had pretty nice hooters. — Joseph Wambaugh, *Finnegan's Week* 1993

lungs *noun, US, 1951*
- We decided that if she had gone to TCU, she would have come from Floydada with big lungs and skinny calves and a lot of chewing gum. — Dan Jenkins, *Semi-Tough* 1972

sweater puppies *noun, US, 1994*
- In the press tent, free copies of The Generation X Field Guide and Lexicon are available for those who don't already know that sweater puppies are breasts[.] — *Playboy* November, 1997

go both ways *adverb*
willing to play both the active and passive role in homosexual sex *US, 1972*
- All the punks go both ways, the queens don't. — Bruce Jackson, *In the Life* 1972

gobstopper *noun*
the penis *UK, 1992*

urination by one person on another for sexual gratification *US, 1943*
- And he would like for me to give 'im golden showers. He liked for me to drink like a sixpack of beer and then after about a good hour then he'd want me to piss all in his mouth[.] — William T. Vollman, *Whores for Gloria* 1991

golden shower queen *noun*
a male homosexual who derives sexual
pleasure from being urinated on *US, 1964*
• Yes, there are those who like to be
peed on (Golden Shower Queens, they
were once known as)[.] — John Francis
Hunter, *The Gay Insider* 1971

gonies *noun*
the testicles *US, 1970*
A diminuitive of 'gonads'.
• "And if I'm permitted to state one more
fact," says Mule, "my goddam gonies
are frozen." — Darryl Ponicsan, *The
Last Detail* 1970

goodbuddy lizard *noun*
a prostitute who works at truck stops *US,
2000*
• Glad's little bits don't have to stand
outside the truck stop like other
goodbuddy lizards usually do.
— J.T. LeRoy, *Sarah* 2000

good choke *noun*
intentional deprivation of oxygen as a sexual fetish *US, 1998*
• You can give "good choke" – erotic
asphyxia – without actually exerting all
that much pressure. — Dan Savage,
Savage Love 1998

goodies *noun*
1 the vagina *US, 1959*
• — Edith A. Folb, *runnin' down some
lines* 1980
2 the female breasts *US, 1969*
• God you wouldn't believe it what some
of them around the house, showing
you the goodies, boy, some of them
just asking for it. — Elmore Leonard,
The Big Bounce 1969

goofer *noun*
a homosexual male prostitute who assumes
the active role in sex *US, 1941*
• — *Male Swinger Number 3* 1981: 'The
complete gay dictionary'

go off *verb*
to ejaculate *UK, 1866*
• One man who wanted to go off using
my rear end, when I told him I would
not allow this, sneered, "You think it's
a perversion, don't you?" — Sara
Harris, *The Lords of Hell* 1967

goolies *noun*
the testicles *UK, 1937*
Originally military, from Hindi *gooli* (a pellet)
in phrases such as 'Beecham Sahib's goolis'

for 'Beechams pills', and so punning on PILLS
(the testicles).
• Thursday, 11 February [1993] Teresa
Gorman [...] knows exactly what should
be done with rapists: "Cut off their
goolies!" — Gyles Brandreth, *Breaking
the Code* 1999

goose *noun*
an act of copulation *UK, 1893*
Rhyming slang for 'goose and duck', FUCK.
• Goes back to when I had my first hole.
First proper goose and all that. — Kevin
Sampson, *Clubland* 2002

gooseberry ranch *noun*
a rural brothel *US, 1930*
• — Dr. R. Frederick West, *God's Gambler*
1964: 'Appendix A'

goose grease *noun*
KY jelly, a lubricant *US, 1985*
• — *Maledicta* 1984–1985: 'Milwaukee
medical maledicta'

gooter *noun*
penis *IRELAND, 1991*
• When Dawn turned to get her glass off
the bar Jimmy Sr. got his hand in under
his gooter and yanked it into an
upright position – and Anne Marie was
looking at him. — Roddy Doyle, *The
Van* 1991

gorilla salad *noun*
thick pubic hair *US, 1981*
• — *Male Swinger Number 3* 1981: 'The
complete gay dictionary'

government-inspected meat *noun*
a soldier as the object of a homosexual's
sexual desire *US, 1981*
• — *Male Swinger Number 3* 1981: 'The
complete gay dictionary'

grand bag *noun*
in homosexual usage, a large scrotum *US,
1981*
• — *Male Swinger Number 3* 1981: 'The
complete gay dictionary'

grand canyon *noun*
in homosexual usage, a loose anus and
rectum *US, 1981*
• — *Male Swinger Number 3* 1981: 'The
complete gay dictionary'

grapefruits *noun*
large female breasts *US, 1964*
• — Roger Blake, *The American Dictionary
of Sexual Terms* 1964

grapes *noun*
1 the testicles *US, 1985*
- Tried to kick him in the grapes, at least. Not sure if I connected. — George V. Higgins, *Penance for Jerry Kennedy* 1985
2 the female breasts *US, 1980*
- — Edith A. Folb, *runnin' down some lines* 1980

grassback *noun*
a promiscuous girl *US, 1969*
- — *Current Slang* Winter, 1969

gravy *noun*
any sexual emission, male or female *UK, 1796*
- Going down for the gravy [oral sex]. — Jack Slater, 1978

gravy strokes *noun*
during sex, the climactic thrusts prior to male ejaculation *NEW ZEALAND, 2003*
- — Chris Lewis, *The Dictionary of Playground Slang* 2003

grease *noun*
any lubricant used in anal sex *US, 1963*
- — Donald Webster Cory and John P. LeRoy, *The Homosexual and His Society* 1963: 'A lexicon of homosexual slang'

grease *verb*
▶ **grease the weasel**
to have sex (from the male perspective) *US, 2003*
- — Chris Lewis, *The Dictionary of Playground Slang* 2003

Greek *noun*
anal sex; a practitioner of anal sex *US, 1967*
- — Dale Gordon, *The Dominion Sex Dictionary* 1967

Greek *adjective*
(of sex) anal *US, 1934*
- They'll give a beating, they'll take a beating, they'll go Greek – and all for the same fifteen, or twenty, or whatever it is. — John Warren Wells, *Tricks of the Trade* 1970

Greek culture; Greek style; Greek way *noun*
anal sex *US, 1967*
- Of course there are requests, especially again from the older men, for the around-the-world trip – the Greek style – and those requests in general. [Quoting Xaviera] — *Screw* 6th March 1972

Greek massage *noun*
anal sex *AUSTRALIA, 1985*
- — Thommo, *The Dictionary of Australian Swearing and Sex Sayings* 1985

grind *noun*
1 sexual intercourse; an act of sexual intercourse *UK, 1870*
- His dick hurt too much for even the most erotic of dreams. A grind was a grind and he could still tell the difference[.] — Donald Gorgon, *Cop Killer* 1994
2 in a striptease or other sexual dance, a rotating movement of the hips, pelvis, and genitals *US, 1931*
- A lot of white vocalists, even some with the big name bands today, are either as stiff as a stuffed owl or else they go through more wringing and twisting than a shake dancer, doing grinds a bumps all over the place[.] — Mezz Mezzrow, *Really the Blues* 1946

grind *verb*
1 to have sex *UK, 1647*
- I can find a grinder any time, that can grind for a while / But tonight I want my love done the Hollywood style. — Roger Abrahams, *Positively Black* 1970
2 in a striptease or other sexual dance, to rotate the hips, pelvis, and genitals in a sensual manner *US, 1928*
- You can pull all the stops out / Till they call the cops out / Grind your behind till you're banned. — Stephen Sondheim, *You Gotta Get a Gimmick* 1960

grind house *noun*
a theatre exhibiting continuous shows or films of a sexual or violent nature *US, 1929*
- The grind houses proclaim their programs in the most explicit terms, glaring posters promote the attractions of topless go-go-dancer joints. — Bernhardt J. Hurwood, *The Sensuous New York* 1973

grind joint *noun*
a brothel *US, 1962*
- It's the snazziest grind joint you ever heard of. And if you happen to catch clap from one of the broads over there, you don't have to worry because it's a higher class of clap. — Charles Perry, *Portrait of a Young Man Drowning* 1962

grine *noun*
sexual intercourse; an act of sexual
intercourse *JAMAICA, 1970*
A variation of GRIND.
- — Glen Adams & The Hippy Boys,
  I Want a Grine 1970

grine *verb*
to have sex *JAMAICA, 1971*
- Look when we used to grine / wooh! /
  You and I — Charlie Ace, *Grine Grine*
  1971

groceries *noun*
the genitals, breasts and/or buttocks,
especially as money-earning features *US,
1965*
- — H. Max, *Gay (S)language* 1988

groom *verb*
to attract children into sexual activity *UK,
1996*
A euphemism that hides a sinister practice.
- [J]ust as monkeys groom each other in
  preparation for mating, "adults intent
  on sexually abusing children first set in
  motion instinctual processes that will
  help them pacify their targets". — *The
  Guardian* 11th February 2003

groove *verb*
to have sex *US, 1960*
- [H]ere was a man who could do a lot of
  good, who had the bread to support
  her bee and give her almost face value
  for the goods she pulled, all for a little
  grooving. — Clarence Cooper Jr,
  The Scene 1960

grope *noun*
an act of sexual fondling, especially when
such fondling is the entire compass of the
sexual contact *US, 1946*
- Her face warn't up to much but she
  were good fer a grope. — Alan
  Titchmarsh, *Trowell and Error*
  2002

growl *verb*
▶ **growl at the badger**
to engage in oral sex on a woman,
especially noisily *UK, 1998*
- — Chris Donald, *Roger's Profanisaurus*
  1998

growl and grunt; growl *noun*
the vulva and vagina *AUSTRALIA, 1941*
Rhyming slang for CUNT.
- — Dale Gordon, *The Dominion Sex
  Dictionary* 1967

grudge-fuck *verb*
to have sex out of spite or anger *US, 1990*
- To avenge the crack about Joe, she
  grudgefucked Dan. — Seth Morgan,
  Homeboy 1990

GS *noun*
a shared act of urine fetishism; the act of
urination by one person on another for sexual gratification *US, 1979*
Used in personal advertising; an
abbreviation of GOLDEN SHOWER.
- Other turn-ons include GS, F [French]
  and S/M [sadomasochism] — Kevin
  Sampson, *Clubland* 2002

G-string *noun*
a small patch of cloth passed between a
woman's legs and supported by a waist
cord, providing a snatch of modesty for a
dancer *US, 1936*
A slight variation on the word 'gee-string'
used in the late C19 to describe the loin
cloth worn by various indigenous peoples.
- G-strings like phosphorescent badges
  etched across the thighs; spread legs
  radiating their unfulfilled invitation[.]
  — John Rechy, *City of Night* 1963

gum it *verb*
to perform oral sex on a woman *US, 1971*
- — Eugene Landy, *The Underground
  Dictionary* 1971

gun *noun*
the penis *UK, 1675*
- This is my rifle/ This is my gun/ One's
  for fightin'/ One's for fun. — *Screw* 11th
  January 1971

gun down *verb*
(used of a male) to masturbate while
looking directly at somebody else *US, 2002*
- They say John got caught on the third
  shift gunnin' down the C.O. — Gary K.
  Farlow, *Prison-ese* 2002

gusset *noun*
the vagina *UK, 1999*
Conventionally, a 'gusset' is a piece of
material that reinforces clothing, particularly
at the crotch and hence in this sense by
association of location.
- With one hand the artist guided his
  shaft into her welcoming gusset.
  — Stewart Home, *Sex Kick [britpulp]*
  1999

gutter slut *noun*
a sexually promiscuous woman *UK, 2003*

- When we bone these gutter-sluts [...] we don't respect them or even think of them as proper people with mums and dads and feelings and shit. — Colin Butts, *Is Harry Still on the Boat?* 2003

gymslip training *noun*
the process of instructing, and conditioning the behaviour of a transvestite who wishes to be treated as an adolescent girl, especially when used in a dominant prostitute's advertising matter *UK*, *2003*
- — Caroline Archer, *Tart Cards* 2003

gyno shot *noun*
a close-up scene in a pornographic movie or a photograph showing a woman's genitals *US*, *1995*
- — *Adult Video News* August, 1995

Hh

hairburger *noun*
the vulva, especially in the context of oral sex *US, 1971*
- — Eugene Landy, *The Underground Dictionary* 1971

haircut *noun*
a sore on a man's penis as the result of a sexually transmitted infection *TRINIDAD AND TOBAGO, 2003*
From the popular belief that the sore was caused by a woman's pubic hair.
- — *Dictionary of the English/Creole of Trinidad & Tobago* 2003

hair pie *noun*
the vulva; oral sex performed on a woman *US, 1938*
Also spelt 'hare' pie or 'hairy' pie.
- You won't believe it when I tell you I haven't seen the old hair pie in twenty-seven years. — Elmore Leonard, *Bandits* 1987

hairy clam *noun*
the vagina *UK, 2000*
- [F]uck off back to Lesbos – to live out the rest of their Dyke Days diving for the hairy clam in the clear blue waters of the Aegean. — Stuart Browne, *Dangerous Parking* 2000

half and half *noun*
oral sex on a man followed by vaginal intercourse *US, 1937*
- When Nicole came into the kitchen she was naked except for her red shirt. – You want a half-and-half? she said. — William T. Vollman, *Whores for Gloria* 1991

half-mast *adjective*
(used of a penis) partially but not completely erect *US, 1972*
- — Robert A. Wilson, *Playboy's Book of Forbidden Words* 1972

halvsies *noun*
mutual oral sex performed simultaneously *US, 1985*
- — *American Speech* Spring, 1985: 'The language of singles bars'

hammer *noun*
the penis *US, 1967*
- — Dale Gordon, *The Dominion Sex Dictionary* 1967

hammer man *noun*
a male of considerable sexual prowess *IRELAND, 1997*
- He's some hammer-man, he must have scooby-dooed half of Abbeytown. — Eamonn Sweeney, *Waiting for the Healer* 1997

Hampton Wick; hampton; wick *noun*
a penis *UK, 1960*
Rhyming slang for PRICK (the penis), after a suburb of London. A polite euphemism in its reduced forms.
- [N]ot much blood comes in and out so your hampton remains small. — Richard Herring, *Talking Cock* 2003

handball *verb*
to insert your lubricated hand into your partner's rectum or vagina, providing sexual pleasure for both *US, 1979*
- — *What Color is Your Handkerchief* 1979

handballing *noun*
the insertion of a hand and fist into a person's rectum or vagina for sexual gratification *US, 1999*
- Anal fisting, also known as handballing, is the gradual process of putting your hand (and for very experienced players, sometimes your forearm) inside someone's ass. — *The Village Voice* 2nd November 1999

hand-doodle *noun*
to masturbate *US, 1968*
- Bab, the most beautiful Jew ever to come out of Fex, took exception to all this hand-doodling. But I maintained that masturbation is an end in itself. — Angelo d'Arcangelo, *The Homosexual Handbook* 1968

hand fuck *verb*
to insert your lubricated fist into a partner's rectum or vagina, leading to sexual pleasure for both *US, 1979*
- — *What Color is Your Handkerchief* 1979

handfuck *verb*
to stimulate another's genitals *US, 2004*
- He went with a tough young man he could grab and handfuck and even kiss

so long as it was some kind of boys' play, not sex but wrestling[.] — China Mieville, *Iron Council* 2004

hand gallop *noun*
an act of male masturbation *US, 1971*
- In Lewisburg he used to tell me he was saving it up, no hand-gallops for him[.] — George V. Higgins, *The Friends of Eddie Doyle* 1971

hand jig; hand gig *noun*
masturbation *US, 1962*
- You know most of the punks, they don't take it in the ass at all. They just give hand-jigs or they'll give blowjobs. — Bruce Jackson, *In the Life* 1972

hand jive *noun*
an act of masturbating a male *UK, 2003*
- I did the hand jive to stop him whining all night. — Chris Lewis, *The Dictionary of Playground Slang* 2003

hand job *noun*
manual stimulation of another's genitals *US, 1937*
- C carved it in with a nail the night she gave him his first hand job in Big Playground. — Richard Price, *The Wanderers* 1974

hand-job *verb*
to masturbate another person *US, 1969*
- In other words, she'd be blowing, fucking, and handjobbing four guys simultaneously, an act that would make her Queen of the Gang-Bang. — Josh Alan Friedman, *Tales of Times Square* 1986

handle *verb*
▶ **handle swollen goods**
(of a male) to masturbate *UK, 2001*
- Saturday night poses, broken noses, wanks (handling swollen goods)[.] — Mark Powell, *Snap* 2001

handmade *noun*
a large penis *US, 1967*
An allusion to the belief that excessive masturbation will produce a larger-than-average penis.
- — Dale Gordon, *The Dominion Sex Dictionary* 1967

hand queen *noun*
a male homosexual who favours masturbating his partner *US, 1964*

- — Roger Blake, *The American Dictionary of Sexual Terms* 1964

hand relief *noun*
masturbation in the context of a hand-massage – a sexual service offered in some massage parlours *UK, 2003*
- VIP massage: massage with hand relief. — Caroline Archer, *Tart Cards* 2003

hand shandy; handy shandy *noun*
an act of male masturbation *UK, 1997*
- Babies be bollocksed. Nowadays it's a quick hand-shandy in a test-tube and you're out the door, mate. — *The Full Monty* 1997

hand thing *noun*
the act of masturbating a man *US, 2001*
- Twenty [dollars] for a hand thing. You go into overtime if you take all day. — Janet Evanovich, *Seven Up* 2001

hand-to-gland combat *noun*
an act of masturbation, especially if conducted with vigour *AUSTRALIA, 1998*
- — Chris Lewis, *The Dictionary of Playground Slang* 2003

hang-down *noun*
the penis *US, 2001*
- Get some stinky on your hang down[.] — Erica Orloff and JoAnn Baker, *Dirty Little Secrets* 2001

hangers *noun*
the female breasts *UK, 1967*
- Chubby took in her jugs again. Nice big hangers. — Richard Price, *Blood Brothers* 1976

hanging bacon *noun*
the outer labia of the vagina *UK, 2002*
- — www.LondonSlang.com June, 2002

hanging Johnny *noun*
the penis in a flaccid state *US, 1980*
- — *Maledicta* Winter, 1980: 'A new erotic vocabulary'

hank *noun*
▶ **take your hank**
to masturbate *US, 1967*
- If taking your hank could destroy someone, I'd of been boiled down to a grease spot years ago. — Malcolm Braly, *On the Yard* 1967

hank book *noun*
a pornographic book or magazine *US, 1974*

- — Paul Glover, *Words from the House of the Dead* 1974

happy valley *noun*
the cleft between the buttock cheeks *US, 1972*
- — Bruce Rodgers, *The Queens' Vernacular* 1972

hard *noun*
an erection *US, 1961*

- — Caroline Archer, *Tart Cards* 2003

hardware shop *noun*
a homosexual male brothel *UK, 1987*
- — *Maledicta* Summer/Winter, 1986–1987: 'Sexual slang: prostitutes, pedophiles, flagellators, transvestites, and necrophiles'

Harry Monk; harry *noun*
semen *UK, 1992*

NIPPLE AND NIPPLES

brown eyes *noun, US, 1932*
the female breasts, especially the nipples
- — Collin Baker et al., *College Undergraduate Slang Study Conducted at Brown University* 1968
bud *noun, US, 1990*
- Your buds is as hard as two frozen huckleberries. — Robert Campbell, *Sweet La-La Land* 1990
high beams *noun, US, 1986*
erect nipples on a woman's breasts seen through a garment
- — Connie Eble (Editor), *UNC-CH Campus Slang* Fall, 1986
knobs *noun, US, 1968*
the female breasts, especially the nipples

- — Collin Baker et al., *College Undergraduate Slang Study Conducted at Brown University* 1968
nip *noun, US, 1965*
The nickname given to the character Elaine Benes (played by Julia Louis-Dreyfus) on *Seinfeld* (NBC, 1990–98) after a snapshot that she took for a Christmas card showed a breast nipple.
- She was a healthy-looking bitch, a jogger type with a great rack ... a couple of real pointers. And I'm not talking about a bra with rubber nipples. I'm talking about a pair of honest-to-Christ pointed nips that must have weighed as much as silver dollars. — Gerald Petievich, *To Die in Beverly Hills* 1983

- He lifts his blanket and he's lying there with a hard. — Herbert Huncke, *Guilty of Everything* 1990

hard leg *noun*
an experienced, cynical prostitute *US, 1967*
- — Kenn 'Naz' Young, *Naz's Underground Dictionary* 1973

hard-on *noun*
the erect penis; an erection *US, 1888*
- And she's getting more relaxed and more flirty, I'm getting a hard-on. And I know where I'm going with this hard-on. — Kevin Sampson, *Outlaws* 2001

hard one *noun*
in necrophile usage, a corpse that has stiffened with rigor mortis *US, 1987*
- — *Maledicta* Summer/Winter, 1986–1987: 'Sexual slang: prostitutes, pedophiles, flagellators, transvestites, and necrophiles'

hard sports *noun*
sadomasochistic sex-play involving defecation *UK, 2003*

Rhyming slang for SPUNK; generally reduced.
- ["]Was she as dirty as she looked?" "Can't really remember. Plenty of Harry on the boat [the face], though." — Colin Butts, *Is Harry on the Boat?* 1997

hatch *noun*
the vagina *US, 1967*
- — Dale Gordon, *The Dominion Sex Dictionary* 1967

haul *verb*
▶ **haul coal**
(used of a white person) to have sex with a black person *US, 1972*
- Some of the relationships in here are interracial, about 25 percent. The whites say, "Okay, if you wanna haul coal." — Bruce Jackson, *In the Life* 1972

have *verb*
1 to have sex with someone *UK, 1594*
- Don't you know that he's married, and that he's had more women than you can count? — Juan Rulfo (translated by Josephine Sacabo), *Pedro Paramo* 1994

▶ **have it off**
2 to have sex *UK, 1937*
- They walk in, have it off with me, say "Ta" and then stroll out again, nice and simple with no complications. Like buying a packet of fags. — *Flame* 1972

Hawaiian disease *noun*
sexual abstinence due to an absence of women *US, 1987*
An allusion to the mythical illness 'lakanuki' (lack of sex).
- "Granddaddy says she is suffering from some terrible old maid's Hawaiian disease." "Oh really? What?" "Something called lackanookie," she said perfectly straight and with no recognizable humor. — Shirley MacLaine, *It's All in the Playing* 1987

Hawaiian muscle fuck; muscle fuck *noun*
to rub and slide the penis in the compressed cleavage between a woman's breasts *US, 1974*
A term used widely in internet "purity tests."
- "Been involved in breast fucking? (aka 'The Hawaiian Muscle Fuck')." — *alt.sex* 17th July 1989

he; him *noun*
the penis *UK, 1970*
- Abby puts her hand under the table, then gives him a squeeze. — Bill Naughton, *Alfie Darling* 1970

head *noun*
1 oral sex *US, 1941*
- Connie probably takes Raymond's little peanut of a cock between her brittle chapped lips and then scrapes her ugly decayed teeth up and down on it while asshole Raymond thinks he's getting the best head on the East Coast. — John Waters, *Pink Flamingos* 1972
▶ **give head**
2 to perform oral sex *US, 1956*
- "Split," Ophelia concluded, "that's the whole trick to giving head. Just split." — Eve Babitz, *L.A. Woman* 1982

head cheese *noun*
smegma in a male *US, 1941*
- I gasped so hard up my nose the head cheese locked into place and he let me breathe, still holding my hair. — Jack Fritscher, *Stand By Your Man* 1999

head cunt *noun*
the mouth (as an object of sexual penetration) *US, 1996*
- [H]is gums are bleeding or he has herpes or a cold sore inside that head cunt. — Peter Sotos, *Index* 1996

header *noun*
oral sex *US, 1976*
- — Mary Corey and Victoria Westermark, *Fer Shurr! How to be a Valley Girl* 1982

headhunter *noun*
1 an oral sex enthusiast *US, 1961*
- Hidden safely behind anthropological images of Amazonian tribes hunting enemy skulls for religious and decorative purposes, as the initiated of the jazz world knew, were the real headhunters, hip guys constantly seeking to receive or administer blow jobs. — Larry Rivers, *What Did I Do?* 1992
2 a homosexual male *US, 1990*
- — Charles Shafer, *Folk Speech in Texas Prisons* 1990

head job *noun*
an act of oral sex *US, 1963*
- The kind who wore a wig and took a man to a back booth and gave him a head job for $10 and a bottle of champagne[.] — Dan Jenkins, *Dead Solid Perfect* 1986

head jockey *noun*
a practitioner of oral sex on a woman *US, 1971*
- — Eugene Landy, *The Underground Dictionary* 1971

heavy *noun*
sexually aroused, especially if aggressively so *UK, 1980*
A sense used by prostitutes.
- He was getting heavy, and I'm trying to get myself together to split from this car. — *Time Out* 30th May 1980

heavy *adjective*
rough, sadistic *US, 1986*
- Because heavy sex is fire, and some people are made of stone and some of paper. — Ethan Morden, *Buddies* 1986

heavy petting *noun*
mutual sexual caressing that stops shy of full intercourse *UK, 1960*
- I should stop. Spare you the counting of the number of fingers a boy

managed to fit up inside his girl, a lad's heavy petting before coming back to "make us all sniff his fingers to show he'd been there". — *The Guardian* 29th March 2003

heavy scene *noun*
  sado-masochistic sex *US, 1979*
  • During one of his periodic excursions to other cities in search of new "heavy scenes" – and his reputation as a top-man precedes his forays – Chas was asked to play an auctioneer at a simulated "slave auction[.]" — John Rechy, *Rushes* 1979

he-girl *noun*
  a person with mixed sexual physiology, usually the genitals of a male and surgically augmented breasts *US, 2004*
  • — www.adultquarter.com/blossary.html January, 2004: 'Glossary of adult Internet terms'

helmet *noun*
  the head of the circumcised penis *US, 1970* From the similarity in shape to a World War II German Army helmet.
  • You get bored you might amuse yourselves by betting quarters whether the next guy in will be a helmet or an anteater. — Joseph Wambaugh, *The New Centurions* 1970

Hershey Bar route *noun*
  the rectum and anus *US, 1973*
  • I ordered him into the shower because of the idea of sleeping with him after he'd gone the Hershey Bar route hardly turned me on. — Xaviera Hollander, *Xaviera* 1973

Hershey Highway *noun*
  the rectum *US, 1973*
  • Then she taught me how to drive the Hershey highway and she masturbated her own clitoris until we both collapsed together in a wave of orgasms. — Harold Robbins, *The Predators* 1998

Hershey road *noun*
  the rectum *US, 1974*
  • There's been so much stick pussy shoved up that Hershey road they could rent it out for a convention center. — Seth Morgan, *Homeboy* 1990

hickey *noun*
  a bruise on the skin caused by a partner's mouth during foreplay; a suction kiss *US, 1942*

  • Hickeys. They were fun to give but a curse to receive [...] And if my parents asked what the hell that was, the answer was always that the faithful curling iron burned me (again). — *Editors of Ben is Dead, Retrohell* 1997

hide-the-baloney *noun*
  sexual intercourse *US, 1973*
  • Man, wouldn't I love to play hide the baloney with that. — Charles Whited, *Chiodo* 1973

hide the salami *noun*
  sexual intercourse *US, 1983* 'Sausage' as 'penis' imagery; a variation of the earlier HIDE-THE-WEENIE.
  • We whipped the doors open and came face-to-face with Ronald DeChooch playing hide-the-salami with the clerical help. — Janet Evanovich, *Seven Up* 2001

hide-the-sausage *noun*
  sexual intercourse *AUSTRALIA, 1971*
  • [A] swift game of hide the sausage in the back stalls [of a cinema]. — Barry Humphries, *Bazza Pulls It Off!* 1971

hide-the-weenie *noun*
  sexual intercourse *US, 1968*
  • He must have flipped because he has a heart-to-heart with his mother about how he's been playing hide-the-weenie with his tutor. — Angelo d'Arcangelo, *The Homosexual Handbook* 1968

high beams *noun*
  erect nipples on a woman's breasts seen through a garment *US, 1986*
  • — Connie Eble (Editor), *UNC-CH Campus Slang* Fall, 1986

high five *noun*
  HIV *US, 2003* A semantic joke based on Roman numerals.
  • — *Oprah Winfrey Show* 2nd October 2003

hit *verb*
  to have sex *US, 2004*
  • — Rick Ayers (Editor), *Berkeley High Slang Dictionary* 2004

hit in the seat *noun*
  an act of anal intercourse *US, 1976*
  • — John R. Armore and Joseph D. Wolfe, *Dictionary of Desperation* 1976

hit on *verb*
to flirt; to proposition *US, 1954*
- [H]e took her to dinner, never mentioned it again, took her home, didn't hit on her in any way. — Terry Southern, *Now Dig This* 1981

ho; hoe *noun*
a sexually available woman; a woman who may be considered sexually available; a prostitute *US, 1959*
Originally black usage, from the southern US pronunciation of 'whore'; now widespread through the influence of rap music.
- "These hos out here think they hos; they ain't hos." She said, "You don't learn how to be a ho, you be born a ho. And I was born a ho." — Christina and Richard Milner, *Black Players* 1972

ho; hoe *verb*
to work as a prostitute *US, 1972*
- But then some again treat them nice, but my cousin even treats his wife like a dog and she's Black, but she got out there and hoed for him. — Christina and Richard Milner, *Black Players* 1972

hog *noun*
1 the penis *US, 1968*
- [S]he snuggled right up to them guys and said to them: "Come on, fellas, take me out in the woods and stick your big black hogs in my mouth and fuck me about twelve times[."] — George V. Higgins, *The Judgment of Deke Hunter* 1976
▶ **beat the hog**
2 (used of a male) to masturbate *US, 1971*
- No, I think they go home and beat the hog over them, is what I think. — George V. Higgins, *The Friends of Eddie Doyle* 1971

hold *verb*
▶ **get hold of**
to have sex with someone *UK, 2003*
- — Susie Dent, *The Language Report* 2003

hole *noun*
1 the vagina; sex with a woman; a woman; women *UK, 1592*
- "Snatch," "hole," "kooze," "slash," "pussy" and "crack" were other terms referring variously to women's genitals, to women as individuals, or to women as a species. — *Screw* 3rd January 1972
2 the anus *UK, 1607*

- [S]tick this f'ing pitchfork up your hole[.] — Graham Linehan and Arthur Matthews, *And God Created Women (Father Ted, Series 1, Episode 5)* 1995

hole-in-one *noun*
sexual intercourse on a first date *US, 1972*
- — Robert A. Wilson, *Playboy's Book of Forbidden Words* 1972

holy of holies *noun*
the vagina *US, 1984*
A crude pun on **HOLE**.
- Look, maybe your method of massage differs from mine, but touchin' his lady's feet, and stickin' your tongue in her holyiest of holyies, ain't the same ballpark, ain't the same league, ain't even the same fuckin' sport. — *Pulp Fiction* 1994

home base; home run *noun*
in the teenage categorisation of sexual activity, sexual intercourse *US, 1963*
- "Did you at least get to home base?" "Who knows. I couldn't tell with that lousy condom." — C.D. Payne, *Youth in Revolt* 1993

homework *noun*
▶ **bit of homework; piece of homework**
a person objectified sexually *UK, 1945*
- — John Ayto, *Oxford Dictionary of Slang* 1998

homo heaven *noun*
a public area where homosexuals congregate in hopes of quick sex *US, 1965*
- Central Park has certain sections known as homo heavens. — Antony James, *America's Homosexual Underground* 1965

honey box *noun*
1 the vagina *US, 1969*
- Ain't none of 'em my bitch unless I got my cock in her honey box. — Cecil Brown, *The Life & Loves of Mr. Jiveass Nigger* 1969
2 the anus *US, 2005*
- He measures them all up and down, including parts you didn't expect, like their nipple size or even their honey box. — Ethan Morden, *How's Your Romance?* 2005

honey dip *noun*
an attractive woman, especially one with a light brown skin colour *US, 1993*
- — *Washington Post* 14th October 1993

honey dipping *noun*
vaginal secretions *US, 1949*
- — Captain Vincent J. Monteleone,
  Criminal Slang 1949

honey-fuck *verb*
to have sex in a slow, affectionate manner
US, 1964
- — Roger Blake, *The American Dictionary
  of Sexual Terms* 1964

honeymoon *noun*
sex *US, 1976*
Used by prostitutes in Southeast Asia during
the Vietnam war.
- Dropped a hundred-thirty last night, on
  the same broad, and all he got outa
  the deal was a steam bath. She
  wouldn't go honeymoon with him.
  — Charles Anderson, *The Grunts* 1976

honeypot *noun*
1 the vagina *US, 1958*
Recorded as rhyming slang for TWAT (the
vagina) It certainly rhymes, but must surely
be influenced — if not inspired — by
senses that are conventional, figurative
and slang. Found once in the UK in 1719,
and then in general slang usage with
'Candy'.
- "Now I am inserting the member," he
  explained, as he parted the tender
  quavering lips of the pink honeypot
  and allowed his stout member to be
  drawn slowly into the seething thermal
  pudding of the darling girl. — Terry
  Southern, *Candy* 1958
2 in male homosexual usage, the anus and
rectum *US, 1981*
- — *Male Swinger Number 3* 1981: 'The
  complete gay dictionary'

honker *noun*
the penis *US, 1968*
- That honker of yours was as ready for
  me as mine was ready for your slick
  butt. — James Harper, *Homo Laws in all
  50 States* 1968

hoochy koochy *noun*
a sexually suggestive dance *US, 1895*
- Sol Bloom, as an entrepreneur at the
  Chicago World's Fair, celebrating the
  400th anniversary of the discovery of
  America, presented "Little Egypt" in a
  series of contortions while she stayed
  on her feet, known as the "hoochy
  koochy." — Jack Lait and Lee Mortimer,
  Chicago Confidential 1950

hoodrat *noun*
a promiscuous girl *US, 1997*
- Talk about how you wanna get back
  with that tramp and how you forgive
  that hoodrat broad/dickhead. — *Hip-
  Hop Connection* July, 2002

hook *noun*
a prostitute *US, 1918*
A shortened 'hooker'.
- The rich are the worst tippers, hooks
  are lousy. — *Taxi Driver* 1976

hook *verb*
to engage in prostitution *US, 1959*
- She was hooking when I met her. So
  I didn't go for that at all. 'Cause
  I never made it with a hooker before.
  — James Mills, *The Panic in Needle
  Park* 1966

hook up *verb*
to meet someone; to meet someone and
have sex *US, 1986*
- You know, like, if we hook up tonight,
  tomorrow I'll just be some girl you go
  telling all your friends about.
  — *American Pie* 1999

hoonah light *noun*
in the pornography industry, a light used to
illuminate the genitals of the performers
US, 1995
- — *Adult Video News* October, 1995

hootchie; hoochie; hootchy mama *noun*
a young woman, especially when easily
available for sex *US, 1990*
- I wanted to get over with one of the
  hootchies over there. — *Boyz N The
  Hood* 1990

hootchie-coo *noun*
sex *US, 1990*
- Y'all gonna do the hootchie-coo?
  — *Boyz N The Hood* 1990

hootchy-kootchy; hootchie-coochie *noun*
a sexually attractive person *US, 1969*
- He was such a hoochie-coochie she
  didn't know what to do. — Steve
  Cannon, *Groove, Bang, and Jive Around*
  1969

hooters *noun*
female breasts *US, 1972*
- She thrust out her chest when she said
  it, and he had to admit she had pretty
  nice hooters. — Joseph Wambaugh,
  Finnegan's Week 1993

hoots *noun*
the female breasts *US, 2002*
- She showed off her luscious hoots again in a topless turn[.] — Mr. Skin, *Mr. Skin's Skincyclopedia* 2005

hoover *verb*
to perform oral sex on a man *UK, 1992*
From the supposed similarity to a 'hoover' (a vacuum cleaner)'s suction.
- Fancy a quick hoover d'amour? — the cast of 'Aspects of Love', Prince of Wales Theatre, *Palare (Boy Dancer Talk) for Beginners* 1989–92

hoover d'amour *noun*
an act of oral sex on a man *UK, 1992*
- Fancy a quick hoover d'amour? — the cast of 'Aspects of Love', Prince of Wales Theatre, *Palare (Boy Dancer Talk) for Beginners* 1989–92

hop *verb*
▶ **hop into the horsecollar**
(from a male perspective) to have sex *AUSTRALIA, 1971*
From HORSECOLLAR (the vagina).
- To "hop into the horsecollar" is to engage in a form of romantic dalliance[.] — Barry Humphries, *Bazza Pulls It Off!* 1971

horizontal bop *noun*
sexual intercourse *US, 2001*
- Whether he [George Washington] and Sally [Fairfax] ever did the horizontal bob has remained a point of speculation for historians[.] — Erica Orloff and JoAnn Baker, *Dirty Little Secrets* 2001

horizontal exercise *noun*
sexual intercourse *US, 1918*
- "I'm not quite so young as I used to be," Leino said at some point that morning when, after several days of horizontal exercises, he failed to rise to the occasion. — Harry Turtledove, *Rulers of the Darkness* 2002

horizontal gymnastics *noun*
sexual intercourse *UK, 2001*
- [A] ruse to get me on my own so she could tell me yet more about her horizontal gymnastics with Sleaze Paul! — *The Guardian* 28th November 2001: 'Teenage Kicks'

horizontal manoeuvres *noun*
sexual intercourse *UK, 1995*

Military origins.
- Then there were all the inter-battalion horizonal manoeuvres. As soon as a battalion was away over the water, all the singlies were straight over to check out the wives. — Andy McNab, *Immediate Action* 1995

horizontal refreshment *noun*
sexual intercourse *UK, 1889*
- [H]e would go to China Town, to further indulge his hankering for horizontal refreshment and whiskey. — H. M. Jacks, *Not All Wanderers Are Lost* 2003

horizontal rumble *noun*
sexual intercourse *US, 2000*
- Nice ass on her. And big blonde hair to her shoulders. Kind of woman he used to chase down for a horizontal rumble. — Christopher Cook, *Robbers* 2000

hormone queen *noun*
a man taking female hormones, usually in the course of a transgender transformation *US, 1972*
- Sometimes a hormone queen will decide she is TS and then have the operation. — *alt.personals.transgendered* 24th July 1998

horn *noun*
the penis; the erect penis; lust *UK, 1594*
- [S]he gives him the horn in a big way. — Kevin Williamson, *Heart of the Bass (Disco Biscuits)* 1996

horndog *noun*
a person who is obsessed with sex *US, 1984*
- "I'm a horn-dog," I say. "I'm into some pretty kinky stuff to be honest." — Marty Beckerman, *Death to All Cheerleaders* 2000

horndog *adjective*
sexually aggressive *US, 1984*
- [A]nd this no matter what kind of scumbag, slutbucket, horndog chick we end up boffing. — Bret Ellis, *American Psycho* 1991

horny *adjective*
desiring sex *US, 1826*
- I know this because when I was pregnant I was able to ball anyone and I was never more horny. — Jefferson Poland and Valerie Alison, *The Records of the San Francisco Sexual Freedom League* 1971

horribles *noun*
the genitals *UK, 2006*
- Someone had taken a right liberty and some grotty mitt was grovelling around in my horribles. — *Uncut* April, 2006

horror *noun*
an extremely unattractive woman who is seen as a sex object, especially one who is ravaged by age *UK, 2002*
- Go for a horror, any fucking day of the week. — Kevin Sampson, *Clubland* 2002

horse *noun*
a prostitute *US, 1957*
An evolution of the STABLE as a group of prostitutes.
- But not for that new horse. I wouldn't give her one of my tricks if she stood on her head. — John M. Murtagh and Sara Harris, *Cast the First Stone* 1957

horsecollar *noun*
the vagina, especially large or distended external female genitals *US, 1994*
- — Michael Dalton Johnson, *Talking Trash with Redd Foxx* 1994

horsefuck *verb*
to have sex from behind and with great vim *US, 1973*
- I'd like to break her open like a shotgun and horsefuck her. — Joseph Wambaugh, *The Blue Knight* 1973

hose *noun*
the penis *US, 1928*
- Jasmin sucks hose as if she's being intubated with anaesthesia (and on the verge of nodding off). — Anthony Petkovich, *The X Factory* 1997

hose *verb*
to copulate, vaginally or anally *US, 1935*
- GARY: So you're a big mover with Diane, are you? BENTLEY: Practically home and hosed. — Alexander Buzo, *Rooted* 1969

hosebag *noun*
a prostitute or promiscuous woman *US, 1978*
- Every time he looked at his wrist he thought about that junkie hose-bag and wondered if he should get a blood test. — Joseph Wambaugh, *Finnegan's Week* 1993

hose job *noun*
oral sex on a man *US, 1978*
- Looks like the hooker was doing a hose job on one of the truckers up at the market. — Carsten Stroud, *Close Pursuit* 1987

hose monster *noun*
a sexually aggressive woman *US, 1984*
- But who wants to admit being a hose monster? — Rajen Persaud, *Why Black Men Love White Women* 2004

hose queen *noun*
a sexually active woman *US, 1984*
- You suddenly realize that he has already slipped out with some rich hose queen. — Kenneth Jackson, *Empire City* 2002

hot *adjective*
sexual, sensuous *US, 1931*
- Don't try to get too hot with a girl in public, or you'll wind up with the cold shoulder. — Jack Lait and Lee Mortimer, *New York Confidential* 1948

hot-arsed *adjective*
feeling an urgent sexual desire, lustful *UK, 1683*
- No hot-arsed Latin lovely tucked away at all? Don't answer that. — John Le Carré, *The Tailor of Panama* 1996

hot bed *noun*
a motel room rented without following proper registration procedures and rented more than once a day; a room in a cheap boarding house *US, 1940*
- Or you can wait till I talk to Dawn Coyote about how you rented her a hot bed tonight. Again. — Joseph Wambaugh, *Floaters* 1996

hot book *noun*
a pornographic book or magazine *US, 1942*
- Hal Griffin has six hot books hidden in the back of his closet which he masturbates over at every opportunity[.] — Stephen King, *Salem's Lot* 1975

hot box *noun*
a sexually excited vagina; a sexually excited female *US, 1964*
- — Roger Blake, *The American Dictionary of Sexual Terms* 1964

hot dog *noun*
a pornographic book or magazine *US, 1974*
- — Paul Glover, *Words from the House of the Dead* 1974

hot-dog *adjective*
obsessed with sex *US, 1975*
- I'd known a lot of hot-dog guys before I got to Bullion, but never had I seen the likes of Maynard Farrell. — James Carr, *Bad* 1975

hotdog book *noun*
a book used for stimulating sexual interest while masturbating *US, 1967*
- Most of these boooks were L and L's, derived from Lewd and Lascivious Conduct, hotdog books heavy with sex, and they were always in demand. — Malcolm Braly, *On the Yard* 1967

hot fish yoghurt *noun*
semen *UK, 2001*
- [L]ean over him to change gear and get all that hot fish yoghurt in her hair. — Garry Bushell, *The Face* 2001

hot karl; hot carl *noun*
an act of defecating on a sexual partner; an act of defecating on a person who is asleep; an act of hitting someone with a sock full of human excrement *US, 2004*
In Chicago, the comedy troupe Hot Karl have been in existence since 1999; a humorous reference to scatalogical practice is inferred but not confirmed. The earliest unequivocal usage is on the Internet in 2002. In 2004 a white rapper called Hot Karl is noted; also tee-shirts with the image of a pile of steaming faeces and the slogan 'hot carl'.
- — *www.popbitch.com* 18th December 2004

hot nuts *noun*
intense male sexual desire *US, 1935*
- — Robert A. Wilson, *Playboy's Book of Forbidden Words* 1972

hot pants *noun*
sexual desire *US, 1929*
- I've still got hot pants for her, if you want to call that love. — Mary McCarthy, *The Group* 1963

hot-pillow *adjective*
said of a hotel or motel that rents rooms for sexual liaisons for cash, without registering the guests using the room *US, 1954*
- Until after World War II, the tourist court was considered the poor cousin of the hotel – a place which catered to the "hot pillow trade," to use J. Edgar Hoover's eloquent phrase. — *Washington Post* 12th January 1979

hots *noun*
sexual desire, intense interest *US, 1947*
- He's a total asshole and he's got the hots for my friend Angela and it's disgusting. — *American Beauty* 1999

hot-sheet *adjective*
said of a motel or hotel that rents rooms for sexual liaisons for cash, without registering the guests using the room *US, 1977*
- Lang returned briefly to his job loading trucks, until one night when he picked up another prostitute at a bar and they slipped into a "hot-sheet" hotel. — *Newsweek* 7th November 1977

house mother *noun*
a madame in a brothel *US, 1987*
- — *Maledicta* Summer/Winter, 1986–1987: 'Sexual slang: prostitutes, pedophiles, flagellators, transvestites, and necrophiles'

how's-your-father *noun*
any act of sexual intimacy from petting to intercourse; unconventional sexual behaviour *UK, 1931*
Originally from the music halls, 'how's your father' or 'howsyerfather' was an all-purpose catchphrase, a euphemism for anything; subsequent usage, especially in the services during World War 2 mainly narrowed the sense to 'a sexual dalliance'.
- Fact is, Jessie, I've met punters that liked 'em dead, oh yeah, snuff muff. It happens, baby, don't think it don't. Necrohowsyourfather. — Ben Elton, *High Society* 2002

huffer *noun*
an act of oral sex on a man *US, 1973*
Probably a mistaken understanding of HUMMER.
- Afterwards, she explained that little extras could be provided for a "tip" – $15 for a "huffer," the quaint idiom for oral sex. — *San Francisco Examiner* 15th January 1973

hum job *noun*
oral sex performed on a male *US, 1964*
- A hum-job is the same as a blow-job however in this case the blower hums a tune, preferably a patriotic one, bringing the blowee off. — *Screw* 29th December 1969

hummer *noun*
an act of oral sex performed on a man *US, 1971*

● Did you check that poony out? I could
parlay this into a hummer at least!
— *Airheads* 1994

hump *noun*
an act of sexual intercourse *US, 1918*
● If you are the dumper, make this last
hump so enjoyable that your ex will
forget how much he hates your guts.
— Anka Radakovich, *The Wild Girls
Club* 1994

hump *verb*
1 **to have sex** *UK, 1785*
● It'll be great, because all those Ph.D.s
are in there, you know, like, discussing
models of alienation and we'll be in
here quietly humping. — *Annie Hall*
1977
2 **to earn money working as a prostitute** *US,
1973*

▶ **hump like a camel**
3 **to engage in sexual intercourse with great
physical enthusiasm** *US, 1970*
● Without you jokers were kicking the
door in, she was humping like a camel.
— Lawrence Block, *No Score [The
Affairs of Chip Harrison Omnibus]*
1970

hump-hump *verb*
to have sex *US, 1997*
A mock pidgin.
● Where'd they teach you to talk like this,
some Panama City "Sailor want to
hump-hump" bar? — *As Good As It
Gets* 1997

humpy-bump *verb*
to have sex *US, 1974*
● I didn't know if you had to humpy-
bump for a job or just know him.

BUTTOCKS

backyard *noun, US, 1972*
● — John A. Holm, *Dictionary of Bahamian
English* 1982
booty; bootie *noun, US, 1928*
● He's Cyndia Lauper's boyfriend, so no skin
search; Cyndi wouldn't want us looking up
his boodie. — James Ellroy, *Suicide Hill*
1986
bumper *noun, US, 1963*
● I'll moor it on the Chicago River and put on
a big sign, "Babes with Big Bumpers
Wanted." — Red Rudensky, *The Gonif* 1970
caboose *noun, US, 1919*
● He cussed her as he drove his needle-toed
shoe into her wide caboose several times.
— Icerberg Slim (Robert Beck), *Pimp* 1969
chair cheeks *noun, US, 2005*
● [H]er exquisitely formed chair cheeks and
her perfecting thrusting, ever-so-slightly
swaying top tier is impossible to look
away from? — Mr. Skin, *Mr. Skin's
Skincyclopedia* 2005
cunt *noun, US, 1972*
**among homosexuals, the buttocks, anus and
rectum**

● Move your cunt — Mama wants to sit down.
— Bruce Rodgers, *The Queen's Vernacular*
1972
moneymaker *noun, UK, 1896*
the genitals; the buttocks
● Shuck my clothes an hop in that fabbroom,
take a fullout shower, wash the jail off my
skin an the funk outa my moneymaker.
— Robert Gover, *JC Saves* 1968
swamp ass *noun, US, 1995*
sweaty genitals and/or buttocks
● Stations that air the Howard Stern Show
were fined $27,000 to $500,000 because he
joked about personal hygiene issues like
"swamp ass" on different shows. — *Daily
News (New York)* 25th January 2005
toilet *noun, BAHAMAS, 1982*
fat buttocks
● — John A. Holm, *Dictionary of Bahamian
English* 1982
turdcutter *noun, US, 1977*
Imprecise and crude physiology.
● Yeah, that bitch sho' has got a helluva
turdcutter on it, ain't she? — Odie Hawkins,
Chicago Hustle 1977

● Back in the days when bad girls
humped good bread into my pockets,
con man, Airtight Willie and pimp ...
me ... lay in a double bunk cell on a
tier in Chicago Cook's County Jail.
— Iceberg Slim (Robert Beck), *Airtight
Willie and Me* 1979

— Edward Lin, *Big Julie of Vegas*
1974

hung *adjective*
endowed with a large penis *UK, 1600*
Shakespeare punned with the term 400
years ago.

- From a certain unevenly rounded thickness at the crotch of his blue jeans, it is safe to assume that he is marvelously hung. — Gore Vidal, *Myra Breckinridge* 1968

hung like a hamster
blessed with a small penis *US*, *2004*
- Brad Pitt has been posing naked for a magazine only days after telling The Sun that he was "hung like a hamster". — *Sunday Times* 9th May 2004

hung like a pimple
blessed with a small penis *US*, *1995*
- I didn't want this new associate seeing that I was hung like a PIMPLE.

— Howard Stern, *Miss America* 1995

hustle *verb*
to engage in prostitution *US*, *1895*
- He put his chick out on the street even though she didn't like to hustle. — Herbert Huncke, *Guilty of Everything* 1990

hustler *noun*
a prostitute, especially a male homosexual *US*, *1924*
- All right, she was a hustler, but she wasn't hustling for me and I did her a favor. — Mickey Spillane, *My Gun is Quick* 1950

Ii

I and I *noun*
used in the military as a jocular substitute for the official 'R and R' (rest and recreation) *US, 1960*
An abbreviation of 'intercourse *and* intoxication', the main activities during rest and recreation.
- [M]en going to Japan turned R&R into the great debauch that came to be known as I&I – intercourse and intoxication. — T.R. Fehrenbach, *This Kind of War* 1963

in-and-out *noun*
sex at its most basic *US, 1996*
- Just in town on business. Just in and out. Ha! A little of the old in-and-out. — *Fargo* 1996

incest *noun*
sex between two similar homosexual types, such as two effeminate men *US, 1972*
- — Bruce Rodgers, *The Queens' Vernacular* 1972

inch boy *noun*
a male who has or is thought to have a small penis *US, 1997*
- — Anna Scotti and Paul Young, *Buzzwords* 1997

interior decorating *noun*
the act of having sex during the day *UK, 1982*
Upper-class society usage.
- — Ann Barr and Peter York, *The Official Sloane Ranger Handbook* 1982

Irish confetti *noun*
semen spilled on a woman's body *US, 1987*
- — *Maledicta* 1986–1987: 'A continuation of a glossary of ethnic slurs in American English'

Irish horse *noun*
a flaccid or impotent penis *US, 1987*
- — *Maledicta* 1986–1987: 'A continuation of a glossary of ethnic slurs in American English'

Irish toothache *noun*
1 an erection *UK, 1882*
- And in case you haven't heard, an Irish toothache is an erection. — Richard Farina, *Letter to Peter Tamony* 24th August 1959
2 pregnancy *US, 1972*
- — Robert A. Wilson, *Playboy's Book of Forbidden Words* 1972

Irish wedding *noun*
masturbation *US, 1987*
- — *Maledicta* 1986–1987: 'A continuation of a glossary of ethnic slurs in American English'

it *noun*
1 sex *UK, 1599*
- Was there something – uh – wrong with me, perhaps? Didn't I like "it"? — Jim Thompson, *Roughneck* 1954
2 the penis *US, 1846*
- MARY'S DAD: You got what stuck? TED: It. MARY'S DAD: It? Oh, it. — *Something About Mary* 1998

itty bitty titties *noun*
small breasts on a female *US, 1992*
- To be held in a blouse with a safety pin or breasts that qualify their owners for membership in the Itty Bitty Titty Committee. — Susan Newman, *Oh God!* 2002

Jj

jabbing jabba *noun*
the act of anal sex *UK, 2001*
A nicely alliterative turn of phrase. Jabba the Hutt, created by George Lucas, is an excrementally ugly character from the *Star Wars* films.

● — *Sky Magazine* July, 2001

jack *noun*
1 an act of masturbation *US, 2003*
● After surviving their first ambush at Al Gharraf, a couple of Marines even admitted to an almost frenzied need to get off combat jacks. — *Rolling Stone* 24th July 2003
2 semen *US, 1997*
Possibly by back-formation from **JACK OFF** (to masturbate).
● Any moke can shoot jack into a woman make a kid. — Joel Rose, *Kill Kill Faster Faster* 1997

jack *verb*
1 (of a male) to masturbate *US, 1995*
● I wanted to take my dick out and start jacking right there. — *Kids* 1995
▶ **jack your joint**
2 to manoeuvre your penis during sex *US, 1997*
● [H]e'd be working, jacking his joint, lost, working at it, and he could feel the come building[.] — Joel Rose, *Kill Kill Faster Faster* 1997

jack-off *noun*
an act of masturbation *US, 1952*
● Whenever I can slip into my office and log on, I'm doing a quick jack-off session. — Howard Stern, *Miss America* 1995

jack off *verb*
(used of a male) to masturbate *US, 1916*
● The one alternative amusement was watching the Melly brothers, George and Ed, who ordinarily spent their lunch hour jacking off in the boy's rest room. — Larry McMurtry, *The Last Picture Show* 1966

jack-off party *noun*
a male gathering for mutual masturbation *UK, 2003*

jack-pack *noun*
a contraption used by a masturbating male to simulate the sensation of penetration *US, 1979*
● — *Maledicta* 1979: 'Kinks and queens: linguistic and cultural aspects of the terminology for gays'

jack picture *noun*
a photograph used while masturbating *US, 1972*
● 'Cause all the punks, every punk that's in our tank has a jack picture, every one of them. A jack picture/ Some picture of a woman. Some of them have just the head of a woman but they jack off with it anyway. — Bruce Jackson, *In the Life* 1972

Jacob's crackers *noun*
the testicles *UK, 2004*
Also shortened form 'jacobs'. Rhyming slang for **KNACKERS**; from the branded savoury biscuits. Usage popularised by comedian Joe Pasquale in the television programme *I'm A Celebrity, Get Me Out of Here*, December 2004.
● [W]hen enjoying a bath with Three Degrees star Sheila Ferguson he [Joe Pasquale] told her; "I'm comfortable with anything, love, but you don't want to see my Jacobs hanging out." — *The Scotsman* 6th December 2004

jaffa *noun*
an infertile man *UK, 2001*
Probably an allusion to a seedless Jaffa orange.
● Somebody been saying I'm a jaffa? Those kids are mine. And the wife hasn't got no complaints. — Liz Evans, *Barking!* 2001

jailbait; gaol-bait *noun*
a sexually alluring girl under the legal age of consent *US, 1930*
● Morty, that fucking chick is jail bait if I ever seen it! I mean, she's a fucking child, for Christ fucking sake! — Terry Southern, *Blue Movie* 1970

jam *noun*
1 sex *US, 1949*

• Everybody plays jam in that park, gets their trim. — Hal Ellson, *Duke* 1949
2 the vagina US, 1980
• — Edith A. Folb, *runnin' down some lines* 1980

jam *verb*
to have sex US, 1972
• — Robert A. Wilson, *Playboy's Book of Forbidden Words* 1972

jammy *noun*
the penis US, 1997
• — Anna Scotti and Paul Young, *Buzzwords* 1997

jammy dodger *verb*
from the male perspective, to have sex UK, 1998
Rhyming slang for ROGER (to have sex), formed from the brand name of a popular biscuit. The noun is 'a jammy dodgering'.
• — Ray Puxley, *Fresh Rabbit* 1998

jampot *noun*
in homosexual usage, the anus and rectum US, 1941
• — *Male Swinger Number 3* 1981: 'The complete gay dictionary'

Jap's eye; japper *noun*
the opening in the glans of the penis UK, 2001
• Make sure u has not bought salty popcorn coz dey will sting your japseye. — Sacha Baron-Cohen, *Da Gospel According to Ali G* 2001

jasper broad *noun*
a lesbian or bisexual woman US, 1972
• You ever hear of what they call a "jasper broad?" That is one who is bisexual, she likes both men and women. — Bruce Jackson, *In the Life* 1972

jaw artist *noun*
a person skilled at the giving of oral sex US, 1972
• — Robert A. Wilson, *Playboy's Book of Forbidden Words* 1972

jawfest *noun*
a prolonged session of oral sex US, 1967
• — Dale Gordon, *The Dominion Sex Dictionary* 1967

jazz *noun*
semen US, 1932
• Momo wipes the jazz off Jasmin. — Anthony Petkovich, *The X Factory* 1997

jazz *verb*
1 to have sex with someone US, 1918
• I say, Baby this daddy was not drinkin, he was on top a me, jazzin! — Robert Gover, *Here Goes Kitten* 1964
2 of a male, to orgasm UK, 2004
After JAZZ (semen).
• [S]o good I jazzed. So if you're listening, boys, you owe me a pair of boxers. — *Kerrang!* 28th August 2004

jelly *noun*
the vagina US, 1926
• The damage had already been done, and what was left just to be pure jelly. — Donald Goines, *The Busting Out of an Ordinary Man* 1985

jelly box *noun*
the vagina AUSTRALIA, 1988
• — James McDonald, *A Dictionary of Obscenity, Taboo and Euphemism* 1988

jelly on the belly *noun*
semen ejaculated on a woman's stomach AUSTRALIA, 1985
• — Thommo, *The Dictionary of Australian Swearing and Sex Sayings* 1985

jelly roll *noun*
the vagina US, 1914
• Say now, if you don't believe my jellyroll is fine / ask Good-Cock Lulu, that's a bitch a mine. — Bruce Jackson, *Get Your Ass in the Water and Swim Like Me* 1964

jelly sandwich *noun*
a sanitary towel US, 1980
• — Edith A. Folb, *runnin' down some lines* 1980

jerk *verb*
▶ **jerk the chicken**
of a male, to masturbate UK, 2003
• [A] final dash to my bedroom and it's a trawl through the pages as I jerk the chicken. Nearly four minutes later, it's all over! — *The FHM Little Book of Bloke* June, 2003
▶ **jerk the gherkin**
of a male, to masturbate UK, 1962
• [W]hile the other bastards are busy getting the dirty waters off their chests [having sex] a bloke like me runs the risk of goin' blind jerkin' the gerkin [sic]!!! — Barry Humphries, *Bazza Pulls It Off!* 1971

▶ **jerk the turk; jerk your turkey**
of a male, to masturbate *UK, 1999*
- — A.D. Peterkin, *The Bald-Headed Hermit & the Artichoke* 1999

jerk-off *noun*
a single act of masturbation, especially by a male *US, 1928*
- The Jerk-off! If you don't know how, let me explain it. — Angelo d'Arcangelo, *The Homosexual Handbook* 1968

jerk off *verb*
to masturbate *UK, 1896*
- I began to wonder if any of them was jerking off while we was sentenced, they all seemed to relish it so much. — John Peter Jones, *Feather Pluckers* 1964

jerk-silly *adjective*
obsessed with masturbation *US, 1962*
- — Joseph E. Ragen and Charles Finston, *Inside the World's Toughest Prison* 1962: 'Penitentiary and underworld glossary'

jewels *noun*
the genitals *US, 1987*
An abbreviation of FAMILY JEWELS.
- But most blacks, and myself, and a few other guys cover the jewels. — Ernest Spencer, *Welcome to Vietnam, Macho Man* 1987

Jewish by hospitalization *noun*
in homosexual usage, circumcised but not Jewish *US, 1987*
- — *Maledicta* 1986–1987: 'A continuation of a glossary of ethnic slurs in American English'

Jewish corned beef *noun*
in homosexual usage, a circumcised penis *US, 1987*
- — *Maledicta* 1986–1987: 'A continuation of a glossary of ethnic slurs in American English'

jig *noun*
sexual intercourse *AUSTRALIA, 1988*
- — James McDonald, *A Dictionary of Obscenity, Taboo and Euphemism* 1988

jig-a-jig; jig-jig *noun*
sexual intercourse *US, 1896*
- I tell 'em how Cholly give me that jig-jig or jail jive[.] — Robert Gover, *JC Saves* 1968

jiggle *noun*
visual sexual content *US, 1978*

- Then again, if "sexy" in the 1970s meant a dash of the "jiggle factor" popularized by Aaron Spelling's Charlie's Angels, she wasn't doing that, either. — Maria Raha, *Cinderella's Big Score* 2005

jigglies *noun*
the female breasts *US, 2002*
- This bubbly blonde with mammoth jigglies has made appearances on Everybody Loves Raymond[.] — Mr. Skin, *Mr. Skin's Skincyclopedia* 2005

Jim *noun*
an interested loiterer and observer in an area where sexual trade is conducted *UK, 1977*
- Wherever prostitutes congregate with their clients [...] there will be other loiterers – the "jims", the "men in raincoats", who watch the transactions and purchased intimacies in a morbid and unhealthy silence. — David Powis, *The Signs of Crime* 1977

jimmy *noun*
the penis *US, 1988*
- "Gimme gimme gimme" / Jumped on my jimmy and rode me like the wild west — Ice-T, *The Girl Tried To Kill Me* 1989

jitney *noun*
a sexually available girl *BAHAMAS, 1982*
Like the bus, anyone can get on if they have the fare.
- — John A. Holm, *Dictionary of Bahamian English* 1982

jiz biz *noun*
the sex industry *US, 2005*
- She has quit the jiz biz three times since then but always seems to come back for more. — Mr. Skin, *Mr. Skin's Skincyclopedia* 2005

jizz *verb*
to ejaculate *US, 1983*
- Then, I want you to flick at my nuts while your friend spanks me into the same Dixie cup Silent Bob jizzed in. — Kevin Smith, *Jay and Silent Bob Strike Back* 2001

jizz; jizzum; jism; jiz; jizm; gism; gizzum *noun*
semen *US, 1941*
Links to an earlier use as 'life-force, energy, spirit'; a meaning that, occasionally, may still be intended.

- Swallowing gism is rather like getting used to raw clams: you have to give it a chance and before you know it, you're addicted. — *Screw* 1st March 1970

jizzer *noun*
a scene in a pornographic film or single photograph showing a man ejaculating *US, 1995*
- — *Adult Video News* August, 1995

An abbreviation of **JERK-OFF**.
- I went two weeks with j/o so I would be really hot. [Letter] — *Drummer* 1979

JO *verb*
(used of a male) to masturbate *US, 1959*
- I tried to "read between the lines" in the famous Nancy Drew books, searching for some deep secret insinuation of erotica so powerful and

---

ANUS/RECTUM

ass cunt *noun, US, 1974*
- Wowee, will you look at that little white kid's ass-cunt. That's a cherry if I ever saw one. — Piri Thomas, *Seven Long Times* 1974

back door; backdoor *noun, UK, 1694*
- She says, "Sweetie, I ain't gonna go three way with you for no sawbuck. You gotta gimme fifteen." He says, "I'll spring for that if you can guarantee a tight back door and quim." — Iceberg Slim (Robert Beck), *Doom Fox* 1978

brown eye *noun, US, 1954*
- The video continues as Stag fucks Trinity's brown eye while she finishes reaming North. — *Adult Video* August/September, 1986

chocolate highway *noun, US, 1977*
- I rode her chocolate highway in eighth gear — Zane, *Carmel Flava* 2006

dirtbox *noun, UK, 1984*
- Is this love at first sight? / I'll let you know when I've seen her dirt-box. — Susan Nickson, *Two Pints of Lager and a Packet of Crisps*, 12th April 2004

Hershey Bar route *noun, US, 1973*
- I ordered him into the shower because of the idea of sleeping with him after he'd gone the Hershey Bar route hardly turned me on. — Xaviera Hollander, *Xaviera* 1973

poop chute; poop shute; poop shooter *noun, US, 1970*
- And if you inform him that your poop chute is a one-way street, he's gotta respect that, or he won't get a taste of your sweet lovin'! — *Seattle Weekly* 9th August 2001

---

jizz joint *noun*
a sex club *US, 2000*
- Because of the way it positions itself, this particular jizz joint is not a haven for working-class girls in a dead-end town or junkies supporting a habit. — *Village Voice* 31st October 2000

jizz-mopper *noun*
an employee in a pornographic video arcade or sex show who cleans up after customers who have come have left *US, 1994*
- You know how much money the average jizz-mopper makes per hour? — *Clerks* 1994

jizz rag *noun*
a rag used for wiping semen *US, 1983*
- "I think you oughta start carrying a jizz rag, Hans," Cecil Higgins said. — Joseph Wambaugh, *The Delta Star* 1983

JO *noun*
an act of male masturbation *US, 1972*

pervasive as to account for the extraordinary popularity of these books, but alas, was able to garner no mileage ("J.O." wise) from this innocuous, and seemingly endless, series. — Terry Southern, *Now Dig This* 1986

job *noun*
▶ **on the job**
having sex, engaged in sexual intercourse *UK, 1966*
- On the job, cripes I wish I was. — Barry Humphries, *Bazza Pulls It Off!* 1971

jock *noun*
the penis; the male genitals *UK, 1790*
- The ugly big-tit broad would stand there [in the dream] buck naked with a jock three times the size of my own. — Iceberg Slim (Robert Beck), *Trick Baby* 1969

jock *verb*
to have sex *UK, 1699*
- — Pamela Munro, *U.C.L.A. Slang* 1989

jock collar *noun*
a rubber ring fitted around the base of the penis *US, 1969*
Later and better known as a COCK RING.
• Pocket was at the back of the poolroom with an old Jewish peddler of French ticklers, Spanish fly, and jock collars. — Iceberg Slim (Robert Beck), *Trick Baby* 1969

jocker *noun*
an aggressive, predatory male homosexual *US, 1893*
• "My, my," the Spook murmured, "not a feather on him. Some jocker's due to score." — Malcolm Braly, *On the Yard* 1967

Jodrell Bank; jodrell *noun*
an act of masturbation *UK, 1992*
Rhyming slang for WANK formed on the observatory located in Cheshire.
• [H]e was having a Jodrell spying on some couple in the shrubbery[.] — Kitty Churchill, *Thinking of England* 1995

Joe the grinder *noun*
used as a generic term for the man that a prisoner's wife or girlfriend takes up with while the man is in prison *US, 1964*
• Jody say, "Don't front me with that shit because it's not anywhere/ and this is Joe the Grinder and damn that square." — Bruce Jackson, *Get Your Ass in the Water and Swim Like Me* 1964

joey *noun*
a youthful, attractive homosexual male prostitute *AUSTRALIA, 1979*
• — *Maledicta* 1979: 'Kinks and queens: linguistic and cultural aspects of the terminology for gays'

john *noun*
a prostitute's client *US, 1906*
From the sense as 'generic man', probably via the criminal use as 'dupe' or 'victim'.
• Russell recognised some of the pavement princesses, whose pitch this normally was [...] livid at missing their regular johns and champagne tricks on their way back from the City. — Greg Williams, *Diamond Geezers* 1997

Johnny *noun*
the penis *US, 1972*
• Or a girl would pick a guy out of the audience – it was always a pimp but she would let on that he was just an average tourist – pull his johnny out of

his pants and start treating it like a lollipop. — Robert Byrne, *McGoorty* 1972

Johnny Long Shoes *noun*
the man who steals a prisoner's girlfriend or wife after incarceration *US, 1991*
• — Lee McNelis, *30 + And a Wake-Up* 1991

johnson *noun*
the penis *UK, 1862*
Despite an 1862 citation, the word was not widely used in this sense until the 1970s.
• I wanna set Heather on my Johnson and just start spinning her like a fucking pinwheel. — *Heathers* 1988

Johnson Ronson *noun*
the penis *US, 1975*
• I had to put down the damn book because Johnson Ronson was ripping through my cheap underwear. — Miguel Pinero, *Short Eyes* 1975

John Thomas; john *noun*
the penis *UK, 1879*
• [S]neakin' around scribblin' John Thomas's on the wall? — Barry Humphries, *Bazza Pulls It Off!* 1971

John Wayne's hairy saddle bags *noun*
the testicles hanging in the scrotum *UK, 1997*
• — *Roger's Profanisaurus* December, 1997

joint *noun*
the penis *US, 1931*
• When one lonely night a man came walking down the street / He had about a yard and a half of joint hanging down by his feet. — Anonymous ("Arthur"), *Shine and the Titanic; The Signifying Monkey; Stackolee* 1971

Joliet Josie *noun*
a sexually attractive girl under the legal age of consent *US, 1950*
Joliet is the site of the major prison in Illinois.
• — Jack Lait and Lee Mortimer, *Chicago Confidential* 1950: 'Loop lexicon'

jollies *noun*
the female breasts *UK, 2002*
• Any bird who gets her jollies out for GQ wants to be in the papers so bad it in't funny[.] — Ben Elton, *High Society* 2002

jones *noun*
the penis *US, 1966*
- He crossed his legs, trying to push his hardening jones down between his thighs. To keep his thang cooled out, like, after all, three months was a pretty good piece of time to remain unfucked. — Odie Hawkins, *Chicago Hustle* 1977

joog *verb*
to have sex *JAMAICA, 1942*
- Jooged plenty women too. — Edwin Torres, *After Hours* 1979

joy bags *noun*
the female breasts *US, 2005*
- Joey bares her juicy little joy-bags in a dressing room before a guy's head comes crashing through the wall. — Mr. Skin, *Mr. Skin's Skincyclopedia* 2005

joyboy *noun*
a young male homosexual, especially a young male homosexual prostitute *UK, 1961*
- There were many other ways; masturbation was first but homosexuals or prisonmade "joy-boys" came in second. — Piri Thomas, *Seven Long Times* 1974

joy button *noun*
the clitoris *US, 1972*
- Although it's sometimes called "the joy button," the clitoris is actually more than a single spot. — Boston Women's Health Book Collective, *Our Bodies, Ourselves* 1984

joy hole *noun*
the vagina *US, 1939*
- At first I slowly pumped her joy hole, but it wasn't long before the momentum picked up. — *alt.sex.stories* 4th April 1993

joy juice *noun*
semen *US, 1969*
- He wanted her ass to be good and strong and filled to the brim with the joy juice of the men she'd had that day, and the more the merrier. — A.S. Jackson, *Gentleman Pimp* 1973

joy knob *noun*
1 the penis *US, 1960*
- Mike's joy knob let go and I had to swallow fast to get down his massive load of sweet boy-cream. — *alt.sex.stories.gay* 31st May 2002

2 the prostate gland *US, 1997*
- I found his joy knob on about the second poke and started working it, his grunts of sheer animal pleasure making my balls tingle. — *alt.sex.stories.gay* 2nd August 1997

3 the clitoris *US, 1998*
- I imagined licking her clitoral bone until her joy knob stood straight out, then I'd lick until she screamed. — *alt.sex.stories.moderated* 23rd December 1998

joystick *noun*
the penis *US, 1916*
Probably derived from mechanical imagery, but there is a suggestion (Ray Puxley, *Cockney Rabbit*, 1992) that this may be rhyming slang for PRICK.
- She may have one arm around him, or have one hand busy squeezing his gonads and the other hand busy rubbing his joystick augmenting the sucking action of her lips — *Screw* 1st December 1969

joy water *noun*
vaginal lubricant produced as a result of sexual arousal *US, 1973*
- [W]hen she climaxed she hollered and screamed and her tasty ass became quite sloppy with joy water. — A.S. Jackson, *Gentleman Pimp* 1973

jubilee *noun*
the buttocks *US, 1967*
- — Dale Gordon, *The Dominion Sex Dictionary* 1967

jug; jugg *verb*
to have sex with *US, 1965*
- There were few women around the neighborhood that Jonny wanted to jugg and didn't jugg, even if they were married. — Claude Brown, *Manchild in the Promised Land* 1965

juggles *noun*
the female breasts *US, 2005*
- Jen's juggles make a nice appearance when she's in bed with her dude[.] — Mr. Skin, *Mr. Skin's Skincyclopedia* 2005

jugs; milk jugs *noun*
the female breasts *US, 1957*
A reference to the source of mother's milk; widely known and used.
- Daddy says tits. Daddy says knockers and jugs and bazooms and

dingleberries and jujubes. And then he
laughs and goes "wuff! wuff!"
— *Journal of British Photography* 9th
May 1980

juice *noun*
1 semen *US, 1969*
- She was afraid, because he'd shot a lot
of juice into her, that she might be
knocked up. — Juan Carmel Cosmes,
Memoir of a Whoremaster 1969
2 sex *BAHAMAS, 1982*
- — John A. Holm, *Dictionary of
Bahamian English* 1982

juice *verb*
1 to have sex *BAHAMAS, 1982*
- — John A. Holm, *Dictionary of
Bahamian English* 1982
▶ juice the G-spot
2 to engage in oral sex on a woman *US,
2001*
- Another way to say "cunnilingus" [...]
Juicing the G-spot[.] — Erica Orloff and
JoAnn Baker, *Dirty Little Secrets* 2001

juice box *noun*
the vagina *CANADA, 2002*
- — Bill Casselman, *Canadian Sayings*
2002

juicy *adjective*
(used of a woman) sexually aroused *US,
1970*
- Over in the corner sat Sweet Jaw Lucy,
looking all juicy. — Roger Abrahams,
Positively Black 1970

jumbo *noun*
the buttocks *NEW ZEALAND, 1998*
- — David McGill, *David McGill's
Complete Kiwi Slang Dictionary* 1998

jump *noun*
an act of sexual intercourse *US, 1931*
- I was just showering your mother's
stink off me after I gave her a quick
jump and sent her home. — Kevin
Smith, *Jay and Silent Bob Strike Back*
2001

jump *verb*
1 to have sex *US, 1999*
- On the bright Sunday afternoon we
visited West Point, Strauss wore a pair
of tortoiseshell prescription sunglasses
that made me want to jump him.
— Rita Ciresi, *Pink Slip* 1999
▶ jump someone's bones

2 to have sex *US, 1965*
- Failing that, he would have thoroughly
enjoyed jumping on her elegant bones.
— Max Shulman, *Anyone Got a Match?*
1964

jumper bumps *noun*
the female breasts *UK, 2005*
- There's no way I would be tempted to
flash my jumper bumps, no matter how
politely I was asked. — *The Guardian*
14th June 2005

jungle *noun*
the female pubic hair; hence the vagina *US,
2001*
- — Erica Orloff and JoAnn Baker *Dirty
Little Secrets* 2001

jungle job *noun*
sex outdoors *US, 1966*
- Studs in New York, particularly those
working the Public Library and Bryant
Park areas, call a frantic quickie in the
bushes a "jungle job" or a "Tarzan."
— Johnny Shearer, *The Male Hustler*
1966

jungle light *noun*
in the pornography industry, a light used to
illuminate the genitals of the performers
US, 1995
- — *Adult Video News* October, 1995

jungle meat *noun*
in homosexual usage, a black man *US, 1981*
- — *Male Swinger Number 3* 1981: 'The
complete gay dictionary'

jungle pussy *noun*
a black woman's vagina; hence black
women objectified sexually *US, 1974*
- First she said the black thing, like she
understood his urge to check out some
jungle pussy. — John Williams, *Cardiff
Dead* 2000

junk *noun*
the genitals *US, 1997*
- She was all over my junk. — Judi
Sanders, *Da Bomb!* 1997

junk in the trunk *noun*
said of a woman with prominent buttocks
US, 2001
- She be wearin some little shorts and
her butt meat be hangin out a little bit.
Yellow whisper to me, "Girl got some
junk in the trunk." — Percival Everett,
Erasure 2001

Kk

K noun

oral sex on a woman performed according to the strictures of the 'Kivin Method' *US, 2001*

- And while you're giving good K, you'll need to place your fingertips on her perineum[.] — *Drugs An Adult Guide* December, 2001

Kansas yummy noun

an attractive woman who is not easily seduced *US, 1985*

A term that need not, and usually does not, apply to a woman actually from Kansas.

- — *American Speech* Spring, 1985: 'The language of singles bars'

keki noun

the vagina *TRINIDAD AND TOBAGO, 2003*

From the Hindi.

- — Lise Winer, *Dictionary of the English/Creole of Trinidad & Tobago* 2003

khaki wacky adjective

attracted to men in military uniform *US, 1944*

- — *Yank* 24th March 1945

kick verb

▶ **kick mud**

to work as a prostitute *US, 1963*

- Chuck had two girls kicking mud around the city of Detroit. — A.S. Jackson, *Gentleman Pimp* 1973

kiddie fiddler noun

a paedophile *UK, 2003*

- The man who's going to die is a kiddie fiddler. — Danny King, *The Hitman Diaries* 2003

kid fruit noun

a male homosexual who achieves gratification from performing oral sex on young men or boys *US, 1961*

- Head-hunters, cannibals and kid-fruits are fellators[.] — Arthur V. Huffman, *New York Mattachine Newsletter* June, 1961

kidney-wiper; kidney-scraper noun

the penis *US, 1888*

A ribald celebration of a penis of heroic dimensions. A clue to the derivation of the word may rest in the tune to which 'The Tinker' is sung: 'Rosin the Beau', an English folk song (with a wonderfully punning title).

- With his jolly great kidney-wiper / And his balls the size of three — Ed Cray, 'The Tinker (II)', 'Bawdy Ballads' 1978

kid-simple noun

a male homosexual who is obsessively attracted to young men and boys *US, 1962*

- — Joseph E. Ragen and Charles Finston, *Inside the World's Toughest Prison* 1962: 'Penitentiary and underworld glossary'

kielbasa noun

the penis *US, 1978*

From *kielbasa* (a red skinned Polish sausage).

- Believing I could do something for her career, she would be ready to please my kielbasa[.] — Howard Stern, *Miss America* 1995

kill noun

semen *US, 1998*

- — Ethan Hilderbrant, *Prison Slang* 1998

king noun

an aggressive, 'mannish' lesbian *US, 1964*

- — Florida Legislative Investigation Committee (Johns Committee), *Homosexuality and Citizenship in Florida* 1964: 'Glossary of homosexual terms and deviate acts'

kink noun

non-conventional sexuality, especially when fetishistic or sado-masochistic *UK, 1959*

- I was the United Kingdom's most fervent new convert to kink. — Claire Mansfield and John Mendelssohn, *Dominatrix* 2002

kinky adjective

used for describing any sexual activity that deviates from the speaker's sense of sexually 'normal'; also of any article, enhancement or manner of dress that may be used in such activity *US, 1942*

- On wash day I have to keep a look out in case some kinky boy comes and steals some of my undies off the line. — Geoff Brown, *I Want What I Want* 1966

kipper noun

the vagina *UK, 1984*

From the tired comparison between the smell of fish and the smell of the vagina.

- A cockney fellow-soldier, on reading of the birth of Siamese twins, 1954, exclaimed pityingly of the mother, "Poor cow! I bet that split 'er old kipper." — Beale, 1984

kipper feast *noun*
oral sex performed on a woman *UK, 1983*
- — Tom Hibbert, *Rockspeak!* 1983

kiss *verb*
to perform oral sex *US, 1941*
- This euphemism has even been employed by medical and technical writers, who call oragenitalism the genital kiss, or, with even greater periphrastic timidity, the kiss of genital stimulation. — G. Legman, *The Language of Homsexuality* 1941

kissing Mrs *noun*
the act of rubbing the clitoris with the penis *UK, 2001*
- — *Sky* July, 2001

kitty *noun*
the vagina *US, 2000*
A diminutive of PUSSY.
- When it comes to mowing our lickable lawns, the hairstyle you choose for your kitty can be an expression of your personal taste. — *The Village Voice* 8th–14th November 2000

kleenex *noun*
a youthful, sexually inexperienced male who is temporarily the object of an older homosexual's desire *US, 1987*
The joke is that you blow once and then throw away.
- — *Maledicta* Summer/Winter, 1986–1987: 'Sexual slang: prostitutes, pedophiles, flagellators, transvestites, and necrophiles'

knackers *noun*
the testicles *UK, 1866*
From an earlier sense (castanets).
- I turned again, and – yeeeoooowww! – a spade handle leapt up at me as I stepped on the end of it, and gave me a resounding whack in the crutch, right in the knackers, de-balling me. — *Alvin Purple* 1974

knead *verb*
▶ **knead the noodle**
(of a male) to masturbate *US, 2001*

- "The boy is masturbating" [...] Kneading the noodle[.] — Erica Orloff and JoAnn Baker *Dirty Little Secrets* 2001

knee-trembler *noun*
1 sex while standing *AUSTRALIA, 1896*
- They disappeared round the corner and Bob gave her a knee-trembler and ten minutes later they were back talking as if they'd never been anywhere. — Bluey *Bush Contractors* 1975
2 a sexually attractive woman *UK, 1999*
- [T]he little Asian bird on the till was a touch of a knee trembler so I just finished chatting her and getting nowhere[.] — Jeremy Cameron, *Brown Bread in Wengen* 1999

knives *noun*
▶ **at it like knives**
very sexually active *UK, 1985*
- [C]onvent girls are at it like knives. — Henry Sloane, *Sloane's Inside Guide to Sex & Drugs & Rock 'n' Roll* 1985

knob *noun*
1 the penis *UK, 1660*
- That cheesyprick pays overtime about as often as my old lady does my knob, and that bitch ain't gave me some knobbin' since she told me she wants a firm commitment. — Joseph Wambaugh, *Finnegan's Week* 1993
▶ **polish a knob**
2 to perform oral sex on a man *US, 1947*
- When you finish with them come on back around to me, and I'll let you polish this knob until it spits. — Donald Goines, *Dopefiend* 1971

knob *verb*
to have sex with someone *UK, 1988*
Derives from KNOB (the penis) but usage is not gender-specific.
- What, you're still knobbing old Alison? — Colin Butts, *Is Harry Still on the Boat?* 2003

knobber *noun*
1 a transvestite prostitute *US*
- In the meantime, prostitution continued unabated there and elsewhere, transvestite or "knobbers" crowing that they needed only hallways in which to satisfy their patrons efficiently and manually. — William Taylor, *Inventing Times Square* 1991
2 oral sex performed on a male *US, 1989*
- — Pamela Munro, *U.C.L.A. Slang* 1989

knob job *noun*
oral sex performed on a man *US, 1968*
- Joe dropping his pants in the car for a quick knob job during my "smoke break" at the restaurant. — R.J. March, *Hard* 2002

knob-jockey *noun*
a homosexual male; a promiscuous heterosexual female *UK, 1998*
- — Chris Donald, *Roger's Profanisaurus* 1998

knobs *noun*
the female breasts, especially the nipples *US, 1968*
- — Collin Baker et al., *College Undergraduate Slang Study Conducted at Brown University* 1968

was laying up in a hotel room knocking a chunk off some bubble-assed taxi dancer he was going with. — Joseph Wambaugh, *The Blue Knight* 1973
▶ **knock boots**
3 to have sex, especially anal sex *US, 1994*
- JAY: I tell you what, though, I don't care if she is my cousin, I'm gonna knock those boots again tonight. — *Clerks* 1994
▶ **knock it out**
4 to have sex *US, 1980*
- — Edith A. Folb, *runnin' down some lines* 1980
▶ **knock one off**
5 to have sex, especially in a perfunctory manner *US, 1924*

PROMISCUOUS PERSON

bike *noun, AUSTRALIA, 1945*
Suggests 'easy availability for a ride'. Often in compound as 'office bike', 'school bike', 'town bike', 'village bike', etc; occasionally, if reputation demands, 'the bike'.
- What an ugly old bike. I wouldn't ride her for practice!!! — Barry Humphries, *Bazza Pulls It Off!* 1971

dartboard *adjective, UK, 1982*
▶ **had more pricks than a second-hand dartboard**
used of a sexually promiscuous woman
As the punch line of a joke from the early 1980s 'second-hand' is dispensable.
- — Ted Walker, *High Path* 1982

punchboard *noun, US, 1977*
A 'punchboard' is a game which used to be found in shops, where for a price the customer punched one of many holes on the board in the hope of winning a prize.
- Claymore Face, the platoon punchboard, was there too. — Larry Heinemann, *Close Quarters* 1977

slut *noun, UK, 1450*
- Well, a slut is one who will go to a bar that's known to be a place for mostly guys – and walk in alone and sit at the bar. — Murray Kaufman, *Murray the K Tells It Like It Is, Baby,* 1966

knob throb *noun*
(of a male) an intense desire for sex *UK, 1998*
- [W]hen he has a knob throb for her and she has a clitwobble for him. — Ray Puxley, *Fresh Rabbit* 1998

knock *verb*
1 to have sexual intercourse with someone *UK, 1598*
- It was more important to back up your mates than to knock a sheila. — William Dick, *A Bunch of Ratbags* 1965
▶ **knock a chunk off**
2 to have sex from the male perspective *US, 1973*
- I was alone because my partner, a piss-poor excuse for a cop named Syd Bacon,

- The moment was there. I wanted to, but I couldn't just ... knock one off. Okay? — Elmore Leonard, *Be Cool* 1999
▶ **knock one out**
6 to masturbate to orgasm *UK, 1990*
- I've never had a wank over the picture me'self, you know what I mean? I'm not sure that I've got her picture out and purposefully knocked one out over her. — *Q* May, 2001

knockers *noun*
1 the testicles *UK, 1889*
- He run right down the road and told it all over the neighborhood how the crazy woman tried to cut his knockers off. — Vance Randolph, *Pissing in the Snow* 1976

2 the female breasts, especially large ones
US, 1934
- Her name was Lillian Simmons.
  My brother D.B. used to go around with
  her for a while. She had very big
  knockers. — J.D. Salinger, *Catcher in
  the Rye* 1951

knocking shop *noun*
a brothel *UK, 1860*
- Don't give me all that crap. You run a
  glorified knocking shop. — Anthony
  Masters, *Minder* 1984

knock off *verb*
1 of a male, to have sex *AUSTRALIA, 1965*
- I took her down to Basin Street and to
  a movie, then took her to my room
  and knocked her off. I was ready to
  go after I'd knocked her off one time.
  But the chick was really something –
  she couldn't see anybody just
  knocking her off one time. — Claude
  Brown, *Manchild in the Promised Land*
  1965
▶ **knock off a piece**
2 to have sex *US, 1921*
- Doin' the short change scene with the
  Geech, the grabbing, back to the pad,
  knocking off a li'l piece with Leelah...
  — Odie Hawkins, *Chicago Hustle* 1977

knockwurst *noun*
the penis *US, 1972*
- Well, I shined my light in there and
  here's these two down on the seat, the
  old boy throwing the knockwurst to his
  girlfriend. — Joseph Wambaugh,
  The Blue Knight 1972

knot-flashing *noun*
**public self-exposure by a male for sexual
thrills** *UK, 1968*

Police slang, formed on an otherwise obsolete
use of 'knot' (the head of the) penis).
- — James Fraser, *The Evergreen Death*
  1968

knuckle shuffle *noun*
an act of male masturbation *US, 2000*
- Copperknob doing a five knuckle
  shuffle in the loo[.] — Jack Allen,
  When the Whistle Blows 2000

knuckle-shuffle *verb*
to masturbate *UK, 2002*
- Okay, okay, I admit it, I knuckle-
  shuffled the FSA [Financial Services
  Advisor]. — Christopher Brookmyre,
  The Sacred Art of Stealing 2002

Kojak *noun*
▶ **the Kojak**
a totally depilated pubic mound *UK, 2002*
Kojak, a television detective of the 1970s,
was played by bald-headed actor Telly
Savalas, 1924–94.
- The Kojak or Full [Bikini Wax:] All hair
  is removed from the pubic and bottom
  area. — *Loaded* June, 2002

Kojak's moneybox *noun*
the penis *UK, 2003*
- — Richard Herring, *Talking Cock* 2003

koochie *noun*
the vagina, *2001*
- Beautifully Shaved Koochies
  — *Pornographic website* 3rd December
  2001

kosher *adjective*
in homosexual usage, circumcised *US, 1987*
- — *Maledicta* 1986–1987: 'A continuation of a glossary of ethnic slurs in
  American English'

Ll

lace *verb*
to have sexual intercourse *US, 1996*
- Think that I should lace her "Nah it's much safer orally" — Sadat X, Fat Joe and Diamond D, *Nasty Hoes* 1996

lace card *noun*
the foreskin of an uncircumcised penis *US, 1941*
- — Donald Webster Cory and John P. LeRoy, *The Homosexual and His Society* 1963: 'A lexicon of homosexual slang'

lace queen *noun*
a homosexual who prefers men with uncircumcised penises *US, 1988*
- — H. Max, *Gay (S)language* 1988

lack-a-nookie *noun*
a notional disease resulting from a lack of sex *US, 1952*
- Peggy said, "And you look like you're suffering from that rare Hawaiian disease." "What disease?" Cockeye was concerned. Peggy looked at Cockeye, smiling at him from head to toe. "Lack a nooky, Chump." — Harry Grey, *The Hoods* 1952

lad *noun*
▶ **the lad**
the penis *UK, 2001*
- I stands back and pulls the lad out[.] — Kevin Sampson, *Clubland* 2002

ladybits *noun*
the female genitals *UK, 2003*
- Do you have any other piercings? Yes, here (points at her ear), here (points at her belly button) and here (points at her ladybits! But then starts laughing) ha ha! I'm only joking. — FHM June, 2003

lady five fingers *noun*
a boy's or man's hand in the context of masturbation; masturbation *US, 1969*
- I wondered if it were a capital crime in this joint to get caught having an affair with "lady five fingers." — Iceberg Slim (Robert Beck), *Pimp* 1969

lady in waiting *noun*
in male homosexual usage, a man who loiters in or near public toilets in the hope of sexual encounters *US, 1981*
- — *Male Swinger Number 3* 1981: 'The complete gay dictionary'

laid, relayed and parlayed *adjective*
thoroughly taken advantage of *US, 1957*
There are multiple variants of the third element — 'waylaid', 'marmalade', etc.
- We been laid, relayed, and waylaid and nobody wants to hear about it. — Edwin Torres, *Carlito's Way* 1975

landlady *noun*
a brothel madame *US, 1879*
- LANDLADIES' NIGHT AT THE CLUB ALABAM! – FUN AND FROLIC! – COME ONE AND ALL! — Mezz Mezzrow, *Really the Blues* 1946

lap dance *noun*
an intimate sexual performance, involving some degree of physical contact between a female performer and a sitting male *US, 1988*
- There's no constitutional right to a lap-dance. That's the gist of a divided Oregon Court of Appeals ruling[.] — *Associated Press* 31st October 2002

lap dance *verb*
to engage in a sexual performance in which a woman dancer, scantily clad if at all, grinds her buttocks into a sitting male customer's lap *US, 1994*
- Lap dancing – where the dancer rubs herself against the customer for a longer time – brings in more money. — James Ridgeway, *Red Light* 1996

lap job *noun*
an act of oral sex on a woman *US, 1969*
- Like my second lap job a year later was on a neighborhood chick, a year older than me. — Screw 7th March 1969

lasting mark *noun*
a welt or bruise produced in sadomasochistic sex *US, 1987*
- If a man says "no lasting marks" he is put through a gradual build-up of increasingly painful procedures. — Frederique Delacoste, *Sex Work* 1987

laundry *noun*
in homosexual usage, a bulge in a man's crotch *US, 1964*

Humorous, suggesting that the bulge is produced by something other than the man's genitals.

● — Guy Strait, *The Lavendar Lexicon* 1st June 1964

lawn *noun*

a woman's pubic hair *US, 1964*

● When it comes to mowing our lickable lawns, the hairstyle you choose for your kitty can be an expression of your personal taste. — *The Village Voice* 8th–14th November 2000

lay *noun*

1 an act of sexual intercourse *US, 1928*

● I was about ten and she was probably less, and at the time a lay seemed like such a big deal[.] — Ken Kesey, *One Flew Over the Cuckoo's Nest* 1962

2 a girl or a woman regarded as a sexpartner, usually with a modifying adjective such as easy, good, great, etc *UK, 1635*

● But all things considered I look good. I like men's bums and penises. At 67 years old, I am what you might call an easy lay. — *The Guardian* 17th November 2003

lay *verb*

1 to have sex *UK, 1800*

Most often heard in the passive.

● I rarely make love / I mostly get laid — Loudon Wainwright III, *Suicide Song* 1971

▶ **lay pipe**

2 (used of a male) to have sex *US, 1939*

● Gonna lay some pipe, six inches at a time. — Joseph Wambaugh, *The Choirboys* 1975

lay-for-pay *noun*

sex with a prostitute *US, 1956*

● "Who's behind all the muscle, Mamie?" I was going too fast for her. "In the past two weeks we've hauled at least three of you lay-for-pay dames into Bellevue to get patched up." — *Rogue for Men* June, 1956

lazy lob *noun*

a partial erection *UK, 1998*

● He got a lazy lob on. Kara reached down and stroked his penis. — Garry Bushell, *The Face* 2001

lead in the pencil *noun*

the ability of a man to achieve an erection and ejaculate *UK, 1925*

● "Hot tea," he declared. "All natural herbs. Here, it'll put lead in your pencil." Keyes shook his head. "No thanks." — Carl Hiaasen, *Tourist Season* 1995

leather *noun*

in homosexual usage, the anus *US, 1941*

● — *Male Swinger Number 3* 1981: 'The complete gay dictionary'

leather *adjective*

used for denoting leather fetishistic and sado-masochistic symbolism in sexual relationships *US, 1964*

● The hostility of the minority "leather" crowd toward the rest of the "gay" world is exceeded by the bitterness of individual homosexuals toward the "straight" world. — *Life* 26th June 1964

leather bar *noun*

a bar with a homosexual clientele whose fashion sense is leather-oriented and whose sexual tastes are sado-masochistic *US, 1963*

● And there are, too, the "leather bars": black-jacketed mesh inside, moving pictures of young men wrestling realistically, murals of motorcyclists at a race[.] — John Rechy, *City of Night* 1963

leather hustler *noun*

a male prostitute willing to engage in sado-masochistic sex *US, 1994*

● The most important thing in being a leather hustler, he explained to me, was the costuming. — John Preston, *Hustling* 1994

leather queen *noun*

a homosexual with a leather fetish *US, 1972*

● Wealthy and perfectly coiffed men sauntered to their seats with leather queens and drag queens and lesbians in fashionable attire. — Randy Shilts, *And the Band Played On* 1988

leg *noun*

1 sex; women as sex objects *US, 1966*

● A place like college – all that leg around campus – you should be sowing your wild oats. — *Mallrats* 1995

▶ **get the leg over; get your leg over; get a leg over**

2 to have sex, generally from a male perspective *UK, 1975*

● Maybe just once he'd like to get the leg over one of these kind of women[.]
— Roddy Doyle, *The Van* 1991

leggins *noun*
the rubbing of the penis between the thighs of another man until reaching orgasm *US, 1934*
● [I]n leggins men reach ejaculation from the insertion of the penis between one another's legs in a face-to-face, usually horizontal, position. — *New York Mattachine Newsletter* June, 1961

legover; leg over *noun*
(from a male perspective) conventional sexual intercourse *UK, 1969*
● I'm strictly a legover man, myself.
— Mike Stott, *Soldiers Talking, Cleanly* 1978

leg-spreader *noun*
a military aviator's wings insignia *US, 1967*
The suggestion is that women find fliers sexually irresistible.
● Women are just impressed with these fliers. There's a reason those wings they wear are known as leg spreaders.
— Harry Stein, *The Girl Watchers Club* 2004

let *verb*
▶ **let the eel swim upstream**
to have sex *US, 2001*
● Another way to say "intercourse" [...] Letting the eel swim upstream[.]
— Erica Orloff and JoAnn Baker, *Dirty Little Secrets* 2001

letch water *noun*
pre-orgasm penile secretions; semen *UK, 2002*
Ultimately comes from 'lechery'.
● — Paul Baker, *Polari* 2002

Levy and Frank; levy *noun*
an act of masturbation; also used as a verb *UK, 1958*
Rhyming slang for WANK, formed, according to Julian Franklyn, *A Dictionary of Rhyming Slang*, 1960, from the name of a well-known firm of public house and restaurant proprietors.
● I'll have a leavy [levy] at the same time and imagine I'm haveing [sic] a bunk up instead of you. — Frank Norman, *Bang To Rights* 1958

Lewinsky *noun*
an act of oral sex *US, 1999*

In 1995 Monica Lewinsky was a White House intern; she was a central figure in US President Bill Clinton's later attempt to exclude oral sex from a general definition of sexual relations.
● In a recent episode of [...] Law & Order: Special Victims Unit, a detective uses the phrase "getting a Lewinsky" to describe oral sex. — *The Guardian* 17th October 1999

lez *verb*
▶ **lez it up**
to behave (sexually) as lesbians *UK, 2003*
● Three in a bed! Menage a trois! You two lezzing it up! It'd be great.
— Richard Herring, *Talking Cock* 2003

lezz off *verb*
to engage in lesbian sex *UK, 2006*
● He wants to watch her lezz off with some lass who looks like Pamela Anderson. — Ashley Lister, *Swingers* 2006

lick *noun*
oral sex *US, 1973*
● — Kenn 'Naz' Young, *Naz's Underground Dictionary* 1973

lick *verb*
▶ **lick the cat**
to perform oral sex on a woman *US, 2001*
● — Erica Orloff and JoAnn Baker, *Dirty Little Secrets* 2001

lick-box *noun*
a person who performs oral sex on women *US, 1949*
● — Vincent J. Monteleone, *Criminal Slang* 1949

licking the dew off her lily *noun*
to engage in oral sex on a woman *US, 2001*
● Another way to say "cunnilingus" [...] Licking the dew off her lily[.] — Erica Orloff and JoAnn Baker, *Dirty Little Secrets* 2001

light off *verb*
to experience an orgasm *US, 1971*
● The broad's great in the sack and she lights off real easy. — George V. Higgins, *The Friends of Eddie Doyle* 1971

lils *noun*
the female breasts *UK, 2003*
Usually in the plural.
● She's got magnificent lils. — Davina McCall, *The Brits* 20th February 2003

limit *noun*
▶ **go the limit**
to have sexual intercourse *US, 1922*
● Several times then, she had nearly gone the limit, as they used to call it, but something had always saved her – once a campus policeman but mostly the boy himself, who had scruples. — Mary McCarthy, *The Group* 1960

Lincoln *noun*
a five-dollar prostitute *US, 1965*
● A resident prostitute of any stature won't take his clothes off for less than $10. And frequently they get $15 and $20. Sailors are usually what are called LINCOLNS. They are eager to supplement their income with homosexual acts for as little as five dollars. — *KFRC radio, San Francisco* 8th November 1965: 'The market street proposition'

Lincoln Tunnel *noun*
in homosexual usage, a loose anus and rectum *US, 1981*
Homage to the tunnel connecting New Jersey and Manhattan.
● — *Male Swinger Number 3* 1981: 'The complete gay dictionary'

line-up *noun*
serial sex between one person and multiple partners *US, 1913*
● So this rape was in fact a line-up? Yes. It was against my will. You have been a party to line-ups on several occasions? I probably have, but if so, I was under the influence of alcohol and I can't remember them. — *Truth* 3rd February 1970

lingy *noun*
the penis *BAHAMAS, 1982*
● — John A. Holm, *Dictionary of Bahamian English* 1982

lip-lock *noun*
oral sex performed on a man *US, 1976*
● Why, there's a broad there who'll whip a lip lock on you that'll scorch your shorts and curl the hairs on the back of your neck to look like pig's tails[.] — Larry Heinemann, *Close Quarters* 1977

lip service *noun*
oral sex *US, 1975*
● — Xaviera Hollander, *The Best Part of a Man* 1975

lipstick *noun*
▶ **lipstick on your dipstick**
oral sex performed on a man *US, 1970*
● — *Current Slang* Spring, 1970

lip work *noun*
oral sex on a woman *US, 1967*
● — Dale Gordon, *The Dominion Sex Dictionary* 1967

little death *noun*
an orgasm *UK, 1999*
● Five images that will stop the "Little Death". Hold them in your head to mentally prevent nature taking its course. — *Loaded* June, 2002

little guy with the helmet *noun*
the penis *US, 2001*
● — Erica Orloff and JoAnne Baker, *Dirty Little Secrets* 2001

little man *noun*
the penis *UK, 1998*
● — A.D. Peterkin, *The Bald-Headed Hermit & The Artichoke* 1999

little ploughman *noun*
the clitoris *US, 1980*
● — *Maledicta* Winter, 1980: 'A new erotic vocabulary'

live *verb*
▶ **live caseo**
to cohabit for sexual purposes *UK, 1956*
From 'caseo' (a brothel/overnight hire of a prostitute).
● They picked up a pair of judies who were attracted to their soldierly bearing, and lived caseo with them. — Charles Raven, *Underworld Nights* 1956

live gig *verb*
to masturbate; to have sex *UK, 2003*
Rhyming slang for 'frig'.
● — Bodmin Dark, *Dirty Cockney Rhyming Slang* 2003

lizard *noun*
1 a prostitute *US, 2001*
● I won't be gettin' my arm broke while you're doin' some goddamn lizard. — J.T. LeRoy, *The Heart is Deceitful Above All Things* 2001
2 the penis *US, 1962*
● — Eugene Landy, *The Underground Dictionary* 1971

load *noun*
1 an ejaculation's-worth of semen *US, 1927*

- And when she mounts him, displaying one of the roundest, hottest, most perfect butts in creation (the ancient Greeks would have deified her), it's hard to resist shooting your second load. — *Adult Video* August/September, 1986

2 any sexually transmitted infection *AUSTRALIA, 1936*
- — Thommo, *The Dictionary of Australian Swearing and Sex Sayings* 1985

load exchange *noun*
the passing of semen to its maker, mouth to mouth *US, 1972*
- — Bruce Rodgers, *The Queens' Vernacular* 1972

lob on; lob *noun*
a full or partial erection of the penis *UK, 1896*
- Well, get me dick out and give it a jostle or something, darling, I've had a lob on all the way up here. — Bushell, *The Face* 2001

lobster *noun*
an unexpected and unwelcome erection *UK, 2004*
- — Jonathan Blyth, *The Law of the Playground* 2004

local *noun*
during a massage, hand stimulation of the penis until ejaculation *US, 1972*
- — Robert A. Wilson, *Playboy's Book of Forbidden Words* 1972

log-flogger *noun*
a male masturbator *UK, 2003*
- That young log-flogger, however, was not the only one who foresaw dire consequences for his masturbatory habits. — Richard Herring, *Talking Cock* 2003

Lolita *noun*
a young teenage girl objectified sexually; a girl of any age up to the legal age of consent who dresses in a manner that is considered sexually provocative or predatory *UK, 1959*
Generic use of a proper name, after the sexually aware 12-year-old girl in Vladimir Nabokov's controversial 1955 novel *Lolita*.
- One thinks of bouncing a "Lolita" on one's lap, but hardly a big-breasted pom-pom girl of one hundred and thirty pounds. — Angelo d'Arcangelo, *The Homosexual Handbook* 1968

lollipop stop *noun*
a rest stop on a motorway known as a place where male homosexuals may be found for sexual encounters *US, 1985*
- Lollipop means penis, the principal activity being fellatio. — Wayne Dynes, *Homolexis* 1985

lolly *noun*
the vagina *BAHAMAS, 1982*
- — John A. Holm, *Dictionary of Bahamian English* 1982

long-dick *verb*
to win a woman away from another; to cuckold *US, 1994*
- Poor ol' Elroy got long-dicked, and now his wife won't even look at him. — Ken Weaver, *Texas Crude* 1984

long eye *noun*
the vulva *AUSTRALIA, 1988*
- — James McDonald, *A Dictionary of Obscenity, Taboo and Euphemism* 1988

long jump *noun*
an act of sexual intercourse *UK, 1999*
- Elvis reckoned he never believed his luck, Paulette got to give him the long jump after that. — Jeremy Cameron, *Brown Bread in Wengen* 1999

long-winded *adjective*
in homosexual usage, said of a man who takes a long time to reach orgasm *US, 1981*
- — *Male Swinger Number 3* 1981: 'The complete gay dictionary'

loop-de-loop *noun*
simultaneous, reciprocal oral sex between two people *US, 1971*
- — Eugene Landy, *The Underground Dictionary* 1971

loop joint *noun*
an arcade showing recurring pornographic videos in private booths *US, 1986*
- A woman in San Francisco who has worked as a stripper in most of the live sex shows all over the West, including loop joints and brothels in Nevada, insists that no connection exists betwen sex and violence[.] — Hunter S. Thompson, *Generation of Swine* 16th June 1986

loosie goosie *noun*
a sexually promiscuous young woman *US, 1979*
- I saw Brad weaving off through the bushes with some Loosie Goosie and

I remember laughing and thinking that now I could forget about the little padlock I'd planned on getting him for his zipper. — Beatrice Sparks, *Jay's Journal* 1979

lope *verb*
1 **to stroke** *US, 1974*
- Tompkins had such a peeny pecker he'd of had to lope it with forefinger and thumb. — Earl Thompson, *Tattoo* 1974
▶ **lope your donkey**
2 **(of a male) to masturbate** *US, 1985*
- Old Chester going "Ain't it woooooonderful" while he's loping that old rubber donkey! — Joseph Wambaugh, *The Secrets of Harry Bright* 1985
▶ **lope your mule**
3 **(of a male) to masturbate** *US, 1967*
- "Pithead's queer for soap," he told his buddies on the yard. "He sleeps with a

- Truckers who don't want solicitations from hookers, he explains, put a decal on their windshield depicting a lizard behind a red circle with a bar through it. (The creature is a reference to the slang term for truck-stop prostitutes: lot lizards.) — *Riverfront Times (St. Louis)* 6th August 2003

love button *noun*
the clitoris *US, 1994*
- Swirl your tongue around the hood, circumscribing the love button. Then get your whole mouth around her clitoris. — Amy Goddard, *Lesbian Sex Secrets for Men* 2001

love cherry *noun*
a bruise from a suction kiss *US, 1951*
- When Rocky took off his shirt I saw that he had a big red love cherry on his shoulder. — Ethel Waters, *His Eye is on the Sparrow* 1951

MASTURBATION

circle jerk *noun, US, 1958*
group male masturbation, sometimes mutual and sometimes simply a shared solitary experience
- If there are several persons present, and somehow it has been determined that all are "O.K.", a circle jerk will result. — John Francis Hunter, *The Gay Insider* 1971

dishonorable discharge *noun, US, 1964*
- When I was in the army, a sergeant caught me in the shower in the process of giving my dick a dishonorable discharge. I looked him straight in the eye and told him it was my dick and I could wash it as fast as I wanted to. — Ken Weaver, *Texas Crude* 1984

fist-fucking; fisting *noun, UK, 1891*
- FIST FUCKING! [Headline] — *Screw* 1st September 1969

hand gallop *noun, US, 1971*
- In Lewisburg he used to tell me he was saving it up, no hand-gallops for him[.] — George V. Higgins, *The Friends of Eddie Doyle* 1971

Irish wedding *noun, US, 1987*
- — *Maledicta* 1986–1987: 'A continuation of a glossary of ethnic slurs in American English'

Rosie Palm and her five sisters; Rosie Palm; Rosie *noun, US, 1977*
the male hand as the instrument of masturbation
- FRIEND: why don't you be a gentleman and ask Rosey? TED: Who? FRIEND: Rosey Palm, your girlfriend. God knows you spend enough fucking time with her. — *Something About Mary* 1998

bar under his pillow and sniffs it while he lopes his mule." — Malcolm Braly, *On the Yard* 1967

lose *verb*
▶ **lose a load**
to ejaculate *US, 1964*
- — *American Speech* May, 1964: 'Problems in the study of campus slang'

lot lizard *noun*
a prostitute who works at transport cafes *US, 1987*

love hole *noun*
the vagina *US, 1986*
- The feel of the fabric against my love-hole was making me cream again. — Penthouse Magazine, *Letters to Penthouse XXII* 2004

love juice *noun*
semen *UK, 1882*
- To man, sperm is "nature's love juice." — Anka Radakovich, *The Wild Girls Club* 1994

love lips *noun*
the vaginal labia *UK, 2003*
- Unsexy... coarse... clumsy... I mean your use of "love-lips" – oh dear! And as for "came the morning he took me again", words fail me! — *The Guardian* 5th July 2003

love machine *noun*
an energetic lover with great stamina *US, 1969*
- It's almost too good to be true. I'm a love machine. — Mantak Ciha, *The Multi-Orgasmic Man* 1996

love muffin *noun*
the vagina *UK, 2001*
- However, the category edibility glosses over the variability within it, which, for FGTs [female genital terms] included frequent reference to meat (e.g., bacon rashers, kebab, meat curtains); fish/seafood (e.g., tuna waterfall; fish, clam); and "sweet tidbits" (e.g., love muffin, fudge, cake-hole). — *Journal of Sex Research* 2001

love mussel *noun*
the vagina *US, 2001*
A neat pun on 'love muscle' (the penis) and FISH (the vagina).
- — Erica Orloff and JoAnn Baker, *Dirty Little Secrets* 2001

love nest *noun*
the vagina *US, 1994*
- In addition to oral moves, some women occasionally like a finger or two inserted into the love nest. — Anka Radakovich, *The Wild Girls Club* 1994

love nuts *noun*
testicles that ache because of sexual stimulation that has not led to ejaculation; sexual frustration *US, 1971*
- He then had to walk around for two days with his love-nuts trapped in glassware[.] — *FHM* June, 2003

love pillows *noun*
the female breasts *US, 2005*
- Dr. Bess drops her scrubs, showing us her pert li'l love-pillows. — Mr. Skin, *Mr. Skin's Skincyclopedia* 2005

love plank *noun*
the penis *UK, 2000*
Popularised in the film '*Kevin & Perry Go Large*', (2000).

- KEVIN: Suck my candy! PERRY: Lick my love plank! — Richard Topping, *Havin' It Large* 2000

love pole *noun*
the penis, *1999*
- His love pole lingered a moment at the embouchement, then glided past into the clinging folds of her sheath. — Stewart Home, *Sex Kick [britpulp]* 1999

love pump *noun*
the penis *US, 1984*
Popularised if not coined for the film *This Is Spinal Tap*.
- This piece is called "Lick My Love Pump." — Christopher Guest, *This Is Spinal Tap* 1984

lover *noun*
a prostitute's customer who is determined to arouse the prostitute's sexual interest *US, 1971*
- A "lover" is a customer who is determined to arouse the prostitute or to get her to respond to him. — Charles Winick, *The Lively Commerce* 1971

love rocket *noun*
the penis *UK, 2003*
- What do men actually say about their love rockets? — Richard Herring, *Talking Cock* 2003

lovers' nuts *noun*
testicles that ache because of sexual stimulation that has not led to ejaculation; sexual frustration *US, 1961*
- — Helen Dahlskog (Editor), *A Dictionary of Contemporary and Colloquial Usage* 1972

love sacks *noun*
the testicles *UK, 2002*
- — *A-Z of Rude Health* 11th January 2002

love sausage *noun*
the penis *US, 2001*
- — Erica Orloff and JoAnn Baker, *Dirty Little Secrets* 2001

love spuds; spuds *noun*
the testicles *UK, 1998*
- A Scottish farmer faces legal charges after his wife [...] discovered him spuds-deep in her Rhodesian Ridgeback. — *Loaded* June, 2003

lovesteak *noun*
the penis *US, 1989*
- — Pamela Munro, *U.C.L.A. Slang* 1989

love stick *noun*
the penis *US, 1924*
- She let my spent love-stick slide out of her mouth and sat up. — *Penthouse Magazine, Letters to Penthouse V* 1995

love trumpet *noun*
the penis *US, 2001*
Especially in the phrase 'blowing the love trumpet' (performing oral sex).
- — Erica Orloff and JoAnn Baker, *Dirty Little Secrets* 2001

love truncheon *noun*
the penis *UK, 1999*
- I batter her twat with my love truncheon. — Stewart Home, *Sex Kick [britpulp]* 1999

lower deck *noun*
the genitals, male or female *US, 1967*
- — Dale Gordon, *The Dominion Sex Dictionary* 1967

low-hangers *noun*
testicles that dangle well below the body *US, 2000*
Used in *Sex and the City*, a late 1990s television comedy to indicate testicles that may get in the way of sexual penetration.
- You really showed those dykes who's got the low hangers. — *Queer as Folk (US version)* 17th December 2000

low neck; low neck and short sleeves *noun*
an uncircumcised penis *US, 1941*
- — *Male Swinger Number 3* 1981: 'The complete gay dictionary'

lube *noun*
a lubricant *US, 1970*
- "So by the end of the day I totalled nine anals." "Yeeow! That must've hurt. Lotsa lube I imagine?" "Lotsa lube". — Anthony Petkovich, *The X Factory* 1997

lube job *noun*
sex *US, 1973*
- I'm in the mood for a Menage a Trois. This girl needs a Lube Job bad tonight. — Cameron Tuttle, *The Bad Girl's Guide to Getting What You Want* 2000

lucky Pierre *noun*
the man (or the woman) sandwiched between the outer layers of a sexually active threesome *US, 1942*

Glorified in the following lyric: 'Pierre gave it to Sheila, / Who must have brought it there. / He got it from Francois and Jacques, / A-ha, Lucky Pierre!' (Tom Lehrer, 'I Got It From Agnes', 1953). Predominately gay male usage.
- [C]an be substituted with a female name if the dynamics require it. "Lucky Pauline" has a certain ring to it. — *Sky Magazine* July, 2001

lunch *noun*
1 the male genitals, especially as may be hinted at or imagined when dressed *AUSTRALIA, 1944*
- — Paul Baker, *Polari* 2002

2 oral sex performed on a woman *US, 1995*
- — *Adult Video News* August, 1995

lunch *verb*
to perform oral sex *UK, 1996*
- — A.D Peterkin, *The Bald-Headed Hermit and the Artichoke* 1999

lunchbox *noun*
the male genitalia, especially when generously presented in tight clothing *UK, 1992*
An indiscreet euphemism that makes people smile; perhaps its most famous usage occurred during commentary and reports of track athlete Linford Christie's impressive performance, in figure-hugging lycra, at the 1992 Olympic Games, when he took gold in the 100 metres. Christie later claimed that references to 'Linford's lunchbox' are racial stereotyping.
- That, Gentlemen, is a lunch-box to be proud of. — *The Full Monty* 1997

lunching *noun*
the act of oral sex *UK, 1996*
- Most of the time the lunching breaks down before a full hard-on is reached. — Peter Sotos, *Index* 1996

lunchmeat *noun*
in the pornography industry, an extremely appealing and sexual woman *US, 1995*
- — *Adult Video News* August, 1995

lunch out *verb*
to perform oral sex *US, 1986*
- There, finally, Anthony let down the drawbridge whereby men could touch, or in fact lunch out on the participating strippers[.] — Josh Alan Friedman, *Tales of Times Square* 1986

lung balloons *noun*
  the female breasts *US*, *2005*
  - Lisa busts out her lung balloons and dances for a tux-clad dandy while he's taking a dump on a toilet.
    — Mr. Skin, *Mr. Skin's Skincyclopedia* 2005

lungs *noun*
  the female breasts *US*, *1951*
  - We decided that if she had gone to TCU, she would have come from Floydada with big lungs and skinny calves and a lot of chewing gum.
    — Dan Jenkins, *Semi-Tough* 1972

Mm

mack *noun*
a pimp *US, 1903*
- In being a mack, you're supposedly the supreme being of a man. Man rules woman. In being a mack, you acknowledge this fact. — Susan Hall, *Gentleman of Leisure* 1972

magic wand *noun*
the penis *UK, 1969*
- — *The Observer* 29th June 1969

maid training *noun*
the process of instructing, and conditioning the behaviour of, a sexual submissive *UK, 2003*
The submissive's menial service becomes part of a sexual relationship (in which an element of transvestism is usually implied).
- — Caroline Archer, *Tart Cards* 2003

main vein *noun*
the penis *US, 2001*
- Another way to say "penis" [...] The main vein[.] — Erica Orloff and JoAnn Baker, *Dirty Little Secrets* 2001

make *verb*
1 to seduce or have sex with *US, 1923*
- We picked up two girls, a pretty young blonde and a fat brunette. They were dumb and sullen, but we wanted to make them. — Jack Kerouac, *On the Road* 1957
▶ **make it**
2 to have sex *US, 1952*
- Once, because it seemed logical, Jessica and I had tried to make it, but the chemistry just wasn't there. — Clancy Sigal, *Going Away* 1961
▶ **make smiles**
3 to have sex *UK, 2003*
- Making smiles with Gloria had left me famished. — Jonathan Gash, *The Ten Word Game* 2003

male beaver *noun*
featuring shots of the naked male genitals *US, 1969*
- I was viewing two hours of male beaver films. — *Screw* 31st July 1969

mams *noun*
the female breasts *US, 2005*
- A-N bares her legendary mams in bed, then lights up the screen with her magnificent seat-meat as she rises to join Jack Nicholson in the shower. — Mr. Skin, *Mr. Skin's Skincyclopedia* 2005

man *noun*
a pimp *US, 1973*
- Sometimes me and my man Daddy drive up Park Avenue in his car. — Susan Hall, *Ladies of the Night* 1973

M and G track *noun*
in a pornographic film, additions to the sound track amplifying moans and groans *US, 1991*
- They [later with editing] put in a groan. The M and G track. — Robert Stoller and I.S. Levine, *Coming Attractions* 1991

man-eater *noun*
a woman with a strong sexual appetite *UK, 1906*
- (Oh-oh, here she comes) Watch out boy she'll chew you up / (Oh-oh, here she comes) She's a maneater. — Hall & Oates *Maneater* 1982

manhole *noun*
the vagina *US, 1916*
- Had some dope shoved in her manhole? — *alt.prisons* 17th November 1998

manhole cover *noun*
a sanitary napkin *US, 1948*
- "Hey. You Gals want to loan me a Sanitary Napkin to staunch the flow? That's right. Those Manhole Covers!" — *alt.utensils.spork* 27th June 2000

manhood *noun*
the penis *UK, 1997*
- Veronica squeezed his manhood so hard he almost winced. — Colin Butts, *Is Harry on the Boat?* 1997

man meat *noun*
the penis *US, 2005*
- It's sort of dark (and there's a lot of man meat in the shot). — Mr. Skin, *Mr. Skin's Skincyclopedia* 2005

man oil *noun*
semen *US, 1949*
- — Captain Vincent J. Monteleone, *Criminal Slang* 1949

manthrax *noun*
unfaithful men *US, 2002*
A combination of 'man' and 'anthrax' coined
for *Sex and the City*, a late 1990s television
comedy.
- — *The Times* 27th July 2002

manual exercises *noun*
masturbation *US, 1964*
- — Roger Blake, *The American Dictionary of Sexual Terms* 1964

manual release *noun*
manual stimulation of a man's genitals *US, 1996*
- The rates are $20 for the manual release, $30 for the manual release with top off, $40 for manual release with top and bottom off. — James Ridgeway, *Red Light* 1996

maracas *noun*
the female breasts *US, 1940*
- See, Lola shakes her maracas, and Rosa bounces her bongos, while Nena is all hands. — Barbara Novak, *Down with Love* 2003

marbles *noun*
the testicles *US, 1916*
- — James McDonald, *A Dictionary of Obscenity, Taboo and Euphemism* 1988

marking *noun*
a welt or bruise produced in sadomasochistic sex *US, 1987*
- Sometimes a man will want "markings" to jog his fantasies if he travels or lives alone. — Frederique Delacoste, *Sex Work* 1987

Marmite motorway *noun*
the rectum *UK, 2003*
From 'marmite' (excrement).
- — Chris Lewis, *The Dictionary of Playground Slang* 2003

marshmallows *noun*
1 the female breasts *US, 1971*
- — Eugene Landy, *The Underground Dictionary* 1971
2 the testicles *US, 1971*
- — Eugene Landy, *The Underground Dictionary* 1971

masher *noun*
a person who takes sexual pleasure from physical contact with strangers in crowded places *US, 1875*
- — Anon., *King Smut's Wet Dreams Interpreted* 1978

massage *noun*
sexual services *US, 2001*
- Melanie specialising in the moodiest massages in town. — John King, *White Trash* 2001

masturbation mansion *noun*
a movie theatre showing pornographic films *US, 1972*
- The early skin-flick houses became known humorously among much of the trade as "masturbation mansions." — Roger Blake, *What you always wanted to know about porno-movies* 1972

matinee *noun*
a sexual encounter in the mid-afternoon *US, 1944*
- From theatrical usage and a 1930s recipe for an ideal marriage: "Once a day, plus matinee." — Robert A. Wilson, *Playboy's Book of Forbidden Words* 1972

mattress *noun*
a sexually active, promiscuous girl from a nearby village *CANADA, 1992*
- The Mattress was the nickname of a girl who was sexy, easy, promiscuous in a nearby village in the Eastern Townships of Quebec. — Lewis Poteet, *Talking Country* 1992

mattressback *noun*
a promiscuous woman *US, 1960*
- "Mattressback!" — John Barth, *The Sot-Weed Factor* 1960

mattress joint *noun*
a hotel catering to prostitutes *US, 1956*
- When the clerk in a mattress joint like the Beloit was reluctant to furnish the police with a guest's room number, the pressure was really on. — *Rogue for Men* June, 1956

Mavis Fritter *noun*
the anus *UK, 2003*
Rhyming slang with shitter.
- If I ask you nicely will you take it up the Mavis? — Bodmin Dark, *Dirty Cockney Rhyming Slang* 2003

meat *noun*
1 the penis *UK, 1595*
- Ron Jeremy is sucked off before ramming his meat into Patti Petite in Blonde on the Run. — *Adult Video* August/September, 1986

2 the vagina *US, 1973*
- — Ruth Todasco et al., *The Intelligent Woman's Guide to Dirty Words* 1973

meat *verb*
▶ **be on a meat-free diet**
to be a lesbian *UK, 1995*
A euphemism formed on **MEAT** (the penis).
- "She's on a meat free diet, that one," she said. I told Gladys I didn't understand why the caretaker's vegetarianism was worthy of a mention. "No, she's a lesbian," said Gladys. — Kitty Churchill, *Thinking of England* 1995

meat curtains *noun*
the vagina *UK, 2001*
- However, the category edibility glosses over the variability within it, which, for FGTs [female genital terms] included frequent reference to meat (e.g., bacon rashers, kebab, meat curtains); fish/seafood (e.g., tuna waterfall; fish, clam); and "sweet tidbits" (e.g., love muffin, fudge, cake-hole). — *Journal of Sex Research* 2001

meat district *noun*
an area where sex is available *US, 1984*
- Down Forty-Second Street, through the meat district. — Jay McInerney, *Bright Lights, Big City* 1984

meat mag *noun*
a homoerotic, often pornographic, magazine *US, 1979*
- — *Maledicta* 1979: 'Kinks and queens: linguistic and cultural aspects of the terminology for gays'

meat market *noun*
a place where people gather with sexual activity as a stated primary goal *US, 1998*
- And we don't go to meat markets to buy drinks for dick teasers. — Dan Savage, *Savage Love* 1998

meat puppet *noun*
the penis *UK, 2003*
- I landed on the handle of the cart and hurt my meat puppet. — Richard Herring, *Talking Cock* 2003

meat rack *noun*
1 the female breasts *US, 2005*
- Check out that meat rack! — Mr. Skin, *Mr. Skin's Skincyclopedia* 2005
2 a restaurant, bar or other public place where people gather in search of sexual partners *US, 1962*

- Soon, we got up, walked around the west side – toward the "meat rack" – the gay part of the park. — John Rechy, *City of Night* 1963

meat seat *noun*
the vagina *UK, 2001*
- Abjection was invoked in various ways: through reference to dirtiness (e.g., front bum, dirt box), uncooked (bloody?) meat (e.g., meat seat, chopped liver), vaginal secretions of all types (e.g., slushing fuck pit, the snail trail), smell (e.g., smelly hole, stench trench), and wounds (e.g., gash, gaping axe wound). — *Journal of Sex Research* 2001

meat shot *noun*
a photograph or scene in a pornographic film focusing on a penis *US, 1974*
- Despite the relative absence of hardcore action in it – some oral sex and an occasional discreet meat shot – Little Sisters ran into some legal trouble[.] — Kenneth Turan and Stephen E. Zito, *Sinema* 1974

meat whistle *noun*
the penis *US, 1965*
- "What're you going to do on the variety show," Red wanted to know. "Perform on the meat whistle?" — Malcolm Braly, *On the Yard* 1967

meat with two vegetables; meat and two veg *noun*
the penis and testicles *US, 1964*
- One storey down / Is the maestro James Brown / Displaying his meat and two veg. — *I'm Sorry I Haven't a Clue, the Official Limerick Collection* 1998

mechanic *noun*
an accomplished, skilled lover *US, 1985*
- "Mechanic" – a man who's good with his bird [penis]; a ladies' man. — *Washington Post* 17th January 1985

medical shot *noun*
in a pornographic movie, an extreme close-up of genitals *US, 1977*
- Use your first camera from a more or less fixed position, and your handheld camera for the ever-important closeups, or, as some refer to them, the "medical shots." — Stephen Ziplow, *The Film Maker's Guide to Pornography* 1977

melons noun
 large female breasts US, 1957
 ● I remember lying in bed one morning, staring at my new developments and wondering, "Who ordered the melons?" — Anka Radakovich, *The Wild Girls Club* 1994

menage à moi noun
 an act of female masturbation UK, 2004
 ● — Michelle Baker and Steven Tropiano, *Queer Facts* 2004

● — David McGill, *David McGill's Complete Kiwi Slang Dictionary* 1998

mickey noun
 the penis IRELAND, 1909
 ● [D]o you agree that the average Irish man is an indolent shit-bag who never thinks about anything but his gut and his mickey[?] — Joseph O'Connor, *The Irish Make at Home and Abroad* 1996

ORGASM

Big O noun, US, 1968
 ● Then, just as I was about to reach the big O, shrieking with pleasure, he hurled me down the stairs[.] — Gore Vidal, *Myra Breckinridge* 1968

bust verb, US, 1964
 ▶ **bust your nut**
 ● She lay with her arms spread, like a female Christ or a woman who has just busted her nuts[.] — Clarence Cooper Jr, *The Farm* 1967

come; cum verb, UK, 1600
 to experience an orgasm
 ● In a jiff I was in; but for some strange reason I couldn't come; all 19-year-old cockmasters can't come, you know this as

well as I do. — Jack Kerouac, *Letter to Neal Cassady* 10th January 1951

pop verb, US, 1969
 ▶ **pop your nuts**
 ● [A] girl is more likely to pop her nuts with a prick buried in her tail than in her mouth. — Juan Carmel Cosmes, *Memoir of a Whoremaster* 1969

shoot verb, US, 1972
 ▶ **shoot your wad**
 to ejaculate
 ● Did you get any action? Did you slam it to her? Did you stick her? Did you hump her? Did you run it down her throat? Did you jam it up her ass? Did you shoot your wad? — *Screw* 29th may 1972

menu noun
 the list of services available in a brothel US, 1993
 ● The menu can help "break the ice" for first-timers, and is a conversation piece[.] — J.R. Schwartz, *The Official Guide to the Best Cat Houses in Nevada* 1993

mercy fuck noun
 sex motivated by a sense of pity US, 1968
 ● Why hadn't she at least given Adam a decent kiss on the lips, a mercy kiss – the way Beverly bestowed her mercy fucks, or so she claimed – instead of that pathetic little vesper-service peck on the cheek? — Tom Wolfe, *I Am Charlotte Williams* 2004

michael noun
 the vagina NEW ZEALAND, 1998
 ● — David McGill, *David McGill's Complete Kiwi Slang Dictionary* 1998

mick noun
 the vagina NEW ZEALAND, 1998

middle leg noun
 the penis UK, 1896
 Still in popular use.
 ● — *Roger's Profanisaurus* 2002

midnight cowboy noun
 a homosexual prostitute, originally one who wears cowboy clothes; hence a homosexual man US, 1972
 Brought from gay subculture into wider use by the film *Midnight Cowboy*, 1969. The less subtle, general sense resulted from the film's success.
 ● The clothes chosen by the fetishists epitomize masculinity: cowboys, sailors, etc. The model acting out the cowboy then is a midnight cowboy[.] — Bruce Rodgers, *The Queens' Vernacular* 1972

Mile High Club noun
 a collective noun for people who claim to have had sex on an airborne plane US, 1972
 A notional association of people who claim to have had sex on an airborne plane.

- I made a few attempts at trying to charm the hostesses into initiating us into their legendary "Mile High Club" but they weren't wearing it. — Dean Cavanagh, *Mile High Meltdown (Disco Biscuits)* 1996

milf; MILF *noun*
a sexually appealing mother *US, 1999*
- "Dude, that chick's a MILF." "What the hell is that?" "Mom I'd like to fuck." — *American Pie* 1999

milk *verb*
1 to masturbate *UK, 1616*
- — Helen Dahlskog (Editor), *A Dictionary of Contemporary and Colloquial Usage* 1972
▶ **milk it**
2 to squeeze the shaft of the penis towards the head of the penis *US, 1978*
- — Anon., *King Smut's Wet Dreams Interpreted* 1978
▶ **milk the anaconda**
3 (of a male) to masturbate *US, 1985*
- A signal meant they'd caught some guy milking the anaconda. — Joseph Wambaugh, *The Secrets of Harry Bright* 1985
▶ **milk the lizard**
4 (of a male) to masturbate *UK, 1997*
- [L]ooks at the pictures and milks his lizard. — Tami Hoag, *The Thin Line* 1997

milk route *noun*
▶ **do the milk route**
as a prostitute, to visit late-night venues in search of customers *US, 1987*
- — *Maledicta* Summer/Winter, 1986–1987: 'Sexual slang: prostitutes, pedophiles, flagellators, transvestites, and necrophiles'

milkshake *noun*
oral sex performed on a male *NEW ZEALAND, 1998*
- — David McGill, *David McGill's Complete Kiwi Slang Dictionary* 1998

millennium domes *noun*
female breasts that are enhanced to misleading dimensions *UK, 2002*
After the UK's much criticised celebration of 2000 years: the Millennium Dome.
- The contents of a Wonderbra, i.e. like the dome, extremely impressive when viewed from the outside, but there's actually fuck-all in there worth seeing. — Chris Lewis, *The Dictionary of Playground Slang* 2003

minge *noun*
1 the vagina *UK, 1903*
From the Latin *mingere* (to urinate) and the mistaken belief that urine passes through the vagina.
- If nothing else, most women will feel they have cut their losses if you get down there and lick her minge! — Richard Herring, *Talking Cock* 2003
2 the pubic hair *UK, 1903*
Extends from the previous sense to include the general pubic area. A natural redhead is known as a 'ginger minge'.
- [A] little contest to see who can shave their minge in the most eye-catching way. — Kevin Sampson, *Outlaws* 2001

mini-moo *noun*
the vagina *UK, 2001*
'Moo' (an unpleasant woman) playing on Mini-Me, the miniature alter-ego of the villainous Dr. Evil in the film *Austin Powers, The Spy Who Shagged Me*, 1999.
- — *Sky Magazine* July, 2001

minky *noun*
the vagina *UK, 2001*
- Nonsense slang referred to vague, inoffensive terms that had little or no meaning in standard English: terms like biff, foo-foo, minky and winkie in FGTs [female genital terms], and chod, dongce, spondoolies and winks in MGTs [male genital terms]. — *Journal of Sex Research* 2001

Minnesota mule *noun*
a prostitute recently arrived in New York City from a small town or city *US, 1987*
- — *Maledicta* Summer/Winter, 1986–1987: 'Sexual slang: prostitutes, pedophiles, flagellators, transvestites, and necrophiles'

Minnie Mouse *noun*
of a woman, the pubic hair *UK, 2003*
- Tommy [Ford of Gucci] can persuade model Louise Pedersen to pose with a 'G' shaved in her Minnie Mouse[.] — *The Guardian* 24th May 2003

minty *adjective*
homosexual, effeminate *US, 1965*
- Freddy was just a minty cunt. — Kevin Sampson, *Outlaws* 2001

miracle meat *noun*
a penis that is almost as large flaccid as erect *US, 1970*

● — *American Speech* Spring-Summer, 1970: 'Homosexual slang'

misfire *noun*
an instance of sexual impotence or premature ejaculation *US, 1981*
● Perhaps Al Mackey's misfire at the Chinatown motel was inevitable. — Joseph Wambaugh, *The Glitter Dome* 1981

mish *noun*
the missionary position for sexual intercourse – man on top of prone woman *US, 1995*
● After a steamy run munch and a wicked b.j., they engage in some nut-slappin' mish capped off with – you guess it – major anal penetration. — *Adult Video News* August, 1995

miss *verb*
▶ **miss the pink and pot the brown**
to engage in heterosexual anal intercourse *UK, 1997*
A snooker metaphor playing on 'pink' (the open vagina) and 'brown' (the anus).
● Yeah, y'know, threesomes, missing the pink and potting the brown. — Colin Butts, *Is Harry on the Boat?* 1997

Miss Palmer and her five daughters *noun*
masturbation *BAHAMAS, 1971*
● — John A. Holm, *Dictionary of Bahamian English* 1982

Mister Floppy; Mr Floppy *noun*
the penis that has become flaccid when an erection is to be preferred *UK, 2003*
● [A]nxiety causes us to say hello to Mr Floppy[.] — Richard Herring, *Talking Cock* 2003

Mister Foot; Mr Foot *noun*
the penis *UK, 2001*
● — *Sky Magazine* July, 2001

Mister Geezer; Mr Geezer *noun*
the penis *US, 2001*
Both parts of this combination indicate 'a man'.
● Sure would make me feel a lot happier if I didn't have to worry about seeing your Mr Geezer hanging out of your boxer shorts. — Janet Evanovich, *Seven Up* 2001

Mister Happy; Mr Happy *noun*
the penis *US, 1984*

Adopted from the character created by UK cartoonist Roger Hargreaves (1935–88) for his *Mr Men* children's books.
● She reached down and grabbed his cock. "How's Mr Happy?" — Garry Bushell, *The Face* 2001

Mister Nasty; Mr Nasty *noun*
the penis *US, 2001*
● A while back, after a short consultation with his johnson [penis], Vinnie agreed to hire Joyce [...] Mr. Nasty was still happy with the decision, but the rest of Vinnie didn't know what to do with Joyce. — Janet Evanovich, *Seven Up* 2001

Mister Softy; Mr Softy *noun*
a flaccid penis *US, 1995*
● — *Adult Video News* September, 1995

moneymaker *noun*
the genitals; the buttocks *UK, 1896*
● Shuck my clothes an hop in that fabbroom, take a fullout shower, wash the jail off my skin an the funk outa my moneymaker. — Robert Gover, *JC Saves* 1968

money shot *noun*
a scene in a pornographic film or photograph of a man ejaculating outside his partner *US, 1977*
Perhaps because it is the one shot that justifies the cost of the scene.
● LEE: We gotta see arses goin' up and down. MOON: Gotta see that mate. JAMIE: Just not my bollocks 'angin' down. MOON: An' push 'er out the way for the money shot. — Chris Baker and Andrew Day, *Lock, Stock... & Spaghetti Sauce* 2000

Mongolian clusterfuck *noun*
an orgy *US, 1986*
● I'm startin' to feel like the bottom man in a Mongolian cluster fuck. — James Ellroy, *Suicide Hill* 1986

monkey *noun*
1 the vagina *US, 1888*
● — Charles Shafer, *Folk Speech in Texas Prisons* 1990
▶ **marinate the monkey**
2 to perform oral sex *US, 2001*
● Another way to say "fellatio" [...] Marinating the monkey[.] — Erica Orloff and JoAnn Baker, *Dirty Little Secrets* 2001

monkey box *noun*
the vagina *US, 1998*
- There's [a...] "toadie," "dee dee," "nishi," "dignity," "monkey box["."]
— Eve Ensler, *The Vagina Monologues* 1998

monkey spank *noun*
of a male, an act of masturbation *UK, 2005*
- There's a bishop's bash, a Jodrell Bank, a slimey slap and a monkey spank[.]
— Anonymous *Blasphemy* August, 2005

monster *noun*
an extremely unattractive woman who is seen as a sex object, especially one who is ravaged by age *UK, 2002*
- I'll admit it. I like Monsters. I don't mind saying so. You know exactly where the fuck you are with a Monster.
— Kevin Sampson, *Clubland* 2002

monster munch *noun*
the vagina *UK, 2001*
Derives, probably, from Monster Munch™, a branded savoury snack food.
- — *Sky Magazine* July, 2001

monster shot *noun*
in pornography, a close-up shot of genitals *US, 1970*
- And he [Randy] is rock hard. So we go monster shots, the graphic close-up.
— Robert Stoller and I.S. Levine, *Coming Attractions* 1991

moonshot *noun*
1 anal sex *US, 1972*
- — Robert A. Wilson, *Playboy's Book of Forbidden Words* 1972
2 outdoor sex at night *US, 1986*
- [A]nd who was to say that they might not be able to go to the powder room simultaneously, and thereby slip off for a ten-minute moonshot? — Dan Jenkins, *Dead Solid Perfect* 1986

mop booth *noun*
a private booth where pornographic films are shown for a fee *US, 2001*
- If public pudpulling is your thing, try a "spooge booth" or "mop booth."
— Rob Cohen, *Etiquette for Outlaws* 2001

mop-up boy *noun*
a worker performing janitorial work at an arcade where men masturbate while watching videos *US, 1997*

- It's not fair. If you're the mop-up boy at a peep show, it's obvious the government is not working for you.
— Chris Rock, *Rock This!* 1997

more pricks than a pincushion
an alleged achievement of a promiscuous woman *AUSTRALIA, 1971*
- Your little Aussie rosebud has had more pricks than a pincushion.
— Barry Humphries, *Bazza Pulls It Off!* 1971

moresome *noun*
in the context of consensual group sex, an indeterminate number *UK, 2006*
- Swinging and the terms threesomes, foursomes and moresomes are all synonyms for the same phenomenon[.] — Ashley Lister, *Swingers* 2006

morning glory *noun*
an erection upon waking up in the morning *UK, 1992*
Rhyming slang for COREY (the penis), formed from the name of a popular garden flower (*Ipomoea violacea*).
- Elaine stubbed her fag out and sunk under the duvet to nosh amicably on his morning glory. — Garry Bushell, *The Face* 2001

morning wood *noun*
an erection experienced upon waking *US, 1997*
- — Pamela Munro, *U.C.L.A. Slang* 1997

morphy *noun*
an hermaphrodite *BARBADOS, 1965*
- — Frank A. Collymore, *Barbadian Dialect* 1965

mossback *noun*
a promiscuous girl *US, 1982*
- — Connie Eble (Editor), *UNC-CH Campus Slang* Spring, 1982

mother-fucking *noun*
sexual intercourse between a son and his mother *UK, 2000*
The literal sense which precedes the rest.
- These women are usually fat with grey hair and tightly packed into puce or black stretch-velour dresses. A man would have to be seriously into mother-fucking to want any of them. — Fiona Pitt-Kethley, *Red Light Districts of the World* 2000

mother thumb and her four lovely daughters
noun
the hand in the context of masturbation *US*,
1967
- It originates from the old Army barracks
shenanigan where you hear a comrade
entertaining Mother Thumb and her
Four Lovely Daughters. — Ken Kesey,
Kesey's Jail Journal 1967

mott *noun*
the female genitalia *UK*, *1984*
- "Her great big, hairy mott", in a mock-
Irish accent was a pun on the insect
moth. — Beale (remembering his mid-
C20 National Service), 1984

mouthfuck *verb*
to take the active role in oral sex *UK*, *1866*
- She wanted me to mouthfuck her and
I kept wondering when she would want
me to pull out to pull down her pants
and fuck her ass from behind.
— J. Price Vincenz, *Anything That
Moves* 2001

mowed lawn *noun*
a shaved vulva *US*, *1964*
- — Robert A. Wilson, *Playboy's Book of
Forbidden Words* 1972

**Mrs Palm and her five lovely daughters; Mrs
Palmer and her five daughters** *noun*
the hand (seen in the context of male
masturbation) *AUSTRALIA*, *1955*
- Oh, Mrs Palm and your five lovely
daughters / Thank you for having me
and being oh, so kind[.] — Ivor Biggun,
The Winker's Song (Misprint) 1978

MSM *noun*
homosexual males *UK*, *1998*
Initialism formed from '*m*en who have *s*ex
with *m*en'.
- — David Rowan, *A Glossary for the 90s*
1998

muck *noun*
semen *UK*, *1997*
- Mario was very much in the dump-me-
muck-and-turf-'em-out camp, whereas
Arabella belonged to the doey-eyed-
let's-have-a-cuddle-and-plan-the-rest-of-
the-day-together school of thought.
— Colin Butts, *Is Harry Still on the
Boat?* 2003

muddy fuck *noun*
anal sex that brings forth faeces or faecal
stains on the penis *US*, *1979*

- — *Maledicta* 1979: 'Kinks and queens:
linguistic and cultural aspects of the
terminology for gays'

mudkicker *noun*
a prostitute, especially of the street-walking
variety *US*, *1932*
- She was three-quarter Kelsey with
mossy glossy hair / she was a
stompdown mudkicker and her mug
was fair. — Bruce Jackson, *Get Your Ass
in the Water and Swim Like Me* 1964

muff *noun*
1 the vulva; a woman as a sex object *UK*,
1699
- "She's maybe got more moves than
you or me got." "That's because she's
got a pair of tits and a muff."
— RobertCampbell, *Juice* 1988
▶ **buff the muff**
2 to manually stimulate a woman's genitals
US, *1999*
- I even got to the point where I could
pop during sex – but only if somebody
was buffing the muff while we were
going at it. — Amy Sohn, *Run Catch
Kiss* 1999

muff *verb*
to perform oral sex on a woman *US*, *1968*
- I just happen to know a guy who
muffed her. — L. Reinhard, *Oral Sex
Techniques and Sex Practices Illustrated*
196

muff-diver *noun*
a person who performs oral sex on a
woman *US*, *1930*
- Jack said to Jimmy I could tell just by
looking at you you're a muff diver[.]
— William T. Vollman, *Whores for Gloria*
1991

muffin *noun*
a woman objectified sexually *US*, *1870*
- I know your sort you see Nicky. Men
you know they do always like a bit of
muffin on the side as you say. Always.
— Jeremy Cameron, *Brown Bread in
Wengen* 1999

muff job *noun*
oral sex on a woman *US*, *1990*
- — Charles Shafer, *Folk Speech in Texas
Prisons* 1990

muffler burn *noun*
a bruise on the skin caused by sucking *US*,
1982

Hawaiian youth usage.
- I got dis muffler burn las' night Diamon' Head! — Douglas Simonson, *Pidgin to da Max Hana Hou* 1982

muff mag *noun*
a magazine featuring photographs of naked women, focusing on their pubic hair and vulvas *US, 1972*
- (Headline) Muff Mags for the Meat and Potatoes Man — *Screw* 3rd July 1972

muff merchant *noun*
a procurer of prostitutes; a man who makes his living off the earnings of prostitutes *US, 1987*
- — *Maledicta* Summer/Winter, 1986–1987: 'Sexual slang: prostitutes, pedophiles, flagellators, transvestites, and necrophiles'

munch *verb*
▶ **munch the trunch**
to perform oral sex on a man *UK, 2003*
Formed on an abbreviation of 'truncheon', as in LOVE TRUNCHEON.
- — Chris Lewis, *The Dictionary of Playground Slang* 2003

mungers *noun*
the female breasts, especially when of above average dimensions *UK, 2003*
Possibly derived from 'humungous'.
- — Chris Lewis, *The Dictionary of Playground Slang* 2003

munter; munta; munt *noun*
an unattractive person who adds to the personal allure with drunkenness and/or promiscuity, especially but not exclusively of young women *UK, 1998*
Student usage.
- A munter is a drunk minger. — Lucy Kenyon Jones, 7th July 2002

mustache ride *noun*
an act of oral sex *US, 1981*

- Another way to say "cunnilingus" [...] Giving her a moustache ride[.] — Erica Orloff and JoAnn Baker, *Dirty Little Secrets* 2001

mustache rider *noun*
a woman as the object of oral sex with a man *AUSTRALIA, 1985*
- — Thommo, *The Dictionary of Australian Swearing and Sex Sayings* 1985

mustard pot *noun*
the vagina *UK, 1896*
Rhyming slang for 'twot' (TWAT).
- — Ray Puxley, *Cockney Rabbit* 1992

mustard road *noun*
▶ **up the mustard road**
engaging in some form of anal sex *US, 1972*
- [W]hat really hurt was being taken up the old mustard road without KY by the one individual I had actually trusted. — R.J. Pineiro, *Havoc* 2005

mute *noun*
the vagina *UK, 1972*
- — Bruce Rodgers, *Queens' Vernacular* 1972

mutton *noun*
the penis *AUSTRALIA, 1971*
- — Barry Humphries, *Bazza Pulls It Off!* 1971

mutton flaps *noun*
the *labia majora* NEW ZEALAND, 1998
- — David McGill, *David McGill's Complete Kiwi Slang Dictionary* 1998

mutton merchant *noun*
a male sexual exhibitionist *AUSTRALIA, 1971*
- I hope he's not a perve or a mutton merchant! — Barry Humphries, *Bazza Pulls It Off!* 1971

Nn

nadgers *noun*
the testicles *UK, 1998*
Possibly deriving from 'gonads', and with a similarity to KNACKERS, 'nadgers' was an all-purpose nonsense word used by the radio comedy series *The Goon Show* during the 1950s.
- The Pole chose to knock Bowe out by hitting him in the nadgers with a punishing three-punch salvo. — *FHM* June, 2003

nads *noun*
the testicles *US, 1964*
From 'gonads'.
- [T]o protect the innocent – ie, his newly shackled nads from the wrath of his young bride. — *FHM* June, 2003

nail *verb*
to have sex *US, 1957*
- Name me one chick in our senior class that Rick Derris didn't nail, for Christ's sake. — *Chasing Amy* 1997

na-na's *noun*
the female breasts *US, 2005*
- Maddy shows off an extremely fluffy muff as her kissy sissy nuzzles her na-nas. — Mr. Skin, *Mr. Skin's Skincyclopedia* 2005

nanny *noun*
a prostitute who will, by arrangement, dress and treat a client as an infant *UK, 2003*
- — Caroline Archer, *Tart Cards* 2003

nappy dugout *noun*
(of a black woman) the vagina *US, 1998*
- There's [a...] "wee wee," "horsespot," "nappy dugout," "mongo[".] — Eve Ensler, *The Vagina Monologues* 1998

nards *noun*
the male genitals *US, 1970*
- [F]reezing my nards off every weekend. — Frank Zappa, *The Real Frank Zappa Book* 1989

nasty *noun*
1 the vagina *NEW ZEALAND, 1998*
A usage that calls to mind Grose's definition of c**t – 'a nasty name for a nasty thing'.

- — David McGill, *David McGill's Complete Kiwi Slang Dictionary* 1998
2 the penis *AUSTRALIA, 1971*
- He's flashin' his flamin' nasty!!! — Barry Humphries, *Bazza Pulls It Off!* 1971
▶ **do the nasty**
3 to have sex *US, 1977*
A squeamish euphemism applied in a jocular manner.
- "He really dating your grandma? [...] Think they did the nasty?" I almost ran the car up on the sidewalk. "No! Yuck!" — Janet Evanovich, *Seven Up* 2001

nasty *adjective*
sexy, attractive, appealing; sluttish *US, 1995*
- And they're Nasty, the kind of girls who want their tasty butts spanked before they drink cum! — Peter Sotos, *Index* 1996

nasty-nasty *noun*
sex *US, 1993*
- — Judi Sanders, *Faced and Faded, Hanging to Hurl* 1993

nates *noun*
the buttocks *US, 1993*
- — J.R. Schwartz, *The Official Guide to the Best Cat Houses in Nevada* 1993: 'Sex glossary'

naughty *verb*
to have sex *AUSTRALIA, 1961*
- — Harry Orsman, *A Dictionary of Modern New Zealand Slang* 1999

naughty Nazi salute *noun*
the fully erect penis *UK, 2003*
A parallel with the arm raised stiffly from the body at a similar angle.
- For most of us, failure to execute the naughty Nazi salute is an ego-crushing disaster[.] — Richard Herring, *Talking Cock* 2003

Navy cake *noun*
homosexual anal sex *US, 1964*
- — Anon, *King Smut's Wet Dreams Interpreted* 1978

nay-nays *noun*
a woman's breasts *US, 1967*
- You know, in the backs of those "Fun Shops," you'll see guys looking through racks and racks of pictures of ladies' nay-nays wrapped in cellophane. — Lenny Bruce, *The Essential Lenny Bruce* 1967

neat *adjective + adverb*
(said of sex) without a condom *US, 1997*
- I am totally shocked, let me tell you, that you fucked him neat. Just because he doesn't understand condoms — Ethan Morden, *Some Men Are Lookers* 1997

necro *noun*
a necrophile *US, 1987*
- — *Maledicta* Summer/Winter, 1986–1987: 'Sexual slang: prostitutes, pedophiles, flagellators, transvestites, and necrophiles'

needledick *noun*
a small, thin penis; a man so equipped *US, 1970*

- [F]or some reason the idea of circle jerking [participating in group male masturbation] with a needle-dicked lard-arse didn't appeal. — Kitty Churchill, *Thinking of England* 1995

nerps *noun*
the female breasts *US, 2005*
- Little Nel shows her not-so-little nerps with Roger Daltrey and Ringo Starr. — Mr. Skin, *Mr. Skin's Skincyclopedia* 2005

Niagara Falls; niagaras *noun*
the testicles *UK, 1943*
Rhyming slang.
- I'd like to believe that coming upon me in the boudoir nakedly inspecting the

ORAL SEX

BJ *noun, US, 1949*
an act of oral sex, a blow job
- And what should be this film's finest sex scene, the finale between Ashlyn and Jamie, turns out to be mainly a simple b.j. ending in a facia. — *Adult Video News* February, 1993

box lunch; box lunch at the Y *noun, US, 1964*
The character Y resembles a woman's groin and plays on **box** (the vagina).
- [C]omments such as "likes to make," "frigid," "the picture does her too much justice," "box lunch," "a real roller," "get laid," ad infinitum. — John Nichols, *The Sterile Cuckoo* 1965

cunt-lapping *noun, US, 1970*
- Is Cunt-Lapping Better Than the Pill? (Headline) — *Screw* 22nd March 1970

deep throat *noun, US, 1991*
oral sex performed on a man in which the person doing the performing takes the penis completely into their mouth and throat
A term from the so-named 1972 classic pornography film.
- Once you've mastered the basic techniques of fellatio and cunnilingus, you might want to experiment with '69', deep throat and

other oral tricks for adventurous lovers! — Siobhan Kelly, *The Wild Guide to Sex and Loving* 2002

face *noun, US, 1968*
- — Inez Cardozo-Freeman, *The Joint* 1984

half and half *noun, US, 1937*
oral sex on a man followed by vaginal intercourse
- When Nicole came into the kitchen she was naked except for her red shirt. — You want a half-and-half? she said. — William T. Vollman, *Whores for Gloria* 1991

head *noun, US, 1941*
- Connie probably takes Raymond's little peanut of a cock between her brittle chapped lips and then scrapes her ugly decayed teeth up and down on it while asshole Raymond thinks he's getting the best head on the East Coast. — John Waters, *Pink Flamingos* 1972

suckee-suckee *noun, US, 1987*
From the patois of Vietnamese prostitutes during the war, embraced by soldiers.
- Me suckee-suckee. My love you too much. — *Full Metal Jacket* 1987

- You paddy motherfuckers never make me feel nothin' with yo' needle dicks. — Joseph Wambaugh, *The New Centurions* 1970

needle-dicked *adjective*
endowed with a small penis *UK, 1995*

Niagaras of another man had sent a sudden rush of jealousy coursing through his veins[.] — Kitty Churchill, *Thinking of England* 1995

niggle *verb*
to have sex *US, 1962*

● — Joseph E. Ragen and Charles Finston,
Inside the World's Toughest Prison
1962: 'Penitentiary and underworld
glossary'

niner *noun*
an erect penis that is nine inches long *UK,*
1997
● I reckon it's gorra be 'eading for a
niner. maybe a bit more. And 'e's got
a massive bell end. — Colin Butts, *Is
Harry on the Boat?* 1997

ninety-six *noun*
reciprocal anal sex *US, 1949*
● — Anon., *The Gay Girl's Guide* 1949

ninny *noun*
the vagina or vulva *BAHAMAS, 1982*
● — John A. Holm, *Dictionary of
Bahamian English* 1982

nip *noun*
a nipple, especially a woman's *US, 1965*
The nickname given to the character Elaine
Benes (played by Julia Louis-Dreyfus) on
Seinfeld (NBC, 1990–98) after a snapshot
that she took for a Christmas card showed
a breast nipple.
● She was a healthy-looking bitch,
a jogger type with a great rack ...
a couple of real pointers. And I'm not
talking about a bra with rubber nipples.
I'm talking about a pair of honest-to-
Christ pointed nips that must have
weighed as much as silver dollars.
— Gerald Petievich, *To Die in Beverly
Hills* 1983

nippers *noun*
the female breasts *US, 1968*
● — Collin Baker et al., *College
Undergraduate Slang Study Conducted
at Brown University* 1968

nippie *noun*
the nipple *UK, 1997*
● Because I want to lick your chocolate
button nippies. — Bernadine Evaristo,
Lara 1997

nip slip *noun*
a photograph revealing at least a part of
a woman's nipple *US, 2004*
The premise is that the reveal is accidental;
major usage of the term on Internet photograph sites.
● Now that some of the initial shock of
the Jackson nip slip is over, she said:
"The audience decided they wanted to

see these artists." — *Daily News
(New York)* 26th February 2004

nitty-clitty *noun*
oral sex on a woman *US, 1975*
● [G]et down to the nitty-clitty. — Xaviera
Hollander, *The Best Part of a Man*
1975

nixies *noun*
a female undergarment with a cut-out
crotch permitting vaginal sex while
otherwise clothed *US, 1978*
● — Anon., *King Smut's Wet Dreams
Interpreted* 1978

nob *noun*
the penis *UK, 1961*
● Cheryl's just been looking at men's
nobs. — Caroline Aherne and Craig
Cash, *The Royle Family* 1999

nonce *noun*
a sex offender; a child-molester; a pervert
UK, 1975
● You sick fucking nonce. They're only
kids and you want to bum them.
— John King, *Human Punk* 2000

noodle *noun*
the penis *US, 1975*
● "You're just not getting enough?"
"None! I got a limp noodle,"
he whispered. — Joseph Wambaugh,
The Glitter Dome 1981

nook *noun*
the vagina *US, 1973*
● Then Dove clasped her breasts and
began to ease his sweeper into her
hairless nook[.] — D.M. Perkins, *Deep
Throat* 1973

nook and cranny *noun*
the buttocks, the backside; the vagina *UK,
1979*
Rhyming slang for FANNY.
● You can't roll that tobacco, it's as dry
as a nun's nook & cranny. — Ray
Puxley, *Cockney Rabbit* 1992

nookie; nooky *noun*
the vagina; hence a woman as a sex object;
sexual intercourse *US, 1928*
● "Well," said Mona, grinning at him,
"a little nookie does you a world of
good." — Armistead Maupin, *Tales of
the City* 1978

nooky-nooky *noun*
sex *US, 1974*

● Man, a whole lot of men have pulled time without digging another man's behind and I'd better get my mind on something else beside nooky-nooky. — Piri Thomas, *Seven Long Times* 1974

nooner *noun*
a bout of sex at about noon *US, 1973*
● "Nooners, for Christ sake?" I said. "Coop, I'm middle-aged." — George V. Higgins, *Penance for Jerry Kennedy* 1985

noonies *noun*
the male genitals *UK, 2006*
British Indian (Hindi) urban slang.
● Relax, blud, not everybody b walkin round checkin out other guys' noonies da way u do, batty boy. — Gautam Malkani, *Londonstani* 2006

nosh *noun*
an act of oral sex on a man or, perhaps, a woman *UK, 2001*
● One thing I cannot stand is a girl looking up at us while she's giving us a nosh. — Kevin Sampson, *Outlaws* 2001

nosh *verb*
to perform oral sex *UK, 1998*
● Elaine stubbed her fag out and sunk under the duvet to nosh amicably on his morning glory. — Garry Bushell, *The Face* 2001

nozzle *noun*
the penis *US, 1994*
● She sandwiches your nozzle between her tits, massaging it with a slow rhythm. — *Bunker 13 (excerpted in 'The Guardian' under the headline 'The Bad Sex award shortlisted passages')* 4th December 2003

nub *noun*
the clitoris *UK, 2002*
● I was far too horrified by their sordid tales of throbbing love muscles and red-hot nubs of womanly passion. — Helen Hastings, *Are Friends Electra [Inappropriate Behaviour]* 2002

nubbin *noun*
1 the clitoris *UK, 2004*
Making 'rubbin' the nubbin' female masturbation.
● — Michelle Baker and Steven Tropiano, *Queer Facts* 2004
2 the penis *US, 1968*

● — Erica Orloff and JoAnne Baker, *Dirty Little Secrets* 2001

nubbins *noun*
the female breasts *US, 2005*
● Ample nubbins and side nudity when Angela removes her top and pops onto her guy. — *Mr. Skin, Mr. Skin's Skincyclopedia* 2005

nudger *noun*
the penis *UK, 1984*
● Did anyone ever find out what happened? To his knob, like? Why it was all mangled like that? [...] Some sheep playing hard to get. Snapped out at the end of is nudger. — Niall Griffiths, *Sheepshagger* 2001

nudie *noun*
a performance or film featuring naked women but no sexual activity *US, 1935*
● Usually the "nudies," in contrast to the old-fashioned sun-bathing, nudist colony, sex-exploitation stuff, have a male actor as the central subject or star. — Michael Milner, *Sex on Celluloid* 1964

nuggets *noun*
the testicles *US, 1963*
● Eyes like cold yellow stone at Mark, a regular Sonny Liston prefight hoodoo glare that would sizzle your average bleeding-heart radical's nuggets to a crisp. — John Sayles, *Union Dues* 1977

nugs *noun*
female breasts *US, 1994*
● — Judi Sanders, *Mashing and Munching in Ames* 1994

num-nums *noun*
the female breasts *US, 1993*
● — J.R. Schwartz, *The Official Guide to the Best Cat Houses in Nevada* 1993: 'Sex glossary'

nunga *noun*
the penis *AUSTRALIA, 1971*
● — Barry Humphries, *Bazza Pulls It Off!* 1971

nunga-muncher *noun*
a person who performs oral sex on men *AUSTRALIA, 1971*
● [P]om [British] sheilahs [women] are generally speaking – real bonzer nunga-munchers. — Barry Humphries, *Bazza Pulls It Off!* 1971

nurds *noun*
the testicles *US, 1981*
- — *Maledicta* Summer/Winter, 1981:
  'Five years and 121 dirty words later'

nut *noun*
1 an act of sexual intercourse; sex as an activity *US, 1991*
Extending back from **nut** (an orgasm).
- Nut one, nut two, nut four, five, six / I
  lost the third nut in the mix – fuck it!
  — NWA *Findum, Fuckum & Flee* 1991
2 an orgasm, especially of a male *US, 1968*
- It's not what you think. It won't take but
  five minutes for the guy to reach a nut.
  I mean, it's like takin' candy from a baby.
  — Donald Goines, *Daddy Cool* 1974
3 semen *US, 1991*
- Back up bitch unless you want nut in
  your eye — NWA *Findum, Fuckum &
  Flee* 1991
4 the female breast *UK, 2002*
Usually in the plural.
- Her giving it the tart thing, orange hair,
  big nuts, glasses. — *The Guardian* 10th
  April 2002

nut *verb*
1 to have sex *US, 1971*
- — Eugene Landy, *The Underground
  Dictionary* 1971
2 to orgasm, especially of a male *US, 1999*
- get yo' nails out my back / Slut I'm
  bout to nut — Dr. Dre *Housewife* 1999

nut nectar *noun*
semen *US, 1996*
- SHE DRINKS THE FRESH NUT NECTAR
  DOWN HER THROAT. — Peter Sotos,
  Index 1996

nuts *noun*
1 the testicles; the scrotum *US, 1863*
- If another one of these chairs hits me
  in the nuts, I'm gonna go postal.
  — *Austin Powers* 1999
▶ **get your nuts off**
2 to ejaculate *US, 1932*
- One of them noticed the hunchback
  and gave a derisive snort: "Wha'cha
  doin', Mac – gittin' yer nuts off?"
  — Terry Southern, *Candy* 1958

nut sack *noun*
the scrotum *US, 1971*
- You can pull my nutsack up over my
  dick, so it looks like a bullfrog. — Kevin
  Smith, *Jay and Silent Bob Strike Back*
  2001

nymphet *noun*
a sexually attractive, or sexually
adventurous, young girl *UK, 1999*
First applied to a real, as opposed to mythic,
creature by Vladimir Nabokov, *Lolita*, 1955.
- The thrilling Birgit Nilsson, as the titular
  necrophiliac nymphet [Salome], is a
  ravening animal. — *The Guardian* 5th
  September 1999

Oo

oats *noun*
sexual gratification *UK*, *1923*
- [S]logging all the way across the old Channel every weekend, just to get your oats. — Mike Stott, *Soldiers Talking, Cleanly* 1978

octopus *noun*
a sexually aggressive boy *US*, *1932*
- — *American Speech* December, 1963: 'American Indian student slang'

ofer; o-for *adjective*
used to describe a male pornography performer who either cannot achieve an erection or cannot ejaculate when needed *US*, *1995*
Borrowing from sports lingo, identifying the performer as "oh" (zero) for however many tries.
- — *Adult Video News* September, 1995

OK Corral *noun*
a group of men masturbating while watching a female *US*, *2002*
An extrapolation of the GUN DOWN image, alluding to the site of a famous American gun battle in 1881.
- — Gary K. Farlow, *Prison-ese* 2002

Oklahoma toothbrush *noun*
the penis *US*, *1994*
In Oklahoma, known as a 'Texas toothbrush'.
- — Michael Dalton Johnson, *Talking Trash with Redd Foxx* 1994

old bill *noun*
the penis *UK*, *1998*
- My old bill's up and pointing at me again now. — J.J. Connolly, *Layer Cake* 2000

old chap *noun*
the penis *UK*, *1992*
- "I've shagged some fucking mingers in my time, but I'd rather put a cheese-grater over my knees and crawl around in vinegar than put my old chap..." Before Greg could finish, Arabella had run off in tears. — Colin Butts, *Is Harry Still on the Boat?* 2003

old-fashioned *noun*
conventional vaginal intercourse *US*, *1971*
- A "flat-backer" who offers only coitus ("old-fashioned" or "straight") is likely to lose customers. — Charles Winick, *The Lively Commerce* 1971

old fellow *noun*
the penis *AUSTRALIA*, *1968*
- When she takes off her clothes it'll make the ol' feller stand up. — Dorothy Hewett, *The Chapel Perilous* 1972

old gent *noun*
the penis *UK*, *2000*
- [M]y old gent's getting twitchy at the very thought[.] — J.J. Connolly, *Layer Cake* 2000

old grinder *noun*
a promiscuous woman *UK*, *2000*
- Fuck me, what an old grinder. He knobbed it as well. — John King, *Human Punk* 2000

old Joe *noun*
any sexually transmitted infection *US*, *1967*
- — Dale Gordon, *The Dominion Sex Dictionary* 1967

old man *noun*
the penis *UK*, *1984*
- He'd balance six half crowns along the length of his "old man". — Lenny McLean, *The Guv'nor* 1998

omo; OMO *adjective*
used for signalling that a woman's husband is not at home *UK*, *1995*
OMO™ is an established branded soap powder.
- As soon as a battalion was away over the water, all the singlies were straight over to check out the wives. Boxes of OMO appeared in the windows to advertise Old Man Out. I didn't find it funny. None of the married blokes did. — Andy McNab, *Immediate Action* 1995

one-eye *noun*
the penis *US*, *1961*
- When a woman looks you straight in the one-eye and says, "There's no way you're putting that near my tradesman's," she is really saying, "You're huge!" — *GQ* July, 2001

one-eyed snake *noun*
the penis *US*, *2001*
- Once he [St Augustine] tucked the old one-eyed snake away for good,

he wrote about his experiences[.]
— Erica Orloff and JoAnn Baker, *Dirty Little Secrets* 2001

one off the wrist; quick one off the wrist *noun*
(of a male) an act of masturbation *UK, 1973*
• And he started to shave / And have one off the wrist / And want to see girls / And go out and get pissed[.] — Monty Python *Brian Song* 1979

one over the pocket *noun*
a woman who is easily available for sex *UK, 2002*
Adopted from snooker terminology.
• She's definitely one over the pocket this aul' fox. — Kevin Sampson, *Clubland* 2002

one-shot wonder *noun*
a man who is unable to achieve a second erection within a short time after orgasm *UK, 1997*
• Sorry, darling. I'm a one-shot wonder. You're not going to get any life out of this for a while. — Colin Butts, *Is Harry on the Boat?* 1997

one-way *adjective*
heterosexual *US, 1964*
• — Roger Blake, *The American Dictionary of Sexual Terms* 1964

one-woman show *noun*
(of a female) an act of masturbation *US, 2001*
• — Erica Orloff and JoAnn Baker, *Dirty Little Secrets* 2001

oo-ah *verb*
(used of a woman) to sit or lie with legs spread immodestly *NORFOLK ISLAND, 1992*
• — Beryl Nobbs Palmer, *A Dictionary of Norfolk Words and Usages* 1992

orbit *verb*
to engage in oral sex *US, 1985*
• — *American Speech* Spring, 1985: 'The language of singles bars'

orchestra stalls; orchestras; orchestrals; orks *noun*
the testicles *UK, 1979*
Rhyming slang for **BALLS**, based on the front seating in a theatre auditorium. Probably late C19 or early C20 but not recorded until 1960.

• [A]ll body-hugging Lycra and a butcher's [look] at the orchestrals for the ladies. — Andrew Nickolds, *Back to Basics* 1994

organ grinding *noun*
sex *US, 1972*
• We never had another around-the-clock drunken marathon, but we did a good bit of organ grinding. — Robert Byrne, *McGoorty* 1972

orgy room *noun*
a room designated for group sex *US, 1969*
• These bars generally consist of a large open space containing a bar and dance floor, and a connected "sex room" or "orgy room" where men practice homosexual sexual acts on each other. — *The Knapp Commission Report on Police Corruption* 1972

Oriental dancer *noun*
in circus and carnival usage, a sexually explicit female dancer *US, 1981*
• — Don Wilmeth, *The Language of American Popular Entertainment* 1981

orphan Annie; orphan *noun*
the vagina *UK, 1998*
Rhyming slang for **FANNY** formed from the character Little Orphan Annie, intoduced to the US in comic strip form in 1924, but best known to British audiences from *Annie* the stage-musical, 1977, and film, 1982.
• [A]void it like an infected orphan. — Ray Puxley, *Fresh Rabbit* 1998

outlaw *noun*
a prostitute working without the services of a pimp *US, 1935*
• I don't tell them other bitzes this, but being a lone outlaw in this life, with the johnlaws up one side an the pimps down the other, everybody mouthwaterin for a taste – well you catchin too much mogo at once[.] — Robert Gover, *JC Saves* 1968

oyster *noun*
the vagina *UK, 1707*
• Flap dancin' I call it [lap dancing] 'cos if you're lucky they give you the full two sets of fanny lips even though they in't s'posed to[...] You can't get no bearded clam with your oysters, no way! — Ben Elton, *High Society* 2002

Pp

PA noun
a Prince Albert piercing of the penis US, 1989
- Sooooo, what do I tell my boyfriend when he asks about the PA I got "visiting my aunt in Pittsburgh" for three days? — Dan Savage, *Savage Love* 1998

sofa-filled room aside the projection booth and packing their fudge for prices only the kin of a true superstar can demand. — Jim Carroll, *Forced Entries* 1987

package noun
1 the female posterior US, 2001
- I gotta have a woman with a nice package. A nice ass. — *Sky Magazine* July, 2001
2 a sexually transmitted infection, especially gonorrhea US, 1950
- — Hyman E. Goldin et al., *Dictionary of American Underworld Lingo* 1950
3 AIDS or HIV US, 2002

GROUP SEX, SEX WITH MULTIPLE PARTNERS

bunch punch noun, US, 1975
sex involving multiple males and a single female
- — *American Speech* Spring-Summer, 1975: 'Razorback slang'

caboose noun, US, 1970
the final participant in serial sex
From the phrase PULL A TRAIN used to describe the practice.
- — *Current Slang* Spring, 1970

gangbang verb, US, 1949
to engage in successive, serial copulation with multiple partners
- I used to do it myself, but these perverts would want to gang-bang your broad. — Edwin Torres, *Carlito's Way* 1975

line-up noun, US, 1913
serial sex between one person and multiple partners

- So this rape was in fact a line-up? Yes. It was against my will. You have been a party to line-ups on several occasions? I probably have, but if so, I was under the influence of alcohol and I can't remember them. — *Truth* 3rd February 1970

train noun, US, 1965
▶ **pull a train; run a train**
to engage in serial sex with multiple partners, homosexual or heterosexual, usually consensual
- A girl who squeals on one of the outlaws or who deserts him for somebody wrong can expect to be "turned out," as they say, to "pull the Angel train." — Hunter S. Thompson, *Hell's Angels* 1966

---

pack verb
1 (from the male point of view) to have sex with US, 1947
- "Are you packing her steady?" "Whenever I want." — Willard Motley, *Knock on Any Door* 1947
2 to tuck the male genitals into the left or right trouser leg US, 1972
- [M]en in the armed forces are taught to pack it to the left, but you show more meat when you pack it to the right. — Bruce Rodgers, *The Queens' Vernacular* 1972
▶ **pack fudge**
3 to play the active role in anal sex US, 1987
- He's been making a nice piece of change for himself by taking the wealthy swells of our clientele into a small

- I wouldn't be associating with him if I were you. He's got the package. — Gary K. Farlow, *Prison-ese* 2002

paddle verb
▶ **paddle the pickle**
(of a male) to masturbate US, 1967
- — Dale Gordon, *The Dominion Sex Dictionary* 1967
▶ **paddle the pink canoe**
(of a female) to masturbate UK, 2004
- — Michelle Baker and Steven Tropiano, *Queer Facts* 2004

pain slut noun
a person who derives sexual satisfaction from physical and verbal abuse UK, 1996
- — Jay Wiseman, *SM101: A Realistic Introduction* 1996: 'Glossary'

pair *noun*
a pair of female breasts *US, 1957*
- She had a nice pair though. — Hubert Selby Jr, *Last Exit to Brooklyn* 1957

pajama *noun*
the vagina *US, 1998*
Something you slip into at bedtime.
- There's [a...] "horsespot," "nappy dugout," "mongo," a "pajama," "fannyboo["].] — Eve Ensler, *The Vagina Monologues* 1998

Pakistaner *noun*
a big-breasted girl *SOUTH AFRICA, 2003*
Teen slang.
- — *Sunday Times (South Africa)* 1st June 2003

palming *noun*
masturbation *BAHAMAS, 1982*
- — John A. Holm, *Dictionary of Bahamian English* 1982

pants *noun*
▶ get into someone's pants
to seduce someone; to have sex with someone *US, 1952*
- You know all you'd do is hump her leg for an hour and try to get in her pants. — *Mallrats* 1995

panty apples *noun*
the buttocks *US, 2005*
- She covers her muff, but we get an ass-tonishing shot of her naked panty-apples. — Mr. Skin, *Mr. Skin's Skincyclopedia* 2005

panty hamster *noun*
the vagina *UK, 2002*
- — www.LondonSlang.com June, 2002

papal roulette *noun*
the rhythm method of birth control *US, 1967*
- Long in use by Catholics as the only church-approved contraceptive technique, rhythm has been facetiously called "Papal Roulette." — Jules Griffon, *Orgies American Style* 1967

paradise stroke *noun*
a man's movement just before ejaculating *US, 1972*
- In order to let him penetrate deeper and directer for the paradise stroke, I lay over on my back with a little silk pillow under my hips and my ankles over his shoulders[.] — Xaviera Hollander, *The Happy Hooker* 1972

parfait *noun*
a young male prisoner desired as a sexual object by other prisoners *US, 1975*
- — Miguel Pinero, *Short Eyes* 1975: 'Glossary of Slang'

parloo *verb*
to masturbate *NORFOLK ISLAND, 1992*
- — Beryl Nobbs Palmer, *A Dictionary of Norfolk Words and Usages* 1992

party *noun*
1 sex with more than one prostitute *US, 1973*
- "What's a party?" I'd say, "Two girls. Both of us at the same time." — Susan Hall, *Ladies of the Night* 1973
2 sex, especially with a prostitute *US, 1956*
A prostitute euphemism.
- She's sitting there very quietly for a couple of minutes, she goes, "You want to have a party?" I ask her what kind of party. She goes, "You know" – and looks around to see if anybody's watching – "do it, man, have a good time. Me and you." — Elmore Leonard, *Cat Chaser* 1982

party *verb*
to have sex, especially with a prostitute *US, 1963*
- Me love you long time. You party? — *Full Metal Jacket* 1987

party piece *noun*
a woman who makes herself sexually available at Hell's Angels gatherings *UK, 1982*
A pun formed on PIECE (a woman as a sexual object).
- Women play a distinctly secondary role. They are accepted as wives, girlfriends, or "party pieces". — *The Observer* 12th September 1982

pash rash *noun*
sore lips or irritation of the area surrounding the mouth as a result of kissing *AUSTRALIA, 2002*
- Britney is breaking out in pash rash and there are tongues all over the shop. — *Weekend Australian* 9th November 2002

pasray *verb*
(used of a woman) to sit without care to that which may be seen *TRINIDAD AND TOBAGO, 2003*
- — Lise Winer, *Dictionary of the English/Creole of Trinidad & Tobago* 2003

pasties *noun*
decorative coverings for a female dancer's nipples *US, 1961*
- [B]ush-league sex compared to L.A.; pasties here – total naked public humping in L.A. — Hunter S. Thompson, *Fear and Loathing in Las Vegas* 1971

pastry cutter *noun*
a person who applies pressure with the teeth while performing oral sex on a man *UK, 2002*
- — Paul Baker, *Polari* 2002

patoot *noun*
the vagina *US, 1974*
- Anyways, I get this knife an' some bread and I stuck the knife up her ol' patoot, got a nice gob of clam squirt, an' I spread it on the bread. — Richard Price, *The Wanderers* 1974

Patsy Palmer and her five daughters *noun*
the hand (seen in the context of male masturbation) *UK, 2003*
A variation of MRS PALM AND HER FIVE LOVELY DAUGHTERS, formed on the name of an actress who came to prominence playing Bianca in the BBC television soap opera *EastEnders* from 1994–99.
- — Chris Lewis, *The Dictionary of Playground Slang* 2003

pavement-pounder *noun*
a prostitute who solicits customers on the street *US, 1960*
- The Mayfair pavement-pounders were the class of the crop. — Lee Mortimer, *Women Confidential* 1960

pavement princess *noun*
a prostitute, especially one who works at truck stops *US, 1977*
- The "pavement princess" is out there doing her "thing," also — Gwyneth A. "Dandalion" Seese, *Tijuana Bear in a Smoke 'Um Up Taxi* 1977

pay and lay *noun*
used for describing the exchange of payment and services involved in prostitution *US, 1969*
- I heard Bessie running bath water and I couldn't help wondering if Railhead was just another pay and lay customer like the pullman porters. — Iceberg Slim (Robert Beck), *Mama Black Widow* 1969

payday pussy *noun*
a visit to a prostitute on a working man's payday *US, 1969*
- It's what I call payday pussy. — Juan Carmel Cosmes, *Memoir of a Whoremaster* 1969

PC *noun*
a latex finger glove used during digital examinations *US, 1958*
A 'pinkie cheater'.
- "Good Lord!" said Krankeit exasperated. "If you're going to poke your finger into that girl every three minutes you could at least put a p.c. on." — Terry Southern, *Candy* 1958

peach *noun*
the vagina *US, 1997*
- — Pamela Munro, *U.C.L.A. Slang* 1997

peanut smuggler *noun*
a woman whose nipples, especially when erect, are apparent through her clothing *AUSTRALIA, 2003*
- — Chris Lewis, *The Dictionary of Playground Slang* 2003

pearl diving *noun*
oral sex *US, 1949*
- One orally ambidextrous boyfriend specialized in pearl diving. — Anka Radakovich, *The Wild Girls Club* 1994

pearl necklace *noun*
semen ejaculated on a woman's throat and breasts, especially after penis–breast contact *US, 1984*
- Pearl necklace: stick you penis between her breasts and go to town (use plenty of lube). — Jamie Goddard, *Lesbian Sex Secrets for Men* 2000

pecker *noun*
the penis *UK, 1902*
- Wow! That thing's the fattest, longest, reddest pecker I've ever seen! — James Harper, *Homo Laws in all 50 States* 1968

pecker checker *noun*
a member of a police vice squad targeting homosexual activity *US, 1970*
- Pecker checker pine (Headline) — *Screw* 27th April 1970

pecker tracks *noun*
stains from seminal fluid *US, 1964*
- The goofy bastard borrowed my car and when I got it back there was a

thirteen-inch pecker track on the back
seat. — Ken Weaver, *Texas Crude* 1984

pee-eye *noun*
a pimp *US, 1960*
- He nursed a new rhythm from Kid's
  drums until the prostitutes were doing
  the funkybutt so sexy that even the
  pee-eyes were flashing their money.
  — Patrick Neate, *Twelve Bar Blues* 2001

peek freak *noun*
a voyeur *US, 1967*
- — Dale Gordon, *The Dominion Sex
  Dictionary* 1967

peel *verb*
to perform a striptease *US, 1948*
Originally a term used by and with athletes,
later by and with stripteasers.
- One gal of our acquaintance who had
  made a respectable and comfortable
  living on the road (even in Boston)
  peeling in night clubs and theaters,
  was booked into one of our larger
  cafes. — Jack Lait and Lee Mortimer,
  New York Confidential 1948

peeler *noun*
a striptease dancer *US, 1948*
- They're not all pimping like crazy for a
  peeler with the roundest heels in the
  Borough of Manhattan. — Bernard
  Wolfe, *The Late Risers* 1954

peep *verb*
to watch in a voyeuristic manner *US, 1999*
- [T]hey peeped naked chicks on cable
  for free. — John Ridley, *Everybody
  Smokes in Hell* 1999

pee-pee *noun*
the penis *US, 1967*
Children's toilet vocabulary.
- [S]he did day work and left me with a
  teenaged girl who had me climb up on
  top of her and pushed my lil' peepee
  into a huge, hairy, warm Something.
  — Odie Hawkins, *Scars and Memories*
  1987

peep freak *noun*
a voyeur *US, 1975*
- — Xaviera Hollander, *The Best Part of a
  Man* 1975

peep show *noun*
an arcade where it is possible to view
pornographic videos or a nude woman in
private booths; formerly an arcade where it

was possible to view photographs of
scantily clad women *US, 1947*
- If you're the mop-up boy at a peep
  show, it's obvious the government is
  not working for you. — Chris Rock, *Rock
  This!* 1997

pee-spout *noun*
the penis *UK, 1998*
- Suddenly Andy began to grunt, and
  Bobby looked at him in time to notice
  white stuff shooting out of his pee-
  spout. — Christopher Brookmyre, *Not
  the End of the World* 1998

peewee; pee wee *noun*
the penis *US, 1998*
- Smith holding back the bushes for him
  with his peewee hanging hard as a
  popsicle waiting — Clarence Major, *All-
  Night Visitors* 1998

peg *noun*
the penis *US, 1972*
- I could have swung her over me and
  sat her on the peg, but I had lost all
  interest in that. — Robert Byrne,
  McGoorty 1972

pegs *noun*
the external vaginal lips *TRINIDAD AND
TOBAGO, 2003*
- When she open she leg I like to see
  the little fat pegs. — Lise Winer,
  *Dictionary of the English/Creole of
  Trinidad & Tobago* 2003

pelt *noun*
1 a woman's pubic hair; sex; a woman as a
sex object *US, 1980*
Building on the vulva-as-BEAVER image.
- — Michael Dalton Johnson, *Talking
  Trash with Redd Foxx* 1994
▶ **stroke the pelt**
2 (of a female) to masturbate *US, 2001*
- Another way to say "the girl is
  masturbating" — Stroking the pelt[.]
  — Erica Orloff and JoAnn Baker, *Dirty
  Little Secrets* 2001

pen bait *noun*
a girl under the age of sexual consent *US,
1964*
- — Roger Blake, *The American Dictionary
  of Sexual Terms* 1964

pencil *noun*
the penis *UK, 1937*
Perhaps borrowing a Mark Twain pun:
'the penis mightier than the sword'.

● — Barry Humphries, *Bazza Pulls It Off!* 1971

pencil dick *noun*
a thin penis; used, generally, to insult a man by attacking a perception of his masculinity *US, 1998*
● I'm more woman than you'll ever have, pencil dick. — *The Guru* 2002

pencil-sharpener *noun*
the vagina *UK, 2003*
● — Chris Lewis, *The Dictionary of Playground Slang* 2003

penitentiary punk *noun*
a male who starts taking part in homosexual sex in prison *US, 1972*
● We classify them two ways: penitentiary punk and free-world punk. — Bruce Jackson, *Outside the Law: A Thief's Primer* 1972

penny pimp *noun*
a small-time pimp *US, 1953*
● The pimps and whores – anyhow the penny pimps and two-bit whores – were barred. — Dale Krame, *Teen-Age Gangs* 1953

Pepsi *adjective*
sexually frigid *UK, 2001*
Presumably because Pepsi™ is 'best served chilled'.
● — *Sky Magazine* July, 2001

Percy *noun*
the penis *UK, 1977*
Used as the title of a 1971 British film comedy about a penis-transplant.
● — Richard Herring, *Talking Cock* 2003

perv; perve *verb*
to lust after another person; to behave as a voyeur *AUSTRALIA, 1941*
● [C]os he likes perving over my missus, the dirty cunt[.] — Dave Courtney, *Raving Lunacy* 2000

pet *verb*
▶ **pet the bunny**
(of a woman) to masturbate *US, 1998*
● I "pet the bunny" (the female equivalent of "spank the monkey") at least three times a week about this man. — Dan Savage, *Savage Love* 1998

peter *noun*
the penis *UK, 1902*
● IF YOU DON'T GIVE ME A SEX CHANGE, I'LL CUT OFF YOUR PETER AND SEW IT

ON ME MYSELF!!! — John Waters, *Desperate Living* 1988

peter-eater *noun*
a person who enjoys performing oral sex on men *US, 1978*
● — Anon., *King Smut's Wet Dreams Interpreted* 1978

peter-gazer *noun*
a prisoner who cannot hide his interest in other mens' penises while in the showers *US, 2001*
● — Jim Goad, *Jim Goad's Glossary of Northwestern Prison Slang* December, 2001

peter pan *noun*
a pan used by prostitutes while washing a customer's penis *US, 1974*
A crude if smart allusion to J.M. Barrie.
● I puked in her peter pan. — Earl Thompson, *Tattoo* 1974

peter parade *noun*
a mass inspection of soldiers for signs of sexually transmitted infections *US, 1947*
● — *American Speech* February, 1947: 'Pacific war language'

peter-puffer *noun*
a person who performs oral sex on a man *US, 1987*
● Are you a peter-puffer? — *Full Metal Jacket* 1987

peter tracks *noun*
stains from seminal fluid *US, 1993*
● A few days before, Martha had sneaked into his closet and dribbled motor oil on the crotches of his pants. The stains won't wash out and now all his trousers have permanent peter tracks. — C.D. Payne, *Youth in Revolt* 1993

PI *noun*
a pimp *US, 1955*
● — Robert S. Gold, *A Jazz Lexicon* 1964

pickle tickle *noun*
an act of sexual intercourse *US, 2001*
● Giving her a little pickle tickle[.] — Erica Orloff and JoAnn Baker, *Dirty Little Secrets* 2001

picnic *noun*
1 oral sex, especially on a man *US, 1964*
● — Robert A. Wilson, *Playboy's Book of Forbidden Words* 1972
2 sex involving many people and many acts; an orgy *US, 1964*

- — Anon., *King Smut's Wet Dreams
  Interpreted* 1978

pie *noun*
1 the vulva *US, 1981*
  - — *Maledicta* Summer/Winter, 1981:
    'Five Years and 121 Dirty Words Later'
2 a woman as a sexual object *US, 1975*
  - — *American Speech* Spring-Summer,
    1975: 'Razorback Slang'

piece *noun*
a woman as a sexual object *US, 1942*
  - He said he fucked your cousin, your
    brother, and your niece / And he had
    the nerve enough to ask your
    grandmom for a piece. — Anonymous
    ("Arthur"), *Shine and the Titanic;The
    Signifying Monkey; Stackolee* 1971

piece of ass *noun*
a woman as a sexual object *US, 1930*
  - Son, here's twenty dollars; I want you
    to go to a good whore and get a piece
    of ass off her. — William Burroughs,
    Naked Lunch 1957

piece of cunt *noun*
a woman as a sexual object *US, 1947*
  - A pat on the back and a piece of cunt
    without no passion? — Ralph Ellison,
    Invisible Man 1947

piece of meat *noun*
a woman as a sexual object *US, 1965*
  - That's some sweet piece of meat, ain't
    it? — *Natural Born Killers* 1994

piece of skin; piece of flesh *noun*
a woman as a sexual object *UK, 1956*
  - I meeting that piece of skin tonight,
    you know. — Samuel Selvon, *The
    Lonely Londoners* 1956

piece of trade *noun*
a male who self-identifies as a heterosexual
but will let homosexual men perform oral
sex on him *US, 1965*
  - The humiliating position he would put
    himself in when some piece of trade
    spurned him because he was not able
    to lay on the requisite bread! — Gore
    Vidal, *Myra Breckinridge* 1968

piggle *noun*
the penis *US, 1951*
Children's vocabulary.
  - — Thurston Scott, *Cure it with Honey* 1951

pig meat *noun*
a prostitute *US, 1971*

- "Biffer," "prossie," "she-she," "pig-
  meat" are some other slang
  designations. — Charles Winick, *The
  Lively Commerce* 1971

pig party *noun*
serial consensual sex between one person
and multiple partners *UK, 1988*
  - — James McDonald, *A Dictionary of
    Obscenity, Taboo and Euphemism* 1988

pig pile *noun*
an orgy with homosexual men *US, 1972*
  - — Bruce Rodgers, *The Queens'
    Vernacular* 1972

pike *verb*
(of a man) to tape the penis and testicles to
the body as part of an effort to pass as a
woman *US, 1987*
  - "Why do you pike?" Spinnerman asked.
    "Don't most of your customers just
    want you to go down on them?"
    — Robert Campbell, *Alice in La-La Land*
    1987

pillow-biter *noun*
a homosexual male; specifically the passive
partner in anal intercourse *AUSTRALIA, 1981*
  - Visiting pillow-biters have had a few
    nasty surprises in my homeland[.]
    — Barry Humphries, *The Traveller's Tool*
    1985

pills *noun*
the testicles *UK, 1937*
  - What have we got these great artistic
    skill for that other lands would gladly
    give their pills for? — Barry Humphries,
    A Nice Night's Entertainment 1978

pim *noun*
the clitoris *TRINIDAD AND TOBAGO, 2003*
  - — Lise Winer, *Dictionary of the
    English/Creole of Trinidad & Tobago*
    2003

pimp juice *noun*
the indefinable quality that makes a man
sexually attractive *UK, 2005*
  - — Tim Collins, *Mingin' or Blingin'*
    2005

pin dick *noun*
a male with a small penis *US, 2003*
  - — Chris Lewis, *The Dictionary of
    Playground Slang* 2003

pinga *noun*
the penis *US, 1960*
Cuban-American Spanish.

● [T]hen he was pinching the tip of my
pinga through the fabric of my shorts.
  — Junot Diaz, *Drown* 1996

pink *noun*
the open vagina *US, 1991*
● When I see a naked woman spread out
in the centerfold of Playboy or a porn
queen sitting atop some stud in
reverse-cowgirl position or a sassy
stripper showing her pink in a
gentleman's all-nude club, one burning
question always comes to mind: Who
does her pubic hair? — *The Village
Voice* 8–14 November 2000

pinkie *noun*
the vagina *TRINIDAD AND TOBAGO, 1986*
● — Lise Winer, *Dictionary of the
English/Creole of Trinidad & Tobago*
2003

pink oboe *noun*
the penis *UK, 1979*
Coined by satirist Peter Cook (1937–95) for a
sketch performed in Amnesty International's
The Secret Policeman's Ball.
● A self-confessed player of the pink
oboe. — Peter Cook, *Entirely a Matter
For You* 1979

pink piccolo *noun*
the penis *UK, 2001*
● OK, Steve may have been caught
playing YMCA on the pink piccolo – the
SICK BASTARD! – but he was still
FAMILY. — Garry Bushell, *The Face* 2001

pink shot *noun*
a photograph or video shot of a woman's
vulva that shows the inside of the labia *US,
1974*
● The November 1974 issue was a water-
shed, the first in which Hustler featured
a so-called "pink shot." — Larry Flynt,
An Unseemly Man 1996

pink snapper *noun*
the vagina *US, 2001*
● — Erica Orloff and JoAnn Baker, *Dirty
Little Secrets* 2001

pink torpedo *noun*
the penis, especially when erect *US, 1984*
● My baby fits me like a flesh tuxedo / I
love to sink her with my pink torpedo.
— Spinal Tap, *Big Bottom* 1984

pipe *noun*
the penis *US, 1962*

● When she said that, my pipe jumped to
attention, and I had to have her right
then. — A.S. Jackson, *Gentleman Pimp*
1973

pipe job *noun*
oral sex performed on man *US, 1973*
● They come around, ask what time's
your meal and take you for a ride.
Pipe-job specialists. — Charles Whited,
Chiodo 1973

pippie *noun*
the penis *BAHAMAS, 1982*
● — John A. Holm, *Dictionary of
Bahamian English* 1982

pips *noun*
the female breasts *US, 1981*
● Her pips were hanging there because
she was naked to the waist. — Joseph
Wambaugh, *The Glitter Dome* 1981

pirate's dream *noun*
a flat-chested woman *US, 1972*
From the association of pirates enjoying sex
with captive teenage boys, or perhaps from
the punning association of a girl with 'a
sunken chest and a box full of treasure'.
● — Robert A. Wilson, *Playboy's Book of
Forbidden Words* 1972

piss flaps *noun*
the vaginal lips *AUSTRALIA, 1985*
● [N]aked, her breasts pendulous and
flabby, her legs spread, her piss flaps
all red and hairy and wet[.] — Lisa
Jewell, *Labia Lobelia [Tart Noir]* 2002

piss hard-on *noun*
an erection driven by a full bladder *US,
1969*
● Almost every man is hard when he
wakes up in the morning. We call it a
piss hard-on. — Juan Carmel Cosmes,
Memoir of a Whoremaster 1969

piss play *noun*
sexual behaviour involving urination and
urine *US, 1999*
● Red is for fisting, black for heavy s/m,
light blue for oral sex, dark blue for
anal sex, yellow for piss play, orange
for anything goes, purple for piercing,
and so on. — *The Village Voice* 24th
November 1999

Pistol Pete *noun*
a chronic male masturbator *US, 2002*
● — Gary K. Farlow, *Prison-ese* 2002

pitch *verb*
▶ **pitch a tent**
to have an erection *US, 2001*
- — Don R. McCreary (Editor), *Dawg Speak* 2001

pitcher *noun*
the active partner in homosexual sex *US, 1966*
- — *Maledicta* 1979: 'Kinks and queens: linguistic and cultural aspects of the terminology for gays'

placenta poker *noun*
the penis *UK, 2003*
- [M]en only discuss their placenta pokers in humorous tones (for example by referring to them as placenta

plank *verb*
to have sex with *US, 1972*
- They planked on the cinder riding track near 72nd Street on the west side of Central Park and were interrupted by police horses – again at a critical moment. — Ed Sanders, *Tales of Beatnik Glory* 1975

plaster-caster *noun*
a groupie who makes plaster casts of celebrities' penises *US, 1968*
- The most famous incident in the Hendrix mythos was his encounter with Cynthia Plaster Caster, a college drop-out whose thing was immortalized cocks – rock cocks – in plaster. — *Screw* 5th July 1971

ANAL SEX

butt fucking *noun, US, 1999*
- The Back Door Boys go for all the fag subtext of these homoerotic groups, exploring their interpretation of the hit song "I Want It That Way" – it's all about butt fucking. — *The Village Voice* 5th October 1999

daisy chain *noun, US, 1927*
a group of people, arranged roughly in a circle, in which each person is both actively and passively engaged in oral, anal, or vaginal sex with the person in front of and behind them in the circle
A term that is much more common than the practice.
- Past the Horseshoe Club, with its modified burlesque, and where for five bucks extra you can watch three naked women form a daisy chain on the floor of a basement room anytime after one a.m. — *Rogue for Men* June, 1956

grease *noun, US, 1963*
any lubricant used in anal sex
- — Donald Webster Cory and John P. LeRoy, *The Homosexual and His Society* 1963: 'A lexicon of homosexual slang'

ream job *noun, US, 1995*
- The next time you put an ad in your personals section in the back of your magazine about "ream jobs" show a nice brown or black female ass! — David Kerekes, *Critical Vision* 1995

snap *verb, US, 1972*
to flex, and thus contract, the sphincter during anal sex
- — Bruce Rodgers, *The Queens' Vernacular* 1972

---

pokers). — Richard Herring, *Talking Cock* 2003

plank *noun*
▶ **make the plank**
in homosexual usage, to take the passive position in anal sex *US, 1981*
- — *Male Swinger Number 3* 1981: 'The complete gay dictionary'
▶ **put the plank to**
(from a male perspective) to have sex with someone *UK, 2001*
- No way is he putting the plank to the lovely Nina. — Kevin Sampson, *Outlaws* 2001

plate *verb*
to engage in oral sex *UK, 1968*
Rhyming slang for 'plate of ham', 'gam' (to perform oral sex on a man).
- The various chapter prospects were showing everyone how well they could screw and plate her. — Jamie Mandelkau, *Buttons* 1971

play *verb*
▶ **play mums and dads; play dads and mums**
to have sex *UK, 1967*
- Let's all play mums and dads, come on / Where do babies come from, mum? /

Shut up you naughty boy / And put your clothes back on. — Hazel O'Connor, *We're All Grown-Up* 1981

▶ **play with yourself**
to masturbate *IRELAND, 1922*
The earliest usage recorded of this sweet little euphemism is by James Joyce.

● He kept right on playing with himself, all through high school, in the face of certain insanity. — Larry McMurtry, *The Last Picture Show* 1966

plonker; plonk *noun*
the penis *UK, 1947*
Not recorded in print before 1947.

● Man with the biggest plonker in the world / (Dingle, dangle, strap it to your ankle)[.] — Ivor Biggun, *John Thomas Allcock* 1981

plow *verb*
(used of a male) to have sex *US, 1970*

● He's so horny he'd plow a dead alligator or even a live one if somebody'd hold the tail. — Joseph Wambaugh, *The New Centurions* 1970

pluck *verb*
(used of a male) to have sex with a virgin *BAHAMAS, 1982*

● — John A. Holm, *Dictionary of Bahamian English* 1982

plug *verb*
(of a male) to have sex with someone *UK, 1888*

● Then old Buck comes around and plugs her dog fashion while she's goin down on me. — Earl Thompson, *Tattoo* 1974

plum *noun*
the testicle *UK, 2003*
From its shape and fruitfulness. One notable precursor to its unambiguous sense as a testicle is in the innuendo-laden song 'Please Don't Touch My Plums' by Sammy Cahn, 1913–93, written for the film *The Duchess and the Dirtwater Fox*, 1976, in which it was sung in a Golden Globe-winning performance by Goldie Hawn.

● [A] foolhardy procedure that resulted in him smacking one plum square-on and cutting the other with broken glass — *FHM* June, 2003

plumber *noun*
a male pornography performer *US, 1995*

● — *Adult Video News* September, 1995

plumbing *noun*
the reproductive system *US, 1960*

● Helena had known about sex from a very early age, but treated it as a joke, like what she called your plumbing. — Mary McCarthy, *The Group* 1963

plums *noun*
no sexual contact (when the expectation of intimacy is high) *UK, 1989*
Royal Navy slang.

● "Howja get on with them birds, Taff?" "Plums, mate, nothing but bleeding plums." — Rick Jolly, *Jackspeak* 1989

pocket pool *noun*
used of a man, self-stimulation or masturbation while clothed *US, 1960*
Word play based on ball play; the title of a song by Killer Pussy on the 'Valley Girl' soundtrack.

● For chrissake, I'm a cop, Phil. What do you think I do all day, hang around eating tacos with Missy and playing pocket pool? — Robert Campbell, *Juice* 1988

podger *verb*
to have sex *UK: SCOTLAND, 1996*

● Ah'd podger that aw right! — Michael Munro, *The Complete Patter* 1996

pods *noun*
the female breasts *US, 1968*

● — Fred Hester, *Slang on the 40 Acres* 1968

pogue *noun*
a homosexual male who plays the passive role during anal sex, especially if young *US, 1941*

● — *Maledicta* 1979: 'Kinks and queens: linguistic and cultural aspects of the terminology for gays'

pointers *noun*
female breasts with prominent pointed nipples *US, 1983*

● She was a healthy-looking bitch, a jogger type with a great rack ... a couple of real pointers. And I'm not talking about a bra with rubber nipples. I'm talking about a pair of honest-to-Christ pointed nips that must have weighed as much as silver dollars. — Gerald Petievich, *To Die in Beverly Hills* 1983

poke *verb*
1 (from a man's point of view) to have sex with a woman *UK, 1868*

- BB: Hey, asshole, here's the ultimate fuck-you. I just poked your wife! — *Tin Men* 1987
▶ **poke squid**
2 (of a male) to have sex *US, 1982*
- What, Rory — you wen poke squid las' night? — Douglas Simonson, *Pidgin to da Max Hana Hou* 1982

poker *noun*
the erect penis *US, 1969*
- Gawd, what a poker it was! — *Screw* 17th November 1969

pole *noun*
the penis *UK, 1972*
- "Bitch," I replied coldly, "until you grow a pole you leave the pimping to me." — Donald Goines, *Whoreson* 1972

polish *noun*
oral sex performed on a man *NEW ZEALAND, 1998*
- Whady want, sailor, all the way or just a polish? — David McGill, *David McGill's Complete Kiwi Slang Dictionary* 1998

polish and gloss; polish *verb*
(of a male) to masturbate *UK, 1992*
Rhyming slang for TOSS.
- She wouldn't go all the way but she didn't mind polishing my Grandfather Clock [penis]. — Ray Puxley, *Cockney Rabbit* 1992

poly *noun*
a person who loves and has sex with multiple partners *US, 2000*
An abbreviation of 'polyamorous'.
- Not all neo-pagans are polys and not all polys are neo-pagans[.] — *Nerve* October-November, 2000

pommy cock *noun*
an uncircumcised penis *AUSTRALIA, 1985*
- — Thommo, *The Dictionary of Australian Swearing and Sex Sayings* 1985

pom-pom *noun*
sex *US, 1947*
Used by US soldiers in Japan and the Philippines.
- — *American Speech* February, 1947: 'Pacific war language'

pony *noun*
a female who moves quickly from sexual relationship to sexual relationship, manipulating and using her partners *US, 1999*

- — Connie Eble (Editor), *UNC-CH Campus Slang* Fall, 1999

ponyplay *noun*
an animal transformation sexual fetish, in which the dominants train, ride, and groom people who dress and act like ponies *US, 2000*
- The erotic elements of ponyplay depend on the people involved. — *The Village Voice* 28th November 2000

poo *noun*
the buttocks; the anus *BAHAMAS, 1982*
- — John A. Holm, *Dictionary of Bahamian English* 1982

pooch *noun*
the buttocks *BARBADOS, 1965*
- — Frank A. Collymore, *Barbadian Dialect* 1965

poochi *noun*
the vagina *US, 1998*
- There's [...] a "poochi," a "poopi," a "peepe,", a "poopelu," a "poonani," a "pal" and a "piche[."] — Eve Ensler, *The Vagina Monologues* 1998

pooki *noun*
the vagina *US, 1998*
- In Westchester they called it a pooki, in New Jersey a twat. — Even Ensler, *The Vagina Monologues* 1998

poon *noun*
the vagina; a woman; a woman as a sex object; sex with a woman *US, 1957*
A shortened form of POONTANG.
- [H]e was given excess gambling skim to invest as he saw best and opened a call house specializing in underaged poon dressed up as movie stars. — James Ellroy, *Hollywood Nocturnes* 1994

poon light *noun*
in the pornography industry, a light used to illuminate the genitals of the performers *US, 1995*
- — *Adult Video News* October, 1995

poontang *noun*
the vagina; sex; a woman regarded as a sexual object *US, 1929*
Suggestions that the term comes from an American Indian language, Chinese, Bantu, Peruvian or a Filipino dialect notwithstanding, it almost certainly comes from the French *putain* (prostitute).

• He dug that young poontang – even
though at his age I knew he was
shooting blanks. – Edwin Torres,
Carlito's Way 1975

poony *noun*
the vagina; women as sexual objects *UK,*
1994
• Position her batty (the posterior) over
de subwoofers – at moments of
extreme bass de vibrations will stimulate her poony. – Sacha Baron-Cohen,
Da Gospel According to Ali G 2001

poop chute; poop shute; poop shooter *noun*
the rectum and anus *US, 1970*
• And if you inform him that your poop
chute is a one-way street, he's gotta
respect that, or he won't get a taste of
your sweet lovin'! – *Seattle Weekly* 9th
August 2001

pootenanny; pooties *noun*
the female buttocks *US, 1997*
• [A] tourist from the Home Counties
dancing in jiggling her pooties in front
of der face. – Ben Elton, *High Society*
2002

pootie *noun*
the vagina *US, 1999*
• [Y]oung supple breasts, a tight firm ass
and an uncharted pootie. – *Cruel*
Intentions 1999

pooze *noun*
the vagina *US, 1975*
• Listening to Barry [White]'s unctuous,
pooze-ooze voice, it is conceivable that
this man is dangerous[.] – Lester
Bangs, *Psychotic Reactions and*
Carburetor Dung 1975

pop *noun*
an ejaculation *US, 1986*
• We want the pop. How much time is
left on this cassette? Three minutes.
Okay, give us the pop in two forty-five.
– Robert Stoller and I.S. Levine,
Coming Attractions 1991

pop *verb*
1 to ejaculate; to experience orgasm *US,*
1961
• The cocks pop and the wads fly as
wide-open mouths strain to catch the
steaming jizz. – *Adult Video*
August/September, 1986
2 to have sex with someone *US, 1965*
• Well, did you pop her? You must have
jugged her by now, haven't you?

– Claude Brown, *Manchild in the*
Promised Land 1965
3 (used of a male) to have sex with a virgin
BAHAMAS, 1982
• – John A. Holm, *Dictionary of*
Bahamian English 1982
▶ **pop your nuts**
4 to ejaculate *US, 1970*
• They just want to pop their nuts as fast
as they can. – John Warren Wells,
Tricks of the Trade 1970
▶ **pop your nuts**
5 (of a woman) to experience an orgasm
US, 1969
• [A] girl is more likely to pop her nuts
with a prick buried in her tail than in
her mouth. – Juan Carmel Cosmes,
Memoir of a Whoremaster 1969
▶ **pop your rocks**
6 to ejaculate *US, 1977*
• [H]ere was this guy looking her in the
eye like he wanted something more
than to pop his rocks. – John Sayles,
Union Dues 1977
▶ **pop your water**
7 to ejaculate *BAHAMAS, 1971*
• – John A. Holm, *Dictionary of*
Bahamian English 1982

popcorn pimp *noun*
a small-time pimp; a pimp who fails to live
up to pimp standards *US, 1972*
• One of the bouncers pulled his wallet
out. Popcorn pimp, he didn't have fifty
dollars. – Edwin Torres, *After Hours*
1979

pop shot *noun*
a scene in a pornographic film or photograph depicting a man ejaculating *US, 1991*
• Most of the guys get paid anywhere
from $75 to $300 per pop shot.
– James Ridgeway, *Red Light* 1996

pork *noun*
1 flesh, especially in a sexual context *UK,*
1996
• [S]he'd asked him to don oven gloves
before scratching her pork. – Will Self,
The Sweet Smell of Psychosis 1996
2 the genitals, male or female *BAHAMAS,*
1982
• – John A. Holm, *Dictionary of*
Bahamian English 1982

pork *verb*
to have sex with someone *US, 1968*
• But I think maybe Newt [Gingrich] was
having some trouble at home with his

new wife, the former staffer he started porking while he was still married to his second wife. — Al Franken, *Lies* 2003

pork sword *noun*
the penis *US, 1966*
- Ulrika: Caught in media glare playing hide the pork sword with Sven. — *Rated* June, 2002

porky *noun*
the vagina *BAHAMAS, 1982*
- — John A. Holm, *Dictionary of Bahamian English* 1982

porridge gun *noun*
the penis *UK, 2003*
- Isn't it time for men to celebrate their porridge guns outside the murky confines of the water closet? — Richard Herring, *Talking Cock* 2003

portion *noun*
an act of sexual intercourse as something given to a woman *UK, 2000*
- Thought you'd still be round that sort's place giving her a second portion. — John King, *Human Punk* 2000

portnoy *noun*
a male masturbator *UK, 1970*
A reference to *Portnoy's Complaint*, a novel by Philip Roth, 1969.
- [Suzy Creamcheese's] ascents and descents throughout the afternoon providing a pleasant bonus for us uncomplaining Portnoys below. — Richard Neville, *Play Power* 1970

posh wank *noun*
an act of male masturbation while the penis is sheathed in a condom *UK, 1999*
- He reached for the condoms. A posh wank would put the world to rights. — Kevin Sampson, *Powder* 1999

posteriors *noun*
the penis and testicles *BAHAMAS, 1982*
- — John A. Holm, *Dictionary of Bahamian English* 1982

postop *noun*
a transsexual who has undergone all surgery necessary to complete a sex change *US, 1995*
- As a two-year postop MTF, I can attest life as a woman is no bowl of cherries. — Nancy Tamosaitis, *net.sex* 1995

pot *verb*
▶ **pot the white**
to have sex *UK, 1955*
An allusion to billiards.
- — H.E. Bates, *The Darling Buds of May* 1955

pound *verb*
▶ **pound her pee-hole**
from the male perspective, to have energetic sex *US, 1994*
- — Michael Dalton Johnson, *Talking Trash with Redd Foxx* 1994
▶ **pound the bishop**
(used of a male) to masturbate *US, 1977*
- I stop pounding the bishop now, lest I cross the finish-line right along with him. — *Adam Film World* 1977

pound off *verb*
(used of a male) to masturbate *US, 1969*
- But I've been pounding off over this for a week! — Philip Roth, *Portnoy's Complaint* 1969

pour *verb*
▶ **pour the pork**
(from the male point of view) to have sex *US, 1973*
- [S]he told him she just laid a guy across the hall and had seen a gun under his pillow while he was pouring her the pork. — Joseph Wambaugh, *The Blue Knight* 1973

pozzle *noun*
the vagina *US, 1962*
- I mean, whoever heard of a man gettin' too much pozzle? — *One Flew Over the Cuckoo's Nest* 1962

prawn *noun*
an ugly person with an attractive body *UK, 2004*
- Prawn [...] Tasty body, shame about the face. — *Popbitch* 19th February 2004

pre-cum *noun*
penile secretions prior to orgasm *UK, 1995*
- I keep my motion steady, working him, drinking in his heady pre-cum. — Marcy Sheiner (Editor), *Herotica 4* 1996

premie *noun*
a premature sexual ejaculation; a man who is subject to such a thing *US, 1975*
- — Xaviera Hollander, *The Best Part of a Man* 1975

press *verb*
to have sex *UK, 2006*

- I can't believe someone I've pressed is dead. — Noel Clarke, *Kidulthood* 2006

pretties *noun*
the female breasts *UK, 1973*
- I looked down at my own pink tipped pretties and decided that maybe the peepers wouldn't have much time for me after all. — Petra Christian, *The Sexploiters* 1973

prick *noun*
the penis *UK, 1592*
In conventional English until around 1700. William Shakespeare (1564–1616) played word games with it, Robert Burns (1759–96) used it with vulgar good humour and the Victorians finally hid it away.
- She used candles, Roman candles, and door knobs. Not a prick in the land big enough for her, not one. Men went inside her and curled up. — Henry Miller, *Tropic of Cancer* 1961

prick rag *noun*
a cloth used to clean a man after sex *US, 1987*
- Afterwards I stand there quietly for a moment, still holding his penis in my right hand, my left hand resting on his chest. Then I reach for a prick rag[.] — Frederique Delacoste, *Sex Work* 1987

pricksmith *noun*
a military doctor or medic who inspects male recruits for signs of sexually transmitted disease *US, 1967*
- — Linda Reinberg, *In the Field* 1991

prick-teaser *noun*
a woman who invites sexual advances but does not fulfil that which she seems to promise *US, 1970*
- She was always a prickteaser. Now she stood so closely the pert tips of her tits radiated warm spots on his chest. — Earl Thompson, *Tattoo* 1974

pride of the morning *noun*
the erection experienced by a man upon awakening in the morning *US, 1972*
- — Robert A. Wilson, *Playboy's Book of Forbidden Words* 1972

Prince Albert; Albert *noun*
a piece of jewellery for a penile piercing; also applied to the piercing itself *UK, 2001*
This etymology is the stuff of romantic myth: the procedure and bejewelling is named for Queen Victoria's consort who, it is claimed,

endured the embellishment of his member to enhance his Queen's pleasure.
- Hi, my name is Michael, and I wear a P.A. (Prince Albert) [...] When a P.A. is done the urethra is pierced between glans and shaft and the other side of the ring leaves the penis through the tip. — *www.fortunecity.com/village* 24th June 2001

Princeton rub; Princeton style *noun*
the rubbing of the penis between the thighs of another boy or man until reaching orgasm *US, 1971*
Princeton is a prestigious and cultured East Coast university.
- Princeton rub – Ostensibly reflects the gentlemanly restraint of the Ivy League. — Wayne Dynes, *Homolexis* 1985

pringle *noun*
multiple orgasms *UK, 2001*
From the advertising slogan for Pringles™, a savoury snack: 'once you pop you can't stop'.
- — *Sky Magazine* July, 2001

prison punk *noun*
a formerly heterosexual man who submits to homosexual sex in prison *US, 1954*
- You have the free-world homosexuals like me. You have the strictly prison punks. — John Martin, *Break Down the Walls* 1954

privates *noun*
the genitals of either sex *UK, 1602*
- On one of Schiaparelli's evening dresses, a fastener slices diagonally across the wearer's groin, like an arrow pointing to her privates. — *The Observer* 23rd November 2003

prize jewels carrier *noun*
the scrotum *UK, 2002*
- [A] gaping hole in my prize jewels carrier. I have since paid many visits to hospital[.] — *Mixmag* February, 2002

prod *noun*
the penis *US, 1975*
- — *American Speech* Spring-Summer, 1975: 'Razorback slang'

prong *noun*
the penis *US, 1968*
- "He's got the biggest prong I ever saw on a white man", Gorilla said in honest admiration. — Earl Thompson, *Tattoo* 1974

pronger *noun*
  the penis *US, 1977*
  - I doubt if there are very many gigs where he doesn't end up pogoing his pronger in some sweet honey's hive. — Lester Bangs, *Psychotic Reactions and Carburetor Dung* 1977

prong-on *noun*
  an erection *US, 1974*
  - So I go, and I'm gone a pretty long time, because I got this huge prong on and I gotta practically stand on my head if I wanna piss in the hopper and not in my own fuckin' mouth. — George Higgins, *Cogan's Trade* 1974

proof shot *noun*
  a photograph, or a scene in a pornographic film, of a man ejaculating *US, 1995*
  - Proof Shot stems from old time producers demanding an external ejaculation of sperm so that the customer saw proof that he popped his wad. — *Adult Video News* August, 1995

props *noun*
  false breasts *US, 1967*
  - — Dale Gordon, *The Dominion Sex Dictionary* 1967

pross; pros *noun*
  a prostitute *UK, 1905*
  - Several of her stable prosses were chatting over too hot cups of coffee, eager to break luck, anxious for Leila to tell them where to turn the first trick of their workday. — Emmett Grogan, *Final Score* 1976

prossie *noun*
  a prostitute *US, 1971*
  - "Biffer," "prossie," "she-she," "pig-meat" are some other slang designations. — Charles Winick, *The Lively Commerce* 1971

prosty; prostie *noun*
  a prostitute *US, 1930*
  - And then she was on top of me, working me up like a Paris prostie[.] — Roger Gordon, *Hollywood's Sexual Underground* 1966

protein shake *noun*
  in the pornography industry, semen that is swallowed *US, 1995*
  - — *Adult Video News* October, 1995

prune *noun*
  the anus *US, 1967*

An allusion to the wrinkles found on each.
  - I guess by now you know what MY FANTASY will be about: the old prune, that tight little chocolate path[.] — *Screw* 20th November 1972

prune pusher *noun*
  the active participant in anal sex *US, 1979*
  - — *Maledicta* 1979: 'Kinks and queens: linguistic and cultural aspects of the terminology for gays'

PT *noun*
  a woman who promises more sex than she delivers *US, 1958*
  An abbreviation of PRICK-TEASER.
  - "She's the biggest little PT in town," a tall girl who reminded Jack of one of the Andrew Sisters turned to advise him. — Earl Thompson, *Tattoo* 1974

PTA *noun*
  a hasty washing by a female *US, 1971*
  In the US, the most common association with PTA is the school-support Parent-Teacher Assocation. The PTA in question here refers to the woman's *p*ussy, *t*its and *a*ss.
  - — Eugene Landy, *The Underground Dictionary* 1971

pube *noun*
  ▶ **get pube**
  in the categorisation of sexual activity by teenage boys, to touch a girl's vulva *US, 1986*
  - Next in order of significant intimacy was "getting silk," which meant touching panty-crotch, and then for the more successful, "getting pube." — Terry Southern, *Now Dig This* 1986

pubes *noun*
  pubic hair *US, 1970*
  - A year has passed. I'm older. I'm wiser. Garth got pubes. — *Wayne's World 2* 1993

pubies *noun*
  pubic hairs *US, 1968*
  - He sat up and picked a few pubies like flecks of tobacco from the tip of his tongue — Richard Price, *The Wanderers* 1974

pucker up *verb*
  to tighten your rectal and anal muscles *US, 1972*
  - Well, they like you to squeeze yourself up, you know, so it would be tighter.

They call it puckering up. And they like to put it in and bring it out and you just all the time squeezing on it.
— Bruce Jackson, *In the Life* 1972

pud *noun*
▶ **pound your pud**
(of a male) to masturbate *UK, 1944*
- He picked up Rocky's limp cock, nursed it with his tongue back into a hard-on, and gave him the wildest, frenziedest, freakiest blow job his world had ever seen, while he pounded his own pud.
— Steve Cannon, *Groove, Bang, and Jive Around* 1969
▶ **pull your pud; pull your pudden; pull your pudding**
(of a male), to masturbate *UK, 1944*
- I sat there pulling my pud like a total dip and told her to take her whatchamacallit and go home[.]
— Lawrence Block, *No Score [The Affairs of Chip Harrison Omnibus]* 1970

Plays on 'dragon' (the penis) and the song 'Puff, the Magic Dragon'.
- — Erica Orloff JoAnn Baker *Dirty Little Secrets* 2001

pull *noun*
a woman as a sex object *UK, 1985*
- — Bob Young and Micky Moody, *The Language of Rock 'n' Roll* 1985

pull *verb*
▶ **pull on the rope**
to masturbate a man *US, 1972*
- And then you start pulling on the rope or to throw the bad-headed champ [perform oral sex], boy you have reached rock bottom in my opinion.
— Bruce Jackson, *In the Life* 1972
▶ **pull pud**
(used of a male) to masturbate *UK, 1994*
- I'm not pulling pud here. I know we're gonna be big. — *Airheads* 1994
▶ **pull the head off it**

S&M WORDS

bottom *noun, US, 1961*
the submissive partner in a homosexual or sado-masochistic relationship
- Boots could take either the top or the bottom, without the least show of emotion.
— Donald Goines, *Whoreson* 1972

dump *verb, US, 1957*
to derive sexual pleasure from sadistic acts
- Tricks pay a hundred dollars to dump girls. Sometimes more. I'd never take a dumping myself for less than a hundred. — John M. Murtagh and Sara Harris, *Cast the First Stone* 1957

heavy scene *noun, US, 1979*
sado-masochistic sex
- During one of his periodic excursions to other cities in search of new "heavy scenes" – and his reputation as a top-man precedes his forays – Chas was asked to play an auctioneer at a simulated "slave auction[.]" — John Rechy, *Rushes* 1979

lasting mark *noun, US, 1987*
a welt or bruise produced in sadomasochistic sex
- If a man says "no lasting marks" he is put through a gradual build-up of increasingly painful procedures. — Frederique Delacoste, *Sex Work* 1987

rough trade *noun, US, 1927*
a tough, often sadistic male homosexual, especially as a casual sex-partner
- I had an address book a mile long, packed with tricks from "drag queens" to rough trade, old aunties, little nellie queens that stayed home with mother. — Antony James, *America's Homosexual Underground* 1965

Sadie Masie *noun, US, 1965*
sado-masochism
- A side trip to the "S. & M." (sado-masochistic) or "Sadie-Maisie" homosexual bars — G. Legman, *The Fake Revolt* 1967

pud puller *noun*
a male masturbator *US, 1990*
- A pudpuller at the movies that night said one of them called the other Joe.
— Seth Morgan, *Homeboy* 1990

puff *verb*
▶ **puff the dragon; puff the magic dragon**
to perform oral sex on a man *US, 2001*

(of a male) to masturbate *UK, 2002*
- I cannot wait for her to fuck off out the house so's I can get into some of them little adverts and pull the fucking head off it. — Kevin Sampson, *Clubland* 2002

pull off *verb*
(used of a male) to masturbate *IRELAND, 1922*

- I can't and won't believe it: four or five guys sit around in a circle on the floor, and at Smolka's signal, each begins to pull off – and the first one to come gets the pot, a buck a head. — Philip Roth, *Portnoy's Complaint* 1969

pum *noun*
the female genitals *JAMAICA, 2006*
In UK use among urban black youths.
- Now tell everyone that you're a lesbian. And that lick pum. — Noel Clarke, *Kidulthood* 2006

pump *verb*
to have sex, usually from the male perspective *UK, 1730*
- Think I ought to take along some jelly in case she wants to get pumped in the ass? — Terry Southern, *Now Dig This* 1975

pumps *noun*
the female breasts *US, 1949*
- — Vincent J. Monteleone, *Criminal Slang* 1949

pum-pum *noun*
the vagina *JAMAICA, 1972*
- — Flowers & Alvin, *In A De Pum Pum* 1972

punani; 'nani *noun*
1 the vagina; hence a woman regarded as a sexual object; hence sex with a woman *UK, 1972*
Probably West Indian. The etymology is uncertain, possibly rooted in POONTANG (the vagina, hence sex). Black slang, popularised in the wider community by comedian Ali G (Sacha Baron-Cohen, b. 1970) and rap music.
- He ain't gonna do shit to you, that's my 'nani now, you get me? — Noel Clarke, *Kidulthood* 2006
▶ **ride the punani**
2 to have sex *UK, 2003*
West Indian slang popularised in the UK in the late 1990s by comedy character Ali G (Sacha Baron-Cohen).
- — Susie Dent, *The Language Report* 2003

punch *noun*
an act of sexual intercourse; a person viewed only in terms of sex *US, 1983*
- She was just a punch. — Gerald Petievich, *To Die in Beverly Hills* 1983

punchboard *noun*
a sexually available and promiscuous woman *US, 1977*
A 'punchboard' is a game which used to be found in shops, where for a price the customer punched one of many holes on the board in the hope of winning a prize.
- Claymore Face, the platoon punchboard, was there too. — Larry Heinemann, *Close Quarters* 1977

punk *noun*
a young and/or weak man used as a passive homosexual partner, especially in prison *US, 1904*
- Four years fuckin' punks in the ass made you appreciate rib when you get it. — *Reservoir Dogs* 1992

punk *verb*
to have anal sex with someone *US, 1949*
- I had some Vaseline for my chapped lips and the desk copper leered and asked if we punked each other. — Neal Cassady, *The First Third* 3rd July 1949

puppies *noun*
female breasts *US, 1963*
- Previous posts about her breast size were accurate. Un-be-lievable! Those puppies wanted out of that sweater! — *rec.arts.tv.soaps* 14th September 1992

puppies in a box *noun*
in the pornography business, a group of bare-breasted women cavorting *US, 1991*
- Um-hmmm. Puppies in a box [four young women playing[.] — Robert Stoller and I.S. Levine, *Coming Attractions* 1991

puppy *noun*
a small penis *US, 1980*
- — Edith A. Folb, *runnin' down some lines* 1980

pups *noun*
the female breasts *US, 2005*
- Laura loses her orange bra, then treats us to her pink-nosed pups and she lies back and diddles her cliddle. — Mr. Skin, *Mr. Skin's Skincyclopedia* 2005

purple-headed warrior; purple warrior *noun*
the erect penis *US, 1998*
- Imagine her surprise when you cuddle up to her and she feels your purple-headed warrior preparing for a third battle. — Karl Mark, *The Complete*

A**hole's Guide to Handling Chicks
2003

purple-headed womb ferret *noun*
the penis *UK, 2003*
- — *Red Handed (Cardiff)* Autumn, 2003

purple-helmeted warrior *noun*
▶ **send in the purple-helmeted warrior**
to have sex *US, 2001*
- Another way to say "intercourse" [...] Sending in the purple-helmeted warrior[.] — Erica Orloff and JoAnn Baker, *Dirty Little Secrets* 2001

push *verb*
▶ **push the bush**
(used of a male) to have sex with a woman *US, 1984*
- The bartender spoke slowly, as if to an idiot child. "You know, push the bush? Slake the snake? Drain the train? Siphon the python?" — James Ellroy, *Because the Night* 1984

push in the bush *noun*
vaginal sex *US, 1980*
- — *Maledicta* Winter, 1980: 'A new erotic vocabulary'

puss *noun*
the vagina; a woman; sex with a woman *US, 1981*
An abbreviation of PUSSY.
- It had been awhile since I had any good puss, and I wanted some of this. — Robert Lipkin, *A Brotherhood of Outlaws* 1981

pussy *noun*
1 the vagina; a woman as a sexual object; sex *UK, 1880*
- "You know what they're saying about us in Wormwood Scrubs," Mick [Jagger] confided, "they're saying that when the cops arrived they caught me eating a Mars Bar out of your pussy." — *Uncut* January, 2002
2 the mouth (as an object of sexual penetration) *US, 1988*
- the rough trade type that insisted on calling my mouth his pussy — Peter Sotos, *Index* 1996
▶ **pet the pussy**
3 (of a female) to masturbate *US, 2001*
- Another way to say "the girl is masturbating" [...] Petting the pussy[.] — Erica Orloff and JoAnn Baker, *Dirty Little Secrets* 2001

▶ **push pussy**
4 to work as a pimp *US, 1992*
- I sold dope, and began pimping, pushing pussy at the bar. — Pete Earley, *The Hot House* 1992
▶ **sling pussy**
5 to work as a prostitute *US, 1990*
- Now that she was good for nothing else, she figured why not fulfill Sugarfoot's highest ambition for her and sling pussy on Sunset Strip. — Seth Morgan, *Homeboy* 1990

pussy beard *noun*
female pubic hair *US, 1967*
- — Dale Gordon, *The Dominion Sex Dictionary* 1967

pussy bumping *noun*
genital-to-genital lesbian sex *US, 1949*
- — Vincent J. Monteleone, *Criminal Slang* 1949

pussycat; pussy cat *noun*
the vagina *US, 1980*
- Don't wear panties underneath your pajamas, dear; you need to air out your pussycat — Eve Ensler, *The Vagina Monologues* 1998

pussy cloth *noun*
any improvised sanitary towel *JAMAICA, 1985*
- — Thomas H. Slone, *Rasta is Cuss* 2003

pussy collar *noun*
a desire for sex *US, 1963*
- Yes, dopers and drugmen and dapper mocking Dans – the fuzz and pussy and pussy-collared[.] — Clarence Cooper Jr, *Black* 1963

pussy fart *noun*
an eruption of trapped air from the vagina during sexual intercourse *US, 1995*
- Turning pussy farts into mainstream humor requires intense effort. — Howard Stern, *Miss America* 1995

pussy finger *noun*
the index finger *US, 1977*
- You almost wrecked my pussy finger. — *Saturday Night Fever* 1977

pussy game *noun*
prostitution *US, 1978*
- A pimp is an organizer in the pussy game (prostitution). — Burgess Laughlin, *Job Opportunities in the Black Market* 1978

pussy hair *noun*
  female pubic hair *US, 1969*
  • One of the hottest times ever was
    when I told my lover I wanted to go
    down on her but I wanted to trim her
    pussy hair first. — Violet Blue, *The
    Ultimate Guide to Cunnilingus* 2002

pussy hound *noun*
  a man obsessed with sex and women *US,
  1984*
  • The Stallion was a weight lifter, a party
    animal — a real pussy hound — and a
    damn good shooter. — Richard
    Marcinko, *Rogue Warrior* 1992

pussy juice *noun*
  vaginal secretions *US, 1989*
  • [N]ude photographer Suze Randall
    carefully poses stripper Linda Lee
    Tracey and adds a few drops of "pussy
    juice" to her vulva. — Barry Keith
    Grant, *Voyages of Discovery* 1992

pussy lips *noun*
  the labia *US, 1969*
  • Ugh. All that hair. Then my pussy lips
    be black. — Alice Walker, *The Color
    Purple* 1982

pussy whisker *noun*
  a pubic hair *US, 1986*
  • You got a wild pussy whisker up your
    ass? — Robert Campbell, *In La-La Land
    We Trust* 1986

put *verb*
  ▶ **put it about**
  to be sexually promiscuous *UK, 1975*
  • The simplest explanation was that he
    had just got tired of Jacqui [...] He was
    a man who had always put it about a
    bit. — Simon Brett, *Cast in Order of
    Disappearance* 1975

puta *noun*
  a sexually promiscuous woman; a prostitute
  US, 1964
  From Spanish *puta* (a whore).
  • Liz had been cheating on her. Liz was
    becoming a tramp. A little chippy. A
    puta. — Sheldon Lord, *The Third Way*
    1964

puto *noun*
  a male homosexual *US, 1965*
  Border Spanish used by English-speakers in
  the American southwest.
  • [T]he most derogatory are puto (homo-
    sexual), culero (coward), and relaje
    (informer). — George R. Alvarez,
    *Semiotic Dynamics of an Ethnic-
    American Sub-Cultural Group* 1965

put out *verb*
  to consent to sex *US, 1947*
  • Even if it's true she [Britney Spears]
    doesn't put out (hah!)[.] — *The
    Guardian* 12th March 2002

putz *noun*
  the penis *US, 1934*
  • Dave's professional putz was just too
    big. — Josh Alan Friedman, *Tales of
    Times Square* 1986

pyjama-python *noun*
  the penis *AUSTRALIA, 1971*
  • I flashed the old pyjama-python[.]
    — Barry Humphries, *Bazza Pulls It Off!*
    1971

Qq

quail *noun*
a girl under the legal age of consent *US,
1976*
A shortened form of SAN QUENTIN QUAIL.
- — Radio Shack, *CBer's Handy
Atlas/Dictionary* 1976

queef *noun*
the passing of air from the vagina *US, 2002*
- [D]efending this limp-wristed yuppie
handjob of an album as if it were High
Art, and acting as if the blues were a
queef emitted from the loins of Camryn
Manheim – when she had a yeast
infection[.] — *OC Weekly* 25th October
2002

queen bee *noun*
the manager of a homosexual brothel *US,
1967*
- Customers call the queen bee and
specify the male they want by physical
characteristics and the length of time
he is wanted. — Mark Holden, *Sodom
1967 American Style* 1967

queenie *noun*
a prostitute *US, 1964*
- Rest a us queenies from them eight
places up and down the street, we was
left high and dry, cause they wasn't
gonna open them places up no more.
— Robert Gover, *Here Goes Kitten* 1964

queer *noun*
a homosexual man or a lesbian *US, 1914*
Usually pejorative, but also a male homosexual term of self-reference within the gay
underground and subculture.
- The homosexual, who was playing hard
to get, came to one masquerade party
dressed as Tinkerbelle, the good fairy.
He was what the other queers called a
screamer. — Phyllis and Eberhard
Kronhausen, *Sex Histories of American
College Men* 1960

queer *adjective*
driven by deep and perverse sexual desires
US, 1967

- I say, You not queer, baby. You look
around you and you see, you not the
only one. — Sara Harris, *The Lords of
Hell* 1967

queer's lunch box *noun*
the male crotch *US, 1964*
- — Roger Blake, *The American Dictionary
of Sexual Terms* 1964

queue *noun*
▶ **put on a queue**
(of a woman) to have sex with a line of
partners, one after the other *AUSTRALIA,
1970*
- [A] generous girl will "put on a queue"
behind the sand dunes for a seemingly
unlimited line-up of young men.
— Richard Neville, *Play Power* 1970

quickie *noun*
a sexual encounter that is carried out
quickly *US, 1950*
- We had a quickie; I didn't come & was
only telling of the future where there
were better bed fucks & us living
contentedly as we walked slowly across
town again to her home. — Neal
Cassady, *The First Third* 5th November
1950

quickie *verb*
to have sex in a hurry *US, 1959*
- But I had a little matinee session with
a doll who just won't be quickied.
— Irving Shulman, *The Short End of the
Stick* 1959

quiff *noun*
the vagina; a woman as sex object; a
prostitute *UK, 1923*
Archaic in the US, but understood in
context.
- "Black or blonde," he said. "If it's quiff,
it's all the same to Brain-Brain."
— Thurston Scott, *Cure it with Honey*
1951

quim *noun*
the vagina; used objectively as a collective
noun for women, especially sexually available women *UK, 1735*
- With his pal filling her quim and
Butler's dick sliding in and out of her
luscious lips, Kari gets a heaping
helping of the living needle from both
ends at once. — *Adult Video*
August/September, 1986

Rr

rabbit *noun*
1 a man who ejaculates with little stimulation *US, 1987*
- — *Maledicta* Summer/Winter, 1986–1987: 'Sexual slang: prostitutes, pedophiles, flagellators, transvestites, and necrophiles'
▶ **go like a rabbit**
2 to demonstrate eagerness during sex *UK, 1972*
- I'm gonna do it to you, gonna do it sweet banana, you'll never give up / Yes: Go like a rabbit, gon-na grab it, gon-na do it 'til the night is done — Paul McCartney, *Hi, Hi, Hi* 1972

racehorse *noun*
an accomplished, sought-after prostitute *US, 1972*
- [A] young what-they-call "racehorse," she'd have run in there, got her $20, and have been back in fifteen minutes. — Bruce Jackson, *Outside the Law* 1972

rack *noun*
1 a woman's breasts *US, 1970*
- Up there near the Section 23 sign. Check the rack on that broad. — Jim Bouton, *Ball Four* 1970
▶ **on the rack**
2 available for prostitution *US, 1977*
- Out on the rack nearly an hour and half and she still hadn't broke luck. — John Sayles, *Union Dues* 1977

rag *noun*
a sanitary towel *US, 1966*
- R is for rag to catch the flow from the womb / it substitutes for Kotex when menstruation is in full bloom. — Bruce Jackson, *Get Your Ass in the Water and Swim Like Me* 1966

rainbow *noun*
▶ **go up the rainbow**
to experience sexual ecstasy *UK, 1972*
- — Richard Allen, *Boot Boys* 1972

rainbow party *noun*
oral sex on one male by several females, all wearing different colours of lipstick *US, 2003*
- A rainbow party is an oral sex party. It's a gathering where oral sex is performed. And a rainbow comes from all — all of the girls put on lipstick and each one puts her mouth around the penis of the gentleman or gentlemen who are there to receive favors and make marks in a different place on the penis, hence the term rainbow. — *Oprah Winfrey Show* 2nd October 2003

Raincoat Charlie *noun*
a striptease audience member who masturbates beneath the safety of his raincoat *US, 1981*
- — Don Wilmeth, *The Language of American Popular Entertainment* 1981

ram *verb*
(from a male perspective) to have sex, perhaps violently *UK, 2001*
- "I am. I'm going to ram you hard." [...] I pull her towards myself and slams her back to the wall[.] — Kevin Sampson, *Outlaws* 2001

ramrod *noun*
the penis; the erect penis *UK, 1902*
- My ramrod is me, any man's rod is himself. — Clarence Major, *All-Night Visitors* 1998

randy comedown *noun*
a desire for sex as the effects of drug use wear off *UK, 2002*
- — Paul Baker, *Polari* 2002

rat *noun*
a prostitute *BARBADOS, 1965*
- — Frank A. Collymore, *Barbadian Dialect* 1965

rat bite *noun*
a skin bruise caused by sucking *US, 1982*
Hawaiian youth usage.
- — Douglas Simonson, *Pidgin to da Max Hana Hou* 1982

rattle *noun*
▶ **give a rattle**
to have sexual intercourse with a female *IRELAND, 2001*
- He's giving her a rattle, no doubt about it. — Paul Howard, *The Teenage Dirtbag Years* 2001

rattle *verb*
▶ **rattle someone's knickers**
to have sex *US, 1967*

- I wonder who's rattling her knickers.
  — Elaine Shepard, *The Doom Pussy*
  1967

rattlesnake *noun*
▶ **like a rattlesnake**
of a woman, describes vigorous participation in sexual intercourse *UK, 2000*
- The gorgeous contours of her figure stir

even have the goddamn courtesy to
give him a reach around! — *Full Metal
Jacket* 1987

ream *verb*
to have anal intercourse *US, 1942*
- Night after night, he rooted, rolled, and
  reamed. — Tom Robbins, *Jitterbug
  Perfume* 1984

PROSTITUTE

baby pro *noun, US, 1961*
a very, very young prostitute
- — Burgess Laughlin, *Job Opportunities in
  the Black Market* 1978

boom-boom girl *noun, US, 1966*
- The rest of the day was spent in finding a
  boom-boom girl. — Charles Anderson,
  The Grunts 1976

dirty leg *noun, US, 1966*
a woman with loose sexual mores; a common
prostitute
- A dirty leg is the $5 or $10 trick. — Bruce
  Jackson, *In the Life* 1972

flatback *noun, US, 2002*
- [U]nlike some of his peers, he didn't take
  just any ho – he liked his flatbacks clean
  and innocent-looking. — Tracy Funches,
  Pimpnosis 2002

hard leg *noun, US, 1967*
an experienced, cynical prostitute
- — Kenn 'Naz' Young, *Naz's Underground
  Dictionary* 1973

mudkicker *noun, US, 1932*
a prostitute, especially of the street-walking
variety
- She was three-quarter Kelsey with mossy
  glossy hair / she was a stompdown
  mudkicker and her mug was fair. — Bruce
  Jackson, *Get Your Ass in the Water and
  Swim Like Me* 1964

pross; pros *noun, UK, 1905*
- Several of her stable prosses were
  chatting over too hot cups of coffee, eager
  to break luck, anxious for Leila to tell
  them where to turn the first trick of their
  workday. — Emmett Grogan, *Final Score*
  1976

racehorse *noun, US, 1972*
an accomplished, sought-after prostitute
- [A] young what-they-call "racehorse," she'd
  have run in there, got her $20, and have
  been back in fifteen minutes. — Bruce
  Jackson, *Outside the Law* 1972

a hearty lusting in him. Snuggly fitting
round her waist. Neat. Trim. Like a
rattlesnake, he bets. — Jack Allen,
When the Whistle Blows 2000

raw *adjective*
naked *US, 1931*
- Though we both wore pajamas, he had
  insomnia. Now at least I can sleep raw.
  — Mary McCarthy, *The Group* 1963

razzle-dazzle *noun*
sexual intercourse *UK, 1973*
- [E]very time we indulged in the full
  genital razzle-dazzle, we grew closer to
  each other[.] — Doug Lang, *Freaks* 1973

reach-around *noun*
manual stimulation of the passive partner's
genitals by the male penetrating from
behind *US, 1987*
- I'll bet you're the kind of guy that
  would fuck a person in the ass and not

ream job *noun*
anal sex *US, 1995*
- The next time you put an ad in your
  personals section in the back of your
  magazine about "ream jobs" show a
  nice brown or black female ass!
  — David Kerekes, *Critical Vision*
  1995

rear door delivery *noun*
anal sex *US, 1973*
- [T]hen I was inside him with the
  strange device, making a "rear door
  delivery," as they say. — Jennifer Sills,
  Massage Parlor 1973

red badge of courage *noun*
a notional badge awarded to someone who
performs oral sex on a woman who is
experiencing the bleed period of the
menstrual cycle *US, 1994*
- — Michael Dalton Johnson, *Talking
  Trash with Redd Foxx* 1994

red-eye *noun*
the anus *US, 1966*
- Ben over and crack yo daddy some redeye, punk! — Seth Morgan, *Homeboy* 1990

red-light *adjective*
pertaining to prostitution *US, 1900*
- The District's "red-light" region may be the largest on earth. — Jack Lait and Lee Mortimer, *Washington Confidential* 1951

red wings *noun*
sexual intercourse or oral sex with a woman who is experiencing the bleed period of the menstrual cycle *US, 1971*
From motorcycle gang culture.
- "Not today, H, I can't, the painters are in. I'll be OK tomorrow." "I don't mind getting me red wings." "You filthy sod." — Garry Bushell, *The Face* 2001

reef *verb*
to fondle another person's genitals *UK, 1962*
Probably from the earlier sense 'to pick a pocket'.
- The back row of the cinema was occupied with hot bodies reefing each other[.] — Brian McDonald, *Elephant Boys* 2000

rent *noun*
a youthful, attractive homosexual male prostitute *UK, 1967*
- — Bruce Rodgers, *The Queens' Vernacular* 1972

rent whore *noun*
an occasional prostitute who sells her services when cash is otherwise short *US, 1973*
- Next rung up on the prostitution ladder are rent whores, girls who turn a few tricks to buy clothes or pay the rent. — Gail Sheehy, *Hustling* 1973

reverse cowgirl *noun*
a sexual position in which the woman straddles the prone man, facing his feet *US, 1991*
- When you're working, is there a sexual act or position you won't do. BRITTANY ANDREWS: Reverse cowgirl. I can't stand it. — *Playboy* 1st March 2002

reverse o *noun*
a position for mutual, simultaneous oral sex between two people, or the act itself *UK, 2003*

- — Caroline Archer, *Tart Cards* 2003

rice paddy Hattie *noun*
any rural Chinese prostitute *US, 1949*
- — *American Speech* February, 1949: 'A.V.G. Lingo'

Richard *noun*
the penis *UK, 2001*
An extension of DICK (the penis).
- — *Sky Magazine* July, 2001

ride *verb*
1 to have sex *US, 1994*
Usually from the female perspective.
- I tied him to the bed, then I rode him. He loved it! — Anka Radakovich, *The Wild Girls Club* 1994

2 (used of a lesbian) to straddle your prone partner, rubbing your genitals together *US, 1967*
- Riding is when one girl gets on top of another and their legs are criss-crossed and you just go up and down. — Ruth Allison, *Lesbianism* 1967
▶ **ride the Hershey Highway**
3 to engage in anal sex *US, 1989*
- — Pamela Munro, *U.C.L.A. Slang* 1989
▶ **ride the silver steed**
4 to participate in bismuth subcarbonate and neoarsphenamine therapy for syphilis *US, 1981*
- — *Maledicta* Summer/Winter, 1981: 'Sex and the single soldier'

ride and a rasher *noun*
sexual intercourse followed by breakfast *IRELAND, 1999*
- I'd say she'd give you a ride and a rasher if you played your cards right. — Terence Dolan, *A Dictionary of Hiberno-English* 1999

riding Saint George; the dragon on Saint George *noun*
heterosexual sex with the woman straddling the man, her head upright *US, 1980*
- — *Maledicta* Winter, 1980: 'A new erotic vocabulary'

rig *noun*
1 the penis *US, 1971*
- In fact, I believe the reason we couldn't get his rig out [of the plaster cast] was that it wouldn't GET SOFT. — *Screw* 5th July 1971
2 surgically augmented breasts *US, 1997*
- — Anna Scotti and Paul Young, *Buzzwords* 1997

rim *noun*
the anus *US, 1997*
- Then ... first, that delicious trembling as the head presses against your rim. — Ethan Morden, *Some Men Are Lookers* 1997

rim *verb*
to lick, suck and tongue another's anus *US, 1941*
- Finally, the third man advances to the side of Johnny, licking his chest as the first one did earlier, tongue flitting over his nipples now, then along his back, down, rimming him[.] — John Rechy, *Numbers* 1967

rim job *noun*
the licking of a partner's anus for the purposes of sexual pleasure *US, 1969*
- KYLE'S MOTHER: What was that word, young man? CARTMAN'S MOTHER: Oh, he said rim job. It's when someone licks your ass. — *South Park* 1999

ring *noun*
the anus *UK, 1949*
- I've never liked anyone enough to want to put me entire arm up ther [sic] ring. — Niall Griffiths, *Kelly + Victor* 2002

ringpiece *noun*
the anus *UK, 1949*
- Your basic dildo is a good way to stretch out a rookie ringpiece, because it has no ridges or things to trigger a cut. — Suroosh Alvi et al., *The Vice Guide* 2002

rip *verb*
▶ **rip off a piece (of ass)**
to have sex *US, 1971*
- "Nice piece of ass," the man said. "You ripping off some of that?" — George V. Higgins, *The Friends of Eddie Coyle* 1971

rise *noun*
an erection *US, 1998*
- — Connie Eble (Editor), *UNC-CH Campus Slang* Spring, 1998

roach *verb*
to have sex with someone's spouse or lover; to cuckold someone *BAHAMAS, 1982*
- — John A. Holm, *Dictionary of Bahamian English* 1982

roachy *noun*
the penis *BAHAMAS, 1982*
- — John A. Holm, *Dictionary of Bahamian English* 1982

road head *noun*
oral sex received while driving *US, 2001*
- — Don R. McCreary (Editor), *Dawg Speak* 2001

roar up *verb*
(of a male) to have sex *UK, 1995*
- Every man and his dog was roaring up this bloke's wife. — Andy McNab, *Immediate Action* 1995

roast *verb*
(from an active perspective) to have sex with someone *UK, 2002*
- I come straight away, but I think that's a blessing in disguise. If I'd've roasted her for a bit the poor aul' girl'd've had a heart attack. — Kevin Sampson, *Clubland* 2002

rock *verb*
to have sex *US, 1922*
- you know that I rocked her / But three days later I had to see the doctor — Kool Moe Dee, *Go See The Doctor* 1986

rock-on *noun*
an erection *UK, 1999*
- He made his way over to her as casually as he was able with a semi rock-on in those restrictively snug jeans. — Kevin Sampson, *Powder* 1999

rocks *noun*
1 the testicles *US, 1948*
- "I'm beat to the rocks." "You mean your socks." "I mean my rocks, my nuts, my balls, fachrissakes." — Robert Campbell, *Sweet La-La Land* 1990
▶ **get your rocks off**
2 to ejaculate *US, 1969*
- Baths vary in character, from the Wall Street Sauna, where businessmen go to get their rocks off during the lunch hour (it's called "funch"), to the Beacon[.] — *The Village Voice* 27th September 1976

rod *noun*
the penis; the erect penis *UK, 1902*
- Jim Tom said, "I'm lucky I inherited the same rod my daddy had. When he died, it took seven days to close the casket." — Dan Jenkins, *Life Its Ownself* 1984

rod walloper *noun*
a male masturbator *AUSTRALIA, 1971*

● [D]id you hear the one about the poor
old rod walloper who overwound his
self winding watch. — Barry Humphries,
Bazza Pulls It Off! 1971

rod-walloping *noun*
male masturbation *AUSTRALIA, 1971*
● Blokes can go blind!!! Rod walloping's
got nothin' on what a cove can get
from foreign sheilahs. — Barry
Humphries, *Bazza Pulls It Off!* 1971

roger *verb*
from a male perspective, to have sex *UK,
1711*
From its, now obsolete, use as a slang term
for 'the penis'.
● Auden fantasised, the wonderfully
informative Katherine Bucknell informs
us, about being rogered by his father.
— *The Observer* 31st July 1994

rogering *noun*
from a male perspective, sexual intercourse
UK, 1998
● Matilda Merriman, notorious for her
alleged night of non-stop rogering with
a one-time cabinet member — Ian
Rankin, *Strip Jack* 1998

roll *noun*
an act of sexual intercourse *US, 1962*
An abbreviation of ROLL IN THE HAY.
● Hey, Billy boy, you remember that time
in Seattle you and me picked up those
two twitches? One of the best rolls I
ever had. — Ken Kesey, *One Flew Over
the Cuckoo's Nest* 1962

roll in the hay *noun*
an act of sexual intercourse *US, 1945*
● We had a few rolls in the hay years ago
– nothing much. — Mary McCarthy,
The Group 1963

roll-on *noun*
a secret lover in addition to your regular
partner *SOUTH AFRICA, 2003*
Teen slang.
● Roll-on: Replaces umakhwapheni,
meaning your bit on the side.
— *Sunday Times (South Africa)* 1st June
2003

Roman candle *noun*
in homosexual usage, the penis of an
Italian or Italian-American *US, 1987*
● — *Maledicta* 1986–1987: 'A continu-
ation of a glossary of ethnic slurs in
American English'

Roman culture *noun*
group sex *US, 1967*
● — Dale Gordon, *The Dominion Sex
Dictionary* 1967

Roman engagement *noun*
in homosexual usage, anal sex with a
woman *US, 1987*
● — *Maledicta* 1986–1987: 'A continuation of a glossary of ethnic slurs in
American English'

Roman roulette *noun*
birth control by the rhythm method *UK,
1969*
A variation of VATICAN ROULETTE.
● — Margaret Powell, *Climbing the Stairs*
1969

root *noun*
the penis *US, 1968*
● — Collin Baker et al., *College
Undergraduate Slang Study Conducted
at Brown University* 1968

rosebud *noun*
the anus *US, 1965*
● — Bruce Rodgers, *The Queens'
Vernacular* 1972

**Rosie Palm and her five sisters; Rosie Palm;
Rosie** *noun*
the male hand as the instrument of
masturbation *US, 1977*
● FRIEND: why don't you be a gentleman
and ask Rosey? TED: Who? FRIEND:
Rosey Palm, your girlfriend. God knows
you spend enough fucking time with
her. — *Something About Mary* 1998

rough *verb*
▶ **rough up the suspect**
(of a male) to masturbate *US, 2001*
● "The boy is masturbating" [...]
Roughing up the suspect[.] — Erica
Orloff and JoAnn Baker, *Dirty Little
Secrets* 2001

rough stuff *noun*
violent or sadistic sexual behaviour *US,
1925*
● No rough stuff or fancy fuckin', boys;
Lolita is only sixteen and just startin'
out. — Edwin Torres, *Carlito's Way* 1975

rough trade *noun*
a tough, often sadistic male homosexual,
especially as a casual sex-partner *US, 1927*
● I had an address book a mile long,
packed with tricks from "drag queens"

to rough trade, old aunties, little nellie queens that stayed home with mother.
— Antony James, *America's Homosexual Underground* 1965

round *noun*
an ejaculation TRINIDAD AND TOBAGO, 2003
● I make three rounds with she. — Lise Winer, *Dictionary of the English/Creole of Trinidad & Tobago* 2003

round-brown *noun*
the anus US, 1972
● "Bend over and show me that round brown," Elwood Banks said. — Joseph Wambaugh, *The Choirboys* 1975

round eye *noun*
the anus; by extension, a male homosexual who plays the passive role in anal sex US, 1950
● She had a good round-eye, and that's no lie / How the trickhouse door would swing! — Dennis Wepman et al., *The Life* 1976

round-heeled *adjective*
easily seduced US, 1957
● Jefferson Tatum, who never allowed visitors in his house, unless you count Millie and Esther McCabe, the round-heeled twins from packaging[.] — Max Shulman, *Anyone Got a Match?* 1964

round heels *noun*
a promiscuous or sexually compliant woman US, 1926
Derogatory; from the anatomical notion that a woman with round heels is more easily put on her back.
● [D]irectly on the round heels of the Food and Drug Administration (FDA) approval of the abortion pill[.] — *Insight on the News* 23rd October 2000

rounds *noun*
an ejaculation BAHAMAS, 1982
● — John A. Holm, *Dictionary of Bahamian English* 1982

rousting *noun*
a vigorous act of sexual intercourse UK, 1999
● [T]hey can give a girl a good rousting once in a while[.] — Jeremy Cameron, *Brown Bread in Wengen* 1999

rub 'n' tug *noun*
a massage that includes masturbation US, 2000

● If you really got lucky, maybe a wayward stripper took one of your unmarried groomsmen into the coat room of the Armpit Tavern and gave him a rub 'n' tug for an extra twenty-five bucks. — *Nerve* October-November, 2000

rubyfruit *noun*
the vagina US, 1982
● — *Maledicta* Summer/Winter, 1982: 'Dyke diction: the language of lesbians'

ruck *verb*
to masturbate UK, 1974
Prison slang.
● — John McVicar, *McVicar by Himself* 1974

rude *adjective*
sexual; sexy UK, 1982
Upper-class society use. Not to be confused with 'in the rude' (naked); one condition does not necessarily lead to the next.
● Spunked (spent) £600 on a black leather Adidas tracksuit. Very "rude". — *FHM* June, 2003

ruff *noun*
pubic hair US, 1974
● In the fullness of time a sparse ruff was revealed, but to me the boobs were more interesting. — Anne Steinhardt, *Thunder La Boom* 1974

ruffle *noun*
the passive participant in lesbian sex or a lesbian relationship US, 1970
● — *American Speech* Spring–Summer, 1970: 'Homosexual slang'

rug *noun*
pubic hair, especially on a female US, 1964
● — *Maledicta* Summer/Winter, 1982: 'Dyke diction: the language of lesbians'

rug-muncher *noun*
a lesbian US, 1997
From the image of oral sex as 'munching a hairpiece'.
● Maybe that's just what dykes like to do, fuck around with straight guys' heads, just so she can go back to her little rug-muncher club and have a good laugh with all her man-hating cronies about how fucking stupid and easily duped men are! — *Chasing Amy* 1997

rumpo *noun*
sexual intercourse UK, 1986

Possibly influenced by (or vice versa) Rambling Syd Rumpo, an innuendo-laden character played by Kenneth Williams in *Round the Horne*, BBC radio, 1965–69.

- Her smell, that wonderful Kara fragrance, played around his nose till it twitched. He had a fleeting image of the cartoon kids in the old Bisto ads. Ah, rumpo, he thought to himself.
  — Gary Bushell, *The Face* 2001

rumpy-pumpy *noun*
sexual intercourse *UK, 1983*

- I wish I had a horny young man here with me now, who'd really appreciate a nice bitta rumpy-pumpy. — J.J. Connolly, *Layer Cake* 2000

runs *noun*
a sexually transmitted infection with discharge *TRINIDAD AND TOBAGO, 1951*

- — Thurston Scott, *Cure it with Honey* 1951

Russian roast *noun*
a sexual act in which a woman performs oral sex on a man who is, at the same time, being sodomised by another man *UK, 2004*

- — *Popbitch* 27th May 2004

rusty bullet wound; rusty bullet hole; rusty sheriff's badge; rusty washer *noun*
the anus *UK, 1997*

- Place two fingers up her rusty bullet hole, then pour baby oil down them.
  — *GQ* July, 2001

rusty trombone *noun*
a sexual technique in which a man receives oral stimulation of his anus and manual stimulation of his penis at the same time and from the same person *US, 2002*
Imagery which becomes apparent if you picture the penis as a trombone's slide and the anus as its mouthpiece.

- WHISKY LIPS: ready to get all wet with your juices. Ever play the rusty trombone? JADEDWOM: what's that? WHISKY LIPS: that's when you blow my ass and reach around and stroke.
  — Cris Burks, *SilkyDreamGirl* 2002

Ss

sack *noun*
the scrotum *UK, 1928*
- She just hoofed you in the sack and you're going to leave them alone in a jail cell with one inept guard? — *Austin Powers* 1999

sack *verb*
to take to bed; to have sex with *US, 1967*
- I'd have liked to sack her, though, because she had a good figure. — Robert Newton, *Bondage Clubs U.S.A.* 1967

saddle *noun*
▶ in the saddle
engaged in sexual intercourse *US, 1979*
The term enjoyed widespread popularity in the US during discussions of the 1979 death of former Vice President and New York Governor Nelson Rockefeller.
- Didn't women have to wait six weeks before you could get back into the saddle? — Odie Hawkins, *Black Casanova* 1984

saddles *noun*
the testicles hanging in the scrotum *UK, 2004*
Probably from JOHN WAYNE'S HAIRY SADDLE BAGS.
- Your mother's got a beard, saddles and a penis too. — Goldie Coloured Chain, *Your Mother's Got a Penis* 2004

saddle up *verb*
to engage in mutual oral sex simultaneously *US, 1985*
- — *American Speech* Spring, 1985: 'The language of singles bars'

Sadie Masie *noun*
sadomasochism *US, 1965*
- A side trip to the "S. & M." (sado-masochistic) or "Sadie-Maisie" homo-sexual bars — G. Legman, *The Fake Revolt* 1967

safe word *noun*
a code word, agreed between a sexual dominant and submissive masochistic partner, for use by the masochist as a signal that the current activity should stop *US, 1987*

- "Do you have a safe word with Ben?" she asked. — Kitty Churchill, *Thinking of England* 1995

salad toss *noun*
any of several sexual practices involving oral–anal stimulation *CANADA, 2002*
- If you've got Wet Wipes around, you could even do a little salad tossing but if you're down with that you probably don't need to be reading this. — Suroosh Alvi et al., *The Vice Guide* 2002

salami *noun*
the penis *US, 1998*
- I had been horrified by the drawings in The Joy of Sex, which showed an inexplicably cheerful woman smiling while a giant male salami was stuffed down her throat. — *Nerve* May-June, 2000

sal'ting; saltfish; sal *noun*
the vagina *JAMAICA, 1991*
- Saltfish is renking [offending] me, y'know. — Prison inmate 5th August 2002

S and M; S&M; s-m *noun*
1 in a sadomasochistic relationship, slave and master (or mistress) *US, 1977*
A confusion of meaning with 'sado-masochism' though not of context.
- No, S&M doesn't involve pain; "it involves a new sensation of pleasure." No, S&M doesn't alienate its partici-pants; "it brings two people much closer in a sharing of pain." — John Rechy, *The Sexual Outlaw* 1977
2 sadomasochism *US, 1964*
- Eventually me 'n' a friend / Sorta drifted along into S&M[.] — Frank Zappa, *Bobby Brown Goes Down* 1979

sandwich *noun*
sex involving more than two people, the specific nature of which varies with use, usually sex between one woman and two men, one penetrating her vagina and one penetrating her anus *US, 1971*
A term given a lot of attention in 2000 when actress Cybill Shepherd dedicated a chapter of her autobiography to a description of her having taken the part of the filling in a 'Cybill Sandwich' with two stuntmen.
- It'd be so righteous to be in a Veronica Sawyer-Heather Chandler sandwich. — *Heathers* 1988

San Quentin breakfast *noun*
a male under the age of legal consent as an
object of sexual desire *US, 1976*
San Quentin is California's largest state
prison.

- The man knows he can be sent to San
Quentin for having sexual relations
with a minor. They are known as "San
Quentin breakfast." — *San Francisco
Chronicle* 22nd March 1976

San Quentin quail *noun*
a girl under the age of legal consent *US, 1947*
In the 1940 film *Go West*, Groucho Marx
played a character named S. Quentin Quale,
an inside joke.

scaly leg *noun*
a common prostitute *US, 1972*

- See, ordinarily I don't mess with dirty
legs, or scaly legs, or whatever you
want to call them. Tramps. — Bruce
Jackson, *In the Life* 1972

scarf *verb*
to lick, suck, and tongue a woman's vagina
US, 1966

- He said, "All I have to do is scarf her a
few times and I get anything I want."
Nuttee asked Diehl to explain the word
"scarf." "To eat her box, in other
words." — Richard Honeycutt, *Candy
Mossler* 1966

MALE PROSTITUTE

hustler *noun, US, 1924*

- All right, she was a hustler, but she wasn't
hustling for me and I did her a favor.
— Mickey Spillane, *My Gun is Quick* 1950

joey *noun, AUSTRALIA, 1979*
a youthful, attractive homosexual male
prostitute

- — *Maledicta* 1979: 'Kinks and queens:
linguistic and cultural aspects of the
terminology for gays'

joyboy *noun, UK, 1961*
a young male homosexual, especially a young
male homosexual prostitute

- There were many other ways; masturbation
was first but homosexuals or prisonmade
"joy-boys" came in second. — Piri Thomas,
Seven Long Times 1974

midnight cowboy *noun, US, 1972*
a homosexual prostitute, originally one who
wears cowboy clothes; hence a homosexual man
Brought from gay subculture into wider use by
the film *Midnight Cowboy*, 1969. The less subtle,
general sense resulted from the film's success.

- The clothes chosen by the fetishists epitomize masculinity: cowboys, sailors, etc. The
model acting out the cowboy then is a
midnight cowboy[.] — Bruce Rodgers, *The
Queens' Vernacular* 1972

tea-room cruiser *noun, US, 1982*
a male homosexual prostitute who frequents
public toilets

- — *Maledicta* Summer/Winter, 1982: 'Dyke
diction: the language of lesbians'

- "I'm San Quentin Quail, Mr. Winner,"
Rosalie says. — Oscar Zeta Acosta, *The
Revolt of the Cockroach People* 1973

sausage *noun*
the penis *AUSTRALIA, 1944*

- However, if we are sitting on a crowded
subway and some creep is standing in
front of us shoving his sausage in our
face, the penis becomes the ugliest
human appendage we have ever seen
in our lives. — Anka Radakovich, *The
Wild Girls Club* 1994

scalp *noun*
the appearance of a pornography
performer's photograph on the video box
UK, 1995
From the sense of a 'scalp' as a 'trophy'.

- — *Adult Video News* October, 1995

scarfing *noun*
self-asphyxiation as a masturbatory aid *UK,
1994*

- — John Ayto, *Oxford Dictionary of Slang*
1998

scat *noun*
1 excrement, especially as a sexual fetish
US, 1927
From Greek *skat* (dung).

- Time he will now spend revisiting the
unbelievable Scat pages of that fucking
Internet. — Kevin Sampson, *Clubland*
2002

2 sadomasochistic sex play involving
defecation *US, 1979*

- — *What Color is Your Handkerchief* 1979

scene *noun*
a sexual interlude *US, 1971*

- I saw her in front of the campfire entertaining a few brothers by having a scene with a dog. — Jamie Mandelkau, *Buttons* 1971

schwing!
used as a vocalisation of the sound a penis makes getting suddenly erect at the passing of a beautiful woman *US, 1992*
A gift to teenage slang from Mike Myers and his 'Wayne's World' sketches.
- Garth holds up a poster of Claudia Schiffer. WAYNE: Schwing. GARTH: Schwing — *Wayne's World* 1992

Scotch screw *noun*
a nocturnal emission of semen *US, 1987*
- — *Maledicta* 1986–1987: 'A continuation of a glossary of ethnic slurs in American English'

Scottish *adjective*
sexually uninhibited *CANADA, 2000*
The etymology is a mystery.
- [In Canada] "Scottish" is also used liberally as an inducement in the same way we'd use "Swedish". — Fiona Pitt-Kethley, *Red Light Districts of the World* 2000

scratch *noun*
a masturbatory manipulation of the clitoris *UK, 1979*
- Could have been watching Frankie Vaughan [pornography] on the telly and giving herself a scratch. — Ian Dury, *This is What We Find* 1979

screw *noun*
1 an act of sexual intercourse *US, 1929*
- If you don't like sleeping, and don't want a screw / Then you should take lots of amphetamine too — The Fugs *New Amphetamine Shreik* 1965
2 a sexual partner, potential or actual, of either gender, objected and gauged *UK, 1937*
- And she was a good screw, man. You saw how she was. — Frank Moorhouse, *The State of the Art* 1983

screw *verb*
1 to have sex *UK, 1725*
- What are you going to screw tonight, eh? Who? Your brother-in-law? — George Mandel, *Flee the Angry Strangers* 1952
▶ **screw the arse off**
2 to have vigorous sex with someone *UK, 1967*
- "Lucy!" cried The Journalist. "Pipes of Pangalin! I want to screw the arse off

you!" "STOP IT!" screamed Dan, and he threw himself at The Journalist — Terry Jones, *Douglas Adam's Starship Titanic* 1998
▶ **screw your brains out**
3 to have sex with great regularity and force *US, 1971*
- She didn't talk much but she was quite affectionate. Nearly screwed my brains out is what I'm trying to say. — Tom Robbins, *Another Roadside Attraction* 1971

scuds *noun*
the female breasts *US, 2001*
A comparison with Scud missiles.
- — Don R. McCreary (Editor), *Dawg Speak* 2001

scum *noun*
semen *US, 1965*
- I had to make sure my mother found no stiffened, wrinkled traces of ecstasy's scum. — Larry Rivers, *What Did I Do?* 1992

scumbag *noun*
a prostitute *US, 1973*
- — Ruth Todasco et al., *The Intelligent Woman's Guide to Dirty Words* 1973

scumff *verb*
to massage the genitals through clothing *UK, 2001*
- He's just scumffing her with his four fingers, just fucking rubbing her and grabbing her. — Kevin Sampson, *Outlaws* 2001

scum-scrubber *noun*
an employee of a pornography arcade whose job is to clean up the semen left by customers *US, 1986*
- The adjacent booth is being mopped by professional scum-scrubbers; mop-and-pail Leroys, urban descendants of dung-shoveling stable jockeys. — Josh Alan Friedman, *Tales of Times Square* 1986

seafood *noun*
a sailor as an object of homosexual desire *US, 1963*
- You have plenty of clients because of the great number of military men, especially the sailors, which we commonly call "seafood." — *"The Market Street Proposition" (KFRC radio, San Francisco)* 8th November 1965

seafood breakfast *noun*
oral sex performed on a woman in the
morning *AUSTRALIA, 1985*
- — Thommo, *The Dictionary of Australian
  Swearing and Sex Sayings* 1985

seagull *noun*
a semi-professional prostitute specialising
in customers who are sailors in the US
Navy *US, 1971*
- There are also lots of "sea gulls" [semi-
  amateurs, who follow the fleet from
  port to port] in the bars. — Charles
  Winick, *The Lively Commerce* 1971

seat meat *noun*
the buttocks *US, 2005*
- A-N bares her legendary mams in bed,
  then lights up the screen with her
  magnificent seat-meat as she rises to
  join Jack Nicholson in the shower.
  — Mr. Skin, *Mr. Skin's Skincyclopedia*
  2005

second base *noun*
in a teenage categorisation of sexual activity,
a level of foreplay, most usually referring to
touching a girl's breasts *US, 1977*
The exact degree varies by region or even
school.
- He's too busy going for it with your
  step-mom! Whoa! Second base! — *Bill
  and Ted's Excellent Adventure* 1989

seeing-to *noun*
the act of sexual intercourse, generally considered as the man *doing it* to the woman
UK, 1985
- For God's sake take me back to your
  flat in Knightsbridge and give me the
  most frightful seeing-to. — Henry
  Sloane, *Sloane's Inside Guide to Sex &
  Drugs & Rock 'n' Roll* 1985

self-love *noun*
masturbation *UK, 2003*
- THE SELF-LOVE MIX TAPE - (MUSIC TO
  LOVE YOURSELF TO) — Paul Sullivan,
  Sullivan's Music Trivia 2003

sell *verb*
▶ **sell backside**
to prostitute yourself, literally or figuratively
SINGAPORE, 2002
- — Paik Choo, *The Coxford Singlish
  Dictionary* 2002

serious chep *noun*
intimate sexual contact; sexual intercourse
IRELAND, 2001

An intensified 'chep' (a kiss).
- — John Morton, *Skegs and Skangers*
  2001

set *noun*
a woman's breasts *AUSTRALIA, 1967*
- "Hey, Jow, there's a good set," one will
  cry. (A "set", for your information, is a
  bosom.) — Sue Rhodes, *Now you'll
  think I'm awful* 1967

seventy-eight; 78 *noun*
a prostitute's customer who is quickly satisfied *US, 1971*
From early vinyl records that were played on
a turntable revolving 78 times per minute.
- A customer who worked quickly was
  called a "78" and one with a slower
  response was a "33." — Charles
  Winick, *The Lively Commerce* 1971

sex *verb*
to have sex with someone *US, 1966*
- I gotta girl so there's no need to sex
  a ho[.] — MC Serch, *Mic Techniques*
  1991

sexed up *adjective*
sexually aroused *UK, 1942*
- [S]ix men straight from the Raymond
  Revue bar sexed up to the ears[.]
  — Nell Dunn, *Up the Junction* 1963

sex in *verb*
to initiate a female member into a male
youth gang by group sex *US, 1996*
- If you get sexed in, they consider you a
  Crip ho, and the gang will give you love
  but no respect. — S. Beth Atkin, *Voices
  from the Street* 1996

shack *noun*
a sexual episode *US, 1995*
- I heard about your shack with Matt last
  night. — Connie Eble (Editor), *UNC-CH
  Campus Slang* April, 1995

shack *verb*
1 to live together as an unmarried couple
US, 1935
Very often used in the variant 'shack up'.
- I was 22 years of age and shacking
  with a chick named Julie, I gave her
  one "joint" which she stashed and
  later turned over to the cops – a joint
  that netted me one of the 5-to-life
  sentences. — *The Berkeley Tribe*
  5th–12th September 1969
2 to spend the night with someone, sex
almost always included *US, 1996*

Not the ongoing relationship suggested by the older term SHACK UP.
- — Connie Eble (Editor), *UNC-CH Campus Slang* Fall, 1996

shack job *noun*
a person with whom you are living and enjoying sex without the burdens or blessings of marriage; the arrangement *US, 1960*
- Poor as us, sometimes from mixed marriages and shack jobs. — Joseph Wambaugh, *The New Centurions* 1970

shack-up *noun*
an act of casual sex *US, 1967*
- You'll see him look around a party and pick out the best-looking girl present, to claim he's just come back from a shack-up with her somewhere. — Elaine Shepard, *The Doom Pussy* 1967

shack up *verb*
to provide living quarters for a lover *US, 1960*
- However, he might also shack her up or simply shack her. — *American Speech* May, 1960: 'Korean bamboo English'

shaft *noun*
the penis *UK, 1772*
- With one hand the artist guided his shaft into her welcoming gusset. — Stewart Home, *Sex Kick [britpulp]* 1999

shaft *verb*
from a male perspective, to have sex *UK, 1962*
- Only thing stopping me shafting her she reckoned was I was too midgy [small]. — Jeremy Cameron, *Brown Bread in Wengen* 1999

shag *noun*
1 the vulva and pubic hair *US, 2005*
- Diana scrubs her perky torso pups in the shower, then shows off her snazzy shag when she steps out to towel off! — Mr. Skin, *Mr. Skin's Skincyclopedia* 2005
2 an act of sexual intercourse *UK, 1999*
- Take me to a place where the drugs are free, the clubs have no gravity and every shag guarantees an orgasm! — Justin Kerrigan, *Human Traffic* 1999
3 a sexual partner *UK, 1788*
- Yeh yeh, I know how cool I am ... great shag, yeh ... best ever, aye ... I know all that. — Niall Griffiths, *Sheepshagger* 2002

shag *verb*
1 to have sex *UK, 1788*
Possibly from obsolete 'shag' (to shake); usage is not gender-specific.
- [H]e wants to shag you up the arse. — Danny King, *The Burglar Diaries* 2001
▶ **shag senseless**
2 to have sex to the point of exhaustion *UK, 2000*
- [H]e will fuck the arse off her tonight, he thinks, he will shag her senseless, screw her daft[.] — Niall Griffiths, *Grits* 2000

shagbox *noun*
the vagina *UK, 2001*
- Women's genitalia were represented as (potential) containers (e.g., bucket, box, hair goblet), places to put things in (e.g., furry letterbox, disk drive, socket, slot), containers for semen (e.g., gism pot, spunk bin, honey pot), and containers for the penis/sex (e.g., willy warmer, wank shaft, shagbox). — *Journal of Sex Research* 2001

shake *verb*
▶ **shake hands with the Devil**
(of either sex) to masturbate *US, 1975*
- — Xaviera Hollander, *The Best Part of a Man* 1975

shake 'n vac *noun*
an act of male masturbation, especially when performed by one sexual partner upon another *UK, 2001*
Shake 'n' Vac™ is a household cleaning product that achieved cult status as the result of a 1970s television commercial. During the all-singing and dancing demonstration, 'Do the Shake 'n' Vac / and put the freshness back' an attractive actress shook the tube-shaped packaging and white powder was scattered – the perfect metaphor.
- Adultery meanz shaggin someone elses bitch. Hobviously it don't refer to receivin a blowie or shake 'n' vac. — Sacha Baron-Cohen *Da Gospel According to Ali G* 2001

shampoo *noun*
a scene in a pornographic film or photograph depicting a man ejaculating onto a person's hair *US, 1995*
- — *Adult Video News* October, 1995

sharpie *noun*
an uncircumcised penis *US, 2002*
- — Amy Sohn, *Sex and the City* 2002

sheep *noun*
a woman who volunteers to take part in serial sex with members of a motorcycle club or gang *US, 1972*
● — Robert A. Wilson, *Playboy's Book of Forbidden Words* 1972

sherman tank; sherman *noun*
an act of masturbation *UK, 1992*
Rhyming slang for **WANK**.
● Samuel Pepys had, according to his diary, a quick Sherman during the sermon[.] — James Hawes, *Dead Long Enough* 2000

shishkebob *noun*
the penis *US, 1999*
Rhyming slang for **KNOB** (the penis).
● Women all grabbin' at my shishkebob[.] — Eminem (Marshall Mathers), *Cum On Everybody* 1999

shit box *noun*
the anus *UK, 1997*
● [S]he won't take it up the shit box. — Colin Butts, *Is Harry on the Boat?* 1997

shit-eater *noun*
a person with a fetish for eating excrement *US, 1996*
● If you're looking for a shit. And shit eaters and shitters and shit fuckers and pissers and piss swallowers, you have very few choices. — Peter Sotos, *Index* 1996

shit freak *noun*
a person with a fetish for excrement *US, 1973*
● I had an idea that he was also a shit freak, and I didn't want to get into that. — Jennifer Sills, *Massage Parlor* 1973

shitkicker *noun*
a prostitute *US, 1967*
● Pimps also refer to the women as "cows" and "shitkickers." — Sara Harris, *The Lords of Hell* 1967

shitpacker *noun*
an anal-sex enthusiast *US, 1964*
● Say, there was asshole shellackers and shitpackers / and freaks who drunk blood from a menstruatin' womb. — Bruce Jackson, *Get Your Ass in the Water and Swim Like Me* 1964

shitter *noun*
the anus *UK, 1984*
● Chris gave me a mother-of-pearl trinket box and a pair of ruby studs. Danny

gave me one up the shitter. — Jenny Eclair, *Camberwell Beauty* 2000

shlong *noun*
the penis *US, 1969*
From the Yiddish. Also spelt 'schlong'.
● There's this talking snake and a naked chick and then this dude puts a leaf on his schlong! Heh heh heh. — Mike Judge and Joe Stillman, *Beavis and Butt-Head Do America* 1997

shnitzel; schnitzel *noun*
the penis *US, 1967*
● Dick, all I want to do is make serious movies that explore social issues and turn a profit, and slip the schnitzel to Jane DePugh. — James Ellroy, *Hollywood Nocturnes* 1994

shoop *verb*
to have sex *US, 1994*
From the song by Salt-N-Pepa.
● — Connie Eble (Editor), *UNC-CH Campus Slang* Spring, 1994

shoot *verb*
1 to ejaculate *IRELAND, 1922*
Most likely a shortened form of the C19 'shooting one's roe'.
● "I don't care how many broads he uses at once," states Butch to the room at large, "or how he fucks 'em as long as he pulls outta their mouth or cunt before he shoots, so we can see it." — Josh Alan Friedman, *Tales of Times Square* 1986
▶ **shoot a beaver**
2 to look for and see a girl's crotch *US, 1966*
● — *Current Slang* Summer, 1966
▶ **shoot blanks**
3 (said of a male) to engage in sex with a low or non-existent sperm count *US, 1960*
● He dug that young poontang – even though at his age I knew he was shooting blanks. — Edwin Torres, *Carlito's Way* 1975
▶ **shoot your wad**
4 to ejaculate *US, 1972*
● Did you get any action? Did you slam it to her? Did you stick her? Did you hump her? Did you run it down her throat? Did you jam it up her ass? Did you shoot your wad? — *Screw* 29th May 1972

shoot off *verb*
to ejaculate *US, 1969*

● You know how it is with a lot of kids –
sometimes, they barely get the head of
their pricks in, and – pow! – they shoot
off. – Joey V., *Portrait of Joey* 1969

shore dinner *noun*
a sailor, as seen by a homosexual *US, 1965*
● — *Fact* January-February, 1965

short-and-curlies *noun*
pubic hair *US, 1967*
● — Dale Gordon, *The Dominion Sex
Dictionary* 1967

short-arm inspection; small-arm inspection
noun
an inspection for a sexually transmitted
infection *UK, 1919*
Soldiers or prisoners are lined up, each
holding his penis. At the command 'Skin it
back and milk it down', each man 'milks'
down his penis from the base to the tip so
that the inspecting doctor can check for pus
at the tip of the urethra.
● There was a crowd in the kitchen,
a mob in the hall / A short-arm
inspection by the shithouse wall.
— Dennis Wepman et al., *The Life*
1976

short heist *noun*
an act of masturbation *US, 1974*
● Who's that with the funny white collar
band? / What's that, a short-heist book
in his hand? — Dennis Wepman et al.,
The Life 1976

short-sleeves *noun*
in homosexual usage, an uncircumcised
penis *US, 1981*
● — *Male Swinger Number 3* 1981: 'The
complete gay dictionary'

short time *noun*
a brief session with a prostitute, long
enough for sex and nothing more *US,
1965*
● Their return English is always
questioning, in the few broken phrases
they know: "How much you got?"
"Short time." "All night?" "Costume
show?" — Lenny Bruce, *How to Talk
Dirty and Influence People* 1965

shot *noun*
an ejaculation *US, 2001*
● If it'll get me a few hundred miles
across country, I'll take a shot in the
mouth. — Kevin Smith, *Jay and Silent
Bob Strike Back* 2001

shot on the swings *noun*
an instance of sexual intercourse *UK:
SCOTLAND, 1988*
● Good weekend, was it? D'ye get a shot
on the swings, aye? — Michael Munro,
The Patter, Another Blast 1988

shove *verb*
to have sex *UK, 1969*
● So it's dirty, a whitey shoving a dinge?
— Alan Hunter, *Gently Coloured* 1969

show *noun*
a sexual performance in a brothel *US, 1997*
● "Two Girl Shows", (as opposed to "Two
Girl Parties") are where two girls each
do each other and the men watch, and
participate later if they have paid extra
for that activity. — Sisters of the Heart,
The Brothel Bible 1997

show *verb*
▶ **show hard**
to reveal to other men that you have an
erection *US, 1975*
● For example, a simplified expression of
the primary tearoom strategy is
frequently inscribed on the walls:
"Show hard – get sucked." — Laud
Humphreys, *Tearoom Trade* 1975

showers *noun*
urination by one person on another, or
other acts of urine fetishism *UK, 2003*
● — Caroline Archer, *Tart Cards* 2003

shower-spank *verb*
(of a male) to masturbate in the shower *US,
1989*
● — Pamela Munro, *U.C.L.A. Slang* 1989

shrimp *noun*
a small penis *US, 1972*
● — Bruce Rodgers, *The Queens'
Vernacular* 1972

shrimp *verb*
to suck another's toes *US, 2002*
A sexual fetish.
● "Victor Alexander" (Spalding Gray) as El
Sharif gets shrimped in Ilsa, Harem
Keeper of the Oil Sheiks. — Bill Landis,
Sleazoid Express 2002

shrimp job; shrimp *noun*
the act of toe-sucking for sexual pleasure
UK, 1999
● "How about letting shoot a famous
artist giving you a shrimp job?" the
Mexican leered [...] Howard got down

on his knees and licked the Rock
Chick's tootsies. The actress getting the
shrimp managed to keep a straight
face[.] — Stewart Home, *Sex Kick
[britpulp]* 1999

shtup *noun*
an act of sexual intercourse *US, 1986*
- He gives them all a good shtup. — Josh
  Alan Friedman, *Tales of Times Square*
  1986

shtup; shtoop; schtup *verb*
to have sex *US, 1965*
Yiddish from the German for 'to push'.
- It was funny, because when we first
  got married, I had never slept with a
  woman before. I had schtupped
  plenty of women, but I had never
  slept with one. — Lenny Bruce, *How
  to Talk Dirty and Influence People*
  1965

shvontz; shwantz *noun*
the penis *US, 1965*
- I think this portrays you as a good-
  looking, hot-headed gavonne who's
  probably – excuse me, ladies – got a
  schvanze that's a yard long.
  — James Ellroy, *Hollywood Nocturnes*
  1994

side boob *noun*
a photograph showing the exposed side of
a clothed woman's breast *US, 1997*
A voyeuristic fetish fuelled by exhibitionists
such as Lindsay Lohan.
- Even the side boob of Cassandra at the
  end of "Prophecy" didn't instigate a
  thread. — *alt.tv.highlander* 20th
  January 1997

sidewalk Susie *noun*
a prostitute *US, 1949*
- — Vincent J. Monteleone, *Criminal
  Slang* 1949

sidewinder *noun*
a South Asian prostitute; a promiscuous
South Asian female *US, 1997*
The allusion is to a poisonous snake found
in North America.
- — Judi Sanders, *Da Bomb* 1997

siff *noun*
syphilis *US, 1972*
- There was a young lawyer of note /
  Who thought he had siff of the throat[.]
  — Robert A. Wilson, *Playboy's Book of
  Forbidden Words* 1972

silk *noun*
in the categorisation of sexual activity by
teenage boys, a touch of a girl's crotch
outside her underwear *US, 1986*
- Next in order of significant intimacy
  was "getting silk," which meant
  touching panty-crotch, and then for the
  more successful, "getting pube."
  — Terry Southern, *Now Dig This* 1986

sin city *noun*
the neighbourhood in An Khe, Vietnam,
housing brothels, bars and other vice dens
US, 1968
- — Carl Fleischhauer, *A Glossary of Army
  Slang* 1968

sixty-nine *noun*
simultaneous, mutual oral-genital sex
between two people *US, 1883*
- May engage in mutual oral-genital
  contact ("sixty-nine") as a prelude[.]
  — Herant A. Katschadourian,
  Fundamentals of Human Sexuality 1975

sixty-nine; 69 *verb*
to engage in simultaneous, mutual oral sex
with someone *US, 1971*
- Kim and I had had the uncommon thrill
  of watching brothers sixty-nine each
  other[.] — John Francis Hunter, *The Gay
  Insider* 1971

size queen *noun*
a homosexual male or a woman who is
attracted to men with large penises *US,
1963*
- Two things I detest – size queens and
  small cocks. — Bruce Rodgers, *The
  Queens' Vernacular* 1972

skeet *verb*
to ejaculate *US, 2002*
- — Gary K. Farlow, *Prison-ese* 2002

skeeze *verb*
to have sex *US, 1990*
- So you skeezin', or what? — *New Jack
  City* 1990

skin *noun*
1 sex *US, 1976*
- The numbers were all in, and there
  wasn't any skin / Crime was on a
  sudden decrease. — Dennis Wepman et
  al., *The Life* 1976
2 a woman as a sex object *TRINIDAD AND
TOBAGO, 1936*
- — *Dictionary of the English/Creole of
  Trinidad & Tobago* 2003

skin *verb*

▶ **skin (it) back**
to withdraw the foreskin from your penis, either as part of a medical inspection or masturbation *US, 2002*
- — Gary K. Farlow, *Prison-ese* 2002

skin book *noun*
a sex-themed book *US, 1970*

skin one; skin two; skin three *noun*
used as a rating system by US forces in Vietnam for the films shown on base; the system evaluated films on the amount of nudity *US, 1990*
Higher ratings reflected higher amounts of nudity.
- — Gregory Clark, *Words of the Vietnam War* 1990

PROSTITUTE'S CUSTOMER

baby *noun, US, 1957*
- Still and all, she had a small minute of indecision when he brought the first hundred-dollar baby to his apartment to meet her. — John M. Murtagh and Sara Harris, *Cast the First Stone* 1957

freak trick *noun, US, 1971*
a prostitute's customer who pays for unusual sex
- — Eugene Landy, *The Underground Dictionary* 1971

geek *noun, US, 1993*
a prostitute's customer with fetishistic desires
- — *Washington Post* 7th November 1993

john *noun, US, 1906*
From the sense as 'generic man', probably via the criminal use as 'dupe' or 'victim'.
- Russell recognised some of the pavement princesses, whose pitch this normally was [...] livid at missing their regular johns and champagne tricks on their way back from

the City. — Greg Williams, *Diamond Geezers* 1997

lover *noun, US, 1971*
- A "lover" is a customer who is determined to arouse the prostitute or to get her to respond to him. — Charles Winick, *The Lively Commerce* 1971

seventy-eight; 78 *noun, US, 1971*
a prostitute's customer who is quickly satisfied
From early vinyl records that were played on a turntable revolving 78 times per minute.
- A customer who worked quickly was called a "78" and one with a slower response was a "33." — Charles Winick, *The Lively Commerce* 1971

trick *noun, US, 1925*
- They had to keep an eye on the cops all the time, because they weren't allow to call the tricks like the girls in Storyville. — Louis Armstrong, *Satchmo: My Life in New Orleans* 1954

- Where'd you learn that? You really ought be writing skin books. — Darryl Ponicsan, *The Last Detail* 1970

skin boy *noun*
an uncircumcised male *NEW ZEALAND, 1999*
- — Harry Orsman, *A Dictionary of Modern New Zealand Slang* 1999

skin diver *noun*
a person who performs oral sex on a male *US, 1969*
The reverse of a 'muff diver'.
- — *Current Slang* Winter, 1969

skin flute *noun*
the penis *US, 1941*
Often arises in the phrase 'play the skin flute' (to perform oral sex).
- I asked her if she'd play "Flight of the Bumblebee" on my skin flute and she slapped me. — Ken Weaver, *Texas Crude* 1984

skin show *noun*
a show featuring women approaching or reaching nudity *US, 1973*
- A good SKIN SHOW is a sought after attraction for a Racket Carnival, for the better the FIX, the wilder the show, often including complete nudity and a little body contact as the girls hover at the edge of the stage. — Gene Sorrows, *All About Carnivals* 1985

skin trade *noun*
the sex industry in all its facets *US, 1986*
- He didn't get where he was in the skin trade just by scaring pussy to death. — Robert Campbell, *In La-La Land We Trust* 1986

skinz *noun*
a sexually attractive woman *US, 1993*
- — *Washingnton Post* 14th October 1993

skull *noun*
oral sex *US, 1973*
- The Manager gave him all the free bourbon he could guzzle and, if he could still get it up, some Oblivious backbooth skull just to discourage the likes of these two Clevelands from filing complaints. — Seth Morgan, *Homeboy* 1990

skullfuck *verb*
to perform oral sex on a man; (from the male perspective) to receive oral sex *CANADA, 2002*
- It's important at this point to make sure you avoid getting skull-fucked. Control the tempo yourself. — Suroosh Alvi et al., *The Vice Guide* 2002

skull job *noun*
an act of oral sex *US, 1971*
- — Eugene Landy, *The Underground Dictionary* 1971

slab boy *noun*
a necrophile *US, 1987*
- — *Maledicta* Summer/Winter, 1986–1987: 'Sexual slang: prostitutes, pedophiles, flagellators, transvestites, and necrophiles'

slake *verb*
▶ **slake the snake**
(of a male) to have sex *US, 1984*
- The bartender spoke slowly, as if to an idiot child. "You know, push the bush? Slake the snake? Drain the train? Siphon the python?" — James Ellroy, *Because the Night* 1984

slam *noun*
sexual intercourse *US, 1982*
- — Connie Eble (Editor), *UNC-CH Campus Slang* Spring, 1982

slam clams *verb*
in lesbian sex, to rub genitals one against the other's *US, 2006*
- — *Wikipedia* 2006

slam partner *noun*
a partner for sex, pure and simple *US, 1993*
- — Judi Sanders, *Faced and Faded, Hanging to Hurl* 1993

slap *verb*
▶ **slap the monkey**
(of a male) to masturbate *UK, 2002*
- [E]very lad in the country is slapping his monkey over Emily's knockers

[breasts] in GQ magazine[.] — Ben Elton, *High Society* 2002

slap-happy *adjective*
obsessed with masturbation *US, 1962*
- — Joseph E. Ragen and Charles Finston, *Inside the World's Toughest Prison* 1962: 'Penitentiary and underworld glossary'

slash *noun*
1 the vagina *US, 1972*
- She acts like any paid hooker [...] Paid for her slash. — Peter Sotos, *Index* 1996
2 an attractive, white woman *US, 1987*
- — Carsten Stroud, *Close Pursuit* 1987

slave *noun*
in a sadomasochistic relationship, a person who endures many forms of humiliation, including extreme pain and public displays of submission *US, 1963*
- There is also jealousy among my slaves. In America, I had three slaves, a Wall Street banker, a telephone company executive and a little printer. — *Screw* 8th February 1971

slave training *noun*
the process of instructing a sexual submissive in order that the submissive's menial service and status become part of a sexual relationship *UK, 2003*
- — Caroline Archer, *Tart Cards* 2003

sleep *verb*
▶ **sleep with**
to have sex with *UK, 1819*
- A woman is much more comfortable taking her current man around guys she's slept with than a guy is taking his woman around women he's had sex with. ("Slept with"/"sex with." Isn't that it in a nutshell?) — Chris Rock, *Rock This!* 1997

slice *noun*
1 an act of sexual intercourse (with a woman) *UK, 1955*
- He'd give his arm to tumble her [and] I wouldn't mind a slice myself, if it comes to that. — Alan Hunter, *Gently Does It* 1955
▶ **cut off a slice**
2 to have sex (with a woman) *UK, 1980*
- There's plenty never gets to see any [girls], you know, let alone cut

themselves off a slice. — Red Daniells, 4th January 1980

sliced *adjective*
circumcised *US, 1988*
- — H. Max, *Gay (S)language* 1988

slick leggings *noun*
the rubbing of the penis between the thighs of another man until reaching orgasm *US, 1961*
- Our prison informants consider this and "slick legging" to be statistically insignificant types of release. — *New York Mattachine Newsletter* June, 1961

slick up *verb*
to moisten with vaginal secretions *UK, 2006*
- BECKY Don't lie, did you slick up? ALISA Yeah a little bit, but his thing was small. — Noel Clarke, *Kidulthood* 2006

slimey slap *noun*
of a male, an act of masturbation *UK, 2005*
- There's a bishop's bash, a Jodrell Bank, a slimey slap and a monkey spank[.] — Anonymous *Blasphemy* August, 2005

slip *verb*
▶ **slip a fatty**
to have sex *UK, 1983*
- — Tom Hibbert, *Rockspeak!* 1983
▶ **slip it to**
(of a male) to have sex with someone *US, 1952*
- Could my father have been slipping it to this lady on the side? — Philip Roth, *Portnoy's Complaint* 1969
▶ **slip one to**
(of a male) to have sex with someone *UK, 2001*
- [H]e was slipping one to Denise in the travel agent's at the time. — Danny King, *The Burglar Diaries* 2001

slip-in *noun*
any lubricant used for faciliating sex, especially anal sex *US, 1962*
- — Joseph E. Ragen and Charles Finston, *Inside the World's Toughest Prison* 1962: 'Penitentiary and underworld glossary'

slipper-training *noun*
spanking with an old-fashioned gym shoe, especially when advertised as a service offered by a prostitute *UK, 2003*
- — Caroline Archer, *Tart Cards* 2003

slit *noun*
the vagina *UK, 1648*
- Nicole gazed up at him and pulled the lips of her slit taut and up to show him the ragged pear of pinkness inside[.] — William T. Vollman, *Whores for Gloria* 1991

sloppy seconds *noun*
sex with someone who has just had sex with someone else *US, 1969*
- Sloppy seconds I think they call it. (Not really sloppy, because she would wash up first, but even so it used to bother me.) — Lawrence Block, *No Score* 1970

sluice *noun*
an act of sexual intercourse; sex *UK, 1970*
- I asked her would she like a sluice. She wasn't quite sure what I meant. — Bill Naughton, *Alfie Darling* 1970

slurp *verb*
▶ **slurp at the sideways smile**
to perform oral sex on a woman *US, 2001*
- Another way to say "cunnilingus" [...] Slurping at the sideways smile[.] — Erica Orloff and JoAnn Baker, *Dirty Little Secrets* 2001

slut *noun*
1 a promiscuous girl or woman *UK, 1450*
- Well, a slut is one who will go to a bar that's known to be a place for mostly guys — and walk in alone and sit at the bar. — Murray Kaufman, *Murray the K Tells It Like It Is, Baby,* 1966
2 a promiscuous boy or man *US, 2002*
- I was a little slut back then, trying to taste all the flavors, so I told her, "Wow, I'd love to fuck in that thing." — Tommy Lee, *The Dirt* 2002
3 a prostitute *US, 1961*
- Now that's the kind of girl you ought to be associating with, and not with common sluts like that one. Why, she didn't even look clean. — Joseph Heller, *Catch 22* 1961

slut puppy *noun*
a promiscuous girl *US, 1990*
- — Connie Eble (Editor), *UNC-CH Campus Slang* Spring, 1990

smack *verb*
▶ **smack the pony**
(of a female), to masturbate *UK, 2002*
Smack the Pony is an all-women television sketch show, first broadcast on Channel 4 in 1999.

● What would I think if I returned home from work to find her smacking the pony in front of a George Clooney film[?] — Andrew Holmes, *Sleb* 2002

smash-mouth *verb*
to kiss passionately *US, 1968*
● — Collin Baker et al., *College Undergraduate Slang Study Conducted at Brown University* 1968

smell *noun*
digital-vaginal contact *US, 1974*
● But Buck's havin a little trouble with his. Won't give him smell. — Earl Thompson, *Tattoo* 1974

smelly hole *noun*
the vagina *UK, 2001*
● Abjection was invoked in various ways: through reference to dirtiness (e.g., front bum, dirt box), uncooked (bloody?) meat (e.g., meat seat, chopped liver), vaginal secretions of all types (e.g., slushing fuck pit, the snail trail), smell (e.g., smelly hole, stench trench), and wounds (e.g., gash, gaping axe wound). — *Journal of Sex Research, Vol. 38, Issue 2.* 2001

smoker *noun*
a social gathering, limited to men, especially one with sexual entertainment; a film shown during such a gathering *UK, 1887*
● There were still smokers, stag movies, it wasn't as commonplace, but I guarantee if you wanted to find hardcore in 1930 you could. — Robert Stoller and I.S. Levine, *Coming Attractions* 1991

smoker film *noun*
a pornographic movie shown at an all-male social gathering *US, 1970*
● But this was no illegal stag or smoker film[.] — Roger Blake, *The Porno Movies* 1970

smooch *verb*
to kiss in a lingering manner *US, 1932*
● "Nuts," replied Dewey. "College kids are still college kids. They're still smooching and driving convertibles and cutting classes and looking for laughs." — Max Shulman, *The Many Loves of Dobie Gillis* 1951

smoothie *noun*
the complete removal of a woman's pubic hair; the result thereof *US, 2001*

● Completely bare: sometimes call the Full Monty, the Sphynx, or the Smoothie, this variation on the Brazilian Wax leaves the entire area hair-free. — *Real Simple* May, 2001

smut *noun*
pornography *UK, 1698*
● Stagliano sits atop the porn heap like a waggish imp, daring us to step over the line of eroticism and enter the taboo world of no-holes-barred smut. — *The Penthouse Erotic Video Guide* 2003

smuts *noun*
sexually explicit photographs or postcards *US, 1962*
● — Joseph E. Ragen and Charles Finston, *Inside the World's Toughest Prison* 1962: 'Penitentiary and underworld glossary'

snackpack *noun*
the male genitals as seen in a jockstrap or tight, skimpy underwear *US, 1988*
● — H. Max, *Gay (S)language* 1988

snail track *noun*
the residue of vaginal secretions, semen and/or saliva on a woman's thighs after sex *US, 1986*
● There was drying snail track on her thigh. — Robert Campbell, *In La-La Land We Trust* 1986

snail trail *noun*
the vagina *UK, 2001*
● Abjection was invoked in various ways: through reference to dirtiness (e.g., front bum, dirt box), uncooked (bloody?) meat (e.g., meat seat, chopped liver), vaginal secretions of all types (e.g., slushing fuck pit, the snail trail), smell (e.g., smelly hole, stench trench), and wounds (e.g., gash, gaping axe wound). — Virginia Braun and Celia Kitzinger, *Journal of Sex Research, Vol. 38, Issue 2.* 2001

snake *noun*
1 the penis *US, 1997*
● You fucking better get on my team, Gus, or you're gonna have a fucking scar down there where you snake used to play. — Stephen J. Cannell, *King Con* 1997
2 a homosexual man *US, 1975*
● — Miguel Pinero, *Short Eyes* 1975: Glossary of Slang

snake verb
to have sex from the male perspective US,
2001
- She's been getting snaked by half the
fuckin' department. — Stephen J.
Cannell, The Tin Collectors 2001

snakey-snakey noun
sexual intercourse UK, 2001
- "So why d'you marry her in the first
place?" "Price she put on her virtue.
No white dress, no snakey-snakey."
— Chris Ryan, The Watchman 2001

snap verb
to flex, and thus contract, the sphincter
during anal sex US, 1972
- — Bruce Rodgers, The Queens'
Vernacular 1972

snapper noun
the vagina, especially one with exceptional
muscular control US, 1975
- — Xaviera Hollander, The Best Part of a
Man 1975

snatch noun
the vagina; sex; a woman (or women) as a
sexual object UK, 1904
- Then we had a boy wanted to see a
pussy – he was a boss, had bread, so
he put up a hundred dollars for
anybody to get his old lady to show
her snatch in the visiting room.
— Edwin Torres, Carlito's Way 1975

snatch 22 noun
a woman who is considered so sexually
unattractive that a man would have to be
drunk to attempt sex with her, but too
drunk to perform UK, 2002
A logical knot, formed on SNATCH (the vagina);
after Catch 22, the novel by Joseph Heller,
1961, and the conventional usage it
inspired.
- — Roger's Profanisaurus 2002

sneeze and squeeze noun
cocaine and sex US, 1984
- A little too early for Odeon, but once
we're downtown, it's happy hunting
ground for sneeze and squeeze. — Jay
McInerney, Bright Lights, Big City
1984

sniffer noun
an outsider who tries to be part of the
pornography industry US, 1995
- — Adult Video News October,
1995

sniper noun
a sexually promiscuous girl of limited
intellect BAHAMAS, 1982
- — John A. Holm, Dictionary of
Bahamian English 1982

snootch noun
the vagina CANADA, 2002
- I wonder what he'd pay for a picture of
my snootch. — Queen Latifah, V
Graham Norton 28th May 2003

snorbs noun
the female breasts US, 1969
- — Current Slang Fall, 1969

snowball verb
to pass semen to the donor through a kiss
US, 1972
- VERONICA: That was Snowball. DANTE:
Why do you call him that? VERONICA:
Sylvan made it up. It's a blow job
thing. DANTE: What do you mean?
VERONICA: After he gets a blow job,
he likes to have the cum spit back
into his mouth while kissing. — Clerks
1994

snowballing; snowdropping noun
after oral sex, passing semen to the donor
by kissing US, 1972
- Snowballing simply means you unload
in your girlfriend's mouth, she swishes
it about then spits in yours — FHM
June, 2003

snuff-dipper noun
a prostitute who works at truckstops US,
1976
- — Lanie Dills, The Official CB
Slanguage Language Dictionary
1976

snuff muff noun
a dead woman used for sex UK, 2002
- Fact is, Jessie, I've met punters that
liked 'em dead, oh yeah, snuff muff. It
happens, baby, don't think it don't.
Necrohowsyourfather. — Ben Elton,
High Society 2002

socket noun
the vagina UK, 2001
- Women's genitalia were represented as
(potential) containers (e.g., bucket, box,
hair goblet), places to put things in
(e.g., furry letterbox, disk drive, socket,
slot), containers for semen (e.g., gism
pot, spunk bin, honey pot), and
containers for the penis/sex (e.g., willy

warmer, wank shaft, shagbox).
— *Journal of Sex Research* 2001

socks *noun*
▶ **give socks**
to copulate *IRELAND, 1984*
● For three days and nights he gave her socks and a reliable source informed me afterwards that it took three vets and a female member of the Knights of Malta to wipe the smile off her face. — Billy Roche, *Tumbling Down* 1984

Socrates' pleasure *noun*
anal sex *US, 1993*
● If you want "Socrates' Pleasures" (anal sex), and the lady of your choice declines, complaining about rectal fissures, lesions, poor sphincter control, foreign bodies in the anus, or perforated anal walls, and you're still determined, ask her to recommend someone else who will oblige you. — J.R. Schwartz, *The Official Guide to the Best Cat Houses in Nevada* 1993

soft swinging *noun*
sexual activity between existing partners while others are present *UK, 2006*
● Whether it's soft swinging, dogging, visiting clubs, orgies or simply meeting a likeminded couple[.] — Ashley Lister, *Swingers* 2006

softy *noun*
a flaccid penis *US, 1995*
● — *Adult Video News* October, 1995

soixante-neuf *noun*
mutual and simultaneous oral sex *UK, 1888*
A direct translation into French of synonymous **69**; perhaps with euphemistic intention, or to lend sophistication to the act.
● [B]efore the film came smoking out of the projector we had seen episodes of lesbianism, homosexuality, soixante-neuf, and group sex. — Roger Gordon, *Hollywood's Sexual Underground* 1966

sort *verb*
to have sex with someone; to satisfy someone's sexual requirements *UK, 2001*
● If Nina Perkins-West is getting sorted then it's not her fella that's doing the honours [...] no way in the world is he sorting Nina. — Kevin Sampson, *Outlaws* 2001

soss; sossy *noun*
the penis *NEW ZEALAND, 1998*

From an abbreviation of 'sausage'.
● — David McGill, *David McGill's Complete Kiwi Slang Dictionary* 1998

soul kiss *noun*
a sustained, open-mouthed kiss *US, 1948*
● They looked at a Roy Lichtenstein blowup of a love-comic panel showing a young blood couple with their lips parted in the moment before a profound, tongue-probing, post-teen, American soul kiss. — Tom Wolfe, *The Painted Word* 1975

Southern love *noun*
mouth-to-penis contact immediately after the penis is withdrawn from a rectum *US, 1995*
● — *Adult Video News* September, 1995

south of the border *adverb*
in or to the area of the genitals, especially a woman's *US, 1945*
● On the bottom of the report the doctor noted that "these women were examined from the waist up." The Stars and Stripes headlined the story: DEPENDS ON HOW YOU LOOK AT IT, SAYS JAP DOC WHO DIDN'T GO SOUTH OF BORDER. — *Newsweek* 19th November 1945

spaff *verb*
to ejaculate semen *UK, 2003*
● [T]his could indeed be smut even Hitler spaffed over. — *FHM* June, 2003

spaghetti and macaroni *noun*
sadomasochism *US, 1989*
Disguising the initialism **S AND M.**
● — Thomas E. Murray and Thomas R. Murrell, *The Language of Sadomasochism* 1989

spam fritters *noun*
the vaginal labia *UK, 2002*
A pink highlight of UK cuisine.
● — *Rogers Profanisaurus* 2002

spam javelin *noun*
the erect penis *UK, 1997*
● [Keith Emerson] regales us with lurid tales of "spam javelins" and unorthodox cures for pubic lice. — *Uncut* October, 2003

spam lance *noun*
the penis, especially when erect *UK, 2005*
● Interfering with himself like. Helping himself along as it were. Giving it six-

nil on the old spam lance. — Niall Griffiths, *Sheepshagger* 2001

Spanish *noun*
sex with a man's penis stimulated between a woman's breasts until he ejaculates *US, 1981*
- [S]tick to Swedish massage (by hand), or French (by mouth), and only go Spanish (between the breasts), Russian (between the thighs), American (a body roll) or Danish (inside) if it's worth the money. — Alix Shulman, *On the Stroll* 1981

spank *verb*
1 (used of a male) to masturbate *US, 1994*
- JAY: "Not in me." That's what she says. I gotta pull out and spank it to get it on. — *Clerks* 1994
▶ **spank the monkey**
2 (used of a male) to masturbate *US, 1999*
- Spanking the monkey. Flogging the bishop. Choking the chicken. Jerking the gherkin. — *American Beauty* 1999

spank bank *noun*
a notional collection of fantasies to rely upon while masturbating *US, 1999*
- Now my mother just became part of his spank bank. — Jill Ferguson, *Sometimes Art Can't Save You* 2005

spank off *verb*
(of a male) to masturbate *UK, 2002*
- Could get that Prince Edward spanking off over the phone, she could. — Kevin Sampson, *Clubland* 2002

spark scene *noun*
a sexual fantasy; the imagined or remembered *scene* that *sparks* or enhances a sexual reaction *UK, 2001*
- I still think about it now when I'm wanking or if there's no fireworks with the girl I'm with. It's still my favourite spark scene, me and their Debbi that time. — Kevin Sampson, *Outlaws* 2001

spear *verb*
▶ **spear the bearded clam**
(from a male perspective) to have sex *AUSTRALIA, 1971*
- If youse get jack [bored] of stropping the Mulligan and feel like spearing the bearded clam [...] tell the tart you love her! — Barry Humphries, *Bazza Pulls It Off!* 1971

spearak headwad *noun*
▶ **hit in the seat**
an act of anal intercourse *US, 1976*

- — John R. Armore and Joseph D. Wolfe, *Dictionary of Desperation* 1976

speed bumps *noun*
small female breasts *US, 2003*
- — Chris Lewis, *The Dictionary of Playground Slang* 2003

spelunk *verb*
▶ **spelunk without a partner**
(of a female) to masturbate *US, 2001*
Figurative sense of 'spelunking' (caving as a sport), hence this solo exploration of a 'grotto' (the vagina).
- Another way to say "the girl is masturbating" [...] Spelunking without a partner[.] — Erica Orloff and JoAnne Baker, *Dirty Little Secrets* 2001

sperm wail *noun*
an involuntary cry from a male experiencing an orgasm *UK, 2002*
- — *Roger's Profanisaurus* 2002

spew *noun*
semen *US, 1989*
- — Pamela Munro, *U.C.L.A. Slang* 1989

spew *verb*
to ejaculate *US, 1989*
Adopted from the more common sense 'to vomit', suggesting a more than generous ejaculation.
- — Pamela Munro, *U.C.L.A. Slang* 1989

sphynx *noun*
the removal by wax of all of a woman's pubic hair; the results thereof *US, 2001*
- The Sphynx – it's the name of a hairless cat from Egypt. I must tell you: The Sphynx takes guts and not everyone has a lover who deserves a Sphynx wax. — *Nerve* December 2000 January, 2001

spit fuck *verb*
to penetrate a rectum or vagina using only saliva as a lubricant *US, 1979*
- — *Maledicta* 1979: 'Kinks and queens: linguistic and cultural aspects of the terminology for gays'

spit-roast *noun*
a sexual position in which a woman (or a man) performs oral sex on one man being penetrated by receiving another from behind; the woman (or man) receiving such attention *UK, 1998*
The two erect penises necessary for this activity create the illusory image of a single

spit going in one end and out the other.
Mainly heterosexual usage.

- That Lucky Pierre had a spit-roast last
  night. — *Sky Magazine* July, 2001

spit-roast *verb*
**to have sex as an active participant in the
spit-roast position** *UK, 2003*

- About an hour after she left my room
  Ace and Hughie ended up spit-roasting
  her. — Colin Butts, *Is Harry Still on the
  Boat?* 2003

splack *noun*
sex *US, 1994*

- — Linda Meyer, *Teenspeak!* 1994

split *verb*
from a male perspective, to have sex *UK, 1937*

- [W]hen [an army vehicle] passes a girl,
  aged six years upwards, the usual
  [soldierly] remark is "Cor, I'd like to
  split that one." — *New Statesman* 2nd
  October 1981

split beaver; spread beaver *noun*
the vagina displayed with lips parted *US,
1969*
A familiar cliché of pornography.

- Then came the split beaver shot, which
  is where the girl has lubricated her
  pussy so that the mons fold apart to
  reveal the inner lips, clitoris, urethral

PIMP

cigarette pimp *noun, US, 1972*
**a pimp whose lack of professional pride leads
him to solicit customers for his prostitutes**

- Black pimps never solicit for their women if
  they are "true pimps," and call a man who
  does a cigarette pimp, popcorn pimp, or
  chile pimp. — Christina and Richard Milner,
  Black Players 1972

easy rider *noun, US, 1914*

- — Robert A. Wilson, *Playboy's Book of
  Forbidden Words* 1972

mack *noun, US, 1903*

- In being a mack, you're supposedly the
  supreme being of a man. Man rules woman.
  In being a mack, you acknowledge this fact.
  — Susan Hall, *Gentleman of Leisure* 1972

man *noun, US, 1973*

- Sometimes me and my man Daddy drive up
  Park Avenue in his car. — Susan Hall,
  Ladies of the Night 1973

pee-eye *noun, US, 1960*

- He nursed a new rhythm from Kid's drums
  until the prostitutes were doing the
  funkybutt so sexy that even the pee-eyes
  were flashing their money. — Patrick Neate,
  Twelve Bar Blues 2001

popcorn pimp *noun, US, 1972*
**a small-time pimp; a pimp who fails to live up to
pimp standards**

- One of the bouncers pulled his wallet out.
  Popcorn pimp, he didn't have fifty dollars.
  — Edwin Torres, *After Hours* 1979

splack *verb*
to ejaculate in sexual climax *US, 2001*

- No, no... I didn't splack. — *Sky
  Magazine* July, 2001

splash *verb*
to ejaculate *US, 1970*

- The point is that if you usually splash
  early and you know you're going to get
  laid, then jerk off. — *Screw* 15th June
  1970

splashing *noun*
**in a prostitute's advertising, semen, urine and
other fluids secreted at orgasm** *UK, 2003*

- — Caroline Archer, *Tart Cards* 2003

split *noun*
the vagina *US, 1967*

- — Dale Gordon, *The Dominion Sex
  Dictionary* 1967

opening and vagina. — *Screw* 13th
October 1969

splooge *noun*
semen *US, 1989*

- The slobs could even kiss her (if they
  so dared, with all that splooge floating
  about her mug). — Anthony Petkovich,
  The X Factory 1997

splooge *verb*
to ejaculate *US, 1989*

- That's right – there is no wacky
  splooging on her face or in her mouth,
  which is, of course, considered the
  Money Shot in almost all straight porn.
  — *The Village Voice* 22nd August 2000

sponk *noun*
semen *UK, 2001*
A variation of SPUNK.

• The sponk I rubbed into my belly has gone dry and flaky white, but I'm still half tossing myself off. — Kevin Sampson, *Outlaws* 2001

spooge *noun*
semen *US, 1987*
• One cock in my face, one inside me, the smell of other men's spooge in my nostrils. — Amy Sohn, *Run Catch Kiss* 1999

spooge booth *noun*
a private booth in a pornography arcade *US, 2001*
• Sex shops range from smutty bookstores with "spooge booths" to higher-end retailers specializing in erotic tools, toys and garments. — Rob Cohen, *Etiquette for Outlaws* 2001

spoon *verb*
to tongue a woman's vagina and clitoris *US, 1971*
• — Eugene Landy, *The Underground Dictionary* 1971

sport fuck *noun*
sex for the sake of sex *US, 1990*
• More often, though, lesbians who end up doing what some call a "sport fuck" with a man have been in a situation, such as travel, in which a good time with a kindred spirit just happened along. — Loraine Hutchins, *Bi Any Other Name* 328

sporting girl *noun*
a prostitute *US, 1938*
• But have you ever known a pimp to take a barmaid and make a sportin' girl outta her? — A.S. Jackson, *Gentleman Pimp* 1973

sporting house *noun*
a brothel *US, 1894*
• "Why hell, woman, time I was his age I'd been to ever cathouse — 'sportin-house' we called 'em then — in this county." — Terry Southern, *Texas Summer* 1991

sporting lady *noun*
a prostitute *US, 1972*
• Ladies is the polite form, and carries the connotations of "ladies of the evening" and sportin' lady, that is, a kind of gallant euphemism.
— Christina and Richard Milner, *Black Players* 1972

sporting life *noun*
the business and lifestyle of prostitution and pimping *US, 1973*
• His name was famous in sportin' life up 'til the time he died, and then he became a legend. — A.S. Jackson, *Gentleman Pimp* 1973

sportsman *noun*
a pimp *US, 1967*
• She told me one night, just after I got into the life through her, that Bible John was her sportsman. "Sportsman? What's that?" I asked. She shrugged her shoulders. "Fancy word for pimp." — Sara Harris, *The Lords of Hell* 1967

spray *verb*
to ejaculate semen onto a sexual partner *UK, 2001*
• [I]t comes into my head that I want to spray her. All over her and that, good style. — Kevin Sampson, *Outlaws* 2001

spread *noun*
a photograph of a naked woman exposing her genitals *US, 1969*
• For those interested in semantics, the pictures with the legs in normal position showing only the pubic bush are called "beaver pictures" but if the legs are spread apart and the camera angle shows the vaginal aperture or clitoris, then it is called "spread." — *Screw* 18th August 1969

spreader *noun*
the vagina displayed with lips parted *US, 1970*
• By 1967 or 1968, a whole group of magazines featured nude females in a manner which emphasized their genitalia in complete detail (known in the industry as "spreader" or "split beaver" magazines). — *The Presidential Commission on Obscenity and Pornography* 1970

spread shot *noun*
a photograph or scene in a pornographic film showing a woman's spread vagina *US, 1971*
• As an example, inspector Guido cited a set of glossy spread shots that sold under the counter for $8. — *Screw* 10th May 1971

spreck up *verb*
(of a male) to orgasm *UK, 2002*

A possible pun on 'ejaculate' based on German *sprechen* (to speak).

- I feel like I'm going to spreck up there and then. — Kevin Sampson, *Clubland* 2002

spunk *noun*
semen *UK, 1888*

- An overweight, faggy-looking Filipino in his early thirties – who was the "floater" at Annabel's gang bang – wipes up any and all spunk sprayed upon Jasmin today. — Anthony Petkovich, *The X Factory* 1997

squab *noun*
a young girl or woman *US, 1948*
From the standard sense (a newly hatched or very young bird).

- The table is so situated that the town's aging and more prosperous squab-hunters who congregate at it nightly can case the door and ogle the bims brought in by younger and more energetic men. — Jack Lait and Lee Mortimer, *New York Confidential* 1948

squack *noun*
a woman; sex with a woman *US, 1972*

- (Caption): WHEN HE GET some fine Ofay squack in the sheets, what he make her do? She suck his joint, man. — *Screw* 30th October 1972

squack *verb*
to ejaculate *US, 1993*

- I'm squacking in my pants. — *Airheads* 1993

squirter *noun*
a scene in a pornographic film or photograph depicting a man ejaculating *US, 1995*

- — *Adult Video News* August, 1995

stable *noun*
1 a group of prostitutes working for a single pimp or madam *US, 1937*

- He could watch and keep tabs on his stable of scrawny, junkie whores working the four corners of the intersection. — Iceberg Slim (Robert Beck), *Pimp* 1969

2 a group of 'slaves' in the control of, or at the disposal of, a dominatrix; a collection of masochists in the control of, a sadist *US, 1989*

- — Thomas E. Murray and Thomas R. Murrell, *The Language of Sadomasochism* 1989

stable sister *noun*
one prostitute in relation to the other prostitutes in a pimp's stable *US, 1972*

- Usually the player relies on one to help him recruit new additions, known as stable sisters. — Christina and Richard Milner, *Black Players* 1972

stacked *adjective*
possessing large breasts *US, 1942*
Sometimes intensified with phrases such as 'stone to the bone' or rhymed as in 'stacked and packed' (the name of a photographic calendar produced by former Nixon operative G. Gordon Liddy, featuring nearly naked women holding guns).

- Harry gave the blonde a seven, but you only gave her a six because you didn't think she was stacked enough for a seven. — Max Shulman, *Guided Tour of Campus Humor* 1955

stag *noun*
a pornographic film *US, 1966*

- You could see better stuff in any Times Square sex joint than those stags they were turning out. — Mickey Spillane, *Last Cop Out* 1972

stag movie *noun*
a pornographic film made for and enjoyed by men *US, 1960*

- Now, the stag movie, the dirty movie – the sixteen millimeter reduction print that you drag from lodge hall, the dirty movie that the Kefauver Committee would destroy and then recreate for private parties. — Lenny Bruce, *The Essential Lenny Bruce* 1967

stag party *noun*
a party for men only, usually organised to view pornography, tell sexual jokes and/or be entertained by strippers or prostitutes *US, 1856*

- College fraternities, volunteer fire companies, lodges, businessmen's associations, conventions, bachelor and stag parties comprise the most common customers for this strictly illegal film fare. — Michael Milner, *Sex on Celluloid* 1964

stalk *noun*
the penis, especially when in a state of erection *UK, 1961*

- Mrs Elizabeth Walk of Lambeth Walk / Had a husband who was jubblified with only half a stalk[.] — Ian Dury, *This is What We Find* 1979

stank noun
1 the vagina; sex US, 1980
Usually said unkindly.
- The answer is, it's gonna be interracial, which means it'll offer a few token liberal white broads a chance to give up a lil' stank... — Odie Hawkins, *The Busting Out of an Ordinary Man* 1985
▶ **get your stank on**
2 (from a female perspective) to have sex UK, 2002
Reclaiming STANK (the vagina) for women.
- If there is one thing that actually is better than getting walloped on brain-rotting chemical stimulants, then it's doing the nasty/getting your stank on* with a lady/man* (*delete as applicable). — *Ministry* October, 2002

stanky noun
sex US, 2002
- He insists he did have time for sex with Lucindreth. He smiles shyly when he tells us he "got some stanky on the hang-low." — Jimmy Lerner, *You Got Nothing Coming* 2002

starfish noun
the anus UK, 2001
- [Y]ou'll need to place your fingertips on her perineum (the smooth skin between pussy and starfish) so that you feel her internal contractions. — *Drugs An Adult Guide* December, 2001

starkers adjective
totally naked NEW ZEALAND, 1923
- — Louis S. Leland, *A Personal Kiwi-Yankee Dictionary* 1984

steak drapes noun
the vaginal labia UK, 1998
- — www.LondonSlang.com June, 2002

steam and cream; steam job noun
during the Vietnam war, a bath and sex with a prostitute US, 1991
- — Linda Reinberg, *In the Field* 1991

steamer noun
an act of oral sex performed on a man UK, 2003
- She doesnt go all the way but she'll definitely give you a steamer! — Chris Lewis, *The Dictionary of Playground Slang* 2003

stem noun
the penis US, 1972

- [N]obody to my knowledge spoke of "choad," "rod," "stem" or any other more strictly pornographic term. — *Screw* 3rd January 1972

stick noun
a prostitute US, 1972
- — Christina and Richard Milner, *Black Players* 1972

stick verb
(from the male perspective) to have sex US, 1972
- Did you get any action? Did you slam it to her? Did you stick her? Did you hump her? Did you run it down her throat? Did you jam it up her ass? Did you shoot your wad? — *Screw* 29th May 1972

stickspin noun
a scene in a pornographic film in which a woman changes positions without losing her vaginal grip on the man's penis US, 1995
- — *Adult Video News* September, 1995

stiffy noun
an erection UK, 1980
Also variants 'stiffie' and 'stiff'.
- TRISTE: only had to touch you and you had a stiffy like GARY: the Blackpool tower? — Patrick Jones, *Unprotected Sex* 1999

sting verb
▶ **sting between the toes**
(from a male perspective) to have sex AUSTRALIA, 1971
- So if youse tell a potato [woman] youse love her she'll let you sting her between the toes with the old pyjama python-shit! — Barry Humphries, *Bazza Pulls It Off!* 1971

stinger noun
the penis US, 1967
- — Dale Gordon, *The Dominion Sex Dictionary* 1967

stink-finger noun
the insertion of a finger or fingers into a woman's vagina UK, 1903
- I could see a black ugly stud playing "stink finger" with an angel-faced broad in a booth behind me. — Iceberg Slim (Robert Beck), *Pimp* 1969

stink pot noun
the vagina US, 1980
- — Edith A. Folb, *runnin' down some lines* 1980

stinky *noun*
a promiscuous woman *BERMUDA, 1985*
- — Peter Smith and Fred M. Barritt, *Bermewjan Vurds* 1985

stinky pinky *noun*
a finger enriched with the aroma of vagina *US, 1993*
- My phone rang. "In Framingham, some boys call themselves the Stinky Pinky Pussy Posse," the caller said. Geeze, what happened to the Boy Scouts? As far as the posse goes, suffice it to say that the boys, students at Framingham High School, like to do things with their hands, and we're not talking about building campfires or lean-tos. — *Boston Globe* 7th April 1993

stir *verb*
1 to have sex *US, 1973*
- I ain't stirred the old lady for a couple years, but I swear when I'm with Irma I get the urge like a young stallion[.] — Joseph Wambaugh, *The Blue Knight* 1973
▶ **stir the porridge**
2 (of a man) to have sex with a woman whose vagina is newly awash with the semen of her previous partner(s), especially if the final man in the line; to have sex with a woman who is in a sexual relationship with another man *AUSTRALIA, 1970*
- On festive occasions, such as a surf carnival, a generous girl will "put on a queue" behind the sand dunes for a seemingly unlimited line-up of young men. The boy on the end is said to be "stirring the porridge". — Richard Neville, *Play Power* 1970

stocks and bonds
a slogan used by prostitutes to advertise bondage services *UK, 2001*
- Instead of soliciting passing males, the hookers of London remained out of sight, if not out of mind, advertising their services on discreetly euphemistic postcards in the windows of local newsagents. "French Lessons", "Large Chest for Sale", "Stocks and Bonds". — Mick Farren (recalling London in the late 1960s), *Give the Anarchist a Cigarette* 2001

stones *noun*
the testicles *UK, 1154*
- They could have heard you squealing over in Cunt Lick County, just a squealing like a stoat with his stones cut off. — William Burroughs, *Naked Lunch* 1957

stonker *noun*
the erect penis *UK, 2001*
- Harry would be on the bed with a stonker, watching Lesley entertain Colin the candle. — Garry Bushell, *The Face* 2001

stonk-on *noun*
the erect penis *UK, 2003*
- [W]e really have to understand what goes in to making a successful stonk-on. — Richard Herring, *Talking Cock* 2003

stovepipe *noun*
a distended, gaping anus produced by recent anal intercourse *US, 1995*
- — *Adult Video News* September, 1995

straight *noun*
1 a heterosexual *US, 1941*
- [T]he pool-playing dykes and femmes sit at tables in one corner away from the juke-box, and the "straights" fill out the rest of the bar. — Roger Gordon, *Hollywood's Sexual Underground* 1966
2 simple vaginal intercourse *US, 1961*
- At first she figured she'd play it open-and-shut, bring him off and charge him twenty for a fifteen-dollar straight without dropping anything but her panties. — John Sayles, *Union Dues* 1977

straight date *noun*
conventional vaginal sex with a prostitute *US, 1972*
- At the hotel, if it's a straight date it's usually $10, and a French date, a blow job, is $20. — Bruce Jackson, *Outside the Law* 1972

straight-fuck *verb*
to engage in conventional vaginal intercourse *US, 1969*
- Mr. Smith got on top of Lisa, put his prick in her, and started straight-fucking her. — Joey V., *Portrait of Joey* 1969

straight lay *noun*
conventional vaginal sexual intercourse *US, 1997*
- Often times a guy would come in for a "Straight Lay", then during the medical

check, he would turn out to be an "Oh My God." — Sisters of the Heart, *The Brothel Bible* 1997

straight trade *noun*
homosexual sex with a man who considers himself heterosexual *US, 1972*
● One of the principal arguments that will be made, according to Martin, is that "homosexual behavior, by homosexuals, but especially also by sailors who consider themselves and are generally considered to be heterosexual – 'straight trade' – is widespread."
— *The Advocate* 19th January 1972

straight trick *noun*
vaginal sex between a prostitute and customer *US, 1972*
● In a joint most of them are straight tricks, but on call about half of them are straight and the other half a little other than straight. — Bruce Jackson, *In the Life* 1972

strange *noun*
a new and unknown sexual partner *US, 1967*
● Once qualifies as strange. More than once you might as well pop your old lady for all the surprises you get with whoo-ers. — James Ellroy, *White Jazz* 1992

strange stuff *noun*
a new and different sex-partner *US, 1950*
● "Do you want to bust in on the church dance?" Steven said. "It's Friday night. There ought to be some strange stuff there?" — Hal Ellson, *Tomboy* 1950

strap-on *noun*
a dildo that is harnessed to a person's body *UK, 1999*
● Eve was sitting on the edge of one of the twin beds, stark naked and with a strap-on sticking up from her cunt. — Stewart Home, *Sex Kick [britpulp]* 1999

strawberry *noun*
1 a woman who trades sex for crack cocaine *US, 1989*
● They would only say that they were investigating a series of crimes that involved women who traded sex for drugs. Since August, 1985, at least nine such women, known in street slang as "strawberries," have been found shot to death. — *Los Angeles Times* 24th February 1989

2 the female nipple *US, 1982*
Usually in the plural.
● — *Maledicta* Summer/Winter, 1982: 'Dyke diction': the language of lesbians

streetwalker *noun*
a prostitute who seeks customers on the street *UK, 1592*
● She was a streetwalker and I bought her a coffee in a hash joint. — Mickey Spillane, *My Gun is Quick* 1950

string *noun*
the group of prostitutes working for a particular pimp *US, 1913*
● Shortly before six the pimps parade their strings for all to admire. — Gail Sheehy, *Hustling* 1973

strings *noun*
the female legs *US, 1963*
● — *American Speech* December, 1963: 'American Indian student slang'

stroke *verb*
1 to masturbate *US, 1986*
● While not the greatest menage ever taped, the action is not bad; it certainly provides material for some lazy stroking. — *Adult Video* August/September, 1986
▶ **stroke the lizard**
2 (of a male) to masturbate *US, 1971*
● — Eugene Landy, *The Underground Dictionary* 1971

stroke book *noun*
a magazine or book viewed while masturbating *US, 1967*
● Millions of other stroke books – the antecedent to Playboy, National Geographic with the African chicks – oh yes, they're stroke books. — Lenny Bruce, *The Essential Lenny Bruce* 1967

strong move to the hole *noun*
a direct approach to seducing a girl *US, 1992*
Application of a basketball term to sexual relations.
● — Connie Eble (Editor), *UNC-CH Campus Slang* Spring, 1992

strop *verb*
▶ **strop the Mulligan**
(of a male) to masturbate *AUSTRALIA, 1971*
● If youse get jack [bored] of stropping the Mulligan and feel like spearing the bearded clam [...] tell the tart you love her! — Barry Humphries, *Bazza Pulls It Off!* 1971

strum *verb*
1 to masturbate *UK, 1999*
Also variant 'strum off'. From the up and
down stroking action that is strumming a
guitar.
- God just thinking about your hard dick
  going inside me is making me come...
  She left a half page, a big greasy patch
  smeared across it, then took up where
  she left off. Sorry, I just had to go and
  strum myself off – here's a little
  sample of what'll be waiting for you,
  my darling. – Kevin Sampson, *Powder*
  1999
▶ **strum the banjo**
2 (of a woman) to masturbate *UK, 2001*
- [S]he'll be strummin her banjo wivin
  seconds. – Sacha Baron-Cohen, *Da
  Gospel According to Ali G* 2001

stud hustler *noun*
a male homosexual prostitute who projects
a tough, masculine image *US, 1963*
- And malehustlers "fruithustlers"/
  "studhustlers": the various names for
  the masculine hustlers looking for
  lonely fruits to score from[.] – John
  Rechy, *City of Night* 1963

stuff *noun*
1 the female genitals *US, 1982*
- "Don't try to tell me what to wear!" she
  snapped back and started a slow
  forward stretch that exposed the hairs
  of her stuff. – Odie Hawkins, *Amazing
  Grace* 1993
2 the male genitals *US, 1966*
- "There's enough white stuff around."
  Vess grinned slyly, and as he did it
  occurred to me that the word "stuff"
  involved me more than it was
  comfortable to admit, since it was not
  oriented towards the coozies. – Phil
  Andros (Samuel M. Steward), *Stud*
  1966
3 an effeminate homosexual man *US, 1976*
- – John R. Armore and Joseph D. Wolfe,
  Dictionary of Desperation 1976

stump *noun*
the penis *US, 1993*
In a world where size matters, often but not
always applied to a short penis.
- – Judi Sanders, *Faced and Faded,
  Hanging to Hurl* 1993

stunt cock; stunt dick; stunt *noun*
a male pornography performer who fills in
for another performer who is unable to
maintain an erection or ejaculate when
needed *US, 2000*
- For the most part, cum shots are only
  faked in dire circumstances – like when
  a stunt cock can't be found and no
  one's being paid overtime. – Ana
  Loria, *1 2 3 Be A Porn Star!*

stunt pussy *noun*
a female pornography performer who fills in
for another performer for the purposes of
genital filming only *US, 2000*
- – Ana Loria, *1 2 3 Be A Porn Star!*
  2000: 'Glossary of adult sex industry
  terms'

sub *noun*
a sexual *sub*missive, a willing slave in a
sadomasochistic relationship *US, 1987*
- He's a sub who likes to be tied up,
  whipped, abused, spat on. The usual
  stuff[.] – Niall Griffiths, *Kelly + Victor*
  2002

submarine races *noun*
used as a euphemism for foreplay in a car
at a remote spot *US, 1967*
- – Hy Lit, *Hy Lit's Unbelievable
  Dictionary of Hip Words for Groovy
  People* 1968

Subway Sam *noun*
a man who is partial to sex in subway
toilets *US, 1966*
- A customer who consumates the sex
  act in a subway toilet is called a
  "Subway Sam." – Johnny Shearer, *The
  Male Hustler* 1966

suck *noun*
an act of oral sex *US, 1870*
- I mean, I've had some fabulous suck in
  my time, but this chick ... wow. – Terry
  Southern, *Now Dig This* 1975

suck *verb*
1 to perform oral sex *US, 1881*
- Were you ever caught sucking a girl?
  – *Screw* 7th March 1969
▶ **suck cock**
2 to perform oral sex on a man *US, 1941*
- Sharon was munching wetly, moaning all
  over Lenny's dick, tugging his balls and
  working her mouth – she was born to
  suck cock. – *Letters to Penthouse V* 1995

suckee-suckee *noun*
oral sex performed on a man *US, 1987*
From the patois of Vietnamese prostitutes
during the war, embraced by soldiers.

• Me suckee-suckee. My love you too much. — *Full Metal Jacket* 1987

suckhole *noun*
a hole between private video booths in a pornography arcade or between stalls in a public toilet, designed for anonymous oral sex between men *US, 1987*
• — *Maledicta* Summer/Winter, 1986–1987: 'Sexual slang: prostitutes, pedophiles, flagellators, transvestites, and necrophiles'

suck job *noun*
an act of oral sex *US, 1969*
• Just as jello makes a nice change from oatmeal, a suck job beats a hand job any time. — Samuel West, *Hard-headed Dick* 1975

suck-off *noun*
an act of oral sex *US, 1995*
• A two-way suck-off is just what the doctor ordered. — *Letters to Penthouse V* 1995

BROTHEL

boom-boom house; boom-boom parlor *noun, US, 1966*
• — *American-Statesman (Austin, Texas)* 9th January 1966
chicken ranch *noun, US, 1973*
a rural brothel
Originally the name of a brothel in LaGrange, Texas, and then spread to more generic use.
• Hey, you don't make a thousand bucks tax-free by staying in bed unless you're working at one of those chicken ranches in Nevada. — Joseph Wambaugh, *Fugitive Nights* 1992
creep house *noun, US, 1913*
a brothel where customers are routinely robbed
• Warnings of immorality were probably less effective than warnings that some brothels

were creep houses or panel houses wherein visitors were robbed of money and gold watches. — Irving Lewis Allen, *The City in Slang* 1993
grind joint *noun, US, 1962*
• It's the snazziest grind joint you ever heard of. And if you happen to catch clap from one of the broads over there, you don't have to worry because it's a higher class of clap. — Charles Perry, *Portrait of a Young Man Drowning* 1962
sugar hill *noun, US, 1987*
• — *Maledicta* Summer/Winter, 1986–1987: 'Sexual slang: prostitutes, pedophiles, flagellators, transvestites, and necrophiles'

suckie *noun*
a woman, perceived as a sex object *US, 1981*
• That Karen was a good looking bitch, but I figured she was probably just like all the other young good looking suckies that hang around with bikers[.] — Robert Lipkin, *A Brotherhood of Outlaws* 1981

suckie fuckie *verb*
to perform oral sex on a man followed by sexual intercourse *US, 1987*
Vietnam war usage.
• Suckee, fuckee, smoke cigarette in the pussy, she give you everything you want. Long time. — *Full Metal Jacket* 1987

sucking *noun*
an act of oral sex *UK, 1869*
• Then she gave me a final sucking, draining me dry. — *Letters to Penthouse V* 1995

sucky *noun*
oral sex on a man *US, 2001*
• So the arrogant sergeant first class was going to the sucky room with a boy dressed like a girl and didn't even know it. — Kregg Jorgenson, *Very Crazy G.I.* 2001

sucky-fucky *noun*
a combination of oral and vaginal sex *US, 1981*
• "Mmmm," she said, pursing her lips together. "Sucky-fucky, twenty dollar." — Kregg Jorgenson, *Very Crazy G.I.* 2001

sugar dish *noun*
the vagina *US, 1998*
A variation of C19 obsolete 'sugar basin' (the vagina).
• My mother said no tampons. You couldn't put anything in your sugar dish. — Eve Ensler, *The Vagina Monologues* 1998

sugar hill *noun*
a brothel *US, 1987*
- — *Maledicta* Summer/Winter, 1986–1987: 'Sexual slang: prostitutes, pedophiles, flagellators, transvestites, and necrophiles'

suitcase boy *noun*
the boyfriend/'agent' of a sexual performer *US, 1974*
- He told me that he would be my "suitcase boy," so that people could call him a gigolo and a pimp. — Blaze Starr, *Blaze Starr* 1974

suitcase pimp; suitcase *noun*
a boyfriend, agent or other male who accompanies a female pornography performer to the set *US, 1995*
- Porsche Lynn actually came up with the term suitcase pimp, because a lot of these guys will walk behind the girl carrying her bags. They are essentially leeches. (Quoting Bill Marigold) — Ana Loria, *1 2 3 Be A Porn Star!* 2000

swab *verb*
▶ **swab the deck**
to perform oral sex on a woman *US, 1964*
- — Roger Blake, *The American Dictionary of Sexual Terms* 1964

swamp ass *noun*
sweaty genitals and/or buttocks *US, 1995*
- Stations that air the Howard Stern Show were fined $27,000 to $500,000 because he joked about personal hygiene issues like "swamp ass" on different shows. — *Daily News (New York)* 25th January 2005

swanz *noun*
the penis *US, 1985*
- They wore wigs and tied their cocks up with pantyhose back toward their ass, so if the guy reached down there he couldn't feel the swanz hanging there to give the guy away. — Mark Baker, *Cops* 1985

swap *verb*
▶ **swap cans**
(used of a male homosexual couple) to take turns as the active participant in anal sex *US, 1965*
- — *The Guild Dictionary of Homosexual Terms* 1965

sweater kittens *noun*
the female breasts *US, 2005*

- Not only did she expose a lungful of her fist-sized frisky sweater kittens, but she even flashed some pussy, cats! — Mr. Skin, *Mr. Skin's Skincyclopedia* 2005

sweater meat *noun*
the female breasts *US, 2004*
- — Ben Applebaum and Derrick Pittman, *Turd Ferguson & The Sausage Party* 2004

sweater puppies *noun*
a female breast *US, 1994*
- In the press tent, free copies of The Generation X Field Guide and Lexicon are available for those who don't already know that sweater puppies are breasts[.] — *Playboy* November, 1997

Swedish headache *noun*
an aching in the testicles from sexual activity that does not culminate in ejaculation *US, 1932*
- — *Maledicta* 1979: 'A glossary of ethnic slurs in american English'

Swedish massage *noun*
ejaculation achieved with the man's penis between the woman's breasts *UK, 1973*
- [H]ere's ten pounds, why don't you pop up to the school nurse, present her my compliments and have her give you a deep, relaxing Swedish massage. — Peter Cook, *Crime and Punishment* 1973

sweet thing *noun*
an attractive young woman *US, 1971*
- So Mick [Jagger...] disengages himself from the sweet thing at his side[.] — Lester Bangs, *Psychotic Reactions and Carburetor Dung* 1971

swing *noun*
a consensual orgy *US, 1969*
- But walk into a swing and take a long look around the room. Every broad (if you've got the time and stamina) is yours. — *Screw* 7th February 1969

swing *verb*
1 to enjoy frequent casual sex with different partners *UK, 1964*
- I swung with him and he was a very good lover. I had a marvelous time. — Frank Robinson, *Sex American Style* 1971
▶ **swing both ways**
2 to be bisexual *UK, 1972*

● [I]n North Carolina a hot dog is free to swing both ways. Nothing in France is free from sexual assignment. — David Sedaris, *Me Talk Pretty One Day* 2001

swinger *noun*
someone who engages in spouse or partner swapping *US, 1964*
● I'm talkin' me 'n Dot are Swingers! As in "to swing!" Wife-swappin'! — *Raising Arizona* 1987

swinging *noun*
consensual swapping of sexual partners as a deliberate activity *UK, 1976*
● In two decades of swinging they have slept with at least 200 people between them. Barry [Calvert] has just published his swinging memoirs. — *The Guardian* 29th August 2003

swipe *noun*
the penis *US, 1969*
● But old Franky only laughed, 'cause he was coming at last / And his swipe swole twice its size. — Dennis Wepman et al., *The Life* 1976

switch *noun*
1 a person willing to play any role in a sado-masochistic sexual encounter *US, 2001*

● You can be a spanking top, a bondage bottom, and a sensory-deprivation switch. — Tristan Taormino, *Pucker Up* 2001
2 the buttocks *US, 1949*
● Got nice legs, and a nice switch. — Hal Ellson, *Duke* 1949

switcher *noun*
a bisexual *US, 1966*
● [S]ometimes they're switchers: married men whose wives held out on them the night before. They decide to play the other side of the street before going to the office. — Johnny Shearer, *The Male Hustler* 1966

switch hitter *noun*
1 a bisexual *US, 1960*
● In those days, she was a switch-hitter, now she was straight dyke. — Edwin Torres, *After Hours* 1979
2 a person who masturbates with first one hand and then the other *US, 2002*
● — Gary K. Farlow, *Prison-ese* 2002

sword fighting *noun*
a sexual act in which two erect penises compete for or share the attention of a single person performing oral sex *UK, 2002*
● — www.LondonSlang.com June, 2002

Tt

table dance *noun*
in a strip-club, a semi-private sexual performance near or on a customer's table *US, 1992*
- Some customers request table dances. The dancer leaves the stage and goes to the customer's table, a tiny round table with spindly legs, littered with glasses. She climbs on the table and moves to the music while removing all her clothing. — Marilyn Suriani Futterman, *Dancing Naked in the Material World* 1992

table pussy *noun*
a woman with good looks and manners *US, 1970*
- A stew can come under the heading of class stuff, or table pussy[.] — Jim Bouton, *Ball Four* 1970

tackle *noun*
the male genitalia *UK, 1788*
Originally 'a man's tackle' subsequent familiarity reduced the necessity for 'a man's'.
- Stripe me, Dave, you gonna just stand there while some woofter is waving his tackle at your missus? — *The Full Monty* 1997

tail *noun*
1 a woman, regarded as a sexual object; women, collectively, categorised with the same regard *UK, 1846*
- "They ought to have a youth center in this burg," said Wally, "where a guy could pick up some tail." — Max Shulman, *Rally Round the Flag, Boys!* 1957
2 an act of sexual intercourse or sexual intercourse in a general sense *UK, 1933*
- MR. CHEEKY: Oh, yeah. My brother usually rescues me, if he can keep off the tail for more than twenty minutes. Huh. BRIAN: Ahhh? MR. CHEEKY: Randy little bugger. Up and down like the Assyrian Empire. — Monty Python, *Life of Brian* 1979

taily *noun*
the penis *US, 1982*
- — John A. Holm, *Dictionary of Bahamian English* 1982

taint *noun*
the perineum *US, 1955*
- I had a big round cheek in each hand and I lowered them down until my prick was bobbing somewhere around her taint – you know what a woman's taint is: 'taint asshole and 'taint cunt. — Willie Baron, *Play This Love With Me* 2004

take *verb*
1 (of a male) to have sex with someone *UK, 1915*
- Joe smears Cathie in tomato sauce and custard before taking her from behind in a desperate, loveless manner. — *Empire* September, 2003
▶ **take one for the team**
2 in a social situation, to pay attention to the less attractive of a pair of friends in the hope that your friend will have success with the more attractive member of the pair *US, 2002*
- — Connie Eble (Editor), *UNC-CH Campus Slang* October, 2002
▶ **take yourself in hand**
3 (of a male) to masturbate *UK, 1953*
- [H]is unsated cockstand demanded alleviation. He took himself in hand, positive that he'd achieve more pleasure on his own[.] — Cheryl Holt, *Complete Abandon* 2003

talala *noun*
the vulva and vagina *TRINIDAD AND TOBAGO, 1959*
- — Lise Winer, *Dictionary of the English/Creole of Trinidad & Tobago* 2003

tallywhacker; tallywacker *noun*
the penis *US, 1966*
- [A] brief commercial opened with a full-body shot of an elephant, then zoomed in on the behemoth's tallywacker, which nearly filled the screen. — Jack Seward, *More About the Japanese* 1971

tamboo bamboo *noun*
the penis *TRINIDAD AND TOBAGO, 1980*
An allusion to a musical instrument made from a length of bamboo.
- — Lise Winer, *Dictionary of the English/Creole of Trinidad & Tobago* 2003

T and A *noun*
visual depictions of sexually provocative females *US, 1993*
From TITS AND ASS; TITS AND ARSE.

- Beautiful Girls flashing T&A and BUSH!
  — Peter Sotos, *Index* 1996

tango *verb*
to have sex *US, 1964*
- "You know, I go for dames, but after I
  seen you two tango, I got the hots for
  one of you, or even both," the man
  said, laughing. — K.B. Raul, *Naked to
  the Night* 1964

tank-ass *noun*
buttocks that are disproportionately large
US, 2001
- — Don R. McCreary (Editor), *Dawg
  Speak* 2001

tap *verb*
to have sex *US, 1949*
- I hear he's tapping Edie Finneran.
  — *The Usual Suspects* 1995

tape and tuck *verb*
(used of a male) to tape your penis and
testicles between your legs in an effort to
pass as a woman *AUSTRALIA, 1985*
- — Thommo, *The Dictionary of
  Australian Swearing and Sex Sayings*
  1985

tapioca *noun*
semen; an urgent need to ejaculate semen
UK, 1980
- A day spent in a warm studio with a
  perfumed houri or two is bound to [...]
  send you home with a touch of the
  tapioca, I shouldn't wonder. — *British
  Journal of Photography* 4th January 1980

Tarzan *noun*
sex outdoors *US, 1966*
- Studs in New York, particularly those
  working the Public Library and Bryant
  Park areas, call a frantic quickie in the
  bushes a "jungle job" or a "Tarzan."
  — Johnny Shearer, *The Male Hustler*
  1966

taters *noun*
the buttocks *US, 1999*
- — Connie Eble (Editor), *UNC-CH
  Campus Slang* Fall, 1999

tea-bag *verb*
in the pursuit of sexual pleasure, to take a
man's scrotum completely into the mouth,
sucking and tonguing it *US, 1998*
- I'm gonna finger-fuck her tight little
  asshole! Finger-bang ... and tea-bag my
  balls ... in her mouth! — Kevin Smith,
  Jay and Silent Bob Strike Back 2001

teabagging *noun*
the sucking of a man's entire scrotum *US,
1998*
- Made famous in John Waters's fab flick
  Pecker, teabagging is a remarkably
  accurate description of a top technique
  that involves his balls and your mouth.
  — Dan Anderson, *Sex Tips for Gay Guys*
  2001

tea dance *noun*
a social gathering featuring same-sex
dancing *US, 1965*
- Tea dance. What a helluva name for
  what it really is. It got its name
  because the Sunday dances begin at
  precisely the tea hour. — Joe Houston,
  The Gay Flesh 1965

team cream *noun*
an orgy *US, 1970*
- — *American Speech* Spring-Summer,
  1970: 'Homosexual slang'

tear *verb*
▶ **tear off a chunk**
to have sex *US, 1973*
- Shit, before my Flossie got sick, I used
  to tear off a chunk every night.
  — Joseph Wambaugh, *The Blue Knight*
  1973
▶ **tear off; tear off a piece**
to have sex *US, 1964*
- [W]e quickly tear off several goodies,
  then, I go back to work. — Neal
  Cassady, *The First Third* 1971

tea-room cruiser *noun*
a male homosexual prostitute who
frequents public toilets *US, 1982*
- — *Maledicta* Summer/Winter, 1982:
  'Dyke diction: the language of lesbians'

tea room queen *noun*
a homosexual man who frequents public
restrooms in search of sex *US, 1941*
- I am not a tea-room queen. Besides, I
  am looking for a more lasting relationship. And I don't want no man who
  looks around toilets. — Larry Kramer,
  Faggots 2000

tease and please *noun*
sexual arousal after which satisfaction is
delayed under the pretence that such
gratification is denied *UK, 2003*
- — Caroline Archer, *Tart Cards* 2003

teeter-totter *noun*
a double-headed dildo *US, 1968*

Based on the visual image of two women connected by a dildo rocking up and down.
- Here in the United States it is termed "the teeter-totter." — L. Reinhard, *Oral Sex Techniques and Sex Practices Illustrated* 196

telescope *noun*
the penis *US, 1968*
- — *Current Slang* Spring, 1968

ten-day sweat *noun*
treatment for a sexually transmitted infection, involving heat therapy and sulpha-based drugs *US, 1949*
- — *American Speech* February, 1949: 'A.V.G. lingo'

tent pole *noun*
an erect penis *US, 1992*
From the image of an erect penis pushing up against a sheet.
- Tent pole. She's a babe. — *Wayne's World* 1992

Texas toothbrush *noun*
the penis *US, 1994*
In Texas, known as an 'Oklahoma toothbrush'.
- — Michael Dalton Johnson, *Talking Trash with Redd Foxx* 1994

TFTF
an after-dinner bloated condition unsuited to the advancement of romance *UK, 2002*
A coded message: 'too fat to fuck'.
- — *www.LondonSlang.com* June, 2002

thatch *noun*
a woman's pubic hair *US, 2005*
- Imagine Saturday Night Live with a trim-butt blonde with high, firm, round boobies and a moderate, light-brown thatch cracking jokes with all her sweet bits hanging out. — Mr. Skin, *Mr. Skin's Skincyclopedia* 2005

thimble-titted *adjective*
small breasted *US, 1994*
- — Michael Dalton Johnson, *Talking Trash with Redd Foxx* 1994

thing *noun*
the vagina *US, 1970*
Euphemism. Early use implied in obsolete 'thingstable' (1785) where 'thing' replaces CUNT in a policeman's title.
- His sister would show you her thing for two cigarette cards. — Johnny Speight, *It Stands to Reason* 1973

third base *noun*
in a notional hierarchy of sexual activity, intimate sexual contact short of intercourse *US, 1948*
Generally, but not always, a reference to touching of the genitals.
- I got to third base last night, I'll make her yet. — Norman Mailer, *The Naked and the Dead* 1948

third leg *noun*
the penis *US, 1994*
- Condoms have become an essential part of the modern man's wardrobe, an extra sock for the third leg. — Anka Radakovich, *The Wild Girls Club* 1994

thirty-three; 33 *noun*
a prostitute's customer who is not quickly satisfied *US, 1971*
From long-playing vinyl records.
- A customer who worked quickly was called a "78" and one with a slower response was a "33." — Charles Winick, *The Lively Commerce* 1971

thrap *verb*
of a male to masturbate *UK, 2001*
- Ad a wank in front of us all, dinny? [...] Didn't give a fuck like, just whapped it out and started thrappin. — Niall Griffiths, *Sheepshagger* 2001

three-hairs *noun*
a Vietnamese woman *US, 1991*
From the perception of the US soldier that the pubic hair of Vietnamese women is very sparse.
- — Linda Reinberg, *In the Field* 1991

threesome *noun*
group sex with three participants *US, 1972*
- "What? A threesome?" "Fuckin' right." "Who with?" — Colin Butts, *Is Harry on the Boat?* 1997

three-way *noun*
sex involving three people simultaneously *US, 1985*
- He introduced me to some model he'd gone out with and kept pushing for a three-way, but I started getting jealous at that point and told him I wanted to go home. — Sandra Bernhard, *Confessions of a Pretty Lady* 1988

three-way *adjective*
(used of a woman) willing to engage in vaginal, anal and oral sex *US, 1967*

- She was a three-way wench, played Jasper in a pinch/ And took 'em around the horn. (Collected in 1963). — Dennis Wepman et al., *The Life* 1976

three-way freeway *noun*
a woman who consents to vaginal, anal and oral sex *US, 2001*
- — *Sky Magazine* July, 2001

throw *verb*
▶ **throw it to**
from a male perspective, to have sex *US, 1969*
- My boyfriend and I do it at least once a day, generally oftener, but every now and then he gets a honk out of watching one of his friends throw it to me. — *Screw* 16th May 1969
▶ **throw one**
from the male perspective, to have sex *US, 1954*
- Man, would I like to throw one to her. — Bernard Wolfe, *The Late Risers* 1954
▶ **throw the bald-headed champ**
to perform oral sex on a man *US, 1972*
- And then you start pulling on the rope [masturbating him] or to throw the bald-headed champ [perform fellatio], boy you have reached rock bottom in my opinion. — Bruce Jackson, *In the Life* 1972

ticket *noun*
a woman who accompanies, and validates the entry of, an unattached male to a swingers' party *UK, 2006*
- Consequently, he'd ask me to go as his ticket to Bill and Beverley's party. — Ashley Lister, *Swingers* 2006

tickets *noun*
the female breasts *US, 1977*
A term from the coarse sector of the entertainment industry, recognising the selling power of sex.
- — Connie Eble (Editor), *UNC-CH Campus Slang* April, 1977

tickle *verb*
1 to administer oral sex to a male pornographer performer before or between scenes to help him maintain an erection *US, 2000*
- — Ana Loria, *1 2 3 Be A Porn Star!* 2000: 'Glossary of adult sex industry terms'
▶ **tickle the pickle**
2 from the male perspective, to have sex *US, 1964*

- You and Myra better stop playing tickle the pickle, boy, before you bat your brains out with your balls. — Jim Thompson, *Pop. 1280* 1964

tidy; tidy up *verb*
to wash the vulva and vagina *TRINIDAD AND TOBAGO, 1978*
- — *Dictionary of the English/Creole of Trinidad & Tobago* 2003

tie and tease *noun*
sexual bondage alternating pleasurable stimulation and deliberate frustration *UK, 2003*
- — Caroline Archer, *Tart Cards* 2003

tig ol' bitties *noun*
large breasts *US, 2001*
An intentional Spoonerism of 'big old titties'.
- — Connie Eble (Editor), *UNC-CH Campus Slang* Spring, 2001

Tijuana Bible *noun*
a pornographic comic book *US, 1979*
- — *Maledicta* 1979: 'A glossary of ethnic slurs in American English'

ting-a-ling *noun*
the penis *BAHAMAS, 1982*
- — John A. Holm, *Dictionary of Bahamian English* 1982

tip *verb*
1 to perform oral sex *UK, 2002*
- — Paul Baker, *Polari* 2002
▶ **tip the velvet**
2 to kiss with the tongue, especially to 'tongue a woman' *UK, 1699*
Based on obsolete 'velvet' (the tongue).
- — Sarah Waters, *Tipping the Velvet* 1998

tit *noun*
the female breast *US, 1928*
- I have had two women so far, one American with huge tits and a splendid Mex whore in house. — Jack Kerouac, *Letter to Allen Ginsberg* 10th May 1952

tit and clit chain *noun*
a decorative chain that connects a woman's pierced nipples and clitoris *US, 1996*
- Dawn unzipped her leather skirt, peeled it down, and showed Blaze where the second chain went. "Tit 'n' clit chains. Right now they're only clamped on, but pretty soon I'm gonna get 'em pierced." — Joseph Wambaugh, *Floaters* 1996

titanic *noun*
someone who performs oral sex on first
acquaintance *UK, 2002*
A jokey reference to 'going down'
(performing oral sex) first time out; the RMS
Titanic famously sunk on her maiden
voyage.
- — *Roger's Profanisaurus* 2002

tit-clamp *noun*
a device, designed to cause discomfort or
pain for sexual stimulation, that is attached
to a breast or nipple *UK, 1995*
- Fighting my way through the tit-clamps
  and cire-pouches, I ordered a drink.
  — Kitty Churchill, *Thinking of England*
  1995

tit-fuck *noun*
an act of rubbing the penis in the
compressed cleavage between a woman's
breasts *US, 1972*
- High lights: the scene where Wilder
  jerks off Jamie Gillis, and a magnificent
  tit-fuck between John Leslie and Mona
  Page (a starlet who had an all-too-brief
  career in porn). — *Adult Video*
  August/September, 1986

tit-fuck *verb*
to rub the penis in the compressed cleavage
between a woman's breasts *US, 1986*
- I have always been well endowed
  (38E), so I am well aware of how men
  like to, to put it bluntly, tit-fuck. — Joan
  Elizabeth Lloyd, *Totally Private* 2001

tit magazine *noun*
a magazine featuring photographs of naked
women *US, 1972*
- "Bring me a couple of tit magazines."
  "I'm embarrasssed to buy them,"
  Charley said. — Richard Condon,
  Prizzi's Honor 1982

tit run *noun*
a walk through a crowd in search of
attractive female breasts *US, 1995*
- — *Maledicta* 1995: 'Door whore and
  other New Mexico restaurant slang'

tits and ass; tits and arse *adjective*
said of a film, television programme, or
magazine featuring nudity *US, 1965*
- "Tits and ass! Tits and ass!" Lenny
  Bruce was fond of yelling. — *Screw*
  25th April 1969

titty; tittie *noun*
the female breast *IRELAND, 1922*

- I won't let men touch me. Or suck my
  titties. Hell no. — Susan Hall,
  Gentleman of Leisure 1972

titty bar; tittie bar *noun*
a bar featuring bare-breasted female
servers and/or dancers *US, 1991*
- I told him he better explain those
  places are titty bars. Raji goes, "Not
  when little Minh Linh's dancing. She
  don't have enough to make it a titty
  bar." — Elmore Leonard, *Be Cool* 1999

titty-fuck *noun*
an act of rubbing the penis in the
compressed cleavage between a woman's
breasts *US, 1988*
Elaboration of TIT-FUCK.
- Are you all here playing Titty-Fuck or
  something? — Paul Watkins, *Night Over
  Day Over Night* 1988

titty-fuck *verb*
to rub the penis in the compressed
cleavage between a woman's breasts *US,
1998*
- I'm titty-fuckin' Bette Midler[.]
  — Eminem (Marshall Mathers), *Low
  Down Dirty* 1998

titty hard-ons *noun*
erect nipples *AUSTRALIA, 1996*
- — James Lambert, *The Macquarie Book
  of Slang* 1996

tit-wank *noun*
an act of sexual gratification in which the
penis is rubbed between a female partner's
breasts *UK, 2002*
- There wasn't really enough time for a
  proper shag, so he'd decided to go for
  the slippery tit-wank[.] — Colin Butts, *Is
  Harry Still on the Boat?* 2003

Tobago love *noun*
a relationship in which there is little or no
display of affection *TRINIDAD AND TOBAGO,
1993*
- — *Dictionary of the English/Creole of
  Trinidad & Tobago* 2003

to both ways *adverb*
willing to play both the active and passive
role in homosexual sex *US, 1972*
- All the punks go both ways, the queens
  don't. — Bruce Jackson, *In the Life* 1972

todger *noun*
the penis *UK, 1986*
From the obsolete verb 'todge' (to smash to
a pulp).

● [S]hoving the tiny todger up — *GQ* July, 2001

todger dodger *noun*
a lesbian *UK, 2002*
● — *Roger's Profanisaurus* 2002

toilet *noun*
fat buttocks *BAHAMAS, 1982*
● — John A. Holm, *Dictionary of Bahamian English* 1982

toilet services *noun*
in a prostitute's advertising, the act of urination, or defecation, by one person on another for sadomasochistic gratification *UK, 2003*
● — Caroline Archer, *Tart Cards* 2003

said. — Joseph Wambaugh, *Finnegan's Week* 1993

tommy *noun*
the penis *BAHAMAS, 1982*
● — John A. Holm, *Dictionary of Bahamian English* 1982

Tommy Tucker *noun*
the penis, especially when erect *UK, 1966*
● [C]onstant meths drinking has ruined the muscles that control Tommy Tucker and he will not rise to the occasion, any more than a boiled carrot.
— Geoffrey Fletcher, *Down Among the Meths Men* 1966

tongue *noun*
1 the clitoris *TRINIDAD AND TOBAGO, 2003*

SEXUALLY TRANSMITTED INFECTIONS

big casino *noun, US, 1948*
● Nitti, like Capone, had picked up in his travels the occupational malady of the underworld, euphemistically known as the capital prize, or big casino. — *San Francisco Call-Bulletin* 23rd February 1948

blue balls *noun, US, 1912*
● — Roger Blake, *The American Dictionary of Sexual Terms* 1964

canoe inspection *noun, US, 1964*
a medical inspection of a woman's genitals for signs of a sexually transmitted disease
● — Robert A. Wilson, *Playboy's Book of Forbidden Words* 1972

package *noun, US, 1950*
a sexually transmitted infection, especially gonorrhea

● — Hyman E. Goldin et al., *Dictionary of American Underworld Lingo* 1950

short-arm inspection; small-arm inspection *noun, UK, 1919*
an inspection for a sexually transmitted infection
Soldiers or prisoners are lined up, each holding his penis. At the command 'Skin it back and milk it down', each man 'milks' down his penis from the base to the tip so that the inspecting doctor can check for pus at the tip of the urethra.
● There was a crowd in the kitchen, a mob in the hall / A short-arm inspection by the shithouse wall. — Dennis Wepman et al., *The Life* 1976

---

tomato *noun*
an attractive woman, especially a young one *US, 1929*
● When Ralph Ginzburg began publishing Avant Garde magazine, rival editor Paul Krassner asked sardonically, "How avant garde is a man who still calls women 'tomatoes'?" — Robert A. Wilson, *Playboy's Book of Forbidden Words* 1972

tom-cat; tomcat *verb*
to pursue women for the purpose of fleeting sexual encounters *US, 1927*
● "It doesn't pay to tomcat around in singles bars, not in these times," Fin

● — *Dictionary of the English/Creole of Trinidad & Tobago* 2003
▶ **get tongue**
2 in the categorisation of sexual activity by teenage boys, to kiss with tongue contact *US, 1986*
● There were several degrees of "making out." The first was "tongue." "Did you get tongue?" was a question frequently heard after a first date with an extremely nice, honor-student-type girl. — Terry Southern, *Now Dig This* 1986

tongue bath *noun*
oral stimulation of the body *US, 2005*

- Ursula lies back from an awe-inspiring lesboid tongue-bath from Adriana Vega. — Mr. Skin, *Mr. Skin's Skincyclopedia* 2005

tongue job *noun*
oral sex on a woman *UK, 1984*
- — Xaviera Hollander, *The Best Part of a Man* 1975

tongue wash *noun*
oral sex, especially on a woman *US, 1981*
- A tongue wash now and then made the time go faster, right? — Gerald Petievich, *Money Men* 1981

tonk *noun*
the penis *AUSTRALIA, 1972*
- I feel like a spare tonk in a knock-shop wedding. — *The Adventures of Barry McKenzie* 1972

tonk *verb*
to have sex *UK, 1974*
Euphemistic for FUCK. ·
- If I was really smart I wouldn't be tonking Gerald's old lady. — Ted Lewis, *Jack Carter's Law* 1974

tonky *noun*
the genitals, male or female *BAHAMAS, 1982*
- — John A. Holm, *Dictionary of Bahamian English* 1982

tool *noun*
the penis *UK, 1553*
Conventional English at first – found in Shakespeare's *Henry VIII* – and then rediscovered in the C20 as handy slang.
- Men wake up every morning and look at their tools standing at attention. — Anka Radakovich, *The Wild Girls Club* 1994

tool check *noun*
an inspection by a military doctor or medic of male recruits for signs of sexually transmitted disease *US, 1967*
- — Dale Gordon, *The Dominion Sex Dictionary* 1967

tools of the trade *noun*
any objects used in sadomasochistic activities, especially when advertised by a prostitute *UK, 2003*
- — Caroline Archer, *Tart Cards* 2003

toot *noun*
a prostitute *US, 2001*
- — Rick Ayers (Editor), *Slang Dictionary* 2001

toothing *noun*
anonymous casual sexual activity with any partner arranged over Blue*tooth*™ radio technology-enabled mobile phones *UK, 2004*
- Toothing [...] is a growing trend among rail commuters. Using Bluetooth, impromptu sex sessions are arranged with strangers in the lavatories. — *The Times* 12th June 2004

top *noun*
the dominant partner in a homosexual or sadomasochistic relationship *US, 1961*
- In fact, you make me feel kind of submissive. Usually, I'm a top. — Stewart Home, *Sex Kick [britpulp]* 1999

top *verb*
to take the dominant, controlling role in a sadomasochistic relationship *US, 1997*
- For the man who buys the services of a dominatrix, being "topped" is attractive as long as it's a service. — Jill Nagle, *Whores and Other Feminists* 1997

top bitch *noun*
in a group of prostitutes working for a pimp, the latest addition to the group *US, 1967*
- Oliver had assured her that she was his top bitch but demanded to know why she couldn't catch as many dates as Alice, his bottom bitch. — Joseph Wambaugh, *Floaters* 1996

top bollocks; top ballocks *noun*
the female breasts *UK, 1971*
- Whenever I see a decent jam tart with a good set of top bollocks I'm in like Flynn, NO PROBS! — Barry Humphries, *Bazza Pulls It Off!* 1971

top hats *noun*
erect nipples *US, 1997*
- — Pamela Munro, *U.C.L.A. Slang* 1997

top man *noun*
in a homosexual couple, the partner who plays the active role during sex *US, 1941*
- They are usually long-terms and are familiarly known to inmates by such local cognomens as "wolves," "top men," "jockers" or "daddies." — *Ebony* July, 1951

torch job *noun*
an enema containing a heat-inducing agent such as Vicks Vaporub™, Ben-Gay™, Heet™, or Tobasco™ sauce *US, 1972*

- — Robert A. Wilson, *Playboy's Book of Forbidden Words* 1972

tortoise head *noun*
the erect penis *UK, 2001*
- HER: I love science, Ali. U: Wotever, I iz got a tortoise head, could u direct me to da laboratory. — Sacha Baron-Cohen, *Da Gospel According to Ali G* 2001

toss *noun*
an act of masturbation *UK, 1785*
- If yer need a toss you wait 'til association. We take it in turns, the rest of us go out [of the prison cell]. — Chris Baker and Andrew Day, *Lock, Stock... & A Good Slopping Out* 2000

toss *verb*
1 (of a male) to masturbate *UK, 1879*
Often used with 'off'.
- He closed his eyes, allowed the onanistic thought some breathing space and tossed himself off something stupid. — Nick Earls, *Perfect Skin* 2001
▶ **toss it to**
2 to have sex with a woman *US, 1964*
- You've tossed it to her so often, you've thrown your ass of line with your eyeballs. — Jim Thompson, *Pop. 1280* 1964
▶ **toss salad**
3 to engage in oral stimulation of the anus *US, 2001*
- You know what they make you do in County? Toss the fucking salad! I don't like this fuck's asshole; I'm gonna do it for some stranger. — Kevin Smith, *Jay and Silent Bob Strike Back* 2001

tossed salad *noun*
any of several sexual practices involving oral-anal stimulation *US, 1997*
- OK, a tossed salad is — get ready, hold onto your underwear for this one — oral-anal sex. — *Oprah Winfrey Show* 2nd October 2003

tossle; tossel *noun*
the penis *AUSTRALIA, 1945*
Variant of 'tassle' (something that dangles).
- Then Sodomy, always quickest on the rise, had his terrifying blue-veined tossel out[.] — Frank Hardy, *The Outcasts of Foolgarah* 1971

tot-tots *noun*
the female breasts *TRINIDAD AND TOBAGO, 1974*

- — *Dictionary of the English/Creole of Trinidad & Tobago* 2003

touch *verb*
to have sex with someone *IRELAND, 1984*
- He was the horniest dog I ever met lads. The same fella would touch a cat goin' through a skylight, I'm not coddin' or jokin' ye. — Billy Roche, *Tumbling Down* 1984

touch-on *noun*
an erection *UK, 2001*
- I'm half getting a touch-on from the way she looked at us[.] — Kevin Sampson, *Outlaws* 2001

touch up *verb*
to caress and fondle someone in a sexual manner *UK, 1903*
- I told him that Mr Stanton was touching me up during the night. — BBC TV, *Panorama* 10th March 1997

town bike *noun*
a promiscuous female *AUSTRALIA, 1945*
Everybody has, it seems, 'taken a ride'.
- A sheila with a reputation as the town bike heard he was there, and went to the house, taking a bottle of cologne with her. — Kel Richards, *The Aussie Bible*

town pump *noun*
a very promiscuous woman *US, 1961*
- Would I be jealous of the town pump? — Malcom Braly, *Felony Tank* 1961

town punch *noun*
an extremely promiscuous girl or woman *US, 1975*
- — *American Speech* Spring-Summer, 1975: 'Razorback slang'

toy *noun*
any object that is used for sexual stimulation during masturbation, foreplay, sexual intercourse or fetish-play *US, 1977*
- A significant part of the content of gay magazines is taken over by advertisements for "toys" – a revealing euphemism, evoking childhood, for implements of "torture": steel clamps, branding irons, whips, straps, even handcuffs. — John Rechy, *The Sexual Outlaw* 1977

trade *noun*
a man, self-identified as heterosexual, who engages in active anal homosexual sex or passive oral homosexual sex but will not reciprocate *US, 1927*

• Never back down on trade agreements. ["Trade" are "tricks" who do not, as yet, consider themselves homosexual.] — Laud Humphreys, *Tearoom Trade* 1975

trade queen *noun*
a homosexual man who prefers sex with a seemingly heterosexual man who consents to homosexual sex in the 'male' role, receiving orally or giving anally *US, 1970*
• Some of these "trade queens," because they're gay, think they're not as whole as other guys. They chase "straights" exclusively so they can put one over on them. — *Screw* 22nd June 1970

tradesman's entrance; tradesman's *noun*
the anus, designated as an entry suitable for sex *UK, 2001*
In the grand houses of polite society the tradesman's entrance is traditionally round the back.
• When a woman looks you straight in the one-eye and says, "There's no way you're putting that near my tradesman's," she is really saying, "You're huge!" — *GQ* July, 2001

traditional discipline *noun*
corporal punishment, especially when used in a prostitute's advertising matter *UK, 2003*
• — Caroline Archer, *Tart Cards* 2003

train *noun*
1 multiple orgasms *US, 1985*
• — *American Speech* Spring, 1985: 'The language of singles bars'
▶ **pull a train; run a train**
2 to engage in serial sex with multiple partners, homosexual or heterosexual, usually consensual *US, 1965*
• A girl who squeals on one of the outlaws or who deserts him for somebody wrong can expect to be "turned out," as they say, to "pull the Angel train." — Hunter S. Thompson, *Hell's Angels* 1966

trannie; tranny *noun*
a transvestite *UK, 1984*
• For trannies most of the danger is once you get into the car and they find out you aren't a woman, Neil said[.] — *The Vancouver Sun* 23rd March 1992

traveller's marrow *noun*
an erection brought on while travelling, especially while sleeping *UK, 1985*
• — Bob Young and Micky Moody, *The Language of Rock 'n' Roll* 1985

tribbing *noun*
a lesbian sex act in which the partners' genitals are rubbed each against the other *US, 2005*
Derives from tribadism. In very wide pornographic use.

trick *noun*
1 a prostitute's customer *US, 1925*
• They had to keep an eye on the cops all the time, because they weren't allow to call the tricks like the girls in Storyville. — Louis Armstrong, *Satchmo: My Life in New Orleans* 1954
2 an act of sex between a prostitute and customer *US, 1926*
• Pimps take cops to dinner with free tricks. — *The Digger Papers* August, 1968
3 a short-term homosexual sexual partner, not paying *US, 1963*
• I looked like a bull dyke, or a trick of one, with handcuffs, a leather jacket, metal belts, and levi 501's, so I would try to method act. — Jennifer Blowdryer, *White Trash Debutante* 1997
4 a casual sexual partner *US, 1968*
• If I don't get arrested, my trick announces upon departure that he's been exposed to hepatitis! — Mart Crowley, *The Boys in the Band* 1968

trick *verb*
1 to engage in sex with a paying customer, usually in an expeditious fashion *US, 1960*
• Vickie had tricked with his father at a convention and was embarrassed and ashamed when Andre invited her home to meet his people and they were introduced. — Herbert Huncke, *The Evening Sun Turned Crimson* 1980
2 to have sex with a short-term partner, without emotion or money passed *US, 1968*
• It seems to me that the first time we tricked we met in a gay bar on Third Avenue during your junior year. — Mart Crowley, *The Boys in the Band* 1968

trick book *noun*
a prostitute's list of customers *US, 1972*
• You may work a trick book. You may work that up yourself or you may buy it. — Bruce Jackson, *In the Life* 1972

trick bunk *noun*
in prison, a bed used for sexual encounters
US, *1990*
- So that's what the dorm tender meant warning Joe that he'd been assigned the trick bunk. Of course – it was the furthest from the door, least visible to passing guards, best suited for the quickie clandestine cigarette date. – Seth Morgan, *Homeboy* 1990

trick day *noun*
an agreed time when homosexuals in long-term relationships may have sex outside the relationship *US*, *1964*
- – Florida Legislative Investigation Committee (Johns Committee), *Homosexuality and Citizenship in Florida* 1964: 'Glossary of homosexual terms and deviate acts'

trick dress; trick suit *noun*
a dress that a prostitute can remove easily
US, *1963*
- [S]he hurried to Burbank to get her "trick suit," which she explained was a dress worn by prostitutes to facilitate their work. – Ed Reid and Ovid Demaris, *The Green Felt Jungle* 1963

trick fuck *verb*
to have sex without any emotional content
US, *2001*
- Can't just trick fuck and let it go. Must be a white thing. – Dan Jenkins, *The Money-Whipped Steer-Job Three-Jack Give-Up Artist* 2001

trick off *verb*
to perform oral sex on a man *US*, *1997*
- – Anna Scotti and Paul Young, *Buzzwords* 1997

trick towel *noun*
a towel or wash rag used to clean up after sex *US*, *1970*
- – *American Speech* Spring-Summer, 1970: 'Homosexual slang'

tricky Dick *noun*
the penis *US*, *1984*
- – Inez Cardozo-Freeman, *The Joint* 1984

trim *noun*
the vagina; a woman as a sex object; sex with a woman *US*, *1949*
- Do you know how close I was to getting some trim? – *48 Hours* 1982

trim *verb*
to have sex with a woman *US*, *1972*
- And I trimmed her three or four times as I remember and just had a ball. – Bruce Jackson, *Outside the Law* 1972

triple *noun*
sex involving three people *US*, *1988*
- Ciglianni's dead. Keeled over with a heart attack last year doing triples with two teenage whores he picked up off the hookers' stroll at Hollywood and Vine. – Robert Campbell, *Juice* 1988

triple m *noun*
mutual manual masturbation *US*, *1985*
- – Wayne Dynes, *Homolexis* 1985

trisexual; trysexual *adjective*
willing to try anything sexually; open to any sexual experience *US*, *1988*
Borrowing from 'bisexual', punning 'tri' with 'try'.
- The large one is trisexual; Bunny just does what she's told. What's trisexual? She'll do [try] anything, I suspect. – Robert Stoller and I.S. Levine, *Coming Attractions* 1991

trombone *verb*
to lick the anus of a male partner while caressing his erect penis *UK*, *2001*
The actions involved mimic the playing of a trombone.
- – *Sky Magazine* July, 2001

trophy fuck *verb*
to have sex with a famous person because of that person's celebrity, *2001*
- Gangs of [groupies] went hunting together – "trophy fucking" – keeping a list of everyone they made out with. – Simon Napier-Bell, *Black Vinyl White Powder* 2001

trouser snake *noun*
the penis *US*, *1976*
- JUSTICE: Of course I like snakes. JAY: How about trouser snakes? – Kevin Smith, *Jay and Silent Bob Strike Back* 2001

trouser trout *noun*
the penis *UK*, *1998*
- I think we've already established that when it comes to the trouser trout there is no norm. – Richard Herring, *Talking Cock* 2003

truck stop Annie *noun*
a prostitute working at a truck stop *US,
1977*
- — Bill Davis, *Jawjacking* 1977

tube *noun*
1 a totally unnecessary breast examination
UK, 1999
- — Adam T. Fox, St Mary's Hospital,
London, 10 October 2002
▶ **lay tube**
2 from the male point of view, to have sex
US, 1983
- [A]bout eighty a them's gonna lay more
tube than the motherfuckin Alaska
pipeline. — Joseph Wambaugh, *The
Delta Star* 1983

tube lube *noun*
oral sex on a man *US, 1970*
- Not only did I get three to give me a
"Tube lube" but I got to French out four
of the five swingers. — *Screw* 20th July
1970

tube steak *noun*
the penis *US, 1980*
- I want to slip my tubesteak into your
sister. What'll you take in trade? — *Full
Metal Jacket* 1987

tubs *noun*
▶ **the tubs**
a gay bath house; the gay bath house
scene collectively *US, 1964*
- At times like this, the tubs was an easy
way out. Discreet, dispassionate,
noncommital. — Armistead Maupin,
Tales of the City 1978

tucked and rolled *adjective*
medically transformed from a male to a
female *US, 1990*
- When she paroled, Magdalena had the
sex change operation at Stanford
Medical Center, she's tucked and
rolled, a genuine woman. — Seth
Morgan, *Homeboy* 1990

tug *noun*
an act of masturbation *AUSTRALIA, 2001*
- I'm not saying I always have a morning
tug to get the day started[.] — Kevin
Sampson, *Outlaws* 2001

tug *verb*
to masturbate *NEW ZEALAND, 1998*
- — David McGill, *David McGill's
Complete Kiwi Slang Dictionary*
1998

tumble *noun*
an act of sexual intercourse; an invitation
to engage in sexual intercourse *UK, 1903*
- I saw at least a thousand I'd have
married gladly on the spot if they'd
given me a tumble. — Oscar Zeta
Acosta, *The Autobiography of a Brown
Buffalo* 1972

tuna *noun*
1 the vagina *US, 1986*
- He added that many women insist on
using Saran Wrap when he goes down
to taste the tuna. — Anka Radakovich,
The Wild Girls Club 1994
2 a young sailor as the object of desire of a
homosexual man *US, 1985*
- From the advertising slogan "Chicken
of the Sea." — Wayne Dynes,
Homolexis 1985

tuning *noun*
an instance of sexual intercourse which
the female partner finds satisfying *UK,
1959*
Automotive imagery.
- [H]e'd drop in, calm as you like, give
me a good tuning before he
disappeared back home[.]
— Anonymous, *Streetwalker* 1959

tunnel shot *noun*
a photograph or shot in a film focusing on
a woman's vagina *US, 1970*
- No ugly gaping tunnel shots, no chicks
fingering themselves; just beautiful
men with fine three piece sets.
— *Screw* 5th October 1970

turdcutter *noun*
the buttocks *US, 1977*
Imprecise and crude physiology.
- Yeah, that bitch sho' has got a helluva
turdcutter on it, ain't she? — Odie
Hawkins, *Chicago Hustle* 1977

Turk *verb*
(of a male) to have sex, especially in a
brutal fashion *UK, 1966*
- — Bill Naughton, *One Small Boy*
1966

turkey neck *noun*
the penis *US, 1997*
- That winter a houseguest, his wife
gone shopping, pinned me in my
bedroom by the mirror and as we
both watched, took out to my horror
a great stiff turkey neck, a hairless

thing he wanted to give me.
— Constance Warloe, *From Daughters to Mothers* 1997

Turkish culture *noun*
anal sex *US, 1972*
- — Robert A. Wilson, *Playboy's Book of Forbidden Words* 1972

turn *verb*
▶ **turn Japanese**
to masturbate *UK, 1980*
From the perceived resemblance between a stereotypical Japanese face and the facial expression that accompanies a quest for orgasm.
- — The Vapors *Turning Japanese* 1980

turn on *verb*
to arouse an interest, sexual or abstract in someone; to stimulate someone; to thrill someone *US, 1965*
- One time I was with Jim and we were balling doggie fashion and his roommate came home and got turned on watching us ball. — *Adam Film Quarterly* October, 1973

turnout *noun*
a novice prostitute; a prostitute working in a particular brothel for the first time *US, 1973*
- Til now I never had the time for a turnout. — A.S. Jackson, *Gentleman Pimp* 1973

turn out *verb*
1 to recruit and convert someone to prostitution *US, 1960*
- I just ain't got the time to turn a girl out. When I get a girl, I want her to be ready made in sportin' life. — A.S. Jackson, *Gentleman Pimp* 1973
2 to engage a woman in serial sex with multiple partners *US, 1966*
- Girls who get turned out at Hell's Angels parties don't think of police in terms of protection. — Hunter S. Thompson, *Hell's Angels* 1966

turtleneck *noun*
the foreskin on an uncircumsised penis *US, 1983*
- — Connie Eble (Editor), *UNC-CH Campus Slang* November, 1983

tush hog *noun*
an aggressive homosexual *US, 1971*

- One of them, called Fraulein, vaguely Teutonic, affected some sort of mongrel accent, which seemed to enhance her allure among the "tush hogs." — James Blake, *The Joint* 1971

tut-tuts *noun*
the female breasts *TRINIDAD AND TOBAGO, 1956*
- — *Dictionary of the English/Creole of Trinidad & Tobago* 2003

TV *noun*
a transvestite *UK, 2003*
- TV Heaven[.] Be the Woman of yor dreams! — Caroline Archer, *Tart Cards* 2003

twang *verb*
▶ **twang the wire**
(of a male) to masturbate *AUSTRALIA, 1971*
- If he reckons we're all going to twang the wire he's got another think coming!!! — Barry Humphries, *Bazza Pulls It Off!* 1971

twat *noun*
1 the vagina *UK, 1656*
- I just love the sound of a bird with a posh accent bellowing obscenities as I batter her twat with my love truncheon. — Stewart Home, *Sex Kick [britpulp]* 1999
2 a promiscuous homosexual man *US, 1987*
- "Disgusting the way some of these twats flaunt it, ain't it?" a tough at the next table said. — Robert Campbell, *Alice in La-La Land* 1987

twenty-eight cheeks; 28 cheeks *noun*
girls who are not romantically or sexually faithful to one partner; two timers *SOUTH AFRICA, 2003*
Teen slang, of uncertain origin. This may well also apply in the singular.
- — *Sunday Times (South Africa)* 1st June 2003

twinkie *noun*
a youthful, sexually inexperienced male who is the object of an older homosexual's desire *US, 1979*
The spelling 'twinky' is also used.
- Ned was no fading twinkie, though, when I knew him; he wore his age with an easy, shambling grace that was completely out of sync with the

desperate pretenses of most people in this town. — Armistead Maupin, *Maybe the Moon* 1992

two-pump chump *noun*
a male who ejaculates without much stimulation *US, 2004*

- — Connie Eble (Editor), *UNC-CH Campus Slang* April, 2004

two-way *noun*
a position for mutual, simultaneous oral sex between two people, or the act itself *UK, 2003*

- — Caroline Archer, *Tart Cards* 2003

two-way bondage *noun*
a restriction of movement to facilitate an erotic encounter or sexual intercourse *UK, 2003*

- — Caroline Archer, *Tart Cards* 2003

two-way watersports *noun*
when used in a prostitute's advertising, indicates that the prostitute is willing both to urinate over the client, and be urinated upon *UK, 2003*
A specification of WATER SPORTS (the practice of urophilia and urolagnia).

- — Caroline Archer, *Tart Cards* 2003

Uu

ultimate *noun*
in the coded terminology used in advertising for sexual contact, full sexual intercourse *UK, 2006*
- CPL, 35M, 28F(AC/DC) seek similar or bi-fem for BDSM and ultimate[.] — Ashley Lister, *Swingers* 2006

unbutton *verb*
▶ **unbutton the mutton**
to undo clothing and liberate the penis *AUSTRALIA, 1971*
- I haven't even had the chance to unbutton the mutton!!! — Barry Humphries, *Bazza Pulls It Off!* 1971

uncommon horn *noun*
an unusually urgent sexual appetite *UK, 2001*
- I have an uncommon horn [...] I have. I'm randy as hell. — Kevin Sampson, *Outlaws* 2001

uncunt *verb*
to withdraw the penis from a woman's vagina *US, 1961*
- [H]e could actually make her change places with his wife, all without un-cunting. — Henry Miller, *Tropic of Capricorn* 1961

uncut *adjective*
not circumcised *US, 1957*
- We never fucked, with his uncut penis. — Sandra Bernhard, *Confessions of a Pretty Lady* 1988

unit *noun*
1 the penis *US, 1985*
The slang sense of the word gives special meaning to the nickname 'The Big Unit' given to baseball pitcher Randy Johnson.
- MADONNA: Wow, look at the unit on that guy. — *Saturday Night Live* 11th May 1991
2 the vagina *US, 1978*
- These detectives here can look right up a broad's unit and check her lands and grooves. — Joseph Wambaugh, *The Black Marble* 1978

unload *verb*
(of a male) to ejaculate *US, 1988*
- I'd better be quick about it or else I'd get discovered. I needed to unload fast[.] — Howard Stern, *Miss America* 1995

unsliced *adjective*
not circumcised *US, 1988*
- — H. Max, *Gay (S)language* 1988

uphill gardening *noun*
anal intercourse *UK, 1997*
- ["]Bradley is referring to the rusty bullet-hole," said Mikey. "The what?" Mario was still struggling. "The chocolate starfish." "Backdooring." "Uphill gardening." [...] "What, you mean shoving it up their arse?" exclaimed Mario. — Colin Butts, *Is Harry on the Boat?* 1997

upskirt *noun*
a type of voyeurism devoted to seeing what is beneath a woman's skirt *US, 1995*
- What began as a small photo gallery on the Internet a couple of years ago has rapidly expanded to more than 40 such "Upskirt" sites, including one devoted entirely to shots taken up skirts in Maryland, said Duqueette, who has been tracking the trend. — *Washington Post* 7th June 1998

up the aisle *noun*
a sexual position in which the woman kneels and the man enters her from behind *UK, 2003*
Rhyming slang for DOG-STYLE.
- — Bodmin Dark, *Dirty Cockney Rhyming Slang* 2003

Vv

vage; vag; vadge; vaj *noun*
the vagina *US, 1986*
- It was well nigh impossible to achieve "full-vage-pen" by breeching aside the crotch panel of this snug-fitting garment. — Terry Southern, *Now Dig This* 1986

vanilla *adjective*
of sex, conventional; of homosexual sex, gentle, traditional, emotional *US, 1984*
- I hadn't been wrong about the people who attended these things [fetish-themed nightclubs] – they really were much better behaved than their vanilla counterparts. — Claire Mansfield and John Mendelssohn, *Dominatrix* 2002

Vatican roulette *noun*
birth control by the rhythm method *US, 1979*
- — *Maledicta* 1979: 'A glossary of ethnic slurs in American English'

V-card *noun*
a person's virginity *US, 2001*
- I'm a sophomore in college, and at times guys try to pressure me to turn in my V-card. — *Teenpeople* April, 2004

vee dub *noun*
a completely depillated female pubis *US, 2003*
Also as a verb and, thus, an adjectival participle. From a similarity in shape and finish to the bonnet of a Volkswagen Beetle.
- I screwed Jennie last night – did you know she was vee dubbed? — Chris Lewis, *The Dictionary of Playground Slang* 2003

vertical bacon sandwich *noun*
the vagina *UK, 2002*
From the resemblance.
- — www.LondonSlang.com June, 2002

V girl *noun*
a woman who is attracted to men in military uniform *US, 1960*
- They had dances all over that year, it was a beginning to ease juvenile delinquency, gang rumbles, V-girls. — Gilbert Sorrentino, *Steelwork* 1970

vice versa *noun*
reciprocal oral sex between two lesbians *US, 1963*
The earliest known lesbian periodical in the US (1947) was named *Vice Versa*.
- — Donald Webster Cory and John P. LeRoy, *The Homosexual and His Society* 1963: 'A lexicon of homosexual slang'

village bike *noun*
a promiscuous woman *NEW ZEALAND, 2002*
As with the TOWN BIKE, 'everyone has ridden her'.
- — Sonya Plowman, *Great Kiwi Slang* 2002

village pump *noun*
a girl who is free and easy sexually *CANADA, 1992*
- — Lewis Poteet, *Talking Country* 1992

vinegar stroke; vinegar *noun*
the final penile thrust culminating in ejaculation when copulating or masturbating *AUSTRALIA, 1961*
Alluding to the facial expression of the male. UK comedian Phil Jupitus, who uses this term to describe the closing moments of his act, explains: 'Just before a bloke comes he looks like you've popped a teaspoon of vinegar into his mouth.'
- I was in bed with the wife of a friend of mine, when all of a sudden, just on the vinegar stroke, I heard her husband's car come up the drive. — David Ireland, *The Unknown Political Prisoner* 1972

VIP massage *noun*
a sexual service offered in some massage parlours, in which a hand-massage includes masturbation of the client *UK, 2003*
- — Caroline Archer, *Tart Cards* 2003

VIP services *noun*
sexual intercourse, as distinct from masturbation, when advertised as a service offered by a prostitute *UK, 2003*
- — Caroline Archer, *Tart Cards* 2003

virginia *noun*
the vagina *BAHAMAS, 1982*
- — John A. Holm, *Dictionary of Bahamian English* 1982

Ww

wacky for khaki *adjective*
infatuated with men in military uniform *US, 1967*
- Hello, Janice Lee. Are you still whacky for khaki? Oh, you remember that. I married a Navy man. — Malcolm Braly, *On the Yard* 1967

wad *noun*
the semen ejaculated at orgasm *US, 1969*
- The cocks pop and the wads fly as wide-open mouths train to catch the steaming jizz. — *Adult Video* August/September, 1986

wad *verb*
(of a male) to reach orgasm *UK, 2003*
- [T]his month's CD is so rude you'll probably wad your Calvins [underpants]. — *Mixmag* April, 2003

wag *verb*
▶ **wag wienie; wag your wienie**
to commit indecent exposure *US, 1984*
- He was arrested in Florida for wagging wienie in a porn theater. — Armistead Maupin, *Maybe the Moon* 1992

walloper *noun*
the penis *UK: SCOTLAND, 2002*
- This wan'll never talk. No' wi' his walloper in his mooth, anyway. — Christopher Brookmyre, *The Sacred Art of Stealing* 2002

wand *noun*
the penis *UK, 2001*
- DUANE: How big is your johnson? RAMU: Johnson? DUANE: Your wand, your pork sword, your baloney pony. — *The Guru* 2002

wang; whang *noun*
the penis *US, 1935*
- Filipinos come quick; colored men are built abnormally large ("Their wangs look like a baby's arm with an apple in its fist"); ladies with short hair are Lesbians; if you want to keep your man, rub alum on your pussy. — Lenny Bruce, *How to Talk Dirty and Influence People* 1965

wank *noun*
1 the penis *US, 2004*
- I kept my eye on his wank, and continued to maneuver me and Eleanor away from his fumey breath and eventual ejaculation. — Michelle Tea, *Rent Girl* 2004
2 an act of masturbation; hence, an act of self-indulgence *UK, 1948*
- He's probably having a wank right now, watching us through binoculars, she laughed. — John King, *White Trash* 2001

wank *verb*
to masturbate *UK, 1950*
The Scots dialect word *whank* (to beat) was the usual spelling until the 1970s. Also used with 'off'.
- [L]oads of blokes wank over her, it don't mean a thing. I mean, shit, even I've wanked over her. — Colin Butts, *Is Harry on the Boat?* 1997

wank-bank *noun*
a personal collection of inspirational erotic images *UK, 2003*
- Approaching his vinegar stroke, he was accessing his mental wank-bank for a suitable image to produce a satisfactory climax[.] — Colin Butts, *Is Harry Still on the Boat?* 2003

wanker *noun*
a masturbator *UK, 1978*
- I'm a wanker, I'm a wanker / And it does me good like it bloody well should[.] — Ivor Biggun, *The Winker's Song (Misprint)* 1978

wanker's doom *noun*
the mythological disease that is the inevitable result of excessive masturbation *US, 1977*
- — *Maledicta* Summer, 1977: 'A word for it!'

wanking-spanner *noun*
the hand *UK, 1961*
A masturbatory tool that loosens nuts.
- — *Roger's Profanisaurus* December, 1997

wank sock *noun*
an item of (men's) footwear used to contain the penis during masturbation *UK, 2001*
- — Graham Norton, *V Graham Norton* 21st May 2003

wash up *verb*
in heterosexual intercourse, to enter the
vagina from behind *UK, 2001*
- — *Sky Magazine* July, 2001

water sports *noun*
1 sexual activity involving the giving and
getting of an enema *US, 1969*
- Have you ever heard of "water sports?"
No? Well, people who are into that enjoy
giving, or – more commonly – receiving
enemas. — *Screw* 6th June 1969
2 sexual activity that includes urination *US,
1969*
- Lately a lot of people have made it
pretty trendy to do water sports or
golden shower kind of things.
— Anthony Petkovich, *The X Factory*
1997

way *noun*
▶ **go all the way**
sexual intercourse *US, 1924*
- The first time we tried to go all the way
I got my toe stuck in the ashtray.
— Annie Ample, *The Bare Facts* 1988

weapon *noun*
the penis *UK, 1000*
- When I look at his penis when it's not
erect, it's small and soft, not so much
like a weapon ruling him and me.
— Ellen Bass and Laura Davis, *The
Courage to Heal* 1994

wedding tackle *noun*
the male genitals *UK, 1961*
- No important bits cut off or damaged
at all, if you get my meaning [...]
Wedding tackle all present and correct.
Adèle Geras, — *Troy* 2000

weenie; weeny; wienie *noun*
the penis *US, 1978*
- But in reality, the muff-happy mogul is
merely hidden away in an upstairs
chamber watching their sexual
escapades via a close circuit TV system,
while pulling his weenie[.] — *Adult
Video* August/September, 1986

weenie wagger; weenie waver *noun*
a male sexual exhibitionist *US, 1970*
- Where the wienie wagger shoved it
through at the old babe changing
clothes and she stuck a hatpin clear
through it and the son of a bitch was
pinned right there when the cops
arrived. — Joseph Wambaugh, *The New
Centurions* 1970

wee-wee *noun*
the penis *US, 1969*
- No little "wee-wee" was able to enter
my "hole." — *Screw* 15th December
1969

well-endowed *adjective*
1 of a man, having impressively proportioned
genitals *UK, 1951*
- "Oui. All my lovers have been well
endowed." His lips twitched. "Ye like
big cocks?" "Big cocks are not enough.
I need big brains too." — Virginia
Henley, *Tempted* 1992
2 of a woman, having generously proportioned breasts *UK, 1984*
- I have other fantasies, too, where a
spectacular, well-endowed blond
beauty seduces me, and I her. — Nancy
Friday, *Women on Top* 1991

well hung *adjective*
of a man, having generously proportioned
genitals *UK, 1685*
- [Y]ou need to find a man like that to
marry. Someone so well hung that even
after three or four kids, he'd still be
wall to wall. — Sherrilyn Kenyon, *Night
Embrace* 2003

wet decks *noun*
a woman who has recently had sex with
several men *US, 1972*
- — Robert A. Wilson, *Playboy's Book of
Forbidden Words* 1972

wet dream *noun*
among men, a sleeping fantasy that triggers
orgasm *UK, 1851*
- — Max Romeo, *Wet Dream* 1969

wet-finger *noun*
▶ **get wet-finger**
in the categorisation of sexual activity by
teenage boys, to insert a finger into a girl's
vagina *US, 1986*
- It was almost axiomatic that, under
"normal" circumstances, to "get wet-
finger" meant the girl's defenses would
crumble as she was swept away on a
tide of sheer physical excitement.
— Terry Southern, *Now Dig This* 1986

wet shot *noun*
a scene in a pornographic film or photograph depicting a man ejaculating *US,
1991*
- And here's a hazard of the trade, the
wet shot. You only get one shot at it.
Here comes the framing of that wet

shot. It's a little off. — Robert Stoller and I.S. Levine, *Coming Attractions* 1991

whack *verb*
▶ **whack your doodle**
(of a male) to masturbate *US, 1970*
- [L]eer at passing legs, whack your doodle at home at night[.] — Lester Bangs, *Psychotic Reactions and Carburetor Dung* 1970

whack-off *noun*
an act of masturbation *US, 1969*
- He couldn't afford much beyond a quick whackoff into an old handkerchief[.] — Lester Bangs, *Psychotic Reactions and Carburetor Dung* 1981

whack off *verb*
to masturbate *US, 1969*
- But you don't get some bird comin' on and whackin' herself off with a dildo, do yer? — Shaun Ryder, *Shaun Ryder... in His Own Words* 1997

wham, bam, thank you m'am
used for describing anything done in very short order, especially sex *US, 1942*
Sometimes abbreviated, and sometimes embellished with other rhymes.
- I had ten dollars from my Granny for what they called a 'short date.' And short it was, a regular wham, bam, thank you mam. — Ken Weaver, *Texas Crude* 1984

whanger; wanger *noun*
the penis *US, 1939*
- But if you are going to jack your whanger, make firm determination to do it well and heartily and in an infinite amount of ways and combinations. — *Screw* 9th May 1969

whip *verb*
▶ **whip it out**
to release the penis from the confines of the trousers *US, 1997*
- Now they're trying to get him for sexual harassment. What happened? The girl came to his hotel room, he whipped it out, she said no, and left. And she wants to sue him? He's the one who got turned down. — Chris Rock, *Rock This!* 1997

whip and top; whip *verb*
to masturbate *UK, 1992*
Rhyming slang for STROP.

- Every schoolboy's dread is to be caught "whipping" himself. — Ray Puxley, *Cockney Rabbit* 1992

whistle *verb*
▶ **whistle in the dark**
to perform oral sex on a woman *US, 1967*
- — Dale Gordon, *The Dominion Sex Dictionary* 1967

white meat *noun*
a white person as a sex object; the genitals of a white person; sex with a white person *US, 1957*
- Shoot, whyn't they try to get them some nice white meat from downtown once in a while instead of picking on us all the time? — John M. Murtagh and Sara Harris, *Cast the First Stone* 1957

white Russian *noun*
in homosexual usage, the passing of semen from one mouth to another *US, 1987*
- — *Maledicta* 1986–1987: 'A continuation of a glossary of ethnic slurs in American English'

whoopee *noun*
▶ **make whoopee**
to have sex *US, 1928*
A forced and silly euphemism, but one sanctioned by television censors; it was used with annoying regularity by Bob Eubanks, host of *The Newlywed Game* television programme (ABC, 1966–90).
- BRANDI: If you and I were making whoopie – BRODIE: What's whoopie? BRANDIE: You know, if we were, intimate. BRODIE: What, like fucking? — *Mallrats* 1995

whore-style *adverb*
said when a woman has sex with her underpants still around one leg *US, 1973*
- She took one leg outta her panties, whore style, and I dropped my pants to my knees and mounted her. — A.S. Jackson, *Gentleman Pimp* 1973

wick *noun*
the penis *AUSTRALIA, 1971*
- — Barry Humphries, *Bazza Pulls It Off!* 1971

wide-on *noun*
a state of sexual excitement in a woman *AUSTRALIA, 1987*
- [S]he asked him to give her half [of a Viagra tablet], giggling and wondering if

she'd get a "wide-on". — Colin Butts, *Is Harry Still on the Boat?* 2003

wiener; weiner *noun*
the penis *US, 1960*
• We're looking at a sizable wiener here. — Rita Ciresi, *Pink Slip* 1999

wife beater *noun*
the penis *UK, 2007*
• And the big surprise is that he's pulled it off. No, not his mucky wife beater — we mean the film. — *Maxim* 2007

wife-in-law *noun*
one prostitute in relation to another prostitute working for the same pimp *US, 1957*
• Keeping her wife-in-laws and my scratch straight up there in Toledo was the first acid test for Rachel was a bottom woman [lead prostitute]. — Iceberg Slim (Robert Beck), *Pimp* 1969

wild thing *noun*
▶ do the wild thing
to have sex *US, 1990*
• Man, you ain't gotta take that pussy. She'll do the wild thing for $5. — *New Jack City* 1990

willy *noun*
the penis *UK, 1905*
Originally northern English, not dialect, for 'a child's penis' or a childish name for any penis. Adopted by adults as a jocular reference, now widely used as a non-offensive and broadcastable term. The spelling 'willie' is also used.
• Ben [a dog] was trying to lick her face again [...] not after licking his willy[.] — John King, *White Trash* 2001

wind tunnel *noun*
in homosexual usage, a loose anus and rectum *US, 1981*
• — *Male Swinger Number 3* 1981: 'The complete gay dictionary'

wingman *noun*
when two male friends are flirting with two females, the male who connects with the least attractive female *UK, 2005*
• — Tim Collins, *Mingin' or Blingin'* 2005

wink *noun*
the penis *UK, 2001*
• — *Journal of Sex Research* 2001

winker *noun*
the vagina *UK, 1970*

The imagery of an eye that opens and closes.
• — Paul Bailey, *Trespasses* 1970

winkie *noun*
the vagina *UK, 2001*
• — *Journal of Sex Research* 2001

winkle *noun*
a boy's penis; a small penis *US, 1966*
• Came home to find another gentleman's kippers in the grill / So he sanded off his winkle with a Black and Decker drill[.] — Ian Dury, *This is What We Find* 1979

winkle-trip *noun*
a male striptease act performed for an all-female audience on a Thames pleasure boat *UK, 1980*
• [T]he boys [strippers] on the trip call it a "winkle trip" or "ladies' dingdong night". — *New Society* 24th January 1980

winky; winkie *noun*
the penis; a small penis; a boy's penis *UK, 1984*
Usually juvenile, occasionally derisory.
• How could you ever look a girl in the eye after you've had your winkie up her? — C.D. Payne, *Youth in Revolt* 1993

wizard's sleeve *noun*
a capacious vagina *UK, 1999*
Coined for humorous magazine *Viz*.
• I can't feel a bloody thing. You must have a fanny like a wizard's sleeve. — *Roger's Profanisaurus*, October, 1999

wolf *noun*
1 a sexually aggressive man *US, 1945*
• It was parked on a sofa, a full six feet long. It gave me ideas, which I quickly ignored. It was no time to play wolf. — Mickey Spillane, *I, The Jury* 1947
2 in prison, an aggressive, predatory homosexual *US, 1952*
• A baby-faced, small-framed, good-looking kid who looked about fourteen years old, he was perfect prey for the jailhouse wolves. — Piri Thomas, *Down These Mean Streets* 1967

wood *noun*
the fully erect penis *US, 1991*
• DIRECTOR (of pornographic film): Problem? ACTRESS: We don't have wood. CAMERAMAN: Stand by. Holding on wood. SOUNDMAN: Stand by for

wood. WOMAN IN STREET: We are
holding for wood. — *The Guru* 2002

woody; woodie *noun*
  an erection *US, 1985*
  US pornographer Joey Silvera is given credit
  for coining this term, which did not stay
  within the confines of pornography for long.
  - Who's the old guy with the big woody?
    — *Airheads* 1994

wool *noun*
  pubic hair; by extension, sex *US, 1972*
  - He looks like he could get hisself some
    good wool if he put his mind on it.
    — Dan Jenkins, *Semi-Tough* 1972

working parts *noun*
  the genitals *UK, 1995*

  - [T]wo slappers [sexually available
    women) came by, hollering and
    shouting at the boys inside, flashing
    their arses and working parts. — Andy
    McNab, *Immediate Action* 1995

wrap-up *noun*
  **a female sex-partner who is regularly avail-
  able** *UK, 1970*
  - I can always accommodate a second
    wrap-up. — Bill Naughton, *Alfie Darling*
    1970

wrong 'un *noun*
  the anus, in a sexual context *UK, 2006*
  - [H]e "had to do her up the wrong un"
    to get any feeling at all. — *Popbitch* 7th
    July 2006

Xx

x-dressing *noun*
  cross-dressing *UK, 2003*
  - WELCOME TO THE WONDERFUL WORLD
    OF X DRESSING[.] — Caroline Archer,
    Tart Cards 2003

Yy

yaffle *verb*
to engage in oral sex *UK, 1998*
From the sense 'to eat'.
- Yaffle the yoghurt cannon (the penis).
  — Chris Donald, *Roger's Profanisaurus*
  1998

yardage *noun*
a big penis *US, 1972*
- — Bruce Rodgers, *The Queens'*
  Vernacular 1972

ya-ya's *noun*
the female breasts *US, 2005*
- The brunette hardbody's ya-yas did get
  a nice workout as one of Baywatch's
  first luscious lifeguards[.] — Mr. Skin,
  Mr. Skin's Skincyclopedia 2005

ying yang *noun*
the penis *US, 1981*
- — *Maledicta* Summer/Winter, 1981:
  'Five years and 121 dirty words later'

yodel *verb*
▶ **yodel up the valley**
to perform oral sex on a woman *AUSTRALIA,*
1971
An elaboration of conventional 'yodel'.
- BARRY: Well, I dunno about you Suke –
  but I feel like dining at the Y. SUKE:
  Well darls [darling] if you wanted to
  yodel up the valley youse had your
  chance[.] — Barry Humphries, *Bazza*
  Pulls It Off! 1971

yoyo nickers; yo-yo knickers *noun*
a woman who (allegedly) exhibits a casual
readiness for sexual encounters *UK, 1999*
The image is drawn of panties going up and
down, up and down.
- Come on, let's go and see Beverly yoyo
  nickers then. — Caroline Aherne and
  Craig Cash, *The Royle Family* 1999

Zz

zig-zig *noun*
sexual intercourse *UK, 1918*
Familiar pidgin in the Far, Near and Middle East and Mediterranean, originally military; a variation of JIG-A-JIG. Used by US soldiers in the South Pacific.

- I wanna, I wanna, I wanna, I wanna, / I wanna really really really wanna zigazig ah. — Spice Girls *Wannabe* 1996

zoo *noun*
a zoophile, a person with a sexual interest in animals *UK, 2002*

- The bible of these self-labelled zoophiles is a book entitled Dearest Pet (one reader states, "it provides for us zoo's [sic] a thorough description of our heritage, as it were, dating back to medieval"). — Kathleen Kurik Bryson, *Lap Dogs and Other Perversions [Inappropriate Behaviour]* 2002

zooms *noun*
the female breasts *US, 1968*
A shortened form of BAZOOMS.

- — Collin Baker et al., *College Undergraduate Slang Study Conducted at Brown University* 1968

Related titles from Routledge

The Concise New Partridge Dictionary of Slang
Tom Dalzell and Terry Victor

Praise for the two-volume *New Partridge Dictionary of Slang and Unconventional English:*

'The king is dead. Long live the king!... The old Partridge is not really dead; it remains the best record of British slang antedating 1945... Now, however, the preferred source for information about English slang of the past 60 years is the New Partridge.' – *James Rettig, Booklist, American Library Association*

'Most slang dictionaries are no better than momgrams or a rub of the brush, put together by shmegegges looking to make some moola. The New Partridge Dictionary of Slang and Unconventional English, on the other hand, is the wee babes.' – *Ian Sansom, The Guardian*

The Concise New Partridge presents, for the first time, all the slang terms from *The New Partridge Dictionary of Slang and Unconventional English* in a single volume.

With over 60,000 entries from around the English-speaking world, the *Concise* gives you the language of beats, hipsters, Teddy Boys, mods and rockers, hippies, pimps, druggies, whores, punks, skinheads, ravers, surfers, Valley girls, dudes, pill-popping truck drivers, hackers, rappers and more.

The Concise New Partridge is a spectacular resource infused with humour and learning – it's rude, it's delightful, and it's a prize for anyone with a love of language.

ISBN13: 978-0-415-21259-5

Related titles from Routledge

Vice Slang
Tom Dalzell and Terry Victor

Are you a bit of a chairwarmer? Do you use the wins from a country straight to get scudded on snakebite in a blind tiger? Do you ride the waves on puddle or death drop?

Vice Slang gently eases you into the language of gambling, drugs and alcohol, providing you with 3,000 words to establish yourself firmly in the world of corruption and wickedness.

All words are illustrated by a reference from a variety of sources to prove their existence in alleys and dives throughout the English speaking world. This entertaining book will give you hours of reading pleasure.

ISBN10: 0-415-37181-3

ISBN13: 978-0-415-37181-0

Available at all good bookshops
For ordering and further information please visit:
www.routledge.com